INSIGHT GUIDE

Mexico

APA PUBLICATIONS

Part of the Langenscheidt Publishing Group

L

ABOUT THIS BOOK

Editorial

Project Editor
Felicity Laughton
Managing Editor
Huw Hennessy
Editorial Director
Brian Bell

Distribution

UK & Ireland
GeoCenter International Ltd
The Viables Centre
Harrow Way, Basingstoke
Hants RG22 4BJ
Fax: (44) 1256-817988

United States
Langenscheidt Publishers, Inc.
46–35 54th Road
Maspeth, NY 11378
Fax: (718) 784-0640

Worldwide
**APA Publications GmbH & Co.
Verlag KG (Singapore branch)**
38 Joo Koon Road
Singapore 628990
Tel: (65) 865-1600
Fax: (65) 861-6438

Printing

Insight Print Services (Pte) Ltd
38 Joo Koon Road
Singapore 628990
Tel: (65) 865-1600
Fax: (65) 861-6438

©1999 APA Publications GmbH & Co.
Verlag KG (Singapore branch)
*All Rights Reserved
First Edition 1983
Seventh Edition 1999*

CONTACTING THE EDITORS
Although every effort is made to
provide accurate information in
this publication, we live in a
fast-changing world and would
appreciate it if readers would
call our attention to any errors or
outdated information that may
occur by writing to us at:
**Insight Guides, P.O. Box 7910,
London SE1 8ZB, England.
Fax: (44 171) 620-1074.
e-mail:
insight@apaguide.demon.co.uk**

NO part of this book may be reproduced, stored in a retrieval system or
transmitted in any form or means elec-
tronic, mechanical, photocopying,
recording or otherwise, without prior
written permission of *Apa Publications.*
Brief text quotations with use of
photographs are exempted for book
review purposes only. Information has
been obtained from sources believed to
be reliable, but its accuracy and
completeness, and the opinions based
thereon, are not guaranteed.

Mexico is famous for its magnificent archeological sites,
fabulous beaches, and vibrant mix
of Indian, Spanish, and contemporary cultural influences. In this,
the seventh edition of *Insight Guide:
Mexico*, however, we have attemp-
ted to go beyond the familiar and
offer an insight into the character
of the country and its people,
aspiring to broaden the mind
rather than narrow it to meet
expectations.

How to use this book
Insight Guide: Mexico is
carefully structured to convey an understanding of the
country and to guide readers

through its sights and activities:
♦ To understand Mexico, you need
to know something about its past.
The **Features** section covers the
history and culture of the country
in a series of lively and informative
essays.
♦ The main **Places** section provides a complete guide to all
the sights and areas worth
seeing. Places of special
interest are coordinated by
number with full-colour maps.
♦ The **Travel Tips** listings
section provides a useful
reference for information on
travel, hotels, restaurants,
shops and more.

The **Places** section was completely revised and updated by the project editor, and checked by **Wendy Luft**, a writer and editor based in Mexico City, who has worked on numerous books about Mexico. Wendy wrote several features in this edition, including two picture essays, and she also updated the Travel Tips section at the back of the book.

The Modern Mexico history article was updated, taking into account the political turbulence of recent years, by **Andrea Dubrowski**, a Mexico City-based journalist with 15 years' experience writing about the country. A new feature on Colonial architecture was written by **Chloe Sayers,** who has written several books about Mexican culture, and a new article on the recently-emerged guerrilla movement in Chiapas was written by **Phil Gunson**, Mexico correspondent for the Guardian newspaper. The new picture feature on the colorful and exotic marine wildlife of the Yucatán was written by **Barbara McKinnon**, president of the renown environmental organisation, the Sian Ka'an Biosphere Reserve, Chetumal. **Ron Mader**, based in Mexico City and a specialist in Latin American eco-tourism, wrote the new feature on Adventure tourism, covering everything from whale-watching to river-rafting.

The majority of the stunning photographs in this book were taken by **Kal Müller**, although many new images have been added from **John Brunton**, **Mireille Vautie**r, **Buddy Mays**, **Andreas Gross**, **Marcus Wilson Smith** and **Eric Gill**. Thanks lastly to **Hilary Genin** for picture research, ably assisted by **Monica Allende** and **Joanne Beardwell**.

The contributors

The task of assembling the team who put together this edition of *Insight Guide: Mexico* was taken on with great gusto by project editor **Felicity Laughton**, with 18 years in Mexico, now married to a Mexican artist and based in the Cotswolds. Thoroughly revised and updated, this book builds on the original edition produced by **Kal Müller**, and edited by **Martha Ellen Zenfell** with subsequent contributions from specialist writers **John Wilcock**, **Margaret King**, **Mike Nelson**, **Barbara Ann Rosenberg**, **José-Antonio Guzmán**, **Guillermo García-Oropeza** and **Patricia Díaz**.

Map Legend

— ·· —	International Boundary
– – – –	State Boundary
⊖	Border Crossing
– • –	National Park/Reserve
– – – –	Ferry Route
⊞	Metro
✈ ✈	Airport: International/Regional
🚌	Bus Station
P	Parking
❶	Tourist Information
✉	Post Office
† †	Church/Ruins
†	Monastery
☾	Mosque
✡	Synagogue
🏰	Castle/Ruins
∴	Archaeological Site
∩	Cave
1	Statue/Monument
★	Place of Interest

The main places of interest in the Places section are coordinated by number with a full-colour map (e.g. ❶), and a symbol at the top of every right-hand page tells you where to find the map.

CONTENTS

Maps

A map of Mexico is also on
the inside front cover and one
of Mexico City Center on the
inside back cover.

Introduction

History

People

Features

Looking down
on jungle-covered
canyons, in the
back roads, high
above Puerto
Vallarta

Insight on ...

Information panels

Places

¡QUE VIVA MÉXICO!

Fabulous beaches, spectacular festivals, and
ancient cultures – Mexico is a tropical treasure-trove

Mexico, as we know it today has only existed for 150 years. Before, its borders stretched way up north through Texas, New Mexico, Arizona, and California. Now, although it is only one quarter the size of its northern neighbor, it is still a vast country full of surprises and startling contrasts, both geographical and social.

In Monterrey, Pittsburgh-style factories rise out of the desert; in northern Veracruz and along the Tabasco coast, oil rigs loom up like black exclamation points. Yet, oblivious to the industrial activity, indigenous Mexicans continue to perform age-old rituals; and, on the Pacific, Gulf and Caribbean beaches some 4 million visitors a year bask under tropical suns and *cha-cha* balmy nights away in the wake of ancient Mesoamerican civilizations.

Fiery murals blanket many of Mexico City's public walls, but thick smog blankets the sky, all too often obscuring the snow-capped volcanoes – Popocatépetl and Iztaccíhuatl – only 60 km (37 miles) to the southeast. With a population of over 20 million, Mexico City is the biggest megalopolis on earth; sadly it is no longer a place *Where the Air is Clear*, as Mexican novelist Carlos Fuentes entitled his most popular novel.

Yet beyond the sprawl of the rapidly expanding Distrito Federal, the air is wonderfully clear and, although many parts of the country are remote and inaccessible, there are more than 241,000 km (150,000 miles) of road, making it the most extensive travel network in Latin America.

Two-thirds of Mexico's 95 million people – a figure that grows by almost 3 percent each year – are under the age of 30. But, as well as the majority of Spanish-speaking, mixed-race *mestizos,* some 60 native languages are still spoken by more than 50 indigenous groups.

So, how do you explain it all – this fantastic, frenetic country? "One does not explain Mexico," says the philosopher Manuel Zamacona in *Where the Air is Clear*. "One believes in Mexico, with fury, with passion..."   ❏

PRECEDING PAGES: raising the flag on the Zócalo; festive parade; *charros ,* the ultimate Mexican machos; taking it easy on Xcacel beach;
LEFT: "Popo" with snowcap in January.

SMOKING MOUNTAINS AND BLOOMING DESERTS

A land of extremes, Mexico is both barren and lush,

rugged and pastoral – an untamed ecological paradise

There are many Mexicos, it has often been said. The physical features of the country make for striking divisions. Two great mountain ranges, the Sierra Madre Occidental and the Sierra Madre Oriental, run down from the US border, paralleling the Pacific and Gulf coasts. The mountains give way to the central highlands, the historic heart of Mexico: covering an area of about 640 km (400 miles) from east to west and less than 320 km (200 miles) from north to south this region represents just one-tenth of all Mexico, but it contains almost half the country's population.

Across the center of the Republic, a 160-km (100-mile) belt of mountains stretches between Puerto Vallarta on the Pacific coast and Puerto de Veracruz on the Gulf. This New Volcanic Axis, as it is called, is the boundary between North and Central America. South of that line, lesser mountains form the Sierra Madre del Sur, narrowing down at the Isthmus of Tehuantepec – Mexico's so-called waist with a width of only 160 km (100 miles). East of the Isthmus the mountains surge up again and continue south into Guatemala; to the north, the terrain is very different: the Yucatán Peninsula, ironed flat by nature, consists of a limestone sheet covered by thin soil.

Rainfall and changing climate

Mountains and highlands characterize much of Mexico, but deserts dominate the far north. The Great Arizona Desert continues south of the US border through Sonora, and here, as well as in Baja California and in the northern states of Chihuahua, Coahuila and Durango, crops can be grown only with the help of irrigation.

Many of these areas get as little as 10 cm (4 inches) of rain a year. It seems almost perverse that on the Gulf coast, too much rain –

as much as 6 meters (236 inches) each year – washes the land so that farmers have to hack away unwanted growth. In the central highlands, where most of the staple corn and beans are grown, rainfall is erratic: sometimes a trickle, sometimes a flood, although most of the rain falls between June and October.

Major problems arise from the indiscriminate cutting of timber which continues to denude some Mexican forests. The problem began in colonial times when many areas were stripped of trees for planting crops or for large-scale mining. The silver-mining region of Zacatecas is an example of woodland which was transformed to savannah by tree-cutters. The water table has fallen and climatic change has ensued as a result of the destruction of forests; areas that once had a measure of protection because they were inaccessible are now easily reached by road.

PRECEDING PAGES: patriotic symbols.
LEFT: *charro* gallops at full speed.
ABOVE RIGHT: bandillero flowers and maguey cactus.

Rivers and roads

Apart from in some southern areas, Mexico's rivers are mostly unnavigable. Throughout the colonial period, the road from Mexico City to Veracruz served as the umbilical cord between the New World and Spain; during the 16th century land links were also opened to the agriculturally rich Bajío region north of Mexico City and on to the mining district of Zacatecas. But when new mines were discovered in what is now southern Chihuahua, attempts to colonize New Mexico failed. It took more than a year to make the 2,600-km (1,600-mile) round trip from Zacatecas to New Mexico and neither

Volcanic spectacles

In geological terms, Popocatépetl (altitude: 5,452 meters/17,886 ft) is a child. In 1997, the "smoking mountain", which had lain dormant for many decades, put on a speaular show, sending out high-reaching fumaroles and a thick layer of dust which carpeted the surrounding area as far as Mexico City. As a result, the authorities have closed the access roads from the Paso de Cortés although climbers can still tackle Popo's extinct neighbor, Iztaccíhuatl, the "sleeping woman" (altitude: 5,286 meters/ 17,342 ft). The Pico de Orizaba, or Citlaltépetl ("star mountain" in Náhuatl) is 5,747 meters

Spain nor Mexico had the resources to integrate the great northern reaches which the conquistadores had claimed as theirs. When the time came, Anglo-Americans fought the Mexicans and took over what was then northern Mexico.

During the Díaz dictatorship, foreign capital poured in and helped finance the building of roads and railroads to the north and develop untapped natural resources. It then became economically worthwhile for North American companies to begin bulk ore mining. Foreign capital also financed the exploration for oil. By 1938, when the government expropriated the Mexican oil industry, a basic communications system was in place.

(18,900 ft) high and can be seen from the road between Mexico City and Veracruz, as well as by sailors out at sea off the Gulf coast. West of Mexico City, the Nevado de Toluca, or Xinantécatl, stands 4,680 meters (15,354 ft) tall. A dirt road, passable most of the year, leads right up to the crater and the two lakes, El Sol and La Luna (the Sun and the Moon).

The still smouldering Paricutín, the youngest of Mexico's volcanoes, was born in February, 1943, when, local farmer Dionisio Pulido witnessed its emergence from a cornfield one afternoon. Awestruck, he returned with his *compadres* (friends) the next day to discover a cone 6 meters (20 ft) high. Paricutín erupted soon after, hurling great chunks of molten rock 100 meters (328 ft) into the air and putting on a fiery display of orange lava. During its nine active years the volcano poured out a billion tons of lava, covering the village of San Juan Parangaricutiro, drowning 10 other hamlets and creating a mountain 427 meters (1,400 ft) high. Visitors can reach the site from the Purépecha indian village of Angahuan. En route they will pass the tower of San Juan's church which sticks defiantly out of a black lava bed.

Toward the western edge of the volcanic axis, the Nevado y Fuego (Snow and Fire) crater in Colima is not unusually high (3,326 meters/

10,912 ft), but is topped by two cones, one of which is snow-covered while the other periodically emits fumes. Although the last major eruption occurred in 1913, the mountain rumbled and spewed lava and ashes as recently as 1973. In 1952, the Mariano Bárcena mountain blew its top in the Mexican-owned Revillagigedo Archipelago, some 575 km (357 miles) off the Pacific coast. More recently, in 1982, the Chichonal volcano in Chiapas erupted causing many deaths and much destruction of land and property.

LEFT AND ABOVE: Tarascan girls tending sheep in Michoacán.

Wildlife

Though there is not enough prime land for agriculture, there are vast uninhabited areas that are still isolated and inaccessible, and in which wild animals can roam freely. How refreshingly remote are the vast deserts of Baja California, the mountains of central Mexico or the jungles bordering the Bahía de Campeche.

Mexico is a paradise for the nature-lover. It has no less than 2,896 species of vertebrates, including 520 mammals, 1,424 species of birds, 685 different kinds of reptiles, and 267 amphibians. Of these, 16 mammals, 13 birds and 9 reptiles are on the endangered list. Some are protected in national parks; others in wildlife refuges. In all there are over 50 national parks in Mexico, but many are in the very remotest regions while, around urban areas, rivers continue to be polluted, and the pervasive smog from Mexico City continues to obliterate the sky for much of the year. Deforestation, soil erosion, industrialization and in some cases uncontrolled tourism continue to pose serious ecological threats.

A country the size of Mexico, with its deserts, jungles, mountains, volcanoes, lakes, lagoons and rivers, is bound to offer many exciting options for anyone looking for new and challenging experiences.

Tough hikers can sight great horned sheep in the San Pedro Mártir National Park in the mountainous interior of Baja California. In the Cumbres de Monterrey National Park there are black bear, as well as unconfirmed reports of grizzlies in the wildest reaches of the Sierra Madre Occidental. Also off the Pacific coast of the Baja Peninsula, the islands of San Benito and Guadalupe (the latter has been declared a Biosphere Reserve) are a refuge for elephant seals. The largest male elephant seals can reach over 6 meters (19½ ft) in length. Although they were practically extinct in this part of the world at the beginning of the 20th century, by the late 1970s the elephant seal population on Guadalupe alone exceeded 47,000. A colony of sea lions basks on the beaches of Isla Cedros and the waters off the coast of Baja California are also home to the internationally endangered green turtle (*Chelonia mydas*).

The most spectacular of the mammals is the gray whale, which migrates yearly from Alaska's Bering Sea to Baja California's Pacific bays to mate and calve. For over a hundred years the whales were hunted to near extinction but, thanks to protective policies adopted by the government, there has been a strong recovery in recent decades. At Scammon's Lagoon, the whales' breeding ground, only 250 gray whales were counted in 1937; by 1975 the numbers had increased to 18,000.

From pelicans and eagles in the north and west, to humming birds and vultures further south, birds are never far from view in Mexico; in some parts, wild flocks of parrots are as common a sight (and sound) as the caged and singing canaries or macaws in the patios of restaurants, houses or hotels. As well as hav-

ing hundreds of native species, Mexico is the winter terminus for many more. Some favor the Pacific coast, and all-day boat trips are available to bird sanctuaries like the one on the San Juan Estuary, upstream from San Blas. At the other end of the country, thousands of pink flamingos flock to the Río Lagartos area of northern Yucatán and the bird sanctuary at Celestún, west of Mérida. Boat excursions can be organized from Isla Mujeres to the bird sanctuary on the tiny Isla Contoy, a breeding ground for herons, cormorants, pelicans, flamingos and frigate birds.

The Lagunas de Chacahua National Park west of Puerto Escondido, or the Sumidero Canyon, in Chiapas, are also popular not only for bird watchers, but all nature enthusiasts, and there is a zoo in Tuxtla Gutierrez which specializes in species that are native to Chiapas.

The eco-trend

In recent decades, as visitors' interest in Mexican wildlife has grown, the term "eco-tourism" has become somewhat of a trend in itself. As a result you no longer need to be an explorer to enjoy much of Mexico's wildlife. In many parts of the country, parks encompass a landmark of outstanding interest or beauty and organized trips can be arranged locally.

In the north, for example, there is the well-known Copper Canyon National Park – four times the size of the Grand Canyon – or the Cascada de Basaseáchic National Park, with the highest single drop waterfall in North America.

In the south, a journey along the Río Usumacinta, in the states of Tabasco and Chiapas, reveals dense rainforest, exciting wildlife, and ancient Mayan cities. Also in the south are the jungle waterfalls at Agua Azul National Park and the breathtaking colors of the Lagunas de Montebello where the lakes' varying shades of blue, green and gray depend on mineral deposits and the reflection of the light.

A year-round fairyland of bright fish and corals can be explored in the Caribbean waters off the Yucatán coast, a mecca for divers ever since Jacques Cousteau filmed here in the 1960s.

One of the most ambitious conservation projects is the vast Sian Ka'an Biosphere Reserve, in the State of Quintana Roo. There is a variety of habitats including tropical rain forest, wetlands, coastal lagoons, mangrove swamps and sinkholes, as well as part of the world's second-longest barrier reef system, with 60 different kinds of coral. There are also turtles, howler monkeys, crocodiles, pumas, ocelots, jaguars, and hundreds of species of birds and fish.

But perhaps the most spectacular sight of all is found in Central Mexico. Each November, millions of Monarch butterflies transform the Michoacán landscape when they arrive at their breeding ground – the sanctuary of El Rosario – after flying thousands of miles, all the way from Canada and the United States. ❑

LEFT: fishing boats in Bahía de los Angeles, Baja California.
RIGHT: the village of Tapalpa, Jalisco, at dawn.

PRE-HISPANIC CIVILIZATIONS

The Maya and Aztecs are the best known cultures, but there were

many other ancient peoples in Mexico before the arrival of the Spanish

According to radioactivity and carbon dating, Mexico has been inhabited for over 20,000 years. It all began in Siberia, with ancient peoples crossing the Bering Straits in search of food during the last Ice Age. From Alaska they went south into Canada and the United States, and eventually reached Mexico, Central and South America.

These people were meat and wild plant eaters, usually hunting small or medium-sized animals, although it is known that they also hunted mammoths from time to time.

In the late Cenolithic Age (9000–7000 BC), long after mammoths had become extinct, people in what is now Mexico used a crude stone implement to grind grain. This was the forerunner of the *metate*, the slab upon which most rural Mexicans still grind their corn today. By the year 5000 BC the ancient Mexicans had begun to grow maize and beans, which have been the staples of the Mexican diet ever since.

The mother culture

Until quite recently, the Maya were credited with being the oldest of the Mesoamerican civilizations, but discoveries in the 1930s led to a reshuffle of the historical jigsaw. It is now known that the mysterious Olmec culture of the low-lying jungle regions of southern Veracruz and Tabasco flourished between 1200 BC and 400 BC and was the first of Mexico's great ancient cultures.

The history and lifestyle of the Olmec, or "people from the land of rubber", remains an enigma. We know that they cultivated the soil and channeled water to irrigate the crops. We also know that they developed a strong, centralized organization that was highly elitist. Unlike the Maya, the Olmec had no writing with which to express their history, so we must rely entirely on the testimony of their art.

Their best-known legacy are the astounding,

PRECEDING PAGES: Chichén Itzá glyphs; Edzná Acropolis.
LEFT: Colossal Olmec head.
RIGHT: Coatlicue, the Aztec goddess of the Earth.

monolithic basalt heads, measuring up to 3 meters (10 ft) in height, and weighing between 6 and 50 tons. They are believed to be gigantic portraits of powerful Olmec rulers. Although all 17 of the heads discovered so far present a general similarity of features – flat wide noses, thickened lips, staring eyes – they are all dif-

ferent from each other. All the heads are wearing helmets bearing insignia of rank indicating they were important people. No two helmets are alike either, with carvings depicting human hands, macaw heads, or curved jaguar claws.

The heads, carved out of basalt rock from the Tuxtla mountains, were hauled across hills and rivers over distances of up to 100 km (60 miles) to the ancient ceremonial centers where they were found. The enormous workforce required for such tasks is proof in itself of a highly organized and hierarchical society.

Other Olmec monuments include thrones and stelae, or carved stone slabs. But not all Olmec art is monumental in size; there are also exquisite jadeite miniatures, beautifully carved pottery and delicate obsidian jewelry. The extraordinary thing is that all these pieces were created without the help of any metal tools whatsoever. Furthermore, some of the materials, such as the jade, obsidian and serpentine, were brought from as far afield as Guatemala. Early Olmec manifestations have also been found in Puebla, the Valley of Mexico, Oaxaca and Guerrero.

As in all pre-Hispanic cultures, Olmec art and religion were inseparable. A recurring motif in this ancient art is the jaguar; the snarling, tawny coated big cat which ruled the jungles

and played a leading role in Olmec religion. Many of the sculptures portray the so-called were-jaguar, which Olmec scholar Miguel Covarrubias describes as "a haunting mixture of human and feline characteristics." The Olmec pantheon was populated with many other deities, sometimes mythical or semi-mythical creatures, and mostly monstrous or fearsome. Many of their sculptures portray children, often with physical abnormalities such as those seen with cleft palate or Down's Syndrome. It is thought that these infants were deified as their slanting eyes and split lip likened them to the great jaguar god.

The three main Olmec sites – San Lorenzo, La Venta and Tres Zapotes – spanned more or less consecutive periods before they were abandoned. Today all three, although accessible, are off the beaten path and most of their monuments and artefacts have been removed to the anthropology museums of Villahermosa, Xalapa and Mexico City.

The Olmec civilization came to a violent end around 400 BC. We can only hazard a guess at why so many of the Olmec stone sculptures were so brutally mutilated. Perhaps the lower classes rebelled against their rulers; or maybe the devastating iconoclasm resulted from the struggle for hegemony over the Olmec "heartland." Whatever happened, their art, their gods and their social organization were to influence all subsequent civilizations in Mesoamerica.

Maya

The Mayan culture, which reached its peak during the Classic period (AD 300–900), dominated the Yucatán Peninsula and areas south, including what is now the state of Chiapas, and into Guatemala and Honduras. In the lowlands of the Yucatán, limestone provided the Mayan craftsmen with first-rate material for building and sculpting; their harmoniously proportioned buildings are often beautifully decorated with fine stone carving or stucco. Although the true arch was entirely absent from pre-Hispanic architecture, the Maya invented what is known as the corbelled vault, or "false arch."

The Mayan pyramid is considerably steeper than its counterparts in other areas of Mexico, its verticality emphasized by the temple built at the top. This temple has delicate carving, a sloping roof, and is crowned by a decorative stone crest or comb.

THE BALL GAME

The ball game was an important part of life for all pre-Hispanic cultures, from the time of the Olmecs. The colossal heads themselves may have represented warrior ball-players. The ceremonial game was heavily ritualistic. There is evidence that, during the Classic period, prominent war captives were forced to play the game, with the inevitable outcome being human sacrifice. The players used a heavy rubber ball which had to be propelled with knees, hips and elbows through a stone ring placed high on one of the walls surrounding the grounds. The game was particularly important to the culture of the Maya and in El Tajín, where no less than 17 ballcourts have been discovered.

The discovery in 1952 of a burial chamber in the Temple of the Inscriptions at Palenque led to the speculation that Mexican pyramids, like those in Egypt, were a place for burial and not merely a base for the temple. Another discovery, this time of the vivid floor-to-ceiling battle murals in Bonampak, also revolutionized our knowledge not only of art forms and techniques, but also of the ancient Mayan way of life. These unique mural paintings provide us with infinite detail of Mayan dress, music, warfare and rituals.

BRANCHING OUT

The historian Michael D. Coe once wrote – "The Mesoamerican tree of culture has many branches and many roots, but the main trunk is Olmec civilization."

– and believed that the universe would end when the Great Cycle of the Long Count ran out in the year 2011.

The Mayas needed a precise calendar because coordination of the heavenly bodies determined everything they did, beginning with the agriculture cycle. Since the universe moves in regular cycles, they knew that past movements of stars and planets would be repeated and thus Mayan priests could make predictions and take appropriate action to forestall disaster.

LEFT: "The Wrestler," an Olmec sculpture.
ABOVE: Pyramid of the Magician at the Mayan city of Uxmal, Yucatán Peninsula.

Time keepers

The passage of time was an all-important issue to the Maya, and their calendar was the most sophisticated of any used in Mesoamerica No other culture was so obsessed with recording time. They calculated the solar year at 365.2422 days and the moon's period at 29.5209 days. Both figures are so accurate that it was only in the 20th century that scientists came up with figures infinitesimally more exact. They calculated time from a date zero in the year 3113 BC

Gods of the Maya

The Mayan pantheon was just as complicated as their calendar. We know of 166 named deities, each with four representations corresponding to the cardinal points; there were counterparts for the opposite sex and every astronomical god had an underground avatar, or incarnation. The supreme god seems to have been Itzamná ("Lizard House"), the fire deity, often represented as an old man with a Roman nose. In his embodiment as the Sun, he was the husband of the Moon Goddess, Ixchel, benefactress of weavers, doctors and women. Believing themselves to be descended from people of corn, Yum Kaax, the god of maize, was also important to the Maya, as was Chac, the rain deity. During the post-Classic period, the Toltecs from the central highlands introduced the cult of the feathered serpent, known to the Maya as Kukulkán.

Long-thought to have been peaceful worshippers of the gods, it is now known that the elaborate Mayan rituals included blood-letting (using the tail of a stingray) from ears, tongues or penises, and that fiestas involved dance and sacrifice to win the favor of the gods. Victims in Chichén Itzá

HORSE GODS

The Maya associated the mounted Spaniards with the Chacs; horse and rider were thought to be one creature and their firearms represented thunder and lightning.

Albán. Moving goods by sea in large canoes, and using cocoa beans as a form of currency, they traded textiles, tools, feathers, pottery, precious stones, medicinal herbs, incense and salt.

Classic Maya civilization in the southern lowlands suffered a fatal decline beginning in the 9th century, while the late-Classic Puuc-style architecture was flourishing in northern Yucatán. The Toltec invaders arrived from central Mexico in the late 10th century, and the starker architecture can be felt in Chichén Itzá.

were thrown into the sacred Cenote (a great natural well) in the hope of increasing rainfall.

Common ground

The Mayas had a structured and disciplined society governed by priest-rulers. But they were never united at a single capital or under a single ruler. The autonomous city-states shared a common hieroglyphic script, the concept of zero, and a common religion and cosmology. Their distant ceremonial centers were linked by sacred roads, or *sacbeob*.

Between the 3rd and 6th centuries, the Maya had considerable contact with other parts of Mesoamerica, especially Teotihuacán and Monte

Teotihuacán

The cultures of the central highlands have provided the most detailed knowledge of Mexico's pre-Hispanic history. The last people to dominate the region were the Aztecs; the first great civilization of the highland plateau was Teotihuacán, which emerged some 200 years before the Christian era. Although Teotihuacán was a ghost town when the Aztecs arrived in the 1300s, it was so imposing that the Aztecs called it "The Place of the Gods", and believed the Sun and the Moon had been created there.

Classic Teotihuacán was an important ceremonial center as well as being the first planned urban society in Mesoamerica; its influence, both in religion, art and architecture, was felt as far south as Guatemala.

Influential gods

Tlaloc, the god of rain and fertility, was one of the principal deities of Teotihuacán, like Chac to the Maya or Cocijo to the Zapotecs. The people portrayed in the *Paradise of Tlaloc* mural at Teotihuacán (or reproduced in the Museum of Anthropology, in Mexico City), are frolicking, singing and dancing in a lush, fertile land.

The cult of Quetzalcóatl, the Plumed Serpent, Aztec god of wind and dawn, also developed in Teotihuacán. The many legends about Quetzalcóatl tell how he descended into the Land them with blood and thus created the human race; how he stole maize from the ants and thus introduced food to mankind, and much more.

Teotihuacán was an important commercial center which controlled large deposits of obsidian, used throughout Mesoamerica for making tools and weapons. Trade in this raw material as well as the city's sacred status, helped Teotihuacán gain widespread power and influence. It also resulted in the proliferation of sacred Teotihuacán art: life-size masks made from serpentine or jade by the skilled resident lapidaries from Guerrero; complex incense burners; tripod vessels carved or stuccoed with intricate mythological motifs; the so-called thin-orange ware; and complex figurines, some with movable arms and legs.

Beginning with Teotihuacán in the 8th century, the Classic civilizations of Mexico went into decline, and all had collapsed by the end of the 10th century. The city of Teotihuacán, was burnt and all but abandoned; whether this was the result of internal rebellion or an invasion – perhaps by the Toltecs – remains a mystery.

The Toltecs

In the 10th century, after the destruction of Teotihuacán but before the rise of the Aztecs and Tenochtitlán, a group of Chichimecas, nomadic hunters, came to central Mexico, founded Tula and became Toltecs (craftsmen); there were masons, jade carvers, weavers, metal-smiths, and featherworkers.

The cult of Quetzalcóatl, the feathered serpent, took on an even greater significance than in Teotihuacán. Legend has it that a Quetzalcóatl ruler fled to the East after he was driven out of Tula by the warrior god, Texcatlipoca. The Toltecs became increasingly militaristic; at one time they controlled much of central Mexico, and are thought to be the first to have introduced the practice of mass human sacrifice.

Apart from the serpent, predominant Toltec motifs include the reclining *chacmool*; the famous Atlantes; eagles and jaguars devouring human hearts, and the *tzompantli,* or human skull rack. Many of the architectural and iconographic elements of Tula were repeated in Chichén Itzá by the invading Toltec exiles.

Their commercial ties reached northwards too: emblems and artefacts have been found as far north as Casas Grandes, in Chihuahua, and even further afield in Arizona and northern New Mexico. The Toltec empire was fairly short-lived, however, and Tula, like Teotihucán, was partly destroyed by fire in the 12th century.

The Aztecs

By the time the Spaniards arrived, Aztec culture was in full bloom; their dominance of the Gulf coast was complete, although the West was still putting up a struggle and resisting Aztec rule.

According to legend, the Aztecs – or Mexica – and other Náhuatl-speakers came from

LEFT: Mayan mural painting in Bonampak, Chiapas.
RIGHT: Statue of chacmool, at Chichén Itzá, Yucatán.

the seven caves called Chicomozoc, in the north of Mexico. The Mexica claimed to have migrated from Aztlán, where they first had their vision of an eagle, perched on a cactus and devouring a serpent. This cosmic symbol – the eagle representing the sky and the sun, the snake symbolizing the earth, and the cactus as sustenance of a wandering desert people – is today the national emblem of Mexico.

Place of the Cactus

Led by their tribal god, Huitzilopochtli, they reached the central highlands and, on an island in Lake Texcoco, they saw the prophesied eagle

which was to end over a century of wandering. And so, in about 1345, the Mexica founded what was to be the great city of Tenochtitlán, named for their leader Tenoch, and which means "Place of the Cactus."

At first they lived off snake meat, fish, ducks and even mosquito larva. The aquatic environment was ideal for the *chinampa* system of floating gardens anchored to the lake bottom. The lake also provided easy communication in a land where terrestrial transport, with no pack animals, was complicated.

Around 1429, the Mexicas formed a triple alliance with nearby Tlacopán and Texcoco, establishing the basis of the Aztec Empire. Dur-

ing the reign of Moctezuma I, Tenochtitlán emerged as an imperial capital, and after a series of ambitious military campaigns the Aztecs captured Oaxaca and subdued many Mixtec centers in the south.

Then they headed east and launched campaigns against the Huastecs and the Totonacs on the Gulf Coast. The Aztecs were not interested in occupying the lands of the vanquished. They left the conquered peoples with their own leaders and government but demanded hefty tributes of shells (used for religious rites), quetzal feathers, jaguar skins and precious stones; huge numbers of prisoners were taken to Tenochtitlán to be sacrificed and dedicated to the gods.

The inauguration of the temple-pyramid of Huitzilopochtli in 1487 – 19 years after the death of Moctezuma – was accompanied by the sacrifice of thousands of prisoners who, according to some accounts, were marshalled, four abreast, in a 5-km (3-mile) long file, then driven to the sanctuary on top of the pyramid where priests tore out their hearts. The ritual is said to have lasted for three days and nights.

Five suns

Over 2,000 gods were worshipped in the complex Aztec pantheon, although the main temple at Tenochtitlán was dedicated to Huitzilopochtli – the tribal hummingbird god – and to Tlaloc, the rain god. Two other major temples stood beside the great pyramid: one was dedicated to Tezcatlipoca, the smoking-mirror god, and the other was the round temple of Quetzalcóatl, the plumed serpent. The Aztec believed there were five time-spans, or Suns.

The First Sun lasted 676 years. This was the reign of the god Tezcatlipoca – the Sun of Night and Earth – when the land was inhabited by giants. Quetzalcóatl defeated the First Sun who fell into the water and was transformed into a jaguar that ate the giants.

The Second Sun, Quetzalcóatl, God of the Wind, was overthrown by the same jaguar after ruling for 364 years. A great wind arose and everyone perished except for a few monkeys.

The Third Sun was Tlaloc, the Rain of Fire, whose domination lasted 312 years and ended when Quetzalcóatl conjured up a day-long rain of fire which killed everyone except a few who survived as birds, mostly turkeys.

The Fourth Sun, Chalchiuhtlicue, controlled

the world for 676 years but came to an end when Tlaloc sent a great flood which drowned all but a few who only survived as fish.

The Fifth Sun, the Sun of Movement, is the contemporary ruler whose era first started at Teotihuacán.

In their constant struggle to appease the gods and keep the Fifth Sun alive, the Aztecs provided him with that most sacred and life-giving of food – living human hearts.

> ### DECIPHERING CODICES
>
> The picture-writing of the Aztec codices is quite easy to interpret. Traveling is depicted by footprints, speech is a scroll emerging from the speaker's mouth, and song is indicated by the same scrolls decorated with flowers.

Aztec art

The Aztecs, more often praised for their military prowess than their artistic achievements, developed a strong art style. They were, in fact, skilled sculptors, potters, jewelers and painters, whose books – the codices – are among the most beautiful ever produced. As well as the rigid, highly stylized religious sculptures, there was a strong strain of naturalism in their representation of grasshoppers, coyotes, birds, frogs, rabbits, turtles, monkeys, fish and other animals.

The giant Sun Stone or Aztec Calendar of Tenochtitlán (almost 4 meters/13 ft in diameter) is the synthesis of Aztec astronomic knowledge and there are interpretations of its significance. At the center it exhibits the face of the impassive Sun God surrounded by successive rings containing astronomical symbols. The outermost ring is formed by two fire-serpents facing each other.

Perhaps, however, the greatest masterpiece of Aztec art was the magnificent city of Tenochtitlán they built in the middle of the lake, the proud center of their powerful empire.

Zapotec and Mixtec

The ceremonial center of Monte Albán, the oldest post-Olmec site, was in fact the most enduring of all the Classic civilizations of ancient Mexico. It is also the greatest achievement of the Zapotec culture, which grew and thrived in the southern state of Oaxaca throughout the Classic period. The early phase, when the mountain-top was lopped off to make the huge

platform, shows strong Olmec influence.

Very early on, the Zapotecs developed a fully-fledged writing system of glyphs and used the bar and dot system also used by the Maya. These were the people who created the extraordinary series of bas-reliefs at Monte Albán, called *Los Danzantes* (The Dancers). Their ceramic funerary effigy urns, depicting seated deities wearing flamboyant costumes and jewelry, are unique. The urns were placed in elaborate vaulted stone tombs where they are

believed to have guarded the noble deceased.

In about AD 1000 the Mixtecs, a people who came from the Cholula-Puebla area further north, invaded Monte Albán, already in decline, mixed with the Zapotecs, and took the site over for their own necropolis. They reopened some of the earlier Zapotec tombs and replaced the occupants with their own dead. The best-known of the Mixtec graves, Tomb 7, at Mitla, was excavated in 1932 by the Mexican archeologist Dr Alfonso Caso. He discovered intricate jewelry and other precious artefacts – more than 500 pieces in all – the greatest single treasure trove ever found in Mesoamerica.

The Mixtecs were famed as master craftsmen

LEFT: stone *tzompantli* (skull rack) from the days of human sacrifices.

ABOVE: Mixtec skull overlaid with turquoise mosaic.

and the Aztecs employed them to make gold jewelry and turquoise and feather mosaics. Their finely wrought gold pieces were cast with the lost-wax method, and their superbly painted polychrome pottery was traded and imitated from Central Mexico to Guatemala.

The Mixtec codices measure up to 12 meters (39 ft) in length and are a vital source of all kinds of information. Illustrations and glyphs on the lime-coated deer-skin manuscripts recount historical events, divine knowledge or the genealogies of noble families.

The best example of Mixtec architecture can be seen at Mitla, east of Oaxaca, where the

long, low "palaces" are decorated in finely cut raised stone mosaic; the geometrical patterns suggest textile designs and resemble the Mayan stone latticework at Uxmal in the Yucatán.

Totonacs

The fertile, tropical Gulf Coast of Mexico with its abundant rainfall and year-round warm temperatures was not only home to the Olmecs, the first civilization of Mesoamerica, but also to the Totonacs in Central Veracruz and the Huastecs in the north.

The name Totonac is used as a generic term to refer to cultures that developed in Central Veracruz, principally at Remojadas, El Tajín

and El Zapotal, although there are literally dozens of other archeological sites in this region.

The Remojadas culture, not recognized for its ceremonial centers or monumental architecture, was outstanding for its mastery of clay. Archeological finds show that the ancient tradition of burying the dead with offerings of clay sculptures and vessels was observed in Central Veracruz. The clay figures are usually seated and wearing short skirts; their faces have characteristically slanting eyes with a cross-eyed expression, which was considered a trait of physical beauty. Many of the figurines were in fact whistles or rattles, and were painted with elaborate geometric designs.

The enigmatic smiling figurines are the most characteristic of the Central Veracruz culture. The symbolism of these hollow figurines, which include both men and women, has been studied by many researchers. Some believe they portray the ritualistic use of hallucinogenic substances (hence the smile), while others see them simply as the expression of the festive, happy character of the coastal inhabitants.

The large clay sculptures unearthed at El Zapotal in the 1970s were part of a colossal offering made by the ancient coastal inhabitants to Mictlantecuhtli, god of the underworld. The solemn fleshless figure of "The Lord of the Dead" himself was accompanied by several hundred figures and other objects, including smiling figures and a group of monumental clay sculptures known as Cihuateotl, the women who were deified after dying in childbirth.

The vast city of El Tajín, with its famous Pyramid of the Niches, is, without a doubt, the climax of monumental architecture in Veracruz and one of the most outstanding cities of the pre-Hispanic world.

The ritual ballgame appears to have formed the core of the customs of El Tajín's culture. Some 17 courts have been found at the site, and relief panels are carved with scenes depicting the sacrifice of the players and rituals related to the sacred game. One mural painting depicts a beheaded player with serpents of blood spurting from his neck, symbolizing fertility and the earth. It is thought that the many beautiful but enigmatic carved stone *hachas* (axes), *palmas* (palms) and *yugos* (yokes) were also part of the ballplaying ceremony, or at least had ritual significance. El Tajín was undoubtedly an important regional capital that dominated a vast territory and whose influence was widespread; the cultural and economic relations between El Tajín and contemporary centers such as Teotihuacán and Xochicalco are evident.

Huastecs

The ancient Huastecs occupied an area in the north of Veracruz that also touched on the states of Hidalgo, Puebla, San Luis Potosí and Tamaulipas. Their language, which is still spoken by the Huastec descendents today, was a Mayan tongue that

INSPIRATION

Picasso turned to Africa for his inspiration, whereas sculptor Henry Moore sought his from the monumental sculptures of pre-Hispanic Mexico. His reclining figures are direct descendants of the *chacmool*.

thought to be children's toys. Mexican archeologist José García Payán suggests that the Huastecs were great founders of culture and that many of the deities in the Aztec pantheon, including the origins of the great Quetzalcóatl himself, "the nerve center of Mexican mythology," can be traced to Huastec culture.

But the Aztecs conquered the Huastecs during the reign of Ahuizotl, predecessor of Moctezuma II. The Mexica were shocked by the Huastecs who

had branched off from the main trunk in the remote past.

Comparatively little archaeological work has been carried out on the architecture of the Huastecs, and most knowledge comes from their extraordinary art work. Their highly stylized sandstone sculptures and reliefs depict synthesized body shapes of women and men, with the characteristic conical headdress, and bent-over figures of hunchbacks. There are also engraved shells, delicate clay figurines, bowls, vessels and figures of animals with wheels,

ABOVE LEFT: an eternal smile from a Totonac figure.
ABOVE: Diego Rivera mural depicting the city of El Tajín.

faced their enemy totally naked, their bodies painted with brilliant colors, their heads flattened and deformed, their hair and sharp filed teeth dyed.

Western cultures

Much less is known about the cultures of western Mexico, although effigy pottery found in shaft and chamber tombs have revealed much about the beliefs and rituals of the people who inhabited this area 2,000 years ago. Tombs of a similar kind have been found in Ecuador, and this has sparked the notion that they were first introduced into Mexico by sea voyagers from the south. Colima, Jalisco and Nayarit never merged into unified kingdoms but remained under chieftains who controlled small areas with little cultural exchange between groups.

From their pottery, it is evident they believed in life after death. Thus a man was buried with ceramic replicas of his wife, servants and slaves to enhance his life in the afterworld. The clay figures are among the most charming art of Mexico. Lacking the refinement of the Maya or the technical sophistication of the Mixtecs, the work of the potters of the west is distinctive, thanks to its simplicity and cleanliness of design and to the joyfulness expressed. These potters portrayed everyday life as well as religious themes: a ritual

ball game with a crowd of spectators, lovers embracing, phallic dances, musicians, warriors and animals; one of their most common models was the *itzcuintli*, the plump and hairless, native Mexican dog, said to be very tasty and often served as a delicacy at banquets.

The Tarascans

Thanks to the Spaniards, we know a good deal about the Tarascan culture of Michoacán. Shortly after the Conquest, the first viceroy ordered Vasco de Quiroga to compile a history of the Purépecha, or Tarascans as they were called by the Spanish; *Chronicles of Michoacán* provides an introduction to Tarascan culture.

The Aztecs claimed common ancestry with the Tarascans, saying they were both part of the Chichimeca group of tribes who had originated from caves in the north.

Michoacán means "Place of the Fishermen," and the state of Michoacán is bordered by the Pacific Ocean. However, the ancient religion of the inhabitants was based not on the ocean, but on volcanoes. The cult of fire was central to the Tarascan religion. The chief deity, Curicáueri, the "Great Burner," represented the young Sun. In his honor, the people made human sacrifices and kept fires burning constantly on top of huge stone ceremonial structures they built, called *yácatas*. The largest of these *yácatas* is at Tzintzuntzán, the Tarascan capital, on the shores of Lake Pátzcuaro.

Apart from the *yácatas*, the Tarascans built mainly in wood. They excelled in pottery, woodwork, copperware, and especially in featherwork (modern Tarascans still practise all of these crafts except featherwork, an art form that has been abandoned).

The ancient Tarascans knew how to organize for battle and had well-trained military forces. Tariácuari, the first legendary king, welded the rival clans into a well-knit alliance that twice managed to defeat the Aztec juggernaut.

The Tarascan kingdom ended on a sad note. Converted to Christianity, the last of the Tarascan kings, Tangaxoan II, went humbly to pay homage and submit to Cortés in 1522. Debasing himself, as was the Tarascan custom, he wore soiled and torn clothing. But to no avail; Nuño de Guzmán, the most brutal of the conquistadores, had the king burned alive on the pretext that he had conspired against Spanish rule; in reality it was because the king was unable to produce enough gold.

Modern appreciation

The recent growth of nationalism has kindled an appreciation and enthusiasm for pre-Hispanic art in Mexico; national identity and cultural pride have found a prestigious symbol in the neglected art of the indians, and today pre-Hispanic motifs are everywhere – in the murals on many public buildings, in architecture, interior decoration, and all kinds of design, from coins and stamps to jewelry and clothes. ❑

ABOVE: lifelike pottery dog, Colima culture.
RIGHT: Mayan city of Palenque, Chiapas.

Decisive Dates

PRE-HISPANIC ERA

50,000 BC: First human migrations to the Americas-from Asia over the temporary land bridge joining the two continents across the Bering Straits.

10,000 BC: Human settlements established in the Valley of Mexico. Communities form, based on fishing, hunting and gathering.

9000–1200 BC: The beginning of agriculture with the cultivation of corn. Former hunters and gatherers become farmers with the Mexican 'trinity' of staples – corn, beans and chiles – already their main crops.

1200–400 BC: Pre-Classical period. Olmec culture develops, flowers and declines. Considered to have had great influence on later Mayan peoples, the Olmecs are noted for their colossal stone head sculptures. Chief Olmec centers at La Venta, Tres Zapotes and San Lorenzo. Mayan settlement begins in the southern lowlands, and construction begins at Monte Albán in the Valley of Oaxaca.

300–900 AD: Classical period. Many Mesoamerican cultures flourish: formation of priest caste system with a proliferation of deities; art, ceramics, literature and astronomy reached their peak; urbanism reaches its apex with the building of large cities and complex ceremonial centers. Chichén Itzá and Uxmal in the Yucatán are among chief Mayan sites.

900–1000 AD: Beginning of post-Classical period. Militarization of theocratic societies. Emergence of warlike Toltecs who establish an empire in the Valley of Mexico, founding the cities of Tula and Tulancingo. Development of metallurgy. Most cities are suddenly and mysteriously abandoned, and major cultural changes take place.

1345: Aztecs found city of Tenochtitlán, their capital, on swampy island in Lake Texcoco, site of present-day Mexico City. Immediately begin construction of the Templo Mayor Ceremonial Center.

SPANISH CONQUEST

1517: Spanish navigator Hernández de Córdova makes exploratory expedition along coast of Yucatán, observing signs of Mayan settlement.

1519: Hernán Cortés and his conquistadores arrive at Tenochtitlán and marvel at island city. They are greeted peacefully by Montezuma II and treated as guests of honor. Current population of Mesoamerica estimated at 25 million.

1520: Hundreds of indians murdered in the Templo Mayor by Pedro de Alvarado, in the absence of Cortés. Large numbers of Spanish are subsequently killed as they try to fight their way out of the city. The event becomes known as *Noche Triste*, Sad Night.

August 1521: After a 75-day siege, Tenochtitlán falls to the Spanish and is razed to the ground.

COLONIAL ERA C.1521–1821

1530: King Carlos V declares Mexico City capital of New Spain and residence of the viceroy.

1539: First printing press introduced in Mexico.

1566: Martín Cortés, son of Hernán instigates first revolt of conquistadores against centralized control from Spain.

1571: Spanish Inquisition is established in Mexico.

1573: Construction begins on present cathedral of Mexico City.

1692: Riot in Mexico City. The Viceroyal Palace and City Hall are set on fire by the crowds.

1810-21: Mexico's War of Independence from Spain. Miguel Hidalgo, curate of Dolores, makes his famous *Grito de Dolores* – Cry for Independence.

September 1821: Independence is declared with the triumphant arrival of General Agustín de Iturbide and the Ejército Trigarante in Mexico City.

1822: Iturbide crowned Emperor Agustín I.

1823: Antonio López de Santa Anna campaigns for alternative republican plan and Iturbide abdicates. The Mexican Constitution is announced, with the establishment of a federal republic.

1846-8: President Santa Anna declares war on the

United States. Mexico City invaded. Military cadets in Chapultepec Castle die in battle and are immortalized as the *Niños Héroes* (Boy Heroes). In the concluding Treaty of Guadalupe, Mexico cedes Texas, New Mexico, Arizona and California – half its territory – to the United States.

1855: Benito Juárez orders confiscation of Catholic Church property; Church is separated from State.

1858: Wars for Reform between Conservatives and Liberals. Reform Laws include: nationalisation of Church property; civil marriages; secularization of cemeteries; freedom of worship.

1862: The Battle of Puebla. Invading French forces defeated by National Army.

1864: Maximilian of Hapsburg, sent by Napoleon II to be emperor of Mexico, is received ceremoniously. Executed by firing squad three years later.

1867: Mexican Republic re-established and Zapotec indian Benito Juárez declared president.

1873: Cristero Revolt erupts in Guanajuato and Jalisco, protesting reform measures.

1876-1911: General Porfirio Díaz is president, then dictator. His 35-year administration, the *Porfiriato*, is characterized in the capital by European-style mansions and elsewhere by enormous *haciendas* for the few and poverty for the majority.

November 1910: Armed rebellion finally ousts Díaz from office. He flees to self-imposed exile in Paris.

MEXICAN REVOLUTION, 1910–21

1910: Struggle for *Tierra y Libertad* (Land and Liberty). Charismatic leaders Emiliano Zapata and Pancho Villa occupy Mexico City for several days.

1917: New Constitution announced; Venustiano Carranza elected president.

1919: Emiliano Zapata is assassinated.

1920: Adolfo de la Huerta declared provisional president by Congress.

MODERN ERA, FOUNDING OF PRI, 1929

1929: Formation of the first official political party, the Partido Nacional Revolucionario – now the leading Partido Revolucionario Institucional (PRI).

1938: President Lázaro Cárdenas expropriates petroleum companies and founds the nationalized Petróleos Mexicanos (PEMEX). Nationalization of rail network.

1968: Students killed in demonstration in Tlatelolco,

LEFT: Aztec codex painting showing national symbol of an eagle on a cactus plant.

RIGHT: portrait of indian girl from Oaxaca, photographed by Desiré Charnay.

Mexico City, days before opening ceremony of the Olympic Games. The first subway line is put into operation in Mexico City.

1982: President José López Portillo nationalizes banking system.

1985: Earthquake measuring 8.1 on the Richter Scale strikes Mexico City. Thousands killed but most structures remain intact.

1986: Following the worldwide collapse of petroleum prices, Mexico enters GATT (General Agreement on Tariffs and Trade).

1988: PRI candidate Ernesto Salinas de Gortari, elected president, amid allegations of fraud.

1994: North American Free Trade Agreement between

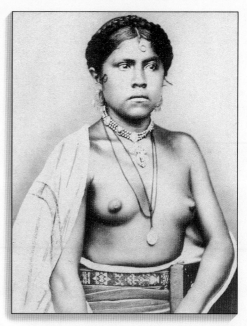

Mexico, the United States and Canada goes into effect, making the region one of the world's largest trading zones.

January 1994: Emergence of indian group Ejército Zapatista de Liberación Nacional (EZLN), campaigning for land distribution and human rights issues, with capture of four towns in Chiapas.

March 1994: Assassination of Luis Donaldo Colosio, presidential candidate of the PRI.

August 1994: Ernesto Zedillo Ponce de León, PRI campaign manager, elected president.

February 1996: EZLN signs the first of six peace accords with the Mexican government, all aimed at improving political and human rights of indigenous groups. ❑

LOS CONQUISTADORES

The culture clash produced when Hernán Cortés met Aztec god-king Moctezuma

can still be felt in Mexico today, nearly 500 years later

The Spanish conquest of Mexico was the result of a violent clash between two empires, both of which were cultured, cruel and well organized. But it was there that the similarities stopped.

From an outsider's point of view, it is one of the most exciting adventure stories of mankind.

Against the tens of thousands of Aztec warriors and allied tribes, Hernán Cortés, the Spanish leader of the conquistadores, had fewer than 400 Spanish soldiers in the beginning, with 16 horses – "fearsome beasts" (as reported in the Spanish chronicles), never before seen in the New World – 10 heavy guns, four lighter pieces of artillery and plenty of ammunition.

Although the sound and fury of the weaponry initially terrified the Aztecs it was not their final undoing. The success of Cortés's expedition would have been impossible without the alliance of indian groups hostile to the Aztecs: most of all the Tlaxcalans, who provided thousands of men to fight alongside the Spaniards.

Burning the boats

Cortés was just 19 years old when he arrived on the island of Hispaniola in 1504. Intelligent, ruthless and ambitious, he craved adventure. Under Diego de Velázquez, the governor of Cuba, he organized an expedition to Mexico. After a battle in Tabasco he landed, with 11 ships (on the Gulf coast) at Veracruz on April 22, 1519.

The first thing Cortés did was to order the destruction of all but one of his ships. It was a daring but intelligent military move to cut himself off from the line of retreat. His men now knew beyond doubt that there was no turning back; they had to conquer the enemy or die in the process.

The journey to Tenochtitlán

The Spaniards were well received by the Totonac indians of Cempoala and they soon began the 312 km (194 mile) march inland to the Aztec capital of Tenochtitlán.

When the invaders finally reached the outskirts of Tenochtitlán, they beheld a marvelous city set in a lake with a wide main street, temples, terraces, gardens and snowcapped blue mountains in the distance. Throngs of curious Aztecs watched them arrive with their armor, cannon and horses.

Bernal Díaz, a soldier in Cortés's army, described in his journal the wonder he felt when he and his fellow comrades first saw the shimmering, shining Aztec capital. "[The city] seemed like an enchanted vision from the tale of Amadis", he wrote. "Indeed some of our soldiers asked whether it was not all a dream." The Spaniards saw the people, the canals, the bridges and the boats gliding on the water carrying produce to market. They saw huge causeways, miles long, wide enough for 10 horses to ride abreast. They visited the great market of Tlatelolco, patronized by some 70,000 people a day, with row upon row of every kind of merchandise laid out for sale.

Moctezuma came out to meet Cortés. The king was about 40 years old, tall and trim, with a wispy beard, his skin lighter than that of his copper-hued subjects. He greeted Cortés courteously and, thinking the Spaniard was a divine envoy from the god Quetzalcóatl, gave him many gifts and arranged for his men to quarter in one of the palaces.

CORTÉS'S ROUTE

Some travel agencies offer organized tours which follow the "Ruta de Cortés" from Veracruz to Mexico City.

There followed a week or so of palaver between Moctezuma and Cortés (the two spoke through Cortés's trusted indian interpreter, La Malinche) but nothing much was accomplished. The king remained polite but Cortés became increasingly bold and his men were growing restive, ready for action. Eventually he and his cohorts decided on a plan and in a highly daring stroke they kidnapped and took Moctezuma hostage. The king, still believing Cortés to be a divine envoy, kept his people from rebelling.

Back in Cuba, Governor Velázquez had heard the reports. Fearing Cortés was becoming too ambitious, he sent an expedition from Cuba to arrest him. Ever the strategist, Cortés sallied forth to meet his countrymen, defeated them, and incorporated them into his army.

Meanwhile, the Spanish troops under Capitán Alvarado, continued to guard the prisoner Moctezuma. But they made the grave mistake of attacking and slaughtering a group of priests and nobles who were taking part in a religious ceremony. As word of the killings spread, the Aztecs rose in rebellion and attacked the Spanish. Cortés pressed Moctezuma to cool down his warriors. According to one version, the king appealed to his people but they reviled and wounded him and he died soon after. Others claim that it was the Spaniards who killed him.

A sad night for Cortés

The Aztecs blockaded the palace, destroyed the bridges over the canals, and trapped the conquistadores. On the night of June 30, 1520, Cortés's men fled the palace. The Aztecs thrust with their long copper-tipped spears; they were experts with the sling and also wielded the *maquahuitl*, a paddle-shaped club inset with razor-like pieces of obsidian. The Spaniards fought back then ran for their lives while the

LEFT: Two schoolbook portraits of Hernan Cortés.
RIGHT: Cortés enters Tenochtitlán (detail of a painted screen from the colonial period).

Aztecs, no longer fearful of the white invaders, harassed them along their road of retreat.

Many Spaniards died from greed; weighed down with Aztec gold, they could not fight or swim to safety or even move effectively.

Bernal Díaz wrote that during this *"Noche Triste"* (Sad Night), as it became known, the Spanish lost more than half their army, all their artillery and munitions, and many of their horses. "We fought very well but they were so strong and had so many bands which relieved one another by turns, that if we

had been ten thousand Trojan Hectors and so many Rolands, even then we should not have been able to break through."

Help from Tlaxcala

The Aztecs failed to follow up their victory and the surviving Spaniards managed to escape. They lived on wild berries and the few ears of corn they could glean from the fields, but they still managed to reach their allies in Tlaxcala.

With reinforcements of men and arms, Cortés was able to devise a strategy for the final assault on Tenochtitlán. He ordered 13 war sloops to be built and armed with cannon. The boats were hauled to Lake Texcoco, where the

Spaniards could control passage on the water, and thus deprive the Aztecs of supplies of food and fresh water.

On their final assault the Spaniards had 86 horsemen, 700 foot soldiers and 118 cross-bowmen and musketeers as well as the thousands of indian warriors from Tlaxcala. The footmen discarded their metal armor and wore the quilted cotton protection of the Aztecs.

The following year, 1521, a reinforced Spanish army laid siege to Tenochtitlán for almost three long months. They conquered the causeways first, then the city, street by street. Besides professional tactics, strength, arms, and

"For some years before the Spanish came, a miasma of doom had hung in the air and a series of omens had portended disaster. One night, the sages said, a huge, flaming ear of corn had appeared in the sky, dripping blood. A comet flared, trailing tails of fire.

A man with two heads was reported walking the streets. The waters of Lake Texcoco had risen without warning on a windless day and flooded the city. A strange bird with a mirror set in his head was captured and taken to Moctezuma. The king looked in the mirror and, though it was daytime, saw the night sky and stars reflected. Clearly something was wrong.

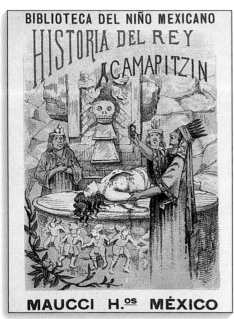

the help of the Tlaxcalan indians, the Spanish cause was aided mightily by a virulent smallpox epidemic that was sweeping through the Aztec population; many others were slowly dying from lack of fresh water as the lake around them was impure and brackish. The Aztec resistance ended when the Spaniards captured the new emperor, Cuauhtémoc, as he tried to flee Tenochtitlán in a canoe.

Omens of disaster

Consider the story of the conquest of Mexico from the point of view of the Aztecs, as described by the Mexican scholar Miguel León Portilla in his book *The Broken Spears:*

He looked again and saw a strange army advancing on his capital. The soldiers were mounted on animals that looked like deer."

Quetzalcóatl's return

It was about this time that reports came of the Spanish landings on the coast. Moctezuma of course knew the legend foretelling the return from the east of the god-king Quetzalcóatl. The description of the Spanish arriving in their floating towers coinicided with the legend; they, like Quetzalcóatl, were both fair-skinned and bearded.

So the invaders arrived and Moctezuma tried to win them with gold. Miguel León Portilla wrote that they "picked up the gold and fingered it like monkeys... they hungered like pigs for that gold."

Broken spears

The destruction of Tenochtitlán was dreadful, the author said. "The cries of the helpless women and children were heart-rending. The Tlaxcalan and the other enemies of the Aztecs revenged themselves pitilessly for old offenses and robbed [the people] of everything they could find... The anguish and bewilderment was piti-

INTERPRETATIONS

La Malinche, Cortés's indian interpreter, aide and lover is considered the arch traitor by Mexicans, even today.

daughter of an indian nobleman, who spoke both Maya and Náhuatl, the language of the Aztecs. She is thought to have learned Spanish from a seaman who had been shipwrecked off the Yucatán coast. Cortés often acted on advice given to him by La Malinche, who had a better understanding of how the Aztecs' minds worked.

The Spanish not only lusted for gold, they also had a sense of divine mission, and wanted to win land for their monarch and in the process to aggrandize his realm. They believed in their

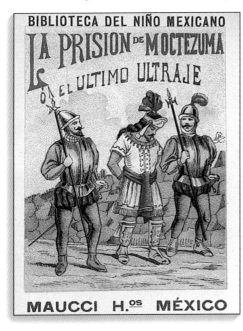

ful to see. The warriors gathered on the rooftops and stared at the ruins of their city in a dazed silence and the women and children and old men were all weeping."

La Malinche

Cortés's most valuable aide was his indian mistress and interpreter, Doña Marina, who was known as "La Malinche." Presented to Cortés after his first battle in Tabasco, she was the

---

FAR LEFT: matchbox art depicts human sacrifice.
LEFT: portrait of Hernan Cortés.
ABOVE: Moctezuma is captured.
ABOVE RIGHT: Cortés weeps on the night of his defeat.

hearts that God was on their side and an important part of this latest mission was to convert the indians to Catholicism.

Bernal Díaz said the Spanish triumph was achieved "not of our volition, but by the guidance of God. For what soldiers in the world, numbering only four hundred – and we were even fewer – would have dared to enter a city as strong as Mexico, which is larger than Venice and more than 4,500 miles away from our own Castile?"

The defeat of Tenochtitlán – certainly one of the most traumatic clashes of culture in world history – ushered in the colonial rule, which lasted for the next three hundred years. ❏

COLONIALISM AND INDEPENDENCE

Colonial society was structured according to an elaborate caste system,

based on race and rigidly controlled by the Spanish Crown

For three centuries Spain governed Mexico. It was hardly an enlightened rule, and often harsh colonialism at its worst. Rebellion flared from time to time, but the rebels – including Hernán Cortés's own son Martín – were always swiftly crushed.

At the beginning of the 16th century, Spain – united after finally driving out the Moors – was one of the most dynamic countries in the world. At home the Church reigned supreme, while small groups of nobles held staunch political power. A rigid hierarchy prevailed and not a breath of democracy was permitted.

And in the colonies Spain ruled with an iron hand. Recognizing the potential of this virgin territory, they were quick to rule out any form of semi-autonomy in the "New Spain", as it was now called. After defeating the Aztecs, the Spanish consolidated their power, subjugated the indians, and reached out for new riches. The Crown not only neglected the conquistadores but eventually took away many of the landgrants which Cortés had given his stalwarts. A nobleman was dispatched to rule New Spain as the viceroy, and the soldiers who had fought so bravely came away with little more than their wounds. "We ought to call ourselves, not the victors of New Spain, but the victims of Hernán Cortés," Bernal Díaz commented bitterly.

Encomiendas and haciendas

Initially a land-grant system was introduced whereby the holder of the grant – called an *encomienda* – was allocated some land and a number of indian workers, whom it was his duty to protect and convert to Christianity. Most of the *encomiendas* were too small to be economically viable and fewer than two percent of the holders could make a living out of them.

PRECEDING PAGES: Mexican Independence, depicted in a mural by Juan O'Gorman.
LEFT: the Palacio de Iturbide, Mexico City, in the 19th century.
RIGHT: *San Rafael and Tobias* by Miguel Cabrera (1695–1768), Mexico's most famous colonial artist.

As agriculture developed, the *encomiendas* gave rise to *haciendas,* larger extensions of land bought from the Crown.

Nobody was much troubled by the master-servant relationship between Spaniard and indian. The Church heartily supported the philosophy that each person had his assigned station in life

and that only by humbly accepting his place could he reap his reward in the next life. It took decades to Christianize the indians. First it had to be acknowledged in a papal bull that they were human beings, descendants of Adam and Eve, and with a soul which could be saved.

The Spanish missionaries concentrated their initial proselytizing efforts on teaching the children of the native aristocracy. In 1528, the Colegio de Santa Cruz in Tlatelolco was founded for this purpose. Many of the students aspired to the priesthood but a decree in 1555 prohibited the ordaining of indians, *mestizos* or *negros.*

But religion was secondary to the fact that the native community was being wiped out, chiefly through disease. With no immunity against the European diseases, and especially hard hit by smallpox, almost 90 percent of the indigenous population disappeared in the decades after the conquest. Moreover, some indian communities refused to accept Spanish rule and there were even instances, in Chiapas for example, where whole groups of disenchanted people committed suicide.

Slaving for silver

It did not take long for the Spanish to discover silver in Zacatecas, Pachuca and Guanajuato, and by 1548 more than 50 silver mines were in

settled, useful for cattle-raising but not much else, extended into what is now Texas, Arizona, New Mexico and California.

In their hunger for wealth and power, ruthless men seized indian farmland and many were killed in endless disputes over land and water rights. Needless to say, the indians came out the losers. Thus, while indian slavery was abolished in New Spain in 1548 – black slaves took their place – many indians remained in bondage. Accumulation of debt meant that an indian family was often compelled to remain in servitude on the same *hacienda* for generations. Sometimes the Church sought to protect them; priests

operation. But even with the forcible recruitment of indians to work in the mines, the labor force was insufficient and black slaves were imported. By 1800 Mexico was producing 66 percent of the world's silver.

A few adventurers pushed into the far north in the hope of finding further deposits of silver or other riches. Being several months' journey from Mexico City and thus well out of reach of the ruling hierarchy, these independent men developed an open society. Usually *criollos* (Mexican-born Spaniards) or *mestizos* (of Spanish and indian blood), they were brazen and self-reliant, much like the pioneers of the American West. The semi-desert and wide-open lands they

of conscience, such as Fray Bartolomé de las Casas in Chiapas, or the bishop Don Vasco de Quiroga in Michoacán, set up organizations to help the indian people.

Church rivalry

The Church itself had its problems, including internal politics and conflict with civil authorities. Several religious orders sent missionaries to convert the indians. By 1559, there were 380 Franciscan monks, 210 Dominicans and 212 Augustinians; others, including the Jesuits, soon followed. Although each order had an assigned area and its own style of evangelizing, rivalry among them was at times acute. The

Church was undeniably wealthy. It received a 10 percent tithe from agriculture, commerce, and from the wealth of the mines, as well as a cut from the native economy, such as it was. It owned sugar mills and *haciendas*, and it even acted as money lender.

Inevitably, there were clashes between the Church and the viceroy, who represented the king of Spain and thus had absolute authority in the colony. The Spanish Crown, interested above all in how well the colony was paying off, introduced laws to help

CONTROLLED ECONOMY

The planting of grape vines and olive trees was forbidden in Mexico in order to protect Spain's export monopoly in wine and olive oil.

overland to Mexico City and on to Veracruz, the only port authorized to trade with Spain. Contraband trade and piracy both flourished and a fair proportion of Mexico's silver was smuggled out.

New crops and people

Sugar cane did well in Mexico, but as early as 1599 a decree was passed restricting the planting of cane in favor of corn and wheat. In the states of Tlaxcala and Hidalgo, *haciendas* produced *pulque,* an alcoholic drink made from the fermented juice of the maguey

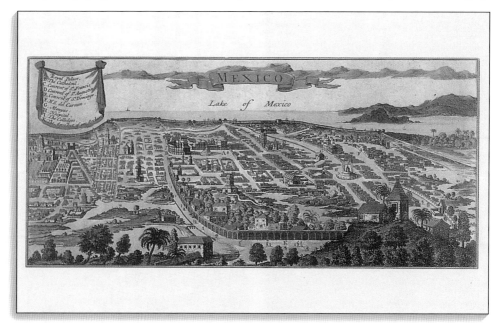

maximize profits from New Spain. Mexico could not legally trade with any European country except Spain, and all inter-colonial trade was banned since it would compete with imports from the Iberian Peninsula.

It was not only silver and goods from New Spain that were being protected. During the Colonial period, Mexico became Spain's route to the riches of the Orient. About once a year, the Manila galleon arrived in Acapulco from the Philippines and the goods were carried

LEFT: the Palacio Nacional by Casimiro Castro.
ABOVE: at the beginning of the 18th century, Mexico City was still surrounded by a lake.

cactus. The Yucatán Peninsula specialized in the production of cotton and indigo; Oaxaca produced cochineal (a red dye from the dried body of a female cactus grub), and other areas cultivated vanilla, cacao and tobacco.

Obviously, the indians did most of the sweat labor. But there were also many poor laborers among the thousands of recently arrived Spanish settlers. Meanwhile, a medley of new peoples was being born: *criollos,* or creoles – Spanish-born Mexicans; *mestizos,* of Spanish and indian blood; and *castas,* with varying degrees of Spanish, indian, black and Oriental blood. The authorities registered these combinations, and had a name for each particular mix. By the 18th century the *mestizos* and creoles accounted for around half the population.

Dreams of independence

Feelings of discontent against the Crown were widespread and the French Revolution, which began in 1789, together with the independence of the British colonies in North America, encouraged the beleaguered people of New Spain to dream of independence. When Napoleon Bonaparte occupied Spain in 1808 and put his own brother on the Spanish throne the feelings of unrest intensified.

The middle-class creoles, who had the most

pulpit he spoke of insurrection and rebellion; he demanded equality among men and land for the landless; death to bad government and to the *gachupines* (a term of contempt for those born in Spain), the only ones legally permitted to hold the highest offices. It was, in fact, the battle cry which ended with his famous *Grito de Dolores*, the "shout" for independence from Spanish rule, and the most famous outcry in Mexican history. The revolution had begun.

Armed with sticks, shovels and slings, Hidalgo's followers marched forth behind the flag of the Virgen de Guadalupe; wherever they went more men joined, and from a few hun-

to gain from a change in the establishment, started to meet and talk of rebellion and independence. Present at one such meeting, which took place in the town of Querétaro, was the quiet parish priest of the town of Dolores, Don Miguel Hidalgo y Costilla; Capitán Ignacio Allende was also there.

The men were planning an uprising for the end of the year (1810), but word of the plot leaked out to the government. Doña Josefa Ortiz de Domínguez, wife of the local governor, warned the conspirators who decided to act immediately. On the morning of September 16th 1810, Padre Hidalgo summoned his congregation in the town of Dolores. From the

dred their numbers soon swelled to many thousands. Within a couple of months the rebel army had captured San Luis Potosí, Valladolid and Zacatecas in central Mexico; when they reached Guadalajara, Hidalgo formed his first administration and issued decrees to emancipate black slaves, to abolish the tributes paid by indians and to eliminate state monopolies of tobacco and gunpowder.

Bitter battles

Hidalgo either ordered, or at least tolerated, the murder of hundreds of Spaniards. He began to lose the support of some wealthy creoles who had initially welcomed the uprising.

In the meantime, General Félix María Calleja, sent by the government to halt the rebels, had arrived with an army and laid siege to Guadalajara. In January 1811, the rebels were routed by Calleja's forces at Puente de Calderón, some 40 km (25 miles) east of Guadalajara. Hidalgo and the remnants of the insurgent troops fled north, but they fell into a trap and were captured and imprisoned in far-off Chihuahua. Hidalgo was condemned to death and executed on July 30th, 1811.

> ### FIGHT FOR A DECADE
>
> "The nation wants to be governed by the creoles and since it has not been heeded, it has taken arms to make itself understood and obeyed."
>
> – José María Morelos

Guerrero). However, the resulting constitution and bill of rights were never put into practice. The implacable General Calleja and the troops of the viceroyalty caught up with Morelos and in 1815 he, like his predecessor, was imprisoned and executed.

With the death of Morelos, the struggle for independence had lost the last of its famous leaders. Many of the creoles accepted defeat and most of the rebel forces dispersed.

An ambitious creole colonel, Agustín de

Creole victories

But the movement for independence did not die. Among the new rebel leaders was José María Morelos y Pavón, also a rural priest and former student of Hidalgo.

Morelos waged brilliant campaigns in the south, capturing first Oaxaca and then Acapulco. Believing the end of Spanish domination to be imminent, he convened a congress in Chilpancingo (now capital of the state of

LEFT: 17th-century view of Acapulco.
ABOVE LEFT: painted tile from colonial Casa Sandoval.
ABOVE RIGHT: royal fiesta in Mexico City's Chapultepec Park (18th century).

Iturbide, was commissioned to crush the remaining rebels in the south, who were led by Vicente Guerrero, one of Morelos's followers.

Fighting continued sporadically until, in 1821, the royalist Iturbide defected, struck a deal and joined forces with the rebel Guerrero. They then announced the Plan de Iguala, which established three guarantees: Roman Catholicism as the only recognized religion; equality of all Mexican citizens; and a constitutional monarchy. The plan was ratified when the newly arrived viceroy, Juan O'Donojú, signed the Treaty of Córdoba which finally converted New Spain into Mexico on August 24th 1821, 11 years after the first uprising. ❑

Architecture from the Conquest to Independence

I n Mexico, the legacy of the past is rarely far away. pre-Christian pyramids, fortified monasteries, Baroque churches and ruined *haciendas* lie off busy highways. After the Spanish Conquest, the resulting fusion of cultures gave rise to a multiplicity of architectural styles. The missionary friars were the most prolific builders of the sixteenth cen-

tury. Far from Spain, in an alien climate and an alien land, they adopted elements from Classical, Romanesque, Gothic, Renaissance and other Old World architectures. Mudéjar (Muslim-influenced art made for Spanish Christians) also left its mark in Mexico. At Acolman, Actopan, Huejotzingo and Yecapixtla, majestic and immense monasteries still dominate the landscape. With their heavily buttressed walls, these fortress-like structures were often built with stones from "pagan" pyramids and temples. Friars also supervised the construction of chapels, hospitals and schools.

Work was carried out by native craftsmen, who received instruction in carpentry, masonry, painting, metal-working and other European skills. The glory of the Church Militant found expression in immense altarpieces, gilded images, mural paintings, and carved decoration of wood and stone. Such creations were not mere copies of European models. They revealed an artistic sensibility inherited from native civilizations. This intermingling of Old World and indian styles is called *tequitqui* by art historians.

Throughout the 17th century, Mexican architecture became increasingly ornate. Baroque fashions, introduced from Spain, encouraged exuberance and invention. By 1750, Baroque styles had become Ultra-Baroque, or Churrigueresque (named after the 18th-century Spanish architect José Churriguera). Characterized by lavish complexity and richness of detail, churches and cathedrals reflected 18th-century prosperity. Gold-clad altarpieces – replete with twisted columns, saints, angels and medallions – dazzled the faithful of Amecameca, Tepotzotlán, Taxco or Querétaro.

In outlying districts, local craftsmen drew inspiration from urban trends. Their imaginative and eclectic creations are described as *barroco popular*. Stucco, carved in the manner of stone, embellished façades in the Sierra Gorda of Querétaro. Glazed polychrome tiles covered church exteriors in the state of Puebla: at San Francisco Acatepec, they encased cornices, capitals and columns. In and around Puebla City, church interiors were often encrusted with plaster relief in gold and color. Clusters of flowers, fruit, animals and cherubs cover the walls and ceiling at Santa María Tonantzintla.

Neo–Classicism, officially imported to the viceroyalty at the end of the eighteenth century, condemned Baroque tastes as showy and vulgar. As academic circles embraced Greco–roman ideals, building styles entered a period of artistic severity. Some church interiors were stripped of decoration, replaced by pseudo–classical forms and materials such as marble. Yet, despite the dictates of of European rationalism, many Baroque churches and cathedrals survived intact. Decked out today with flowers, candles and plaster saints – sometimes even with neon crosses – they meet the aesthetic and spiritual needs of modern Mexican worshippers.

CITIES AND PALACES

In the capital of viceregal Mexico, the ruling class displayed an appetite for luxury. An ambitious building program followed the destruction of Tenochtitlán. Aztec edifices were replaced by grand residences and government buildings. Fray Alonso Ponce, who saw the city in 1585, praised its "very good houses and handsome streets." Today, little remains of 16th-century civil architecture. Buildings that were not demolished by later generations have been modified to suit changing tastes.

Palatial dwellings of the Baroque period had two or more stories. Lavish exteriors incorporated corner towers, statues in niches, balconies with wrought ironwork, and monumental entrances surrounded by coats of arms. Inside, an imposing stairway led from the main patio to the highest level. Horses and carriges were kept on the back patio. Wealthy families ran their urban mansions with the income generated by country estates. The Condes del Valle de Orizaba owned sugar plantations. During the 18th century, they reconstructed and redecorated their 16th-century house in Baroque style. Popularly known today as *La Casa de los Azulejos* (House of Tiles), because blue and white tiles embellish the façade, this former residence of the Count of Tales de Orizaba in Mexico City, now operates as a shop and restaurant. Other palaces have been renovated to serve as museums. Outside the capital, fine houses were built in cities such as Puebla. Here, during the Baroque period, façades were often encrusted with stucco. One such mansion, resplendent with icing–like ornamentation, is aptly known as *La Casa del Alfeñique* (Sugar-Frosted House).

During the rule of neo–Classicism, which extended beyond 1821 and the Wars for Independence, classical models inspired the erection of grand residences, government buildings and theaters in Mexico City and beyond. During the second half of the 19th century, however, French influences brought a return to the ornamental style of architecture and decoration.

HACIENDAS AND NATIVE HOMES

Landowners with large *haciendas*, or country estates, made fortunes from farming and mining. Throughout the Colonial era, existing structures were constantly remolded to meet prevailing needs. This process accelerated after 1876, during the administration of Porfirio Díaz. Many surviving *hacienda* buildings have thus acquired a timeless quality as a result, which makes them hard to date.

LEFT: the unadorned stone façade of the church of San Roque, Guanajuato.
RIGHT: the Baroque magnificence of the Rosary Chapel of Santo Domingo, Puebla.

Autonomous and self-sufficient, *haciendas* operated along feudal lines. Thick and powerful walls protected the great house, with its lofty rooms and plant-filled patios. The walls also encircled the chapel, the labourers' dwellings, the school, the cemetery, the stables and cattle yards, the warehouses and granaries. The *espadaña* – a section of wall with arched openings for bells – was a striking feature. Today some *haciendas* survive as hotels or private residences; the former *Hacienda de San Gabriel*, on the outskirts of Guanajuato, is now a four-star hotel, with delightful gardens, a chapel, and a museum. The *Hacienda de Santa Ana*, outside Xalapa, is a museum, with its

original furniture. Others, sacked and destroyed during the Mexican Revolution, lie in ruins.

Beyond the limits of viceregal towns and the outer walls of country estates, native populations relied on local materials to build their houses in a traditional manner. Even now, in areas with heavy rainfall, roofs of grass or palm overhang walls made from poles, planks or wattle-and-daub. In dry regions, where *campesinos* build with stone or adobe (sun-dried mud-bricks), some houses are roofed with Spanish-style tiles or terracotta. A coat of rough plaster offers protection against insects and the elements. In villages in the Yucatán or Oaxaca, popular architecture of this type conserves the imprint of the past. ❏

THE NINETEENTH CENTURY

In its first century of independence, Mexico was juggled between emperors, presidents and dictators and was invaded by the US, France, Spain and Britain

The first decades of the 19th century were a time of bloodshed in Mexico; hundreds of thousands of lives were lost, the country was left exhausted and drained, commerce ruined and the land devastated.

After the signing of the Treaty of Córdoba and the consummation of Independence, there

was great enthusiasm and rejoicing. Iturbide led his victorious army into Mexico City and was appointed head of the first independent government; the following year, in a lavish coronation ceremony, he had himself crowned Emperor Agustín I. But his rejoicing was short-lived; less than a year later one of his cronies, General Antonio López de Santa Anna, rebelled, forced him to abdicate, and called for a republic. Iturbide was executed soon after.

Shaky republic

The Constitution of 1824 finally established Mexico as a federal republic and Guadalupe Victoria, a stalwart of the Independence Wars,

became the first elected president. But it was General Santa Anna who was to dominate the political scene for the next three decades.

After Independence, Mexico found itself to be a vast country with vast problems. Maritime traffic with Europe and the Far East had been paralyzed during the wars, and mining, agricultural and industrial production had all been cut drastically. The road network, for what it was worth, had deteriorated, and communications in the huge, disunited, troubled land were almost impossible. The majority of the country's six million inhabitants at the beginning of the 20th century were *mestizos* and indians living in dire poverty, apathetic towards and cut off from politics.

From 1821 to 1850 Mexico was in a state of constant turmoil. In 30 years there were 50 governments, almost all the result of military coups, and 11 of them presided over by the megalomanic General Santa Anna, who earned himself the title of "perpetual dictator."

It was a time of internal and external struggles: long and bitter contests between liberals and conservatives weakened the country and tempted ambitious foreign powers to intervene (thanks to popular myths about the country's boundless mineral riches).

Santa Anna is mostly remembered in Mexico as being the man who gave away half the nation's territory to the United States. In 1835, the non-Mexican settlers of Texas – most of whom were from the United States – declared Texas to be an independent state. Santa Anna, then president, personally marched north to conquer the rebels. His massacre of the Texans at the Alamo mission earned him the hatred of Texans in perpetuity. In turn, he was badly beaten by Sam Houston at San Jacinto soon after and Texas gained its independence.

In 1845 the US Congress voted to annex Texas and to extend its borders to include most of Arizona, New Mexico and California. This sparked the Mexican-American war, a classic example of the old saying "might makes right". US troops moved south from New Mexico and captured Chihuahua; more came from Texas and captured Monterrey, Coahuila and points further south; others, supported by a fleet in the Pacific, entered California. The bulk of the American forces, under General Winfield Scott, disembarked in Veracruz, marched inland and captured Mexico City.

In 1848, by the Treaty of Guadalupe, Mexico ceded Texas, California and most of New Mexico and Arizona – more than half of its entire national territory – to the United States. The sale, in 1853, of the rest of

PERSONAL LOSS

As well as losing half of Mexico to the US, Santa Anna lost his left leg in a battle against the French in 1838, known as the "Pastry War".

Juárez and the Reform

Benito Juárez, a Zapotec indian from Oaxaca, has been likened to Abraham Lincoln as one of his country's great leaders.

Born in 1806 in a hill village near Oaxaca, Juárez spoke only Zapotec as a child. He was taken in and educated by a local priest, and later became a lawyer, with a reputation for being incorruptible, and for having a cold but logical legal mind.

Juárez became a key figure of the new liberal government. He was largely responsible

New Mexico and Arizona for $10 million under the conditions of the Gadsden Purchase proved to be Santa Anna's final undoing; he was driven into exile by the liberals in 1855.

There had been serious problems at the other end of the country too. On the Yucatán Peninsula, which resisted central government control until 1876, the Mayan indians, savagely exploited by their creole overlords, had rebelled in 1847 in the so-called War of the Castes.

LEFT: 19th-century portrait of General Antonio López de Santa Anna, the "perpetual dictator."
ABOVE: naïve painting of national hero, President Benito Juárez.

for drafting the Liberal's Plan de Ayutla and for the exile of Santa Anna. Under the new regime Juárez became minister of justice. His Reform Laws attacked the privileges of the Catholic Church, Mexico's untouchable bastion of power; they nationalized church properties and emphasized individual liberties and agricultural reform.

Understandably, Juárez's revolutionary venture met with fierce opposition from the conservatives and for three years, from 1858–61, the two parties were engaged in the bitter and savage War of Reform. Juárez emerged triumphant, and on January 1 1861, the liberal forces marched into Mexico City.

French invasion

But this victory was short-lived. At the end of the civil war, the new liberal government was bankrupt and Juárez had to suspend payment of the foreign debt. Spain, Great Britain and France protested against the measure and sent a joint force to Mexico to secure payment of the debts.

But Napoleon III's ambitions went beyond that of financial recompense. Allied with the conservatives (who hated Juárez more than they hated the idea of foreign rule), he ordered his

troops to advance on Mexico City. After a brief though famous defeat by the Mexicans under General Ignacio Zaragoza in Puebla, the French took over most of the country. Napoleon invited Maximilian of Hapsburg, the young Austrian archduke, to become emperor of Mexico, under French protection.

Emperor Maximilian and Empress Charlotte moved into Chapultepec Castle (*see page 164*) in 1864, but their reign was to be brief. Ironically, Maximilian acted much more like a liberal than a conservative. He endorsed Juárez's reforms, lost the support of the conservatives, and the US – which had finished its bloody civil war – put pressure on Napoleon, who

> **NATIONAL HERO**
>
> March 21 is a national holiday in Mexico, not because it is the first day of spring, but because it is the birthday of Benito Juárez.

withdrew his troops. Without the French army to support him, Maximilian, who refused to leave, was defeated and captured in Querétaro by the Liberal forces loyal to Juárez. The 35-year-old prince was executed on June 19 1867. He is said to have given a gold coin to each member of the firing squad.

The Republic was restored, and Juárez reassumed power and set about putting his Reform Laws into practice. He died in office in 1872, having been re-elected a year earlier, and was succeeded by Sebastián Lerdo de Tejada.

Don Porfirio Díaz, who had been a prominent military leader under Juárez, was also from the southern state of Oaxaca. He had left the army to run against Juárez in the presidential elections of 1867 and again in 1871. He lost both times but, after the death of Juárez, and after successful armed intervention during the 1876 elections, he had himself proclaimed President. He was to dominate Mexico's political scene for more than three decades, a period that has come to be known as the *Porfiriato*.

Díaz was ruthless but his rule was efficient and effective. He immediately snuffed out any opposition and doled out land to his favorite henchmen and trusted supporters. Capital poured in from countries abroad, with three-quarters of the nation's mineral rights being sold off to foreigners. Roads were built, and a highly impressive 19,000-km (12,000-mile) railroad network was laid.

He used the army and the *rurales*, his much-feared rural police force, to enforce his program at any cost. At the beginning of his rule, Díaz stressed the pacification of his strife-torn country. Political liberty would come later, he promised; what the country needed now, Díaz claimed, was strict administration and very little politicking.

Industrial development

Once he had things under control, Díaz pressed for modernization and moved Mexico into the industrial age. The rail system revolutionized the transportation of goods. Steel mills were built in Monterrey with iron ore railed in from Durango. It suddenly became economically feasible to transport cotton by railroad from the fields of the north to textile plants in central

Mexico. Railroads also made it possible to develop mining, not only of gold and silver but also coal, lead, antimony and copper. American companies made huge investments – and huge profits – in mining. By the end of the Porfiriato, foreign investment in Mexico amounted to $1.7 billion, of which 38 percent was American, 29 percent British and 19 percent French.

NEIGHBORS

"Poor Mexico! So far from God and so close to the United States."

– Porfirio Díaz

Impressive and grandiose architecture, with pronounced French or Italian influence, was much favored by the Europeanized elite during the Porfiriato. In Mexico City, buildings such as the Palacio de Bellas Artes, the central Post Office and the massive Art Deco Monumento a la Revolución all date from this period of flamboyant expansion.

Wealthy hacendados

Mining, banking and the oil industry all fell into foreign hands, whilst wealthy Mexican landowners generally neglected basic agriculture – with the result that corn, which was (and still is) the staple, had to be imported.

During the Porfiriato, the indian communities were particularly affected by a disposition whereby land could be taken away from anyone who did not have legal title to it and, as a result of the complicated bureaucratic system, very few people did.

This way, most of the productive land wound up in the hands of some 6,000 *hacendados*, whose holdings ranged from 2,500 acres to areas the size of a small European country. William Randolph Hearst, the American publisher, bought 1 million hectares (2.5 million acres) for a song, in return for supporting Díaz in his newspapers. Governor Terraza of Chihuahua was said to control 6 million hectares (15 million acres).

These landowners raised cattle and grew exportable cash crops such as mahogany, sugar, coffee, tobacco, rubber and *henequén,* a cactus fiber used to make rope. Foreigners invested in coffee and cotton plantations. A few wealthy Mexicans controlled the economy, while rural dwellers and most people in the cities barely managed to survive.

LEFT: Emperor Maximilian of Mexico.
RIGHT: a mural of Porfirio Díaz by David Siqueiros.

Looking to gain influential conservative support, Díaz shrewdly sought a rapprochement with the Church and, although he did not allow it to regain all its previous holdings (which at one time had included half of settled Mexico), he restored some of its lost powers and privileges. He also allowed the expelled Jesuits to return and offered no objection when the Bishop of Querétaro started the custom of an annual pilgrimage to the shrine of Our Lady of Guadalupe (*see pages 118–19.*)

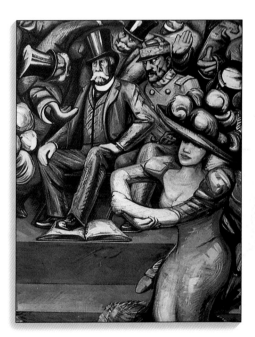

End of an era

Díaz ruled with an iron hand. The only real opposition came from radical liberals, who were forced into exile in the USA.

In a much-reported interview with an American journalist in 1908, Díaz said that Mexico was now ready for democracy and that he would welcome real opposition. However, in 1910, at the age of 80, Porfirio Díaz had himself re-elected president of Mexico for the sixth consecutive time. This sparked the armed rebellion of November 20 1910.

The next six months saw the collapse of a system of government that had remained in power for 34 years. ❑

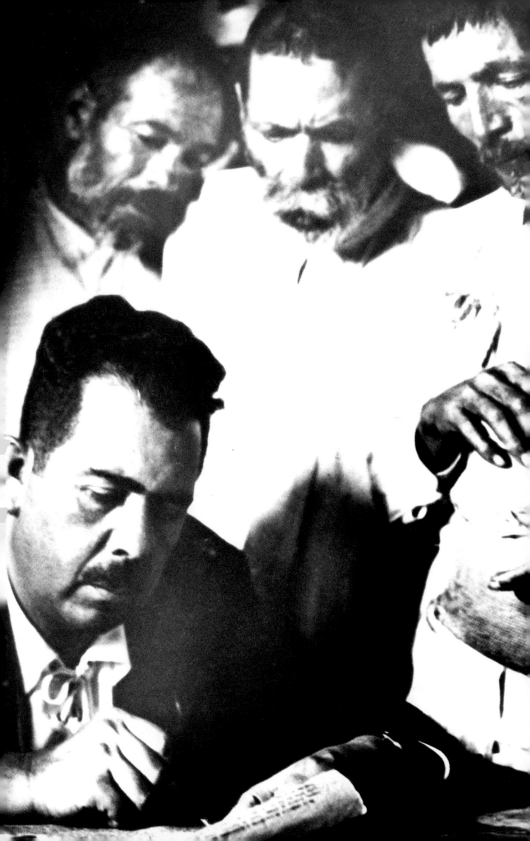

THE REVOLUTION AND ITS AFTERMATH

One out of every ten Mexicans lost his life during the decade that followed the reign of Don Porfirio Díaz

The Mexican Revolution was no straightforward, united fight for freedom and democracy against the oppressive regime of the Porfiriato. It was a decade of violence and starvation. People went hungry, were tortured and shot, and over a million died.

Porfirio Díaz was finally ousted in 1911 when, under the slogan "Effective Suffrage and No Reelection," the Madero revolution triumphed. Francisco Madero, who had been helped by men like Francisco Villa in the north and Emiliano Zapata in the south, assumed the presidency. A wealthy and cultivated *hacienda* owner from Coahuila, with a degree from the University of California, Madero was a liberal reformer who championed democracy and wanted an end to social injustice. But he lacked conviction and a sense of urgency, and instead of making a clean sweep of the Díaz sycophants, he tried unsuccessfully to bargain with them.

"Tierra y Libertad"

Emiliano Zapata, on the other hand, was a peasant leader from the state of Morelos who demanded immediate land reform. His creed was a simple one to which he remained forever loyal: throw out the *hacienda* owners and divide the land among the peasant farmers. In 1910 Zapata had taken up arms against the Díaz government with the cry of "Tierra y Libertad" ("Land and Freedom"). And when he thought the new president was dragging his feet on land reform, Zapata's support for Madero disappeared.

Zapata proclaimed the Plan de Ayala, his radical land reform project, barely a month after Madero had taken office, and took control of most of Morelos. To this day, he is (to most Mexicans) the hero of the agrarian movement.

The situation became more complicated. The national and foreign investors in the economy were desperate to restore order as well as the privileges they had enjoyed under the old regime (such as exemption from payment of taxes). US ambassador Henry Lane Wilson negotiated for

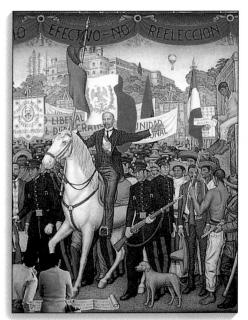

DRAMATIS PERSONAE

- **Francisco Madero**: wealthy liberal; led opposition to Díaz regime; president 1911–13; assassinated.
- **Victoriano Huerta**: Madero's general; switched sides and became president; resigned in 1914.
- **Pancho Villa**: *bandido*-style revolutionary in the north; assassinated in 1923.
- **Emiliano Zapata**: peasant leader in the south with slogan *Tierra y Libertad*; assassinated in 1919.
- **Venustiano Carranza**: Constitutionalist leader; president from 1917–20; assassinated in 1920.
- **Alvaro Obregón**: supported Carranza but later rebelled; president 1920–24; assassinated in 1928.

PRECEDING PAGES: Zapata's troops at Sanborn's restaurant, Mexico City.
LEFT: Lázaro Cárdenas signs peasants' land deed.
RIGHT: victorious Madero, Chapultepec Castle.

Madero's general, Victoriano Huerta, to switch sides and lead the counter revolution with the Porfirian army, which had survived almost intact. At the end of their successful assault on the government, Madero was assassinated.

New alliances

Huerta became president and formed a government, essentially with the goal of restoring the old regime and the concessions to foreign investment. But he immediately ran into trouble. After the death of Madero, the revolutionaries

PANCHO VILLA

Villa, a revolutionary *bandido* from Durango, was a horse general in the tradition of the great cavalrymen of history. Villa's admirers looked on him as a Robin Hood.

Europe, Villa and Zapata occupied Mexico City. The Zapatistas came in from the mountains; then came Villa's men in boxcars, with their horses and their followers. However, Zapata and Villa never formed a serious alliance, and a month later they left Mexico City.

The Constitutionalists – Obregón and Carranza – gained ground. Obregón pursued Villa and defeated his followers in Celaya by digging trenches, lacing the ground with barbed wire and setting up machine guns. The lesson of the war in Europe had not been

regrouped and formed new alliances: the unplacated Zapata continued to fight and rally support in the south, whilst in the north, Pancho Villa and his men joined forces with Venustiano Carranza, a Madero supporter in Coahuila, and General Alvaro Obregón, in Sonora.

After Huerta relinquished power in 1914, Carranza called a convention in the town of Aguascalientes, trying to weld together all the factions that had fought Huerta. But the delegates agreed only to disagree and the fighting broke out again.

Although Obregón supported Carranza, Zapata and Villa did not. In December 1914, while the world's attention was riveted on the war in

lost on him. Most of Villa's men were slaughtered and, although Villa never recovered, he was still the gadfly; he carried out border raids into the United States, in the hope of provoking an invasion. President Wilson ordered General John J. Pershing to capture Villa, dead or alive, and the US Army pursued the revolutionary for 11 months. But it was a lesson in futility; they never caught up with Villa and, after an encounter with Carranza's troops, they retreated.

Villa mellowed with age, stopped riding on his raids and settled down on a *hacienda* in Parral. Then, one morning in 1923, his Dodge car was ambushed and he and his bodyguard were assassinated.

New liberal constition

Carranza, a moderate and a reformer, tried to consolidate his power and in 1917 he drew up a new constitution. It included several articles that were very liberal and pro-labor for its day; such as the right to strike, an eight-hour working day, equal pay for equal work, housing for employees, and accident insurance. It also aimed at breaking up the *haciendas* and distributing the land among the peasant farmers.

But the fighting continued, especially in the

DECADE OF VIOLENCE

Ten years after the start of the Revolution, Madero, Zapata and Carranza, the three protagonists, had all been assassinated.

Relative stability

General Obregón took over an exhausted country, drained by revolution, ravaged by conflict, plagued by foreign debt and sunk in economic morass. He imposed order and reasserted the power of the central government. Obregón's first job was to make himself secure. Needing foreign capital, he was forced to come to terms with the International Committee of Bankers through which he renegotiated his country's 1.5 billion *peso* debt. Then, in violation of the constitution, he

south, where the Zapatistas continued to demand more radical reforms. In April 1919, one of Carranza's generals tricked Zapata into a meeting and then shot him dead.

What led to Carranza's downfall was that, like Madero, he lacked a sense of urgency in carrying out the promised reforms. He eventually lost the support of Obregón and was forced to step down. Obregón assumed the presidency and Carranza was shot by government forces as he tried to flee the country.

LEFT: Pancho Villa sits in the presidential chair with Emiliano Zapata to his right.
ABOVE: an execution during the Cristero Revolt.

granted rights to foreign oil companies to continue exploration.

For economic reasons Obregón cut down the size of the federal army from 100,000 men to 40,000, a decision that spurred the ambitions of a group of military men who led a revolt. Once more rifle fire resounded in the land. But Obregón obtained arms, ammunition and even a few planes from the United States and, as one historian put it, "there was plenty of work for the firing squads".

Obregón began land reform, pushing it enthusiastically in Morelos and the Yucatán where there were no American landowners, but being very circumspect in his native northern

Mexico. where his personal interests and those of the Americans more or less coincided.

National reconstruction

Obregón's education minister José Vasconcelos built schools all over the country and, believing that art was an important part of the *reconstrucción nacional*, commissioned many of the murals that decorate Mexico's public buildings today.

At the same time, the civil government's never-ending fight with the Catholic Church escalated. During the Porfiriato, the Church had regained some of its power but now the military

After Calles's term in office, Obregón defied the constitution and ran again for president. He was re-elected but a few weeks later, on July 17 1928, he was shot dead, seemingly by a fanatical young Cristero.

Forerunner of the PRI

President Calles became known as the biggest power broker in the history of elected officials of Mexico. During his regime thousands of schools were built, the road network was expanded, irrigation projects were started and 3 million hectares (7 million acres) of land were redistributed. Calles renegotiated his country's

and civil leaders were more fanatically anti-clerical than ever and had the legal support of the constitution itself. In 1923, the Vatican's Apostolic nuncio was expelled, and convents and church schools were closed.

The battle extended into the presidency of Obregón's successor, Plutarco Elías Calles. Catholic guerrillas, the *Cristeros*, whose war cry was *Viva Cristo Rey* ("Long Live Christ the King") clashed with the *federales* in the central states of Jalisco, Michoacán, Guanajuato and Colima, battling to re-establish a pro-cleric constitution. Eventually a compromise was reached and religious services – which had been clandestine – were restored.

debts and gave guarantees to private enterprise.

But his detractors likened him to a fascist dictator. He founded the PNR, or National Revolutionary Party, the forerunner of today's PRI (Institutional Revolutionary Party), and through it he controlled his own and subsequent elections by naming his successors (the practice continues to this day). He brought diverse factions under the PNR umbrella, such as labor, agriculturalists and the military.

Lázaro Cárdenas

Although he was the PNR candidate, Lázaro Cárdenas, who assumed the presidency in 1934, broke with the *Callistas* and, over the next six years, did more for the common man than any president in the history of modern Mexico. A profound nationalist, Cárdenas stepped up the Reform program, set up and sponsored *ejidos* (farm cooperatives) throughout the country and distributed 18 million hectares (45 million acres) of land. Although certificates of exemption (from appropriation) were issued to landowners with the most efficiently run *haciendas*, by the end of his presidential term, Cárdenas had distributed land to almost one-third of the national population.

EXPROPRIATION

Lázaro Cárdenas's single bravest and most significant act was to nationalize the Mexican oil industry in 1938.

Petróleos Mexicanos

In 1936, the CTM had demanded pay raises and fringe benefits from the foreign oil companies. The companies – American and British – agreed to talk, but were not about to give in to the workers' demands. After six months of bickering the union called a strike. Cárdenas intervened, appointed a commission, and the companies were ordered to grant a 27 percent wage increase.

Several more months of appeals and maneuvers achieved nothing until Cárdenas stepped in

Cárdenas encouraged the labor unions and in 1936, the CTM (Confederation of Mexican Workers) was founded by the Marxist Vicente Lombardo Toledano. Cárdenas also welded the agrarian movement into one big, government-sponsored group, the Confederación Nacional de Campesinos (National Federation of Farmers). With those two organizations behind him, representing millions of workers, Cárdenas had a broad political base.

LEFT: General Obregón and his wife.
ABOVE: women donating chickens during a country-wide campaign to raise funds to pay for the nationalization of the petroleum industry.

once more. He broadcast on public radio that he was appropriating the oil companies' property and nationalizing the industry. Mexicans cheered; the British were incensed and Mexico broke off diplomatic relations. President Roosevelt, being the chief advocate of the "Good Neighbor" policy with Latin America, had the US State Department present a comparatively mild note of protest, pointing out that it was Mexico's duty to pay fair compensation. Implementation was long delayed: a settlement with the US oil companies, amounting to $24 million plus interest, was not concluded until 1942. Payment to the British took even longer. It amounted to $81 million. ❑

MODERN MEXICO

Mexico has grown into one of the world's leading petroleum producers,
boosted by the recent discovery of more oil deposits

etween World War II and the late 1990s, Mexico's population jumped from 22 million to 95 million. Such demographic growth means the Mexican economy needs to provide one million new jobs a year.

In addition to the *Distrito Federal* – Mexico City, the nation's capital – the Mexican Republic comprises 31 states. Its constitution was modelled on that of the US and the congress consists of two houses: the senate, with 64 seats, and the chamber of representatives, consisting of 500 members. In reaction to Porfirio Díaz's 35-year dictatorship (1876–1911), under the constitution, the president is allowed to serve only one six-year term in his lifetime. However, during his administration he is endowed with almost unlimited power.

Each *sexenio* (six-year period) is an almost independent unit, with major changes in government functionaries and objectives, which inhibits long-term planning.

Manuel Avila Camacho (1940–46) was president during World War II. A middle-of-the-roader, he stressed economic growth. With the world in flames, it was clear that Mexico had to learn to stand on its own feet, so he encouraged the building of light and heavy industry.

Permanent revolution

It was Miguel Alemán, a wealthy lawyer but a champion of labor, who changed the name of Mexico's ruling political party to the Institutional Revolutionary Party (PRI) during his presidency (1946–52). His reasoning was that the revolution was permanent: the seed planted by the original revolutionaries was still thriving but the goal had not yet been reached. Alemán generally raised the standard of living. With an eye on President Roosevelt's "Brain Trust", he drafted bright young men into government service, modernized the railroad system, and tied the nation together via a highway network.

LEFT: gleaming modern architecture reflects rising business prosperity.
RIGHT: back alley of a poor residential neighborhood.

Perhaps his biggest achievement was the construction of Ciudad Universitaria (University City) in the south of Mexico City. Its modernistic buildings, covering an area of almost 8 sq km (3 sq miles), are adorned with murals by artists such as Diego Rivera, Juan Alfaro Siqueiros and Juan O'Gorman.

The next president, Adolfo Ruiz Cortines (1952–58) tried to consolidate Alemán's gains. He enfranchised women and encouraged foreign investment. American corporate business everybody from Nabisco to Sears hurried down to Mexico. But domestic responsibilities continued to grow: in 24 years the population had doubled.

Leaning on the left

Under Ruiz Cortines, the revolution had stagnated; but under Adolfo López Mateos (1958–64), the next president, it came alive again. He realized there was trouble in the land and that the great promises had gone unfulfilled. Encouraging industry, he sought foreign capital but also distributed 12 million hectares (30 million acres) to the landless, the most since Lázaro Cárdenas had done in the 1930s. He bought out American and Canadian industrial interests. Social welfare projects were stepped up with expanding medical care and old-age assistance programs, and public housing was built. "I lean to the left, but within the constitution," were his famous words.

> ### POLITICAL LIFE
>
> It is said, jokingly, that some politicians perceive their life-spans totally in terms of how many *sexenios* (six-year periods) they have left.

But at the same time he was harsh on *políticos* who were to the left of the constitution. He jailed the Communist muralist Siqueiros and

kicked out the Communist leadership in the railroad and the teachers' unions.

Student massacre

Gustavo Díaz Ordáz (1964–70), a conservative from Puebla, was president during a time of stress. The PRI didn't realize that the student movement which began in June 1968 would spread like wildfire. Students from the National Autonomous University spearheaded a major call for "democratic liberties," and a change in the paternalistic, authoritarian-type government which ruled Mexico under the PRI. The leaders were well organized and could call out hundreds of thousands of people at a rally.

As Mexico was preparing to host the Olympic Games, the government was not willing to risk protest rallies in the streets with an international audience. On October 2nd, a few days before the Games' opening, a massacre took place at the Plaza de las Tres Culturas, better known as Tlatelolco. It was a relatively small demonstration: about 10,000 people. Police and army units arrived with clubs and tear gas.

But then, a special elite military corps, known as the Olympia Battalion, dressed in civilian clothes, moved in and began shooting. People were caught in the crossfire. Newspaper sources quoted the government as saying 43 people were killed. Political observers have since placed the number at 300–400. Two thousand demonstrators were jailed. The year 1968 has never been forgotten. It marked a turning point in Mexico's political life.

To this day, it has also marked Díaz Ordaz's successor, Luis Echeverría Alvarez (1970–76), who was Interior Minister when the Tlatelolco massacre occurred. Although Díaz Ordaz assumed full responsibility for the October 2nd massacre, analysts say there is evidence that implicates Echeverría. Still alive, he has never had to answer for his role at the time; all these years the mantle of protection with which the PRI has traditionally shielded past presidents has allowed him to live in peace in his stately home in Mexico City.

Echeverría's term is often referred to as the start of "populism", the implementation of economic and social measures to make the sitting president popular among the masses, but did little to push the country forward. One such measure was the expropriation of large private properties.

During Echeverría's presidency, the population continued to grow and inflation rose at a rate of 20 percent a year. In September 1976, the peso was devalued for the first time in 22 years, by 100 percent. Since Echevarría's term, every change of *sexenio* has meant a devaluation of the peso and economic turbulence.

Oil-rich Mexico

José López Portillo (1976–82) was far more determined than his predecessor in applying the laws governing foreign investment. A law professor, he had served as finance minister under Echeverría and knew at first hand the financial condition of the country. On becoming president, López Portillo tried to bring a sense of calm and purpose, setting the pattern for his administration early on. Suddenly, a bonanza – new and great reserves of oil were discovered. Mexico, the geologists said, was sitting on an ocean of oil.

The economy grew by almost 8 percent in 1979 and by 7 percent in 1980. New industries sprang up and a new "industrial area" took root along the Mexican–US border. However, a glut on the world oil market in 1982 cut the demand and the price of Mexico's principal export. Mexico nearly defaulted on its foreign debt, which amounted to $80 billion.

To obtain loans from the International Monetary Fund, Mexico was forced to adopt strict fiscal measures. People began to send their money abroad for safekeeping. The value of the peso plummeted rapidly. In response, in a dramatic move which angered businessmen, López Portillo nationalized the banks just before he left office.

Trade agreements

Miguel de la Madrid (1982–88), his successor, inherited a severe economic crisis. He addressed it by promoting policies to gradually open Mexico's economy. Mexico joined the General Agreement on Tariffs and Trade (GATT). Like his predecessor, whose foreign policy in Central America had often gone against US wishes. De la Madrid believed that the prospect of United States military intervention was the most serious threat to strife-torn Central America. At Mexico's initiative, the Contadora group was formed to search for a solution to the region's problems.

The earthquake registering 8.1 on the Richter scale which hit Mexico City on the morning of September 19, 1985, causing thousands of deaths and billions of dollars worth of damage, did nothing to help the economic crisis. It also changed the face of large areas of the capital.

Although the PRI remained the ruling party through all these years, there were other political parties to present at least symbolic opposition.

LEFT: the "colonial-style" is always in fashion.
ABOVE: Cuauhtémoc Cárdenas during his controversial election campaign in 1988.

But that opposition finally became real in 1988 when, in a much-disputed election, Carlos Salinas de Gortari was elected. The results gave him a bare 50.1 percent of the vote over Cuauhtémoc Cárdenas, son of the well-liked 1930s president, Lázaro Cárdenas.

To this day, the official results have never been known. To avoid losing further credibility Salinas, a technocrat with a master's degree from Harvard University, moved fast: conceded several governorships to the conservative National Action Party (PAN), for the first time since the PRI came to power in the 1920s. He lowered spiraling inflation to a single figures, and generally

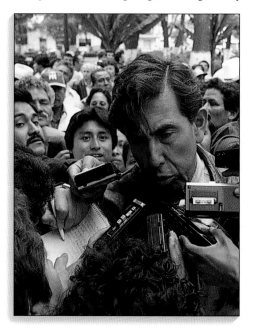

created a sense of renewed confidence in the country's economy. He promoted free-market policies while privatization, the sale of hundreds of State-owned companies, became his motto. Considered a very effective head of state both in Mexico and abroad, Salinas wholeheartedly supported the North American Free Trade Agreement with the United States and Canada, and its passing has been one of the milestones of his administration, bringing Mexico right into the global economy.

However, on New Year's Day 1994, an armed uprising led by the Zapatista Army of National Liberation (EZLN) broke out in the southern state of Chiapas, shattering Salinas's dream administration. The masked indian rebels took over several towns before being ousted by a massive military response.

The Zapatistas were rebelling against the feudal-like exploitation and poverty that afflicted the indians in Chiapas (*see page 90*). The short-lived 12-day war left 193 people dead. Peace negotiations ensued in San Cristóbal de las Casas, but before these concluded, tragedy struck in Tijuana: the PRI's presidential candidate, who would have become Salinas's successor, was felled by an assassin's bullet in an election rally.

The murder of Luis Donaldo Colosio marked

the end of the relative stability which the PRI had provided for more than six decades. Salinas was quick to name a successor, Ernesto Zedillo, who was elected in August 1994.

But a second political assassination later in the same year, this time of the PRI's secretary general, shook the country once again, plunging Mexicans into a prolonged period of political uncertainty. (Soon after the end of his term, Salinas went into voluntary "exile" and has since been living in the Dublin.)

A mere three weeks after President Zedillo took power in December 1994, the Mexican peso was substantially devalued The economic stability achieved under Salinas disappeared overnight, and the ensuing financial crisis had an impact on international capital markets, not to mention causing great distress among the majority of people in Mexico. The US bailed Mexico out with $20 billion dollars and President Zedillo, a Yale-trained technocrat, established severe economic policies.

Turning point

Then, on July 6 1997, important elections in the nation's capital marked a turning point. For the first time ever, the PRI lost its overwhelming majority in the lower house of Congress, while Cuauhtémoc Cárdenas from the leftist PRD (Party of the Democratic Revolution) won the mayor's seat in Mexico City. Until then, the mayorship had always been appointed directly by the president.

In Chiapas, however, the conflict has continued unresolved. In February 1996, both the government and the Zapatistas signed a first phase of the San Andrés peace accords, but negotiations have since been stalled.

The massacre of 45 indians which took place in Acteal, Chiapas, on December 22 1997, reminded Mexicans that trouble continues to brew, and that they must urgently address the issues of social and economic disparity, which remain pending as part of their "democratic transition." This transition requires building the democratic institutions to replace the dwindling presidential power, as well as ensuring that Congress and the judicial powers truly function in an independent manner. ❑

ENVIRONMENTAL PROBLEMS

Mexico suffers from every ecological problem in the book: dumping of toxic waste, deforestation, water depletion, soil erosion, emission of toxic gases. To make matters worse, Mexico City, the world's largest metropolis, is situated in a valley 2,275 meters (7,500 ft) above sea level. Thousands of industries and millions of cars still spew out pollutants into the thin air, and thermal inversion worsens the situation in the winter months. Regulations have been introduced, although not always enforced, and reserves have been created to protect the country's flora and fauna. But clearly, these measures are only a drop in the ocean.

LEFT: Ernesto Zedillo shouts the name of his predecessor, the assassinated Luis Donaldo Colosio, during the March 1994 election campaign.

La Lotería Nacional

Mexico's native inhabitants appear to have been passionate gamblers. Some of their games, like their ritual ball game, had deep spiritual meaning, but also involved much changing of hand of feathers, gold, and cacao beans. The Aztecs even gambled with their own freedom, and sometimes ended up as slaves. A large crowd would gather around to watch the players, who would first shake the *palolli* (beans marked with combinations of dots) and then throw them onto the playing "board" painted on a straw mat, while praying to Macuilochitl, the god of games, for luck.

When the Spanish conquistadores arrived in Mexico, Cortés allowed gambling in the camps to keep his troops entertained. And during colonial rule, some form of gambling was always going on, as everyone wanted to "touch the gates of good fortune." By the middle of the 18th century, King Carlos III realized that the increasingly popular lottery could be yet another lucrative source of revenue for the Spanish crown.

The first drawing of Mexico's state-run lottery was held on May 13, 1771, and even without the benefit of modern marketing techniques, 4,225 tickets were sold. By the beginning of the 19th century, the Mexican lottery had expanded its market abroad and was even selling lottery tickets in Cuba.

After the Mexican Revolution, the new government decided to use lottery revenues to help "noble causes." The result was what is today known as the *Lotería Nacional para la Asistencia Pública*, which was established to provide funds for accredited public and private institutions – both within Mexico and abroad – especially those dedicated to helping homeless children, the aged, and rural schools.

In recent years, even in the wake of the country's worst economic crises in modern times, people's hope of striking it lucky have never been higher, and the National Lottery is selling more tickets than at any other time in its long history. Today, there are many options in addition to the *Lotería Nacional*. You can choose from *Pro Touch, Pro Hit, Pégalo al Gordo,* and *Melate*. But your odds are best (one in 50,000) for winning

the really big one if you play the traditional lottery.

Here's what you need to know to play: tickets are sold in designated shops (*expendios*) and by street vendors. Listen out for their typical sales patter: *¡Mire qué bonitos números! Traigo el número de la suerte.* (Look, what beautiful numbers. I have the lucky number...) Each number is divided into several series and you can buy one *cachito* ("a small piece" – one ticket), several tickets, or a whole series (20 *cachitos*). For each drawing there's a *premio gordo* ("fat" prize) and several lesser ones. Even if you don't have a winning number there's a chance of *reintegro* (getting your money back) if the last number of

your ticket coincides with one of the first three winning numbers.

To find out if you hold the winning ticket, you can check the newspaper on the day following the draw. The winning numbers for each draw are also displayed at the *expendios* and are carried by the street vendors. Remember, the *peso* amount posted next to the winning numbers is for the whole series. If you purchased only one ticket, your winnings will be 1/20 of that amount.

The Mexican Government automatically deducts 21 percent in tax from your winnings (except for the *reintegros, which are tax-free*), but your own country's tax office need never find out about your good fortune *¡Buena Suerte!* Good Luck! ❏

RIGHT: National Lottery ticket from the state of Veracruz – one *cachito*.

PEOPLE AND CULTURE

Mexico's diverse culture reflects the variety of its people,
many of whom still lead pre-Hispanic life-styles

Nine months after the first Spanish conquistadores set foot on Mexican soil, the first mixed-race Mexican, or *mestizo*, was born. The majority of Mexico's 72 million people are now *mestizo*. There is also a large number of indians, a comparatively small number of Spanish and other Caucasians, and a sprinkling of blacks and Orientals. And there are the combinations of all these.

Central Mexico was the melting pot. The Spanish moved large communities – namely the Tlaxcaltecans and Tarascans – north to act as a buffer against hostile indians. Some of the northern indians fiercely resisted the intruder, and still do. The Tarahumaras, the Mayos, the Seris, the Huicholes and the Yaquis, in particular, hang on to their old traditions and the remnants of their tribal lands. The Huastec indians survive in the mountains, while in the fastness of the Chiapas highlands, in the south, the Tzotzils and the Tzeltals also retain their old way of life. However, most of the descendants of the original tribes of central Mexico live in scattered villages around the Valley of Mexico. They include the Nahuas, the Otomí and the Mazahua.In southern Mexico, many indigenous groups have to live on the lands that no one else covets, in the eroded highlands of Guerrero, Oaxaca and Chiapas, and on the thin limestone plateau of the Yucatán peninsula. According to official census figures, the pure indian population of Mexico is between 3 and 4 million. But that number represents just the core, those who speak their native indigenous tongue at home, who have retained their racial purity and their traditions. They live mostly in the marginal lands, the "zone of refuge." Some of these groups have been assimilated by Christianity; others have not. Most have learned to exist in tandem with Christianity; a sort of *modus vivendi*. They worship the Christian saints along with their ancient indian gods. What has survived might be said to be the community spirit of the indigenous people and their emphasis on a harmonious relationship between the physical and the spiritual world.

Perhaps what distinguishes most indians from the rest of the population is their orientation toward the community and not toward the individual. Naturally, the indians who have kept their culture alive are the ones who are most isolated from the rest of the country.

In the essays that follow we discuss a few of the 50 or more tribes who are among the most authentic descendants of the indians of old. Their way of life and the things that motivate them make these tribes the most fascinating people of Mexico. We also look at the European influences on Mexican culture, from art to bullfighting, and from *charros* – Mexican "cowboys" – to religious festivals. ❏

PRECEDING PAGES: a crowd gathers to watch Independence parade; a young Huichol announces the return of the peyote pilgrims.
LEFT: nobody is spared the rush-hour in Mexico City.

PEOPLE

Although the vast majority of the population is of mixed race, many indigenous groups still maintain their traditional life styles in modern Mexico

About two thirds of Mexico's 100 million inhabitants live in cities and the overwhelming majority of the population is *mestizo,* or of mixed race. There are 50 or so indigenous groups that have managed to survive, and these represent a remarkable contrast to their mixed-blood compatriots. Although there are marked differences between the indian groups, they share a common history and are similar in many ways. Indians and *mestizos* often look alike, but in language, in clothing, and most of all, in their basic attitudes towards life, the differences can be profound.

The indian ideal is to come to terms with life and the universe. The *mestizo,* like most westerners, wants to control his destiny. The indian tends to accept things whereas the *mestizo* strives to dominate. While the life of the indian is community oriented, the *mestizo* lives in a more "modern," individualistic society.

A third group, often ignored in Mexico's cultural spectrum, are descendants of the black slaves who have contributed so much to the culture of the coast of Veracruz and stretches of the Pacific coast of Guerrero and Oaxaca.

Machismo and malinchismo

The question of identity is very important to the people of Mexico. It was the Mexican intellectual Samuel Ramos who first took a penetrating look at his compatriots' culture. He said they suffered from a sense of inferiority which they responded to with "virile protest." Ramos blamed the Spanish rule for many of the attitudes still existent, such as the system of privilege. People get ahead in Mexico through their connections with a local boss or a powerful national politician. Ramos believed that this personality cult is "as bloodthirsty as the ancient Aztec ritual; it feeds on human victims."

The Nobel Prize-winning poet Octavio Paz presents an insight into the Mexican culture in *The Labyrinth of Solitude,* a fascinating attempt

at understanding the country's psychological makeup. Paz's thesis is that the macho conduct of the Mexican male is a mask to conceal his solitude. According to Paz, the Mexican perceives that there are only two attitudes to take when dealing with others: take advantage of them, or have them take advantage of you;

"screw or be screwed," in the violent language of the street. His honor requires him to face every adversity – even death – with a certain defiance. He must be aggressive and project an image of strength and devil-may-care. The notion goes back a long time; after all, the country was born from the violent clash of Spanish conquistadores and indian warriors

One woman who was essential to the conquest, Doña Malinche, gave rise to another concept that is considered to be at the heart of the Mexican character. Interpreter, instructor, adviser, and lover of Hernán Cortés, she is the Great Traitor and is reviled by nationalist Mexicans. The word *malinchismo* is used to refer

---

LEFT: ancient traditions at a Huichol gathering.
ABOVE: keeping the peace.

to the preference of all things foreign over anything Mexican.

The Tarahumara

Chihuahua's sierras provide a place of refuge for the Tarahumara indians, who refuse to accept the Mexican way of life. For the Tarahumara, who wanted to keep their own culture, there were only two choices when the Spanish invaded: to fight and die, or retreat into the mountains. There are now about 50,000 Tarahumara living in a 50,000 sq. km

UNUSUAL REMEDIES

According to the Tarahumara's unusual pharmacopoeia, the best remedy for a weakened spirit is to smoke a mixture of tobacco, dried turtle and bat blood.

(19,300 sq. mile) region of the Sierra Madre in northwest Chihuahua.

Apart from fleeting contact with a few Spaniards, the Tarahumara learned about the white man from Jesuits at the beginning of the 17th century. At first the indians were curious and meetings were peaceful, but in 1631, when silver was found in southern Chihuahua, the inevitable rush was on. The Spaniards needed labor for the mine and forced the Tarahumara to work. This triggered a series of revolts that were to last for decades.

Some of the bloodiest revolts and reprisals in the history of Mexico took place in Tarahumara country. The first rebellion was led by Teporaca in 1648 and the first victims were missionaries. There was constant war. Many bands of indians preferred death to surrender; others retreated into the sierras. To survive, some accepted a superficial form of Christianity and were partially assimilated into the white man's culture, on the lowest rung.

Mexican independence saw no relief for the Tarahumara. Spanish power was gone but the Mexican government was preoccupied elsewhere. Thereupon the Apaches began to raid Tarahumara settlements. More trouble came. A new law in 1825 opened up "unused" land to colonization and the best lands of the Tarahumara were taken over.

As in other parts of Mexico, the Tarahumara adoption of Christianity retained an aboriginal flavor, with Christ and the Virgin Mary simply becoming another important male and female in the Tarahumara pantheon.

Known as great long-distance runners, some Tarahumara can run 180 km (100 miles) non-stop – it is no surprise that they should call themselves *Rar'amuri,* meaning "the people with a light foot." Races are held between two teams of up to 20 runners who kick a wooden ball as they run, through the day and night. The Tarahumara bet on these races, and old men may risk their meager flock of goats, sheep or cattle on the outcome.

As with other indigenous groups in the north of Mexico, the Tarahumara still make ritual use of *peyote*. At the turn of the century, Norwegian explorer Carl Lumholtz was told that when God left the earth to live in Heaven, he left *peyote* as a remedy for his people and as a safeguard against witchcraft. When applied externally, it was considered to be a good treatment for snake bites, burns, wounds and rheumatism. The plant was held sacred and offerings were made to it to ensure that it would not provoke insanity.

At present, most Tarahumara live in an enclave in the Sierra Madre Occidental, with some 20 percent of them retaining their traditional way of life. There is now a National Indian Council, and thousands come to large congresses organized by the government. Some of the local leaders demand legal titles to their land and request schools and teachers, better roads, telephones, doctors and medicine, legal help, control over their forestry resources and self-determination on a local level. But other community leaders have no desire to integrate and do not even want schools or roads.

The Seris

Along with the Lacandones, the Seris are among the smallest indigenous groups in Mexico. After centuries of catastrophic contact with Western civilization, most of the tribe has died out. In 1600, there were some 5,000 Seri indians, but by 1930 only about 175 remained. At present there are approximately 500. The survivors have clung to some of their traditions in a part of their homeland on the Gulf of California in western Sonora.

The Seris – the word means "those who live in the sand" – comprise one of six bands that form an ethnic group known as the Kunkaahac, meaning "our great mother race." At one time they lived in the southern part of the Arizona-Sonora desert, along the coast, and on nearby Tiburón island. Hunters and fishermen, they put out to sea in reed boats, killing giant sea turtles with ironwood spears.

In the late 1600s, a German Jesuit, Father Gilg, was given the job of settling and converting the Seris, then calculated to number around 3,000. He was faced with many problems, not the least of which was the small amount of land suitable for agriculture in the semi-desert. He also faced difficulties in his efforts to convert them to Christianity, claiming that the Seris lived "without God, without faith and without houses, like cattle... They have no religious worship, and nor does one find even the shadow of idolatry among them, since they have never known or adored either a true or a false deity." That was not quite true, of course. The Seris, like all Mesoamerican people, worshipped the sun and the moon, and their religion was built around animal deities, headed by the turtle and the pelican.

Father Gilg denigrated the indians for their lack of understanding of the Holy Sacrament and the Christian mysteries of faith, and had little success in teaching them to live like good, obedient subjects and to work happily for their white overlords. In fact, the Seris, a proud peo-

ple, rebelled. In 1662 a band of several hundred Seris fought the Spanish until the last indian man and woman were killed and their children had been sent to the mission villages.

By 1742, only about one-third of the Seris had accepted a settled life in a mission. When the Spanish built a fort at Pitic in 1748, their efforts to persuade Seris to settle on land nearby met with a measure of success. But when the whites took the land from the indians, the Seris protested, albeit peacefully. Thereupon the Spaniards arrested 80 families and shipped the women off to Guatemala and elsewhere. Inflamed, the Seris joined the Pima indians and

destroyed the mission at Guaymas, then carried out numerous raids on Spanish settlements. However, by 1769 a shortage of food had weakened their will to fight and many Seris surrendered, agreeing to submit to Christianity and attend daily Mass.

Near the end of the 19th century, a rancher named Encinas set up a large cattle range on land traditionally hunted for deer and rabbit by the Seris. The indians felt that they could now "hunt" cattle too, and for the next ten years, cowboys and Seri indians fought the Encinas War; extreme penalties were established, and for every head of cattle that was rustled, a Seri was executed.

LEFT: some Tarahumaras still live in caves.
RIGHT: a woman from the long-suffering Seri tribe.

By 1920, only a few of the remaining Seris were nomad hunters. Some of them settled temporarily outside a small village on Kino Bay and became fishermen; responding to a boom in the market for shark livers in the 1930s, they also took up shark hunting.

Then, in the 1950s, wealthy Americans who had discovered the great sports fishing off Kino Bay provided another source of income. By then the Seris

QUEEN OF THE SERI

Lola, the daughter of a prominent white family, was captured by the Seris and became the subject of many tales. She took to the indian way of life, became known as the "Queen of the Seris", and had several children by the shaman Coyote-Iguana.

shape a piece of equipment for their Mauser rifles, using only a file for a tool. Their skill is still alive and they use it to keep their outboard motors in good repair.

The Coras

For 200 years from the time of the fall of the Aztec empire, the fierce Cora indians of Nayarit kept their loosely organized tribal structure and refused to submit to either Spanish arms or to missionary blandishments. Not until 1722 were they defeated. The inhospi-

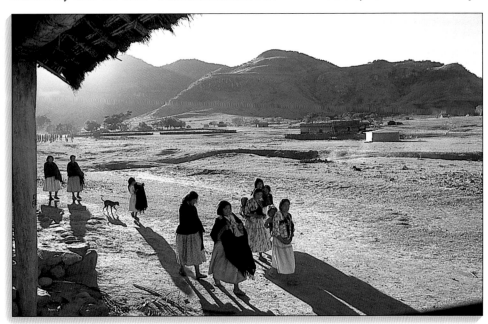

had attracted the interest of many organizations: anthropologists began to study them; linguists translated the New Testament into the Seri language; Protestant missionaries made nominal Christians out of them and – much to the dismay of visitors and anthropologists – prohibited their custom of face painting in the process.

These days, the Seris make their living by selling fish, shell necklaces and beautiful ironwood carvings of animals. The main group of about 300 people lives at Desemboque. They still weave heavy, decorative baskets from a fiber called *torote* and fashion pottery and ceramic figurines. They are also good mechanics. It is said that a century ago they could

table Sierra del Nayar, their homeland in the western range of the Sierra Madre, kept invaders out and allowed them to keep their independence.

Jesuit missionary Father Ortega wrote that Cora country was "so wild and frightful to behold in its ruggedness, even more than the arrows of its warlike inhabitants, that it took away the courage of the conquerors, because not only the ridges and the valleys appear inaccessible, but the extended range of towering mountain peaks confused the eye."

Nuño de Guzmán conquered the lowlands of western Mexico, but left the mountain areas untamed and they remained strongholds of indian rebellion. Except for the Tarascans, there were no tightly organized political entities in western Mexico which could be quickly overcome by the Spaniards' superior arms. Guzmán had the Tarascan king murdered and the Tarascans accepted the Spaniards as their new tribute-greedy overlords. But tribes in western Mexico could not be defeated so easily.

The Cora indians became the most implacable of the rebels in this part of Mexico. Their neighbors, the Huichols, hardly figured in this chronicle of resistance, perhaps because they dwelt in an even more inaccessible region, and were even less closely organized than the Coras.

During the 16th century much of western Mexico was in a state of rebellion and war, and the untamed indians frequently embarked on raids. As a counter-measure, the Spanish moved large groups of submissive indians, including the Christianized Tlaxcalans, into new communities to act as a barrier against wild tribes. In 1616, the Coras joined in the great Tepehuan rebellion and carried out raids on an increasing scale through the rest of the century.

The missionaries tried to tame the Coras, but the indians refused to give up their gods. Next, the Spanish cut off the Coras' salt trade and sent a Jesuit priest to make an offer of peace. The delegation was received by a group of musicians, warriors and elders led by Tonati, the sun priest. But though they were polite, the Coras refused to bend to Spanish authority.

Later, some Cora leaders offered to pledge allegiance to Spanish rule on the condition they could keep their lands in perpetuity, pay no tribute and have the right to pursue the salt trade without paying taxes. Not all Coras were in agreement with this, however, and the Spanish decided to teach the rebellious indians a lesson. The Spaniards' first large-scale expedition achieved only partial success, but in 1722, under Captain Juan Flores de la Torre, they won a clear-cut victory over the Coras. Some survivors fled into the remote mountains but large-scale resistance was over.

The missionaries who followed the army met with the same problem of how to cope with a recalcitrant people – a situation further complicated by the ongoing dispute between the

Jesuits and the Franciscans over who had the right to save souls. The Jesuits won but only for a time; less than half a century later they were expelled from New Spain and the Franciscans took their place, setting up missions in the Coras' religious centers. But these locations were now avoided by the indians except at the time of their important fiestas.

The missionaries did succeed in fostering a Spanish-style civil government of sorts among the indians, and the titles that were bestowed on the officials – *gobernador, alcalde, alguacil* – are retained to this day. The missionaries also introduced Easter, but the adamant Coras con-

verted it into something uniquely their own.

In the final analysis, the missionaries had scant success in taming the people of the mountains. When the Norwegian explorer Carl Lumholtz visited the Coras at the turn of the century, he found that, to a large degree, they still practiced their traditional culture.

The Morning Star remained their principal deity who acted with the other gods to help indians in trouble. Lumholtz wrote that the Coras worshipped old stone figures and a large sacred bowl, which could understand only the Cora language and was considered to be the patron saint of the community, a mother of the tribe.

LEFT: Cora religious and civic centers lie in the few flat areas of the Sierra.
RIGHT: a Huichol man hangs *peyote* out to dry.

Even today the Coras (only a few thousand of them remain) live a traditional life, working subsistence agricultural plots and practising their own religion. They live from cattle-raising and from the sale of their beautiful textiles. Like the Huichols, they engage in the ritual use of *peyote*, a species of thornless, spineless cactus well known for its hallucinogenic effects. The shamans still invoke supernatural beings, and missionaries still try to influence them.

The Huichols

The ritualistic Huichol indians of the rugged Sierra Madre Occidental in northern Jalisco

Nakawe (growth); and Kayaumari (the deer).

Clinging tenaciously to their lifestyle and customs, the Huichols earn a little money by working on the coastal plantations, through the sale of cattle, and by selling their handicrafts.

In the past, they planted corn and hunted deer. Settlements were generally far apart, sometimes as much as half a day's journey from one another.

The Huichols hold their most important ceremonies – for planting, harvesting and *peyote* gathering – in a centrally located *tuki*, or round temple. The *tzauririka* (singing shaman) leads the rites. He and the other temple officials are

offer a window to Mexico's pre-Hispanic past. Anthropologists consider them among the Mexican peoples least affected by Western cultural influences. Their mountain home shut them off from the conquistadores, and missionaries arrived among them belatedly, 200 years after Cortés.

The Huichol have adopted Catholic rituals but with their own embellishment. Some, for example, choose to believe that the biblical Joseph won the right to marry the Virgin Mary by winning a violin-playing contest. Huichol beliefs reflect a Mesoamerican theology dating back to antiquity. The principal deities are the personalized forces of nature: Tatewari (fire);

chosen for a five-year term, and almost every male Huichol holds several of these official positions during his lifetime. Besides being the heart of religious life, the *tuki* serves as the center of social life, where the Huichol can seek help and exchange ideas. Before a ceremony, there is often a ritual deer hunt.

There is little interaction between Huichols and *mestizos*, except during the big fiestas at San Andrés. *Mestizos* come to the festivals, to sell things such as pottery and candy, play music and buy cattle. Huichols sometimes rent land to *mestizos*, who work the land as tenant farmers for half shares.

So far there has been little threat to the Huichol way of life – either from the *mestizos* or the many curious visitors. But the *mestizos* want land for grazing, lumbering and farming and this presents a challenge. To meet it, the Huichols need to find competent and strong leaders and hire the services of professionals, such as lawyers and surveyors. What will eventually happen depends on government attitudes and the forces of economics. If the prices of timber and beef go up sharply, or if minerals are found in the land of the Huichols, then their way of life may be doomed.

The Huichols are most popularly known in and out of Mexico for their traditional ritual use of *peyote* (*see page 239*). Ironically, *peyote* does not grow in their homeland; neither the soil nor the climate is right. So they make an annual pilgrimage northeast to the desert of San Luis Potosí to fetch it. A small "dose" – one to four pieces of *peyote* – takes away hunger, thirst, sexual desire and relieves tiredness. A larger dose – five or more pieces – produces hallucinations.

There have been some signs of change, with different attitudes penetrating even the Sierra Madre. Some Huichols now speak Spanish and wear *mestizo* dress. Tourists have begun to turn up in Huichol country, especially during Easter Week, the only fixed-date festival in their calendar; many are young people attracted by stories of exotic indians and their *peyote*.

The Tarascans

The Tarascan indians have been renowned artisans since pre-Hispanic times. Their home is in northern Michoacán around Lake Pátzcuaro and to the west, on the *meseta* (plateau) of Tarasca. Census figures vary widely but there are probably around 80,000 who still speak their native language; this is unlike any other Mexican indian language, and some researchers have even tried to trace the Tarascan's origins to a Peruvian tribe.

Today's Tarascos are known as fishermen and, particularly, as craftsmen, making pottery, copperware, lacquered bowls and trays, wool weavings, guitars, leather goods, wood masks, hats, mats and furniture.

LEFT: Lake Pátzcuaro has many Tarascan villages along its shores.
RIGHT: the Totonac *voladores* (flyers) design and make their own bird costumes.

Prior to the arrival of the Spanish, the Tarascans had welded together a militaristic empire strong enough to check the Aztec war machine. Shortly after the Spanish conquest, they found a friend and protector in Don Vasco de Quiroga. A lawyer and personal friend of the Spanish monarch, he was appointed to Mexico's Royal High Court of Justice, which had condemned Nuño de Guzmán for his excesses and the assassination of the Tarascan king, Tangaxoan. Consecrated as priest and bishop on the same day, Quiroga went to Michoacán to Christianize the Tarascans and protect them from the excesses of Spanish landlords.

TARASCAN SPECIALTIES

Although Tarascans have been renowned artisans since pre-Hispanic times, it was Bishop Vasco de Quiroga who encouraged each village to set up a co-operative and develop its own craft specialty. The tradition continues to this day. For example, the Tarascan village of Ocumicho specializes in making clay devils in all shapes and manners: devils riding motor-cycles, devils in the form of fish, devils fighting with snakes, and so on. Other villages that have become famous for their particular craft include:

Santa Clara – copperware	Ihuatzio – rush mats
Patamban – green pottery	Paracho – guitars.

Quiroga's ideas of egalitarian communities and self-sufficiency were based directly on Thomas More's Utopian philosophy. Always kind and courteous towards the indian people, Tata ("father") Quiroga – as he was affectionately nicknamed – organized hospitals and schools in the missions and encouraged the Tarascans to pursue their crafts; they created intricate feather mosaics for him and modeled figures of their deities from a paste made of pulverized cornstalks and orchid extract. It may have been Quiroga who encouraged them to fashion corn-paste figures of Christ.

But all was not all Utopia. Caught between

ble for fruitful harvests. Lumholtz observed that the Tarascans were not able to live solely from the land. Many had to devote themselves to making handicrafts, which was exhausting and poorly paid work. Yet the Tarascans persisted with their crafts, and today they continue to demonstrate their skills.

In the 1930s, President Lázaro Cárdenas tried to foster a sense of self-sufficiency among the Tarascan people. His idea was that villagers could participate in the national economy while retaining their traditional way of life. But the situation has not improved. Many Tarascan men still have to leave their villages to find a job

Spanish greed and the strict rules of Christianity, the Tarascans were forced to adapt. Trade was strictly controlled by Spanish merchants, and no direct exchange of goods between indian villages was permitted; everything first had to pass through the markets in white-dominated towns.

Carl Lumholtz, Norwegian chronicler of indian tribes, traveled through the Tarasco land at the beginning of the 20th century. He noted how the Tarascans had adapted to their new religion. Farmers, for example, buried stone replicas of their old deities in the fields to ensure a good crop, while at the same time appealing to Saint Matthew, who was responsi-

and scrape a living; some even make the long trek across the border to seek work in the US.

The Totonacs

The Totonacs, who number perhaps 150,000, have maintained much of their rich cultural tradition. They live in the fertile, tropical coastal lands of Veracruz and in the cool highlands of the Sierra Madre, lands where irrigation is not needed but a lot of hard manual labor is.

The Totonacs trace their ancestry back to one of the most distinguished of the pre-Hispanic civilizations. In ancient times, they excelled at pottery-making, stone sculpture and architecture.

Cortés landed on the coast inhabited by the Totonacs and negotiated an alliance against the Aztecs with their leader at Cempoala. Thus Totonac porters served Cortés's army, lugging supplies and heavy cannons over the mountain passes. Because they aided the Spanish, the Totonacs were given a small measure of autonomy during early colonial rule: they kept their communal lands and their leaders were allowed to exercise some power. But the land of the Totonacs was fertile and yielded much wealth

VOLADORES

You can watch the Volador ritual outside the Museum of Anthropology in Mexico City, at the Acapulco Convention Center, or, more traditionally, at the ruins of El Tajín and in nearby Papantla.

purification rituals with their own magical incantations and offerings of food and liquor. These precautions are to ensure that the pole will not take any performers as victims. As a final insurance measure, a live turkey is dropped into the hole and is ritually crushed as the tree trunk or pole is hoisted into its final position.

The ritual is a comment on the times that the Totonac dancers have had to organize themselves into a union to defend their livelihood and protect the authenticity of their performance.

(they grew sugar cane, tobacco, coffee and vanilla); eventually they were forced into labor on the Spanish-owned estates.

The Totonacs were converted to Catholicism, but, like others, they reinterpreted its rituals. The pre-Christian "Voladores" ritual (*see page 281*), for example, is now performed outside the church of Papantla on the feast day of St Francis.

When the voladores' pole is erected, the Totonacs combine Christian blessings and

LEFT: a photograph of Lacandones by 19th-century French explorer Desiré Charnay.
ABOVE : Zapotec women in Oaxaca.

The Totonacs live a precarious existence, caught up between their traditional lifestyle and the intrusion of the modern world. The discovery of oil in the Gulf, combined with large-scale cattle-raising, has pushed them off the land. They live on a basic diet of corn, beans and chili, supplemented with vegetables and wild plants. They usually kill and eat domestic animals only during fiestas.

The Lacandones

Another tribe that has retained its cultural identity is the Lacandón which, up until comparatively recently, escaped the influence of Western civilization by living in the Chiapas

The Chiapas Problem

Until December 31, 1993, Chiapas was best known for the magnificent Mayan ruins of Palenque and the charming, if somewhat chilly, colonial town of San Cristóbal de las Casas, in Chiapas state.

The present-day indigenous inhabitants of Chiapas – comprising roughly one-third of its three-million population – were a colorful backdrop. They sold handicrafts to the tourists and lived short, impoverished lives, mostly unseen by ordinary visitors, Mexican or foreign.

Then came January 1, 1994, when several thousand indians belonging to the Zapatista National Liberation Army (EZLN) occupied half a dozen Chiapas towns, including San Cristóbal. They declared the region independent, even naming a capital, the small town of La Realidad, deep in the forests of the Lacandon indians, as a symbol of their struggle for political recognition.

After just twelve days of occasionally bloody fighting, President Carlos Salinas declared a truce and offered to negotiate on the Zapatistas' demands for political and economic rights. In the first round a score of armed and hooded peasants, many of them in traditional indian clothing, sat down to talks in San Cristóbal with the former mayor of

Mexico City, Manuel Camacho. Local bishop, Samuel Ruíz, a longtime champion of indigenous rights, acted as mediator.

But the star of the show was "Subcomandante Marcos," the mysterious, pipe-smoking Zapatista leader and the only guerrilla delegate who was clearly not an indian. Later "unmasked" as former teacher, Rafael Sebastian Guillén, Marcos captivated a large audience with his self-deprecatory rhetoric.

Despite their bellicose early statements, the Zapatistas soon declared they were interested only in sparking a peaceful revolution by Mexican "civil society." But, although the talks with Camacho produced an apparently workable agreement, the EZLN later rejected the terms.

In early 1996, resumed negotiations produced an agreement. But the government failed to draft the legislation required to translate the agreement into practice and the EZLN withdrew from the talks. Apparently betting more on a counter insurgency strategy of "low-intensity" warfare than on good-faith negotiations, the government at best permitted – and at worst promoted – the proliferation of anti-Zapatista paramilitary groups.

The federal army and the local police tightened their grip on the "conflict zone," but did nothing to prevent intra-community violence. This combination of harassment and impunity produced a rising death toll: many more have died in Chiapas since January 1994 than in the brief uprising itself. Federal police arrested dozens of suspects but, months later, senior officials who let the paramilitaries roam unchecked still faced no charges. The federal authorities were moved, however, to undertake a new, more active policy in Chiapas. Interior minister Ernesto Chuayffet was sacked and his successor, Francisco Labastida, sought to turn the indigenous rights accord into law.

On the ground in Chiapas, however, harassment of EZLN supporters intensified. Alleging interference in Mexican politics, immigration authorities expelled foreigners sympathetic to the Zapatistas. They also began dismantling the EZLN's network of "automonous municipalities" and jailing supposed ringleaders.

Isolated and surrounded, the Zapatistas' best strategy has seemed to be to survive until the year 2000, in the hope that the general elections would bring a change of government. ❑

ABOVE: masked Zapatista guerrillas at a press conference in San Cristóbal de las Casas.

jungle. However, over the years, lumbermen, hunters, merchants and researchers have traded with the Lacandones, exchanging alcohol, firearms, food and clothing for precious wood, tobacco, and chicle (the original chewing gum). The Lacandones live in two- or three- family units, worshipping their old gods and eking out a living from the jungle. Though the tribe is very small in number, it is still somewhat protected by its formidable surroundings.

The Lacandones were hardly heard of until

GREEN INFERNO

Anthropologist Jacques Soustelle called the Lacandón habitat a "green hell", hard to get into and equally difficult to get out of.

few animals; even insects were scarce, except on river banks.

But the Lacandones are well adapted to their environment. They know which plants are beneficial to them and which are harmful, and by the time a child is 12 years old, he or she is quite able to survive in the jungle.

The word Lacandón comes from *Lacantun,* meaning Great Rock – an island in Lake Miramar and the home of the Lacandones' ancestors, who were a branch of the Itzae Maya.

the French anthropologist Jacques Soustelle and his wife, Georgette, visited them in 1933. Soustelle reported that no sun penetrated the thick carpeting and that the ground was a mass of rotting vegetation that made even walking a struggle.

Yet the Lacandones moved about easily. The trees looked tortured, like something out of a nightmare, and over all towered the giant mahogany. There were innumerable pools of water which never gave off a reflection because the sun rarely penetrated the vegetation, and, apart from the chattering monkeys, there were

ABOVE: modern-day Mayas from the Yucatán.

To the Lacandones the most important deity is the Sun God, who is accompanied by other gods in a complex mythology passed on from father to son. They believe the Sun passes the night in the subterranean world, in a house of stone where he eats and drinks like a human being. They perform rituals and give offerings to ensure that he will appear next morning.

To the Lacandones the ancient Mayan ceremonial centers are objects of special veneration. Because they believe that the god Atchakyum lives in the Yaxchilán complex (Yucatán), small groups go there to offer incense and food.

Soustelle found the Lacandones living in

small clearings, walled in by jungle, with never more than a dozen people to a community. They planted cotton, tobacco, chili, corn, yucca and bananas using the destructive slash-and-burn technique to clear the land, which they then cultivated for three or so years before it was exhausted and they had to move on.

The Lacandones looked for places in the jungle that were thought favorable for women's fertility, but because of a lack of women there were few children. Even today men sometimes "marry" infant girls, with the husband living in his father-in-law's house and working for him for a number of years. As soon as the child

grows up, she cooks for her husband. The Lacandones' concept of wedded life is more about eating together than sleeping together.

The Lacandones used to do a lot of hunting with bow and feathered, silex-tipped arrows. Their quarry was usually monkeys, wild turkeys or wild pigs. But the jungle is not always a healthy place to live, and the Lacandones often suffer from malaria and rheumatism induced by the damp conditions. They also succumb readily to Western diseases and germs, and can often die of influenza and even from a common cold; in fact, no visitor with a cold is allowed into their country.

The Lacandones' contact with white men began in earnest during the latter part of the 19th century, when mahogany became a sought-after material and access roads were built. Some indians worked for the lumber companies to earn money to buy axes, machetes, firearms and liquor.

The few Lacandones who have managed to survive to the present day have seen dramatic changes during the last few years. A dirt road (dry-season only) gives them access to Palenque. and former president Luis Echeverría gave them legal *ejido* title to vast tracts of their jungle; with money received from lumbering concessions, they have bought trucks, clothing and other manufactured goods.

Tzotzils and Tzeltals

Some 200,000 indians, divided almost evenly between the Tzotzils and the Tzeltals, live in the highlands of Chiapas, near San Cristóbal de las Casas. Both groups speak Mayan dialects. Their's is marvelous country; one writer speaks of passing through "layers of cold before entering the cool mountain sunshine of the Chiapas highlands." The Tzeltals live on the lower slopes of Chiapas' central mountains, while most of the Tzotzils live in the same area above the 1,500-meter (5,000-ft) line. Both tribes keep their distinctive style of dress and also their different cultural and social traits.

The community is made up of a central village and outlying farms, often a steep climb and several hours away. The civil officials reside in town with their families, while most of the community lives in the nearby hills. The village comes noisily alive only for Sunday market and the periodic fiestas. Each individual has status in the community and lives on good terms with his fellows and all supernatural beings – the traditional gods, ancestral spirits, and the saints introduced by the Spanish. The villagers offer food, incense and flowers to these gods, and if someone leaves the community, he is considered a traitor.

Over the centuries, the indians have been savagely exploited and treated as second-class citizens. Their lands were seized and they were forced to work on plantations. During colonial times, when no proper roads existed, the Tzeltals were used as porters. They were made to carry heavy loads all the way to Veracruz, a distance of almost 1,000 km (625 miles). Many died from the debilitating heat of the lowlands, and if they tried to rebel they were ruthlessly executed.

Relations between the indians and the Catholic Church were often strained and marked by intolerance. Few of the early missionaries tried to understand the traditional indian rites; they broke up their idols, baptized the heathens, and convinced them to accept an inferior status and serve the Spanish. Their reward would come, they said, in the hereafter.

Apart from a few exceptional missionaries – like Fray Bartolomé de las Casas – the Church backed the exploitation of the indians. On the whole, the missionaries led a life of ease, even of luxury but bloody rebellions flared periodically and sometimes the priests paid for their indolence and were killed.

These uprisings were always local affairs. The uprising of 1994 (*see page 90*) may have had more impact as the whole world saw how badly indian communities are still treated today.

Both the Tzeltals and the Tzotzils have established a *modus vivendi* with Christianity, a live-and-let-live philosophy. In public, the Tzeltals venerate Christ as God, but in their homes they also worship Chulmetic, goddess of earth. They believe in Uch as well, a supernatural being who helps make the corn grow.

The Tzotzils believe in Hz'k'al, a phantasm who is black and has a penis 1 meter (3 feet) long. Some Tzotzils believe that the saints and the gods hold periodic meetings when they decide whether to punish human beings by visiting upon them an ailment or by bringing on a bad crop. The indians believe that the celebration of Mass is a community obligation to the saints. Their civil authorities visit the dwelling places of the supernatural beings – the mountains, caverns, springs – where they pray, play music and appease the gods with food and drink. A man's first and foremost obligation is to plant and care for his field of corn, for it is his relation with corn that distinguishes him from the animals. These indians consider it a waste of time to try to grow anything other than corn, and despair of agronomists who want them to raise a variety of crops.

The indians in the Chiapas highlands wear some of the most exquisite costumes in Mex-

ico, such as finely embroidered blouses and soft woolen shawls. The Zinacantec men wear red cotton ponchos and straw hats festooned with ribbons. The women go barefoot. None likes to be photographed.

Cultural assimilation is an acute problem for these people. It is the same old fallacy – the *malinchismo* – that whatever comes from the "outside" is better than the indigenous. However, there are still many indians who see for themselves the flaw in this reasoning and cherish the value of their traditions. Thanks to their dedication to their ancestors, the Tzotzil and Tzeltal communities continue to survive today.

Surviving against the odds

Many other groups combine to make up the estimated 13 million indians living in Mexico today. There are, for example, nearly one million modern-day Maya in the Yucatán Peninsula; the Zapotecs and Mixtecs in Guerrero and Oaxaca also number a million between them; by far the most numerous of all the groups is the Nahua – descendants of the Ancient Aztecs – whose numbers are estimated at around 1.5 million, and who live mostly in the states of Mexico, Puebla, Hidalgo and San Luis Potosí. Smaller groups, some numbering just a few hundred, include the Mazatecs, the Mazahua, the Huastecs and the Otomí. ❑

LEFT: many people of Afro-Caribbean origin live in Veracruz.
RIGHT: selling seafood with a smile.

LOS CHARROS: MEXICO'S GILDED COWBOYS

These cowboys perform what many believe to be

Mexico's only truly national sport

To define the Mexican *charro* as merely a cowboy is to do him an injustice. The *charro* has his roots in Spain, as do his horses, the cattle he works, and the dress he wears. During colonial times, all Spaniards

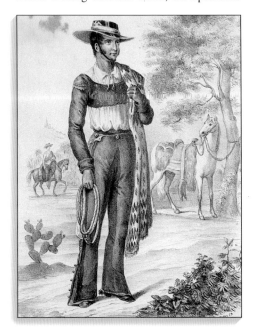

were obliged to own a horse, while a royal decree in 1528 forbade the indians, under penalty of death, from even riding a horse. But over the years, as cattle were introduced into Mexico and indians were needed to work the cattle, this law was abandoned. For both sport and exercise, as well as their daily work, men rode horses and cared for them.

Charros made very fine cavalrymen in Mexico's wars. At the battle of the Alamo, they lassoed and captured Texans, and in the fight against the French, galloping *charros* snagged cannon with their lassos and turned them over. During the Revolution, too, they played an important role, although Pancho Villa's "Golden

Ones" (*Los Dorados*) were eventually stopped by General Alvaro Obregón's trenches, barbed wire and machine guns.

The skilled work that the *charros* did in the field naturally led to competition, and then to sport. It all originated on the cattle ranges: roping, tying, riding and branding. For years bullfighting and *charrería* were intimately associated. Indeed, aficionados of both the *fiesta brava* and the *charros* claimed as their own the great Ponciano Díaz, a bullfighter and *charro extraordinaire*. Probably some of the best known *charros* of all times were the 12 men who took part in Buffalo Bill's Wild West shows in the US. Their leader, Vicente Oropeza, was renowned as the world's greatest artist of the lasso.

Urban charros

After the expropriation of many large cattle ranches during post-Revolution days, the *charro* lost status. Since then, *charrería* has been developed in an urban setting by what one might call "the cowboys of the city," and has become what many consider to be the only truly national Mexican sport. The biggest *lienzos charros* (*charro* rings) are in Mexico City and Guadalajara where competitions are held from 11am to 2pm on Sundays.

The show starts with horsemen riding abreast to salute the judges and the public, in a manner similar to the opening of a bull-fight. The first event, called *cala de caballo*, demonstrates the mastery of rider over horse. The rider comes full gallop down a passageway and brings his horse to an abrupt stop inside a white, chalk-powdered rectangle. The rider turns his mount round and round – to the right, to the left – all the time staying within the rectangle. To top it off, he walks his horse backwards out of the ring.

Then comes the *coleadero,* the thriller. A bull comes charging out of a chute and down the passageway into the ring. Up gallops our hero, the *charro*, who grabs the bull by the tail and then tries to throw him off balance and roll him over on his back. Extra points are given for how swiftly the *charro* can perform the difficult task and how neatly he makes the bull fall and roll over.

Apart from bronco-bucking and bull-riding, everything is now worked with the lasso. The most spectacular event takes place near the end of the show. Three riders drive a wild horse around the edge of the ring. The fourth member of the team stands about 3 meters (10 ft) from the side of the arena, leaving enough room to allow the wild horse and the riders to pass. After the riders and the horse have galloped a

formance is followed by the *paso de la muerte* (the pass of death) which entails a *charro* jumping off his horse onto the back of a wild horse. It is what is known in the trade as "changing horses in midstream."

Women have their own events, called *escaramuza charra*. They dress, naturally, in *charra* style, and mount their horses side-saddle, so as not to lose the "attractiveness of their exquisite femininity," as one Mexican writer put it.

The show sometimes closes with the dancing of the *jarabe tapatío*, the famous Mexican hat dance, which comes from Jalisco and is the all-time *charro* favorite. ❏

few times around the edge of the ring, the man on foot starts twirling his lasso. Then, with incredible, split-second timing, he jumps through a loop in his lasso and in the same breath drops a loop on the ground in front of the horse as it comes thundering by. When the hind legs of the horse are inside the loop, the *charro* jerks his lasso, slips the knot tight, and wraps the rope around his back. The slack is hauled in; the *charro* leans back, digs in his heels, and brings down the wild bronco. Usually this per-

LEFT: a 19th-century engraving of a *hacienda* owner.
ABOVE: a *charro* jumps through his looping lasso before catching a wild horse.

FROM THE HORSE'S MOUTH

Charros tend to be romantic and conservative. They idolize women and are usually fervent nationalists. They are devoted to their horses and love to eat and drink heartily. Teetotal *charros* are considered suspect.

Charros sometimes seem vain and often spend a fortune on their elaborate outfits, particularly the broad-rimmed felt hats. There is an aura of nostalgia about the *charros*, a wish to return to a golden past. They love to perform daring feats to impress the ladies; they are, in fact, the archetypal macho Mexicano and their motto runs "a horse to fill your legs, a fighting cock to fill your pocket, and a woman to fill your arms."

LOS TOROS

The "fiesta brava" – bullfight may not be everybody's idea of fun,

but it has been a part of Mexican culture for nearly 500 years

The bullfight starts promptly at 4.30pm, even if the clock has to be turned back. The opening parade is led by a bailiff who formally asks the authorities for permission to hold the *corrida*. Three *toreros* follow, resplendent in their *trajes de luces* – suits of light – all shiny silk and gold embroidery. Behind

"Veronica" pass (named for the woman who wiped Christ's face). The picadors ride in. They push their lances into the muscular hump on the bull's back. The picadors usually stab twice to expose the "cross" where the bullfighter will thrust his sword in the death stroke. Exit picadors, leaving a raging but weakened bull.

them come their assistants, then the picadors (horsemen armed with lances), and lastly the attendants with their mules, which haul away the dead bulls.

The ring *presidente* waves his handkerchief and the first bull rushes in. Weighing over 500 kg (1,100 lbs), he is a raging muscular combatant, moving along like an express train and itching to fight. The drama unfolds in three acts.

Act 1: The *torero* watches while his assistants handle the bull with their capes. Then he takes a few turns himself to test the animal's behavior, to see how he runs and which way he hooks his horns. The *torero* uses a heavy gold-and-silk cape and will perform the well-known

JUDGING THE PERFORMANCE

Each of the three *toreros* on any afternoon will be assigned two bulls and will be appraised by *aficionados* and judges on the following points:

- ☛ *mandar:* the degree of mastery shown by the *torero* over the bull.
- ☛ *parar:* how well the *torero* stands; whether he is straight, with feet firmly planted and not leaning toward the bull to fake audacity.
- ☛ *templar:* the timing of the *torero*, the slow, rhythmic motion he uses to give the bull maximum time to hook him.
- ☛ the cleanness of the kill.

Act 2: The *torero's* assistants, or in some cases the bullfighter himself, then plant three pairs of *banderillas* (barbed darts) into the bull's hump. The *banderillero* runs to the bull, plants the darts, leans on them, and dexterously gets out of the way of the charging animal, which by this time is bleeding profusely.

Act 3: *La Hora de la Verdad* (the Moment of Truth). The *torero* asks permission to kill the bull and dedicates the kill to a lady friend or anyone else he chooses. He then has 16 minutes to dispatch the bull or be ordered from the ring in disgrace.

SEEING RED

Bulls are color-blind, it is a myth that the cape has to be red; they go for anything that moves.

dies at once, although sometimes a *coup de grâce* has to be delivered.

Depending on his performance, the *torero* can be awarded an ear, two ears, two ears and the tail, and sometimes even the bull's hoof. The *torero* does not always win though; most are gored, sometimes many times; one in four is crippled in the course of his career, and one out of ten will be killed by the bull. If a bull puts up a particularly good fight, he can be pardoned and retired to pasture and stud in the hope that his sons will inherit his courage.

The *torero* works his magic on the bull with his heavy cape, going through a series of daring passes, working even closer to the horns. The *torero* then switches to a smaller flannel cape. When the bull has been so weakened that his head droops, the *torero* aims along his sword and plunges it between the shoulder blades, going over the horns and into the "cross," the place where the sword can penetrate cleanly and sever the artery to the heart or puncture the lung. The bull drops to his knees and usually

LEFT: making the bull see red.
ABOVE: the *torero* swirls his cape to decoy the charging bull

Bullfighting is by no means everyone's favorite entertainment. Ernest Hemingway claimed there were two kinds of spectators at a bullfight: those who identify with the bull and those who identify with the bullfighter. But there is no denying its popularity: there are 225 permanent arenas and 500 improvised ones in Mexico. The Plaza México in Mexico City, the biggest bullfighting arena in the world, can seat 50,000. The season runs from the end of November to March or April, although some good bullfights are also performed in the summer in arenas along the US border, to cater for the *norteamericanos* who have caught the fever. ❑

ARTESANÍA

After sampling the endless variety of crafts in Mexico,
your ideas of beauty and color may never be the same again

The craft tradition in Mexico dates back to long before the arrival of the Spanish, and many of the colorful and decorative *artesanías* can be traced to their pre-Hispanic origins. Often the materials and techniques have survived too, although synthetic fibers and colors have taken over much of the market and mass production is threatening some of the more laborious but infinitely more beautiful, authentic creations.

When the Spaniards came to Mexico, they found the native artisans well organized and selling their wares at great markets called *tianguis*. The Náhuatl word is still in use today, as are the pots, baskets, toys, clothes, sandals, hats, hammocks and other everyday objects made by the modern craftsmen of Mexico.

Among the profound changes wrought by the Spanish newcomers were the introduction of the wheel in pottery-making and the use of metal tools. The Spaniards needed items which were too expensive to import from Spain: saddles and bridles, woolen weavings, furniture and other household items. So, on the heels of the conquistadores came Spanish craftsmen who taught their specialties to indian apprentices. In 1529, a lay brother, Pedro de Gante, established an arts and crafts school in Mexico City for the indians, and in Michoacán Bishop Vasco de Quiroga introduced new techniques for working copper and for producing iron and lacquerware.

Changing fashions

Initially, native craftsmen were scorned and everything Spanish was considered superior. It was not until the early 20th century with the new spirit of nationalism that arose from the Revolution, that the pendulum began to swing the other way.

PRECEDING PAGES: a Huichol artist concentrates on a yarn painting.
LEFT: a mask from Guerrero reflects both Spanish and indian influences.
RIGHT: pottery is one of Mexico's specialties.

In 1921, President Alvaro Obregón opened a crafts exhibition, the first such official recognition given to the native artisan. Diego Rivera, his wife Frida Kahlo and other artists of the time praised the artisans and became collectors of their crafts. All of this hype had its effect. Indigenous handicrafts became fashionable,

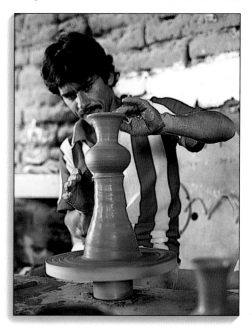

and middle-class Mexicans started to buy them; so did the American visitors. They still do, although the picture is not as rosy as it might seem: so many middlemen get their cut that the craftsman seldom fares well.

The majority of artisans in Mexico are peasant farmers or laborers, who work at their craft part-time to supplement their income and usually make objects for everyday domestic use. Then there is the full-time craftsman, who either has his own shop or works for someone who does. He fashions items that are both decorative and useful, but also supplies the souvenir trade with cheap stuff that appeals to visitors. Next come those engaged in mass-production, and finally there is the unemployed city worker who lives by his wits and, with great ingenuity and skill, fashions toys and trinkets out of factory offcuts and cheap materials such as paper, tin, wire, wood and cork.

Buying crafts

Each region and, in some cases, each town or village in Mexico specializes in one or more particular craft. Sometimes the same village has made the same item since pre-Hispanic times. In many state capitals there is a *Casa de las Artesanías* where you can admire and buy the particular crafts of the region, although prices may

be higher than in the marketplace. Some major cities will have a Fonart shop, too – which are run by a government agency that promotes the work of craftsmen and preserves the quality of the crafts. These, or any of the better tourist shops, will provide a good overall view of what is available as well as an idea of the prices.

However, when possible, it is infinitely more interesting to buy the crafts from their region of origin. Markets all over the country are an important source of handicrafts. The daily or weekly *tianguis* usually have a few stalls selling craft items for everyday use such as pots and baskets, while some towns have markets devoted exlusively to the crafts of that region. Often the most exciting buys of all, though, are the crafts stumbled upon on a street corner or at the roadside in the middle of nowhere.

Regional specialties

Although many of today's handicrafts combine pre-Hispanic, Spanish and contemporary influences, the majority of wonderful *artesanías* are to be found in the areas with a significant indigenous population like Michoacán, Puebla, Oaxaca, Guerrero and Chiapas.

Northern Mexico is not known for its crafts, but exceptions include the ironwood animal carvings of the Seri indians, the woolen belts, baskets and dolls of the Tarahumaras and *serapes* (ponchos) from Coahuila and Zacatecas.

The Cora and Huichol indians travel to Tepic and Guadalajara to sell their woolen belts and bags, superb beadwork, embroidered clothing and yarn paintings. Tlaquepaque, a suburb of Guadalajara, is a center for ceramics – including fine copies of pre-Hispanic pieces – blown glass and furniture. The nearby town of Tonalá specializes in pottery and glass and has a large street market on Thursdays and Sundays.

The best time to buy the delicate *deshilados* (drawn threadwork) and embroidery of Aguascalientes is at the Festival de San Marcos, from April to early May each year. The silk *rebozos* (shawls) of San Luis Potosí are famed for being so fine you can slip them through a wedding ring. In the area known as La Huasteca, the indians weave the traditional white *quechquémetl* (cape for women) with cross-stitch embroidery. They also make rough and inexpensive wool bags and items out of cactus fiber.

Guanajuato has sophisticated Talavera-style pottery, while San Miguel de Allende sells *ser-*

STATES OF THE ARTS

Some of the more widespread crafts can be found all over Mexico but are outstanding in certain states:

- ☛ **Pottery** – Oaxaca, Puebla, Guerrero, Jalisco.
- ☛ **Textiles** – Chiapas, Oaxaca, Puebla, Nayarit, Coahuila.
- ☛ **Leather** – Zacatecas, León, Jalisco, Michoacán.
- ☛ **Woodwork** – Sonora, Michoacán, Morelos.
- ☛ **Lacquerware** – Michoacán (Uruapán), Guerrero (Olinalá), Chiapas (Chiapa de Corzo).
- ☛ **Jewelry/metalwork** – Guerrero (Taxco), Querétaro (San Juan del Río), Michoacán (Santa Clara del Cobre).
- ☛ **Hammocks** – Yucatán, Campeche, Michoacán.
- ☛ **Glassware** – Jalisco, Puebla, Oaxaca.

apes, tinware, *piñatas* (a papier maché figure filled with sweets and toys for children's parties) and masks. Querétaro is famous for its semi-precious stones and silver jewelry, and in Tequisquiapan, craftsmen make baskets, folding stools, and serapes. It can all be bought in the colonial town of San Juan del Río. In the valley of Mezquital (Hidalgo), the Otomí indians use backstrap looms to weave *rebozos* (shawls) and belts, while the town of Ixmiquilpan, also in Hidalgo state, is renowned for its bird cages in the shape of cathedrals.

Michoacán probably has the greatest variety of crafts in all Mexico. Many of the artisans

tery; and Uruapán, masks and lacquerware. In Morelia, capital of Michoacán, some of the state's best handicrafts can be bought at the *Casa de las Artesanías*, located in the former Convento de San Francisco.

The state of Mexico produces warm wool *serapes*, colorful baskets from Lerma and the polychrome ceramic "trees of life" in the town of Metepec. In Ixtapán de la Sal, household utensils and decorative animals are carved out of orange-tree wood. Toluca, the state capital, is known for silverware, and also for chess and domino games made of leather, bone or wood.

The town and state of Tlaxcala, where wool

live near Lake Pátzcuaro and most of the crafts are available in Pátzcuaro town. On November 2, the Plaza Vasco de Quiroga becomes a center for craftsmen. Some artisans work year-round in the nearby Casa de los Once Patios, a former convent.

Some Michoacán towns specialize in particular crafts: Santa Clara del Cobre, copperware; Paracho, guitars; Tzintzuntzán, burnished ceramics; Quiroga, painted wood bowls and household items; Ihuatzio, reed mats and basketry; Patambán, exquisite green-glazed pot-

was first woven in New Spain, is still a center of weaving. Serapes are again a specialty of the house, and hand-carved, brightly painted walking sticks are also popular.

Puebla state is one of the richest in the variety and quality of its crafts. Talavera ceramics (*see page 187*), household crockery and faience tiles are made in the capital, while onyx is cut in Tehuacán and Tecali. The baroque ceramic "tree of life" decorations, often seen on travel posters, are made in the town of Acatlán – especially by Herón Martínez – and in Izúcar de Matamoros, by the Flores and Castillo families. Puebla is also famed for its thick, tree-bark *amate* paper and for its textiles and traditional

LEFT: devil and serpent ceramic figure.
ABOVE: weaving on a backstrap loom.

clothing. The embroidered *huipiles* (tunics) and wall-hangings and the bead-decorated blouses of Cuetzalan and San Pablito Pahuatlán are the best examples. Reed baskets – made in Puebla – are the most frequently purchased tourist items.

South of Mexico City, the state of Morelos concentrates the sale of its craft production in Cuernavaca. Here for sale is locally made, colonial-style furniture, wooden bowls, serapes, palm-leaf strip basketry and combination jewelry. The village of Hueyapan, in the municipality of Tetela del Volcán,

QUALITY CHECK

Before buying, check that wool is wool and that hammocks are cotton, not nylon.

produces wide, embroidered shawls.

The adjoining state of Guerrero specializes in pottery but also produces, in Olinalá, the most beautiful lacquerware in Mexico – gourd bowls, wooden trays, boxes and jaguar masks. Taxco, also in Guerrero, is world famous for its silverware, and it is in the tropical towns further south, that Huapanec indians use bright and even fluorescent colors to paint stories and abstract designs on *amate* bark paper.

Over the border in Oaxaca, the Zapotec indians make elaborate blouses with tiny flowers and miniature dolls which hold the pleats together. The blouses and wrap-around skirts of Yalalag are dyed with natural colors.

In the town of Oaxaca, artisans create exact copies of the intricately beautiful Mixtec jewelry found in the tombs of Monte Albán. The Mixtec coast of Oaxaca is known for its carrying nets, whereas Cuilapan and San Martín Tilcajete produce wooden *animalitos* ("little animals") in bright colors and assorted shapes; the village of San Bartolo Coyotepec is famous for its traditional burnished black pottery, and Santa María Atzompa makes ceramic animal figures and green glazed pottery; Teotitlán del Valle produces Mexico's best *serapes*, either in traditional pre-Hispanic designs or as copies of famous modern art paintings. Oaxaca's handicrafts can be found in the many shops and markets (where the prices are cheaper) and especially during the fiestas in December.

The woven woolen clothing, worn by the indians in the highlands of Chiapas is sold at the Sna Jolobil weavers' cooperative, in San Cristóbal de las Casas; alternatively, there are Sunday markets in San Cristóbal and most of the surrounding hill villages. The Tzotzil village of San Juan Chamula makes much of the woolen clothing sold throughout the state, as well as guitars and harps. The town of Chiapa de Corzo is known for its lacquerware, especially the masks used in the festival of San Sebastián, while Amatenango produces traditional pottery, which is fired without an oven.

The Yucatán Peninsula produces quality mahogany and cedar furniture as well as the county's best hammocks – made either from sisal or cotton – and the best Panama hats come from Becal in Campeche.

Capital crafts

Many of Mexico's wonderful crafts can be found in the capital city, which also has plenty of its own gifted jewelers and artisans. The work of the Linares family, for example, who produce fantastical figures they call *lebrijes*, has become extremely popular in recent years. But there are also the skillful and often ignored urban artisans who create art objects and toys from remnants, such as bottle caps and wire. ❑

LEFT; painting ceramics needs a steady hand.
RIGHT: *amate* bark painting in naïve style is typical artwork from Guerrero state.

MURALISTS

Mural painting has been Mexico's greatest contribution to contemporary art,
with its origins dating back to pre-Hispanic times

Dramatic works of both greater and lesser artists adorn the walls of public buildings all over Mexico. Muralism was a cultural product of the Revolution and flourished in Mexico well into the 1950s. Murals have been painted in Mexico since pre-Hispanic times although many, such as those at Bonampak (*see*

powerful yet humorous engravings reached the very essence and vitality of Mexico's rich tradition of popular art; indeed, they represent the fullest and most penetrating view of Mexican social life in the years before the revolution. Posada, whose skeletons were authentically Mexican (a far cry from the foreign models

page 310) and Cacaxtla (*see pages 188–9*), have only recently been discovered by historians and archeologists.

The explosive murals of the post-Revolution were a new departure; the dramatic works of Diego Rivera, David Alfaro Siqueiros and José Clemente Orozco were to become the most powerful visual expression of the emerging modern Mexico, and were to astound the world.

Influential engravings

Of the Mexican artists who influenced *Los Tres Grandes* (the three great Mexican muralists), none appear to have been more important than José Guadalupe Posada (1852–1913), whose

used by artists of his era), laid the groundwork for a whole school of artistry that was vigorous and obsessively nationalistic. The muralist movement remained close to the folk tradition – the so-called *Mexicanidad* – of Posada's wonderful, popular engravings.

The first murals

In 1921, members of President Alvaro Obregón's new cabinet were keen to spread awareness of Mexico's history and culture. None more so than the radical Education Minister José Vasconcelos, who commissioned murals for the walls of a number of centrally located public buildings. And so the Mexican *Muralismo* movement began and Diego Rivera (1886–1957) painted his first mural at the Escuela Nacional Preparatoria in Mexico City.

Rivera was a contradictory painter who aroused deep feelings and controversy. Though an ideologist (he was a Communist, but was expelled from the party), his work is less political than sensual in style, in the tradition of Paul Gauguin, Henri Rousseau and even Pieter Brueghel the Elder. Rivera's formative artistic influences were by no means exclusively Mexican. In

MURAL MASTERPIECES

The majority of the most famous murals can be seen in Mexico City, although Orozco's finest works were made in Guadalajara and others in the US.

fact, Uccello's *La Battaglia di San Romano* is said to have been one of the most important influences on Mexican mural painting.

Notwithstanding all these European influences, Rivera acknowledged his debt to the Mexican Posada by including the engraver's portrait in some of his most important murals. Rivera was deeply Mexican in his love of color and soft shapes, and in his strong identification with the Mexican indian; he was also profoundly influenced by pre-Hispanic architectural form and

Europe, he had been in touch with avant-garde movements, and the influence of Cubism is apparent in much of his work from that period. However, as a result of the Russian Revolution, and his stated belief in "the need for a popular and socialized art," Rivera distanced himself from the Cubists and sought a more direct and functional artistic style. It is often said that the most important influence on Rivera was not contemporary at all, but came from the frescoes and paintings of the Italian Renaissance. In

sculpture. An excellent draftsman and watercolor artist, he created an idealized and sentimental image of a primitive Mexico, inhabited by brown-skinned girls and dreamy children carrying huge bouquets of exotic flowers.

Rivera himself was a colorful character, a constant source of gossip who loved to shock. One of his works entitled *Dream of a Sunday Afternoon in the Alameda* originally flaunted the words *Dios no existe* ("God does not exist"), causing such an uproar amongst Catholics and church authorities that they had to be removed from exhibition and were expunged (Museo Mural Diego Rivera – *see page 160).*

PRECEDING PAGE: Diego Rivera mural, near San Angel.
LEFT: *Catharsis* by José Clemente Orozco.
ABOVE: David Alfaro Siqueiros's self-portrait.

The ideologue

David Alfaro Siqueiros (1899–1974), like Rivera, continued his art training in Europe. However, unlike Rivera, he had been a combatant in the Mexican Revolution; he was a man of action, a political activist who volunteered for the Spanish Civil War, took part in labor struggles, was involved in a failed attempt to assassinate Leon Trotsky, and was imprisoned several times. His paintings reflect his ideological drive, his taste for bold action, and even for violence. They are so massive and muscular that they become a sort of imprisoned sculpture. Indeed, he experimented with a com-

bination of painting and sculpture which he called *escultopintura*. A constant innovator, Siqueiros was always trying new materials and techniques. Perhaps his best murals are those in Mexico City's Chapultepec Castle (*see page 164*), which offer a baroque and powerful interpretation of Mexican history. His works at the capital's Palacio de Bellas Artes (*see page 158*) are among the best of his easel paintings, although he is best known for his vast, three-dimensional mural in the Poliforum Cultural Siqueiros in Mexico City (*see page 167*).

The satirist

Jose Clemente Orozco (1883–1949), a tragic and passionate artist, is often considered the best of the three. He was a political skeptic, a biting satirist, but also an idealist who was deeply disturbed by the sordidness of history. Orozco used the mural to convey his troubled feelings; his message transcends the national picture and can be understood by everyone. He has been compared to such German artists as Max Beckmann, Otto Dix, and Käthe Kollwitz. Orozco, always an outspoken man, denounced the tendency to convert the Mexican Revolution into a bloody farce that would result in new servitude for the masses.

The first important Orozco mural was painted in the early 1920s at the Escuela Nacional Preparatoria (*see page 157*). Stark and simple, it showed some influence from early Italian Renaissance painting. At the Escuela Preparatoria, Orozco does achieve moments of grandeur, especially in *The Trench*, a powerful image of war and human struggle. On the staircase of the same building, he painted *Cortés y la Malinche*, depicting the naked bodies of the Spanish conquistador and Malintzin, his indian guide, interpreter and mistress. The painting makes a clear statement about the relationship between Spain and Mexico, between conqueror and conquered, a theme to which Orozco returned many times.

From 1927 to 1934, Orozco lived in the US and painted murals for Pomona College, California, the New York School for Social Research and Dartmouth College, New Hampshire. He described the cultural life of the times in his bitter autobiography, and in letters to his friend and fellow artist Jean Charlot. Back in Mexico, at the Palacio de Bellas Artes, Orozco painted *Catharsis*, whose central figure is a colossal prostitute, the symbol of corruption.

Orozco's greatest works were produced in the late 1930s in Guadalajara – in the Palacio de Gobierno, the University *Paraninfo* and on the walls and ceilings of the Hospicio Cabañas (*see pages 250 and 252*). Here he is at the peak of his power, covering straight and curved surfaces with fiery reds and stark blacks, paying homage to Padre Hidalgo, denouncing political manipulation and searching for deep and universal symbols.

Other muralists

Jean Charlot, born in Paris in 1898, was another of the early muralists. His *Massacre in the*

Main Temple, a mural completed in 1923 on the stairway of the west court of the Escuela Nacional Preparatoria, is regarded as the first fresco painted in Mexico since colonial times. Before his move to Hawaii, Charlot painted in the US, helping, with his works, but most of all with his writings, to popularize mural painting during Roosevelt's early days as president.

Juan O'Gorman, a painter and architect of Irish ancestry, transformed the mural into a sort of panorama of miniature scenes. Though modern, his paintings are anchored in Mexico's 19th-century popular art. He is famous chiefly for his murals decorating the Biblioteca Cen-

forms. His decorative murals deal with cosmic and domestic symbology (stars, cats, women) and are indifferent to the direct interpretation of history.

Zacatecas born artist Pedro Coronel (1922–1985) explored much the same ground as Tamayo. His murals are perhaps the best of those painted in recent years. Other mainstream Mexican muralists, whose work is never far removed from realism, include Fernando Leal, Xavier Guerrero, José Chávez Morado, Roberto Montenegro, Raúl Anguiano, Manuel Rodríguez Lozano, Alfredo Zalce and Jorge González Camarena.

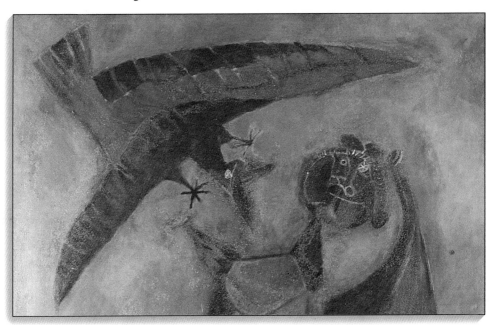

tral (Central Library) of Mexico City's Ciudad Universitaria (*see page 172*). Constructed with colored stone, these giant mosaic-murals describe the culture of the world in a baroque texture that is surprisingly innocent and fresh.

Alongside the paintings of *Los Tres Grandes* there had grown up a second generation of muralists. One of these was Rufino Tamayo, a Zapotec indian from Oaxaca who died in 1991 at the age of 92. Never political, Tamayo soon abandoned realism for poetically simplified

LEFT: Orozco's portrait of Hidalgo, Guadalajara.
ABOVE: detail from *Niña atacada por un pájaro extraño* (Girl attacked by a strange bird), by Rufino Tamayo.

Contemporary murals

The Mexican muralist movement sprang out of the Revolution and, in reality, that emotion is gone and done with. In the second half of the 20th century, the new generations of muralists reacted against the movement that they accused of being too obviously didactic and obsessively nationalistic. But disciples of the great muralists continue to cover the walls of public buildings throughout the country. Mostly, though not always, they repeat the same old formula and sadly, what in Rivera, Siqueiros and Orozco was a revolutionary statement delivered in heat and passion, has now too often become repetitious and bureaucratic, sheer rhetoric. ❑

FIESTAS

*Witness if you can the rituals, costumes, masks, fireworks, song and dance
that make Mexico's fiestas an explosion of exuberance*

There is always a fiesta going on some-where in Mexico. Apart from the national civic celebrations, every city, town, village or *barrio* (neighborhood) has its own fiesta, often in honor of the local patron saint. Visitors have a good chance of happening upon one of Mexico's wonderful fiestas – particularly at certain, more traditionally festive times. The calendar lists over 5,000 every year – that is an average of nearly 14 fiestas per day.

Fiestas are a vital part of community life in Mexico. Many can be traced back to pagan pre-Hispanic rituals which relate to ancient customs and aspects of nature such as fertility or harvest. Others were brought over from Europe with Christianity and have a marked Spanish flavor. But most Mexican fiestas, like the people themselves, are a combination of both.

Fiestas vary greatly from region to region and no two are ever the same, although music, dance, street parades, fireworks and fire-crackers are almost always present. On religious occasions there are also processions, the reciting of rosaries and the chanting of *novenas* (prayers).

Mexican fireworks are quite breathtaking and unlike any display you are ever likely to witness again. As a general rule, the bigger or richer the town the more impressive the show. Specialized craftsmen are brought in for the occasion to make the *castillos* (castles) and *toritos* (little bulls). The *castillos* are enormous wicker structures, up to 20 meters (66 ft) high, to which hundreds of fireworks are wired so as to create a show of spectacular effects. For the *toritos*, especially famous in Cholula, Puebla, the wicker framework, shaped like a bull, is worn by a man who twists, turns and charges at the crowds with the fireworks exploding all around.

Fiestas take place in the center of town, around the church, the main plaza and in the neighboring streets. A marketplace springs up, with stalls selling crafts, trinkets, mementoes and the hard-to-resist *antojitos*. The favorite food of most Mexican people, *antojitos* include a whole range of Mexican food, from beautifully decorative peeled and cut fruits eaten with lime juice, salt and chili powder, to the ubiquitous *tacos*, *tamales* and *quesadillas*.

The *lotería*, a Mexican version of bingo, is usually present too, with its traditional figures of the devil, the moon, the soldier, the señorita, the drunkard, the dandy and, of course, Death. Also common to most parts of the country are bullfighting, horse racing, *charreadas* (*see pages 94–5*) and cock fighting. In some towns – like Huamantla in Tlaxcala or Tlacotalpán in Veracruz – they practice Pamplona-style bull-running through the streets. In Huamantla the bulls run through 12 km (7 miles) of streets which, on *La Noche que Nadie Duerme* ("the night when nobody sleeps"), have been beautifully decorated with colored sawdust and flowers for the feast of the Assumption (August 14).

PRECEDING PAGES: dancers represent conquistadores in Janitzio, Michoacán
LEFT: a conchero dancer in Mexico City
ABOVE: sculptures from the radish festival, Oaxaca

Song and dance

The variety of traditional music and dance performed (at fiestas) is enormous. Apart from the obvious Jarabe Tapatío (Mexican Hat Dance), there are dozens more. Some, like the *concheros*, have survived the Conquest; others interpret it. The masked protagonists of the *Danza de la Conquista* (Dance of the Conquest), in Jalisco and Michoacán, are Moctezuma, Cortés and La Malinche, as well as armed Spanish soldiers and the jaguar and eagle warriors with their feather headdresses.

The best-known of the many dances formerly dedicated to Huehuetéotl, the "Old God", deity

Religious fiestas

Carnaval is celebrated the week before the beginning of Lent, in February or March. It is, traditionally, the last chance to let your hair down before the forty-day abstinence that precedes Easter. The famous carnivals of Veracruz and Mazatlán (the former claims to be the biggest outside Rio de Janeiro), as well as those of Campeche, Mérida and other parts of the Republic, are celebrated with colorful parades, extravagant costumes, fireworks, day-and-night dancing, eating and drinking. The fiesta in Veracruz starts with the ceremonial *Quema del Mal Humor* (Burning of Bad Humor), and reaches

of fire and time, is the extraordinary *Danza de los Viejitos* (Dance of the Old Men) in Michoacán. In Puebla, the Quetzal dancers wear huge, brilliantly colored and feathered headdresses, whilst in Sonora, the Yaqui indians perform the *Danza del Venado* (Stag Dance), and in Veracruz the Voladores "fly" around a 32 meter (105-ft) pole (*see page 281*) in a hypnotic re-enactment of a Totonac ritual.

Other dances, introduced by the Spanish missionaries, pitch Moors against Christians and include such unlikely characters as Charlemagne and the Knights of the Round Table, as well as the more familiar Angel, Devil, Priest, Maiden and Death.

PIÑATAS

The most colorful stall in any Mexican market is the one selling *piñatas,* the terracotta pots decorated with papier maché and brightly colored shredded tissue paper. The *piñata,* shaped like a beautiful three-dimensional star, is a traditional part of Christmas festivities. Nowadays, *piñatas* come in the form of fruit, vegetables, animals, clowns or even the Disney character of the month. The clay pot – filled with candy, fruit, peanuts and sticks of sugar cane – is hung in the patio or street and one by one the children, blindfolded, try to hit and break it with a stick. As soon as the pot breaks, the booty cascades to the ground and the children dive in to grab all they can.

its climax several sleepless days later, on Shrove Tuesday (Mardi Gras). The next day, Ash Wednesday, sees the burial of Juan Carnaval and the symbolic beginning of a new era.

Brightly colored papier maché devils, or Judases, are sold on street corners the week before Easter and are traditionally burned on the Saturday. Easter in Mexico is a time for candle-lit processions and impressive Passion plays that can last for days. Many people flock to Taxco each year, and millions watch the "crucifixion" at Iztapalapa in Mexico City.

The Feria de San Marcos, around 25 April, is a lively affair in Aguascalientes, while Corpus celebrated on the nine days leading up to Christmas, commemorate the journey of Mary and Joseph to Bethlehem and are traditionally accompanied by the breaking of the *piñata*. Christmas itself is celebrated on the night of December 24, with a big dinner and Mass the next morning. Some families still put up the traditional *nacimiento* – or nativity scene – although, influenced by the US, Christmas trees are now more widespread. Customs vary in different regions of the country: in some parts the children receive gifts from the "infant Jesus," while in others it is the Three Kings who bring the gifts on January 6.

Christi – when (all the) children go to church dressed as indians and carrying tiny straw donkeys – is especially interesting in Papantla, Veracruz. The Day of the Dead is Mexico's answer to All Souls' Day, the ultimate combination of pre-Hispanic and Christian ritual (*see pages 262–3*). Even the celebrations on 12 December, when all Mexico commemorates the Virgen de Guadalupe (*see pages 118–19*), has Aztec as well as Catholic origins. The *posadas*,

LEFT: a group of Cora indians, painted black, celebrate Easter.
ABOVE: the Crucifixion is re-enacted at Ixtapalapa, Mexico City, on Good Friday.

Patriotic fiestas

Although religious celebrations are usually the most elaborate, there are lively fiestas in Mexico's political calendar too. National flags are for sale everywhere in September, *el mes de la patria* ("Fatherland Month"), which traditionally begins with the president's state of the nation address (1 September) and builds up to Independence Day celebrations on 16 September.

On 20 November school children parade through the streets dressed as Zapata or Pancho Villa to celebrate the Day of the Revolution, while the 5 May marks the Mexican defeat of the French army (albeit short-lived) at the Battle of Puebla. ❑

LA VIRGEN DE GUADALUPE

Mexico's adored patroness, the Virgin of Guadalupe,

is an expression of the country's racial and cultural mix

A mind-boggling six million pilgrims arrive at the Basílica de Guadalupe, Mexico City, every year to pay tribute to Mexico's patron. Some arrive on foot, after days on the road, from the remotest parts of Mexico. Others walk only the last few kilometers down the Calzada de Guadalupe. It is extraordinary to

witness the devotion of a large group of young men who crawl across the plaza, in one extreme act of faith and self-mortification, whilst pushing the bicycles they have been riding for days.

Individuals come to ask for help or to make a pledge to the Virgin; business groups often send representatives, and sometimes a whole village will arrive. An old man when asked why he has come says clearly: "Señor, I have a hard life, a lot of work and very little money. But whenever I really need anything, I've always asked the Little Virgin and she has always helped me. I am grateful to her. Now that my wife is sick, I have come to ask the Virgin to cure her."

The Virgen de Guadalupe is much more than a patron saint. She is the symbol of national unity, of the racial and cultural mix that is Mexico. Born from the fusion of the Spanish and Indian cultures, she represents pre-Hispanic as well as Catholic beliefs.

Temples and Gods

After the conquest, in an attempt to eradicate the old religion and impose the Catholic faith, the Spaniards tore down the "pagan" temples and built churches, often on the same site and using the very same stones. However, they soon discovered that an edifice does not guarantee devotion, and many of the indians continued to worship their old gods.

In the 16th-century, Father Bernardino de Sahagún set out to rectify what the Church considered a melancholy state of affairs. He reasoned that Catholicism could be implanted only by first understanding, then replacing, the gods of the indians.

During the siege of Tenochtitlán, the conquistadores had set up camp at the bottom of the hill of Tepeyac, just north of the Aztec capital. They had brought with them their own revered Virgin of Guadalupe who, according to legend, was carved by St Luke and had appeared miraculously in Spain, where she was associated with the reconquest of the Iberian Peninsula from the Moors. Her shrine, curiously enough, was built in Extremadura, the home of Cortés's.

On that very same hill of Tepeyac, there was a temple dedicated to one of the most important Aztec deities. She was the goddess of the earth, spring and maize, known by the names of Cihuacóatl (Serpent Woman), Coatlicue (Serpent Skirt), Chicomecóatl (Seven Serpents) or, as was most common, Tonantzín (Our Mother).

The Juan Diego miracle

Not long after the conquest, the Virgin of Guadalupe made her miraculous appearance to a newly converted indian named Juan Diego. Early one morning in 1531, Juan Diego, a simple man of the soil, was walking on the hill of Tepeyac when he heard a sweet voice calling him. It was the Virgin Mary. She said she wanted a temple built there so that everyone could worship and adore her. "Why me?" Diego asked boldly. "Why do you not ask one of the powerful Spaniards?"

The Virgin did not explain but told him to relay her message to Archbishop Zumárraga. As expected, the archbishop scoffed. The next day, the Virgin appeared before Juan Diego again, and the following day. Finally, she gave him the proof he needed. She commanded some roses to bloom – which in itself was a miracle since roses had never been seen there before – and ordered Juan Diego to gather them in his cactus-fiber mantle and take them to the archbishop. He did this, and when he threw the roses down at the archbishop's feet, miracle of miracles, the image of the Virgin appeared on the mantle. By her appearance before a humble indian, the Virgin had shown her favor not only to the Spanish, but to all the people of Mexico. The piece of cloth that is preserved inside the basilica today is said to be the mantle worn by Juan Diego.

Confusing dates

Franciscan monks sought to dispel any confusion between the Virgin of Guadalupe and Tonantzín. It was not an easy task, especially as the shrine built to the Virgin was located at the very site where the Aztec goddess's temple had previously stood.

Furthermore, the pre-Hispanic festival for Tonantzín was held on the first day of the 17th month of the Aztec ritual calendar. That corresponded to December 22 on the Julian calendar, which was used in Mexico until 1582. It was then that Pope Gregory XXIII subtracted 10 days from the calendar date so that it should align better with the solar cycle. Thus December 22 became December 12, the day when all Mexico celebrates the Virgen de Guadalupe.

Tent in the Sinai

Building of the original basilica was begun in 1694, but by the mid-20th century its founda-

---

LEFT: a group of pilgrims complete the last leg of their journey on their knees.

RIGHT: floral offerings to the Virgin of Guadalupe.

> **WELL-LOVED VIRGIN**
>
> Except for the Vatican, the Shrine of the Virgin of Guadalupe in Mexico City is visited by more people than any other religious site in the Christian world.

tions had become unstable and it was beginning to show cracks. The new basilica was conceived by the architect Pedro Ramírez Vásquez, who was also responsible for the Museo Nacional de Antropología in Mexico City (*see page 164*). The basilica was designed to convey the impression of the tent used by Abraham in the Sinai. It took more than 20 months to build the imposing 11,000 sq meter (118,000 sq ft) temple, which can accommodate 10,000 pilgrims, at the cost of over $10 million.

Queen of Mexico

The Virgin de Guadalupe is said to have stopped the flooding of Mexico City in 1629; and to have brought to an end a terrible epidemic in 1736. During the struggle against Spain, she was awarded the rank of general and, after independence, Emperor Iturbide founded the Imperial Order of Guadalupe. The name of Mexico's first president was Guadalupe Victoria, and the dictator Porfirio Díaz had the Virgin crowned Queen of Mexico; not long after, she was hailed as patroness of Emiliano Zapata, who fought against Díaz. Even today, no sensible politician would dare to criticize the Virgin of Guadalupe. ❏

FOOD

Whether it's authentic Mexican food or a Tex-Mex
interpretation, the spice will be in the sauce

Like so many other things in Mexico, the cuisine is the result of centuries of encounters and mixings of cultures and peoples. Along with the essential staples of chilies, beans and corn, the pre-Hispanic indians enjoyed a varied diet that included turkey, wild pig, *itzcuintli* (a plump, hairless dog), fish and iguana, as well as Philippines, and potatoes were brought from South America. Even the brief French occupation is responsible for the addition of several cakes and sweet dishes such as *crème caramel*. Over the centuries, the blending of all these different foods, methods and styles of cooking has become accepted as Mexico's own cuisine.

avocados, tomatoes, the green *tomatillos*, nopal cactus, tropical fruits like pineapple and papaya, vanilla, pumpkins, herbs and cacao.

The Spanish conquistadores and settlers, wanting to maintain their own eating habits, brought to the New World their Mediterranean-style foods with chickens, pigs and cows, cheese and wheat, olive oil and wine, citrus fruits, onions and garlic. New methods of cooking were adopted to integrate the European and native ingredients, although, for the vast majority of Mexicans, the staples of corn, beans and chilies have remained unchanged for centuries.

During the Colonial period, rice and spices arrived on the galleons from China and the

The spice of life

Eating can be one of the chief pleasures in Mexico, where the cuisine is as varied as the country itself. Generally speaking, food in the south is much spicier than in the north. Some dishes, although native to certain regions, can be found all over Mexico, while others are found only locally. A trip to a market is the perfect way to see or sample the huge variety of unusual fruits, vegetables, chilies and other strange or exotic

PRECEDING PAGES: fish, salad and a few beers; corn, tortillas and salsa.
ABOVE: seafood tostadas.
RIGHT: breakfast in Baja California.

ingredients. Mexico City is the culinary melting pot, with many restaurants specializing in regional dishes. As in most big cities, the capital also has plenty of more familiar international cuisine as well as good vegetarian restaurants.

North to south

The characteristically simple, unspicy food of northern Mexico – usually grilled meats – is accompanied by wheatflour rather than corn tortillas. *Cabrito* (baby goat) is the specialty in Monterrey; grilled and greasy but very tasty, it is washed down with another local favorite, cold Carta Blanca beer. But even the sparse northern cooking offers such delicacies as *caldillo*, which is as close as Mexico gets to *chile con carne*.

Cooking in the Central Highlands is more adventurous and includes many traditional dishes, such as *pozole*, a hearty soup made of hominy (large maize kernels) with pork or sometimes chicken. Much of the flavor of a good *pozole* lies in the extravagant garnishing of chile sauce, oregano, avocado, lettuce, onion, radish and lime juice. Other exquisite dishes include the delicate *flor de calabaza* (squash blossom) soup or the *tacos* and crêpes filled with *huitlacoche*, a blackish fungus which grows on corn and which has been savored since the days of the Aztecs.

Puebla is the home of the famous *mole poblano*, the rich, spicy sauce said to have been invented by a nun during colonial times. *Mole* is, in fact, one of the most obvious Spanish-indigenous combinations on any menu. More than two dozen ingredients go into its preparation, including several kinds of chilies, as well as herbs, spices, tortilla, nuts and, most

famously, chocolate. The sauce, served with chicken or the native turkey and accompanied with corn tortillas and rice, is often eaten at parties or wedding feasts. Every variation of *mole* can be sampled at the yearly *mole* festival held in San Pedro Atocpán (Mexico City), including the spicier and more robust Oaxaca version of the dish, and the milder and easier to digest *pipián,* as well as *mole verde* (green mole), which is made with pumpkin seeds.

Chile relleno is another favorite. The large green *poblano* chili peppers are stuffed with cheese or a mixture of ground meat and spices, dipped in egg batter, fried and served with a

---

VERSATILE TORTILLAS

Tortillas, the thin round patties made of cornmeal or wheatflour, are the very soul of Mexican food. They are used as a form of bread with just about everything and are the basic ingredient of many of Mexico's wonderful *antojitos*. Distinguishing between the many dishes made with tortillas can be confusing at first; here are some of the most widely available:

☛ *Tacos*: warm tortillas rolled around any sort of filling; *tacos al pastor* consist of meat rolled in a tortilla and served with chopped coriander, onion and a chunk of pineapple.

☛ *Flautas*: tortillas rolled very tightly around chicken then fried and served topped with lettuce and cream.

☛ *Enchiladas*: tortillas folded around meat, cheese or fish and covered in sauce; *enchiladas suizas* are always served with chicken and a creamy white sauce with cheese.

☛ *Quesadillas*: tortillas folded around cheese (or other fillings) and fried or cooked on a griddle.

☛ *Chilaquiles*: fried tortilla chips in a more or less spicy tomato sauce, served topped with cream and cheese.

☛ *Tostadas*: crispy fried tortillas spread with refried beans and topped with lettuce, chicken, tomato, onion, avocado, chili, sour cream, cheese, or any other combination.

☛ *Sopa de tortilla*: soup with fried tortilla strips, tomato, chili and avocado (also *sopa tlaxcalteca* and *sopa tarasca*.)

tomato sauce. Chilies in Puebla are traditionally served *en nogada* – filled with meat, covered with a white walnut sauce, and garnished with red pomegranate seeds, echoing the three colors of the Mexican flag.

Over 10,000 km (6,200 miles) of coastline provides Mexico with an abundance of seafood. Two of the most popular fish dishes are *ceviche*, (raw fish marinated in lime juice and mixed with onions, chilies, tomatoes and coriander) and *huachinango a la veracruzana*, a classic of red snapper with olives, capers and tomato sauce. As well as the Spanish influence, there is a strong Cuban element in the food from Veracruz, with its characteristic black beans and giant tropical *macho* banana (plantain), eaten fried. Veracruz also boasts the most delicious fruit in Mexico – huge pineapples, exquisite mangoes, and juicy oranges, tangerines and other citrus fruits are sold at the roadside.

Oaxaca is renowned for its *mole negro* and banana-leaf *tamales,* which are bigger and more elaborate than the others (*see below*). Oaxaca cheese, not unlike mozzarella, is the best kind to use in *quesadillas* as it melts beautifully when grilled or fried inside a tortilla.

The inspiration of cooking in the Yucatán dates back to the pre-Hispanic Maya indians. Yucatecan cuisine claims such outstanding dishes as *cochinita pibil,* a sweet and spicy pork dish cooked in banana leaves, and *papadzules* (tortillas filled with egg and pumpkin seeds). There is a magnificent soup made with *limas,* the subtle Mexican lemon. Beer aficionados rate Yucatán's beer as the best in the country – both the light Montejo, and the dark and rich Negro León. *Queso relleno*, another Yucatecan speciality is, surprisingly, Dutch cheese stuffed with spicy minced meat. In comparatively recent times Lebanese immigrants have dipped their own spoon into Mexican cuisine and some of the best restaurants in Mérida offer both Yucatecan and Lebanese dishes.

Antojitos

Similar to the Spanish *tapas*, *antojitos* are the Mexican answer to fast food. These mouthwatering snacks or light dishes can be bought – and eaten – almost anywhere, from north to south and from the best city restaurant or most elegant hacienda to the village plaza, the market, and even on the bus or train.

A whole range of Mexican food is classed as *antojitos*, from succulent corn on the cob, to tortilla chips with *guacamole* and the delicious *tortas*, or filled bread rolls. *Tamales,* are also popular; these little parcels made from corn husks (or banana leaves in Oaxaca) wrapped around a cornmeal mix are stuffed with highly seasoned meat, cheese or chili sauce, and then steamed. *Tamales* can also be sweet, and the meat replaced with strawberries, pineapple, pecan nuts or raisins. But, whether it is *tacos, tostadas, quesadillas* or *enchiladas*, most *antojitos*, like Mexican food in general, rely on the tortilla. ❏

MEAL TIMES

Breakfast can be as simple or elaborate a meal as you want; some Mexicans eat a European-style meal; others wait until mid-morning and then eat a large almuerzo. Lunch is eaten late, between 2 and 4pm, although it is usually available from 1 o'clock. Many restaurants offer a fixed-price menú del día, which includes several courses and can be excellent value. Although the capitalinos of Mexico City no longer take a siesta, in smaller towns most businesses close for two hours. After a large and late lunch, the evening cena or merienda tends to be a lightish meal, often including tacos or other antojitos and pan dulce (sweet bread).

LEFT: a fountain of fruit in Cancún.

Chili Peppers

Chili peppers are everywhere in Mexico – more than 100 varieties. And, far from being alike in taste or spiciness, they are nearly endless in variety, depending on the specific climate in which they are grown, the chemical composition of the soil and even the geographical characteristics of neighboring plantings.

Chilis (chiles) are part of the nightshade family of plants, which also includes capsicums, tomatoes, eggplants and potatoes. Nevertheless, they elude strict description: *chilis* are horticulturally classified as fruits, although botanists refer to them as berries. Produce purveyors count them as vegetables, but when they are dried, the rest of the world thinks of them as spices.

The Aztecs and the Incas domesticated *chilis* about 7,000 years ago, but it is only in recent years that their flavors and uses have been defined for people outside those cultures.

Columbus carried some back to Europe, where Spain and Portugal adopted them for some dishes and passed them on to India and Africa, where they were eagerly incorporated into the native foods. Even then, the problems of identifying *chilis* was complicated by the changes in their characteristics when they were grown in different locales.

It becomes even more complex to attempt to define *chilis* by their "hotness" factor, because these perverse little examples of the genus capsicum vary from location to location and, oddly enough, occasionally from pepper to pepper on the same plant. Nevertheless, it isn't difficult to identify the ones most frequently encountered in the marketplace in Mexico, where you can buy them fresh, dried or pickled.

• **Chile Serrano** is the chili most common in Mexico. As a small green pepper it is used in fresh sauces and added to stews and soups for a touch of piquancy. When it turns red it loses some of its characteristic hotness. Chile de Arbol is occasionally used fresh but is predominantly grown for drying, to be used in table sauces and in cooking.

• **Chile Ancho**, a full-flavored but mild and sweetish tasting chile, is a dried version of the green Poblano pepper, which in its original state is stuffed with cheese or chopped meat, dipped in egg batter, fried and served with a tomato sauce as Chile Relleno.

RIGHT: some Mexican chilis are hotter than others.

• **Chile Chipotle** is the same variety as a jalapeño pepper, only in this version it is first ripened, then smoked and dried. It is used to make a hot and-pungent sauce, part of the recipe for *Albóndigas en chipotle* - meatballs in chipotle sauce – a popular dish in Querétaro

• **Chile Guajillo**, the dried version of the Mirasol chili, adds bite as well as a yellow color to dishes in which it is cooked.

• **Chile Mulato** and chile Pasilla are similar. Pasilla is used in one of the great dishes of Mexico City,

• **Caldo Tlalpeño**, a soup which includes chicken and avocado. Mulato is an essential ingredient for mole sauce, used in the classic Mexican festive

dish, *Mole Poblano de Guajolote* – turkey cooked in a sauce with chilies and unsweetened chocolate.

• **Chile Pequín**, known in other cultures as "cayenne", is very hot in flavor, generally exceeded only by Yucatan's chile Habanero, which is said to be the hottest in the world. The small and flavorful Habanero chile is common in the Yucatán Peninsula, where it used in a sauce called *Ixni-pec*. The Pequín, also known as Chiltepín, frequently grows wild throughout Mexico.

What to do if you find most Mexican food far too hot? If it's already in your mouth, reach for the bread, not the water. Beer also helps. If you are ordering a meal, the key word is *picante* – spicy – not *caliente*, which means hot only in temperature.

MÚSICA MEXICANA

Salsa is the essence, while cumbia, quebradita, danzón and son
are not formation showpieces, but everyday dances in bars and barrios

Music is everywhere in Mexico. Wherever you happen to be, whether it's in a restaurant, on the beach, on the subway or a crowded bus in the rush hour, somebody is likely to produce a guitar and strike up a song.

But you won't hear the same rhythms from Chihuahua to Chiapas. In Mexico the music is as varied as the food, the culture and the country itself; it is as *mestizo* as the Mexican people and has absorbed traditional and popular music from all over the world: Spain, Argentina, Colombia, Cuba and Africa, as well as the more recent influence of rock music from Europe and the USA.

Música popular

In the north of Mexico (and the south of the United States), hugely popular Western-style *Norteño* bands pump out Tex-Mex *corridos* on guitars, accordions, contrabass and drums. The *corrido* always tells a story and its hero is usually on the wrong side of the law; in the old days, the ballads would extol the virtues of the likes of Pancho Villa and Emiliano Zapata; these days, they may tell of an illegal immigrant, the fate of the *mojado* (wetback) across the border.

Canción Ranchera is another all-time favorite; it is Mexico's version of country music which dates back to the Spanish romances or chivalric ballads. Mexican *ranchera* music is passionate by definition; the emotions are up-front and the action is melodramatic: heroes and villains, *bandidos* and *pistoleros,* politics, current affairs and, most of all, tragic and heart-rending love.

Tropical bands play *salsa* music in the dance halls with a selection of percussion instruments – bongos, *tumbas*, *güiros*, rattle-gourds, *timbales* and cowbells – as well as guitars, trumpets, flutes, pianos and even marimbas.

Salsa, or *música tropical,* generically includes

PRECEDING PAGES: playing *norteña* music on the street.
LEFT: violinist – his instrument bears the image of the Virgin of Guadalupe.
RIGHT: a mariachi singer drowns out the competition.

a whole range of rhythms from *mambo* and *cumbia* (probably even more popular in Mexico than in its native Colombia) to the frenetic *merengue* and the sedately seductive danzón.

The *marimba* itself is most popular in the southern states of Chiapas, Oaxaca, Tabasco and Veracruz. This large wooden xylophone-

type instrument is played by up to four musicians, using rubber-tipped batons. The soloist carries the tune; the other three divide the secondary melody in counterpoint. Traditionally all players came from the same family and could play waltzes, *paso dobles,* boleros and even excerpts from operas.

The nostalgic and romantic bolero is probably the most popular type of music in urban Mexico. Its origin goes back to Andalusia, but it was enriched by the tropical beat that came over from Cuba. Agustín Lara, the most famous composer of boleros in this century, is a household name in Mexico, and in Veracruz there is a museum dedicated to his life.

But probably the most Mexican of all is the ubiquitous *son* which is interpreted in many regions and with a variety of instruments throughout Mexico. In Jalisco, the *son* is the music of the *mariachi* bands and is often considered the most representative of Mexican music. In the region known as the Huasteca, the *son* or *huapango huasteco* is sung in falsetto while in southern Veracruz the *son jarocho* (of which *La Bamba* is the most famous example) includes harp, *jarana* and sometimes tambourine with its guitars and violins.

Mexicans, the masters of improvisation, come into their own with the *son* and, although

the lyrics of many *sones* date back to 16th-century Spain, many more verses concerning a particular event or person are ingeniously invented by the *soneros* on the spur of the moment.

Other rhythms may be less well known – the *jarabe* of Jalisco, the *sandunga* of Oaxaca, the *jarana* of the Yucatán, the *pirecua* of Michoacán and many more – but are still popular in their specific regions and are accompanied, like the *son* , by dances.

Noble musical traditions

Musical tradition in Mexico has its roots in both pre-Hispanic and Spanish cultures. Before the arrival of the conquistadores, music was an integral part of religious rituals and was unsuspectedly energetic and varied. It had to be performed, like the dance, in a plaza, on a platform, or on a pyramid. Priests, nobles and even kings took part.

Netzahualcóyotl, king of Texcoco, was a poet and a fine singer who encouraged the composers in his court to narrate the glories of his lineage and the history of his kingdom. Many of the songs dedicated to the gods have survived. Manuscripts and codices with rhythmic annotation were set down by the Spanish friar Bernardino de Sahagún in the 16th century and are the first examples of scored music in the Americas.

The songs were generally accompanied by the *huehuetl* and the *teponaztli,* both of them percussion instruments, as well as by rattles, flutes, conch shells and grooved bones. In some villages of Hidalgo, Veracruz and Tabasco both the *huehuetl* and the *teponaztli* are considered sacred instruments and are still used to accompany the ancient rituals.

Pre-Hispanic wind instruments were sophisticated: reed and clay flutes, multiple flutes, ocarinas, whistle jugs and conch-shell trumpets. In funerary rites, the sound of the conch shells was associated with mourning.

Fray Juan de Torquemada left an excellent description of pre-Hispanic song and dance that had been incorporated into religious rites. Musical instruments for ceremonial use in Mexico-Tenochtitlán were kept in a sacred place called Mixcoacalli. A large number of musicians were employed in the service of the temples; men dedicated themselves to the study of song and dance. So important was music to the indians that a missionary claimed conversions came about more readily through music than through preaching.

Colonial influences

After the Spanish conquest, musicians who had served in the Aztec temples were employed in the churches. The earliest school to teach music to the indians was founded just three years after the conquest by Fray Pedro de Gante. It was not long before New Spain started making its own organs and other secular instruments. Some, such as guitars, violins and harps, became the specialty of certain villages. The Aztecs were a musical people. One early missionary marveled that "at the beginning they did not understand anything nor did the old instructor have an interpreter. In a short time they understood so well that they learned not only plain chants but also the songs of the organ and now there are many choirs and singers who are skillful in modulation and harmony, learning everything by heart."

The secular music of the Renaissance arrived aboard the galleons from Spain. Out of the Caribbean came rhythms and musical forms that mixed Latin, Mediterranean, Arab, African and indigenous music. From all these came the exciting rhythms of the tango,

MARIACHI

The name *mariachi* comes from either *mariage*, the French for wedding, or *mariagero*, the Galician for a musician who performs at a wedding.

Mariachi music, which originated in the 18th century, is still played all over the country but is most popular in Jalisco and central Mexico. At first the players used only string instruments but trumpets were added later for pizazz.

During the 19th century the waltz became popular. The new music spoke of the triumph of the War of Independence. Major composers such as Juventino Rosas gave form to the Mexican version of the waltz combining originality, nostalgia and melodic imagination.

the rumba, the fandango, the chaconne, the saraband, the cumbé, the habanera, the bolero and the *danzón*.

During its 300 years as a colony, Mexico was treated to all kinds of music. In 1711, Mexico City played host to the first opera composed and performed in the New World, *La Parténope*, by Manuel de Zumaya. During late colonial times, the *corrido*, accompanied by guitar and harp, became the most popular musical form.

LEFT: Tarahumara indian playing violin at somber Easter festivities.

RIGHT: colorful folk dancing at Centro Acapulco, entertainment center.

Música moderna

The invasion of North American and British rock music (many Mexicans still claim to have learnt English from Beatles lyrics) has been supplemented by the more recent tradition of *rock en español*. And the long-time Cuban influence is far from faded: the weight of the *Nueva Trova Cubana* can be felt in the compositions of many modern Mexican song-writers.

A revival of interest in Mexican folk music, sparked in the 70s by the arrival of Andean rhythms, has fizzled out now. Instead some musicians attempt to fuse past with present by combining authentic pre-Hispanic instruments with the ultimate in hi-tech sound. ❑

DIVING IN AT THE DEEP END

Whether sub-aquatic adventure is your thing or a more leisurely swing in a palm-shaded hammock, Mexico's beach resorts offer the perfect escape

Except for its borders with the United States and Guatemala, Mexico is entirely surrounded by warm tropical waters: almost 3,600 kilometers (6,000 miles) of coastline on the Pacific, the Gulf of Mexico, and the Caribbean. And into these coasts nature has carved some of her most spectacular creations: places of limitless year-round sunshine, long stretches of silky soft beaches and crystalline warm waters. The choice is endless: from plush hotels and luxurious hideaways to tiny places, blissful in their tropical torpor, where life inches along and "getting away from it all" has become an art.

SNORKELING AND DIVING

Some of the world's top diving spots lie off Mexico's coastlines. In the crystal clear waters of the Caribbean, gaudy fish glide through coral grottoes filling the waters with color. All the major resort areas off the Pacific coast have excellent diving, but it's Cozumel, with the second-largest living coral reef in the world, that gets top awards from scubaphiles.

Mexico's Pacific coast, meanwhile, offers some of the best surfing waters in the world.

△ **BEACH AND CULTURE**
Just a short distance down the coast from the bustling resort of Cancún, the Mayan ruins at Tulum overlook miles of peaceful white beaches. With ifs cliff-top viewpoint, Tulum was the ideal location for the worship of the god of the Setting Sun.

▷ **BASKETS GALORE**
Vendors sell all manner of colorful handicrafts on the beach. Why go shopping when the shopping comes to you?

△ **PELICANS**
Hundreds of species of birds gather along Mexico's Pacific, Atlantic and Caribbean coastlines to feed on the rich sea life attracted by the warm waters.

▽ **SURF'N'TURF**
Seaside dining can mean a pile of fresh shrimp and a cold beer under a *palapa*, or a Beef Wellington in an air-conditioned restaurant, serenaded by romantic ballads.

▽ **SNORKELLERS**
The clear warm waters of Mexico's Caribbean teem with fish and coral reefs. Pacific coast resorts also offer excellent snorkelling and diving conditions, from beginners to advanced.

NIGHTLIFE BY THE BEACH

Mexican resorts really get going after dark. Restaurants begin to fill up after 9pm and the discos don't open until about 10.30pm, fill up around midnight, and keep going until dawn. Acapulco and Cancún are Mexico's undisputed disco capitals, but Mazatlán, Ixtapa, and Puerto Vallarta are not far behind. Even the smaller places offer romantic walks along the beach, a cooling drink in a seaside *palapa*, and one or two spots where you can "shake off the dust," as they say in Mexico. Another option of course, is to simply stretch out in a hammock and gaze at the stars in glorious solitude. There's usually a sunset or moonlight cruise, with dinner and dancing. The Mexican Fiestas – slightly corny but lots of fun – are fine places to meet people and usually feature a buffet, bar, folk dancing, and of course a mariachi group.

◁ **STREET MUSIC**
Wherever you are in Mexico you will not be far from the sound of music. If you are craving peace and quiet, the local watering hole is probably not the place to be; day and night there is music - *latina* and *americana* - everywhere.

◁ **CANCUN AERIAL VIEW**
Not even marked on maps in 1970, Cancún has blossomed from a government-planned creation into one of the world's largest and most popular resorts, with direct flights and tour packages from the US and Europe.

▷ **BEER WITH A TWIST**
Mexican beer can stand proud alongside the world's best. If you want to drink it the local way, take a swig with a twist of lemon or lime and a pinch of salt.

PLACES

*From the Rio Grande to the Yucatán, all Mexico is here, with
specially drawn maps to help you find your way around*

There's no way to see all Mexico on one vacation. The place is far too big, and too diverse. Consider just a few highlights: the world's most remarkable train ride, through a region bigger than the Grand Canyon, from Chihuahua to the Pacific coast; the 45-metre (150-ft) high dive off a cliff into Acapulco Bay; tumultuous Mexico City and the ancient pyramids in the Central Highlands; the Mayan ruins in the southern and eastern regions.

From the arid desert landscapes of Baja California to the mountains of Chiapas, and from the northern border skirting four North American states to the lush jungles of the Yucatán and the turquoise waters off Cancún, Mexico has 9,650 km (6,000 miles) of coastline. Nearly half the country is more than 1,500 metres (5,000 ft) above sea level, and mountain ranges are dotted with still-smoking volcanoes. Mexico's hills and snow-capped mountains are breathtakingly picturesque; its waters – from the Sea of Cortés in the northwest to the Caribbean in the southeast – are filled with some of the world's richest and most spectacular marine life.

The most practical plan is to settle for one region per visit and explore it thoroughly. Or to concentrate on one theme –colonial architecture, the *Ruta Maya* or marine wildlife, for example; or perhaps just settle for one of the wonderful beach resorts. There are now agencies specializing in "Adventure Tourism" which can include mountain climbing, white-water rafting or suba diving; others promote trips along the *Ruta de Cortés*, the route the Spanish conquistadores took from Veracruz to Tenochtitlán, the capital of the Aztec empire and today's Mexico City. There's something for almost everybody in Mexico's 1,968,324 sq. km (760,000 sq. miles).

And Mexico is a year-round destination. The entire western coast, including the 1,770-km (1,100-mile) Baja Peninsula, is bathed in sunshine for at least three-quarters of the year; and the coastal area encompassing Acapulco, Ixtapa/Zihuatanejo and Puerto Vallarta thinks of itself as the Mexican Riviera, with all that that entails. Even in the south, including Mexico City, the torrential summer rains conveniently fall in the afternoons (mostly), leaving the rest of the day clear and usually sunny.

Many of the colonial cities in the central part of the country – Guanajuato, San Miguel de Allende, Morelia – are high enough up to be balmy on even the hottest days. They offer an adventure in history and an ideal climate in which to explore it. Winter is the best time to see the Mayan ruins in the Yucatán, but the powdery soft beaches of Cancún beckon irresistibly at any time of year. ❑

PRECEDING PAGES: Popocatépetl looms above the cornfields of the central plateau; a view of the river from the Misión Mulegé, Baja California; overview of Mexico City prior to 1986 earthquake with "Popo" and "Izta" in the background.
LEFT: wary diver meets moray eel on a barren reef.

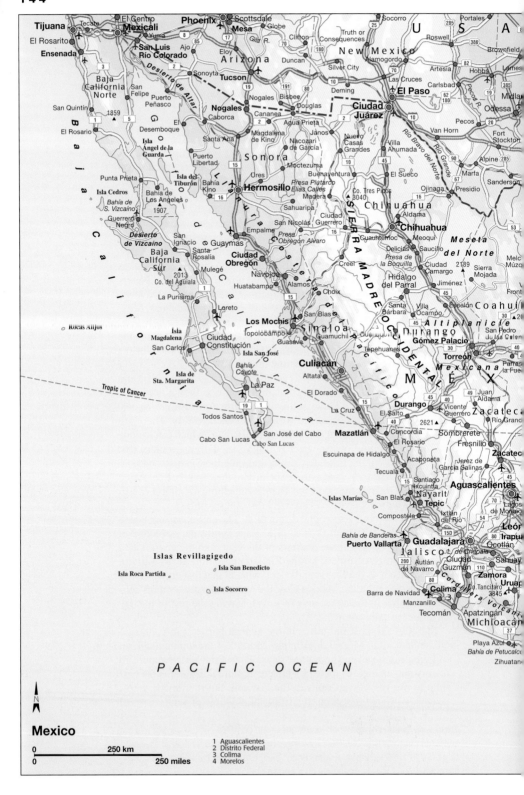

Mexico

0 ———————— 250 km
0 ———————— 250 miles

1 Aguascalientes
2 Distrito Federal
3 Colima
4 Morelos

MEXICO CITY AND ENVIRONS

An overview of the capital and its surrounding state, with cross-referenced maps and street plans to guide you

Referred to by Mexicans simply as México or the Distrito Federal (Federal District) or, even more simply, the D.F., Mexico City lays claim to being the world's most populous city. At an altitude of 2,250 meters (7,380 ft), it is also one of the highest cities on the planet and, sadly, one of the most polluted. Some visitors find they feel tired and short of breath as a result of the high altitude but these symptoms are generally short-lived, unlike those resulting from the high levels of pollution in the air.

Although many beach lovers choose to fly direct to Cancún or Puerto Vallarta, Mexico City is the initial stop for the majority of people arriving by air. It is well worth spending a couple of days in the city, and for anyone interested or planning to visit the pre-Hispanic sites at Teotihuacán or further afield, a few hours browsing through the anthropology museum are strongly recommended.

Most of the major sites in Mexico City are concentrated along a central area that stretches from the Zócalo (main square) and the Aztec Templo Mayor to the east, past the Alameda and the Zona Rosa to Chapultepec Park, with its outstanding Museo Nacional de Antropología, to the west. Also, for anyone who can spare an extra day or two, it is worth making a short trip south, to the *colonias* (neighborhoods) of San Angel – with its colonial mansions and famous Saturday bazaar – and Coyoacán – with its street performers, sidewalk cafés, Bohemian atmosphere and mouth-watering ice creams. The floating gardens of Xochimilco are another favorite destination although, if time is short, you may do better heading straight for one of the "Around Mexico City" sites.

Mexico City makes a convenient base for all kinds of fascinating day and weekend excursions: there are pre-Hispanic ruins, colonial towns, and baroque churches; or there is shopping for silver in Taxco and, for those who want to get away from it all, there are semi-tropical spa resorts or mountain lakes with sailing and a host of other watersports. ❏

PRECEDING PAGES: the Cathedral at night. **LEFT:** veterans from the Mexican Revolution.

MEXICO CITY

Traffic-clogged and polluted it may be, but the capital is the hub of Mexico, with its best museums, superb restaurants and nightlife, and remains of its Aztec origins

Map on page 152

México City

The vast sprawling megalopolis of Mexico City is a love it *and* loathe it kind of place. Much of the the nation's wealth and power is concentrated here, together with the finest in music and the arts. It is a huge, exciting, unpredictable city where people are friendly and adventure seems to linger on every street corner. But being one of the largest and most populated cities in the world has its disadvantages too: traffic congestion and pollution are appalling, and the petty crime of pickpockets and thieves is rife. Visitors are more likely to be robbed in Mexico City than elsewhere in the country and basic precautions should be taken: keep cameras and jewelry out of sight; avoid dimly lit side streets at night and always keep a firm hold of your possessions, especially on buses and subways; and if you are travelling by taxi, make sure it is an authorized "*sitio*" one (based at a taxi rank, can be called by 'phone).

Including both the sordid and the majestic, downtown Mexico City comprises about 100 blocks of Spanish, indian, French romantic and modern architecture; it is a business district, a marketplace, a colonial slum and shopping area all rolled into one. The **Centro Histórico** corresponds roughly to the old Aztec and colonial capital.

LEFT: vintage tour bus or taxi?
BELOW: children phoning home.

House of tiles

Breakfast at the charming **Casa de los Azulejos ❶**, a 16th-century house covered in blue and white tiles, is a good way to start the day. Nowadays, as **Sanborns** restaurant, it may be the best-known eating place in the city, but it has been famous at least since the days of Pancho Villa and Emiliano Zapata, whose troops once ate here in the days of the Revolution. The glass-covered patio section of the restaurant is the most striking, and there is a large mural on the landing of the staircase by José Clemente Orozco (*see pages 108–11*).

A well known photograph of the revolutionaries dining (*see pages 60–61*) can be seen down the block in the **Casasola** photo store; you can also browse through archives of ancient pictures or even pose for a souvenir photo dressed as a revolutionary. Opposite Sanborns, the **Torre Latinoamericana ❷** (open until midnight) was, in 1956, Mexico's first skyscraper. The panoramic view from the 42nd-floor observation platform (and the 41st-floor restaurant) is clearest at night; daytime visitors may well find themselves peering through a murky sea of gray smog.

Busy **Calle Madero** leads from the Alameda to the Zócalo, the hub of Mexico City and the Centro Histórico. It is an interesting street and its occupants include such landmarks as the sinking church of **San Francisco ❸**, once part of the Franciscan monastery

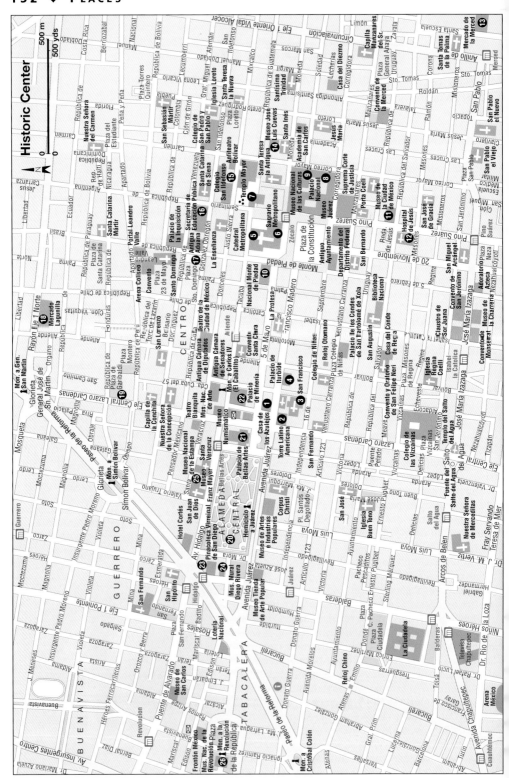

Historic Center

founded by Cortés himself three years after the Conquest, in 1524. Most of the structure, including the stone portal and churrigueresque façade, date from the 18th century.

The heavily adorned **Palacio de Iturbide** ❹ is also 18th-century. Named after "Emperor" Agustín de Iturbide, who lived here in 1821, it now houses the Banamex cultural foundation which stages contemporary art shows in the patio. On the same block, the **American Bookstore**, has a large array of English-language reading material and a good selection of books on Mexican archeology. Nearing the end of Madero, the somber **Templo de la Profesa**, which served as the capital's surrogate cathedral early in the 20th century, has sunk considerably since it was built in 1720.

Once the principal Aztec ceremonial center, with pyramids, palaces and wide open spaces, the **Zócalo** has been transformed many times. Until a few years ago it was a huge, busy square, with palm trees and a tram terminal. Now it is a stark and imposing treeless plaza, a convenient place for military and political rallies. The best view of the Zócalo is from the rooftop restaurant of the **Hotel Majestic** (entrance on Madero), and photographs and models of how it used to be can be seen in the Zócalo metro station.

A mixture of styles

The vast **Catedral Metropolitana** ❺, supposedly the largest religious building on the continent, is an encyclopedia of Mexican colonial art. Construction took around three centuries to complete, beginning in Spanish Renaissance style and finishing in the French neoClassical style of the early 19th century. The upper portion of the elegant façade and the towers crowned with unusual bell-shaped cupolas were designed by the two great neo-Classical architects, Manuel Tolsá and José Damián Ortiz de Castro.

Huge and impressive, the cathedral's somber but magnificent interior is softly illuminated through contemporary stained-glass windows that give off a mellow, golden light. The 100-meter (328-ft) long and 46-meter (151-ft) wide interior is divided into five naves. Close to the main entrance, the **Altar del Perdón** (Altar of Forgiveness) with its huge *retablo* was the work of 17th-century Jerónimo de Balbas. Both the altar and the adjacent choir with its intricately carved choir stalls were severely damaged by fire in 1967 and have been fully restored.

At the end of the central nave the magnificent **Altar de los Reyes** – also designed by Jerónimo de Balbas – is one of the masterpieces of the elaborate, ultra-Baroque, *churrigueresque* style (*see page 54*). Finished in 1737, the altar is like a large, over-decorated niche with gilt carvings, moldings, angels, saints and cherubim. In the center, two paintings represent the Assumption of the Virgin and the Adoration of the Magi. The cathedral has 14 side chapels along the eastern and western walls, many of them unusually dark. Tragically, like many other buildings in Mexico City, the Cathedral is sinking and much of its interior beauty is hidden by the scaffolding that is propping up the entire edifice. The cathedral's neigh-

Map on page 152

Detail on the façade of the Cathedral.

BELOW: flying the flag in the Zócalo.

TIP

The Bar León, just
round the corner from
the cathedral, is one of
the best places to hear
salsa music.

bor, the 18th-century **Sagrario Metropolitano** ⑥, is a graceful building with a highly decorated red and white stone churrigueresque façade. But it too is subsiding and impressive cracks have appeared in the walls.

A picturesque square on the east side of the cathedral has a fountain and a monument honoring Fray Bartolomé de las Casas, the Spanish bishop who dedicated his life to defending the indians. (He suggested, in good faith, that Africans be brought to Mexico to do much of the hard labor; thus contributing to the infamous slave trade.)

Ruins of Tenochtitlán

The **Templo Mayor** ⑦ (open Tues–Sun; entrance fee) to the northeast of the Zócalo stood at the center of the Aztec universe, the exact spot where the eagle was sighted on the cactus (*see pages 33–4*). Excavations began after electricity workers chanced upon an 8-ton stone disc. The carvings on the disc represent the corpse of Coyolxauhqui, goddess of the moon, who was defeated by her brother Huitzilopochtli. Her death symbolized the sun's daily victory over the night. The great circular stone was found at the foot of the pyramid which was divided into two, with two temples at the top dedicated to Huitzilopochtli, god of war, and Tlaloc, god of water. A pathway round the site reveals the temple's multiple levels of construction, although it is hard at first to make out what is what since the Spanish demolished two-thirds of the temple and used the stones to build their churches and palaces. The beautifully designed **museum** (entrance included in ticket to temple) exhibits artefacts found during the excavation work, including the original Coyolxauhqui stone, and helpful models of what Tenochtitlán and the great Templo Mayor looked like before the Spanish Conquest.

BELOW: snakes' heads on the Templo Mayor.

Palacio Nacional

On the Zócalo's east side, the **Palacio Nacional** ❽, built on the site of Moctezuma's palace, is the seat of power in Mexico and home to the offices of the President, the Treasury and the National Archives. Most visitors to the Palace come to admire the murals by Diego Rivera (*see pages 108–11*) that adorn the main staircase and first floor gallery. Painted between 1929 and 1935, the murals dramatically illustrate the history of Mexico, from an idealized pre-Hispanic past through the horrors of the Conquest to Independence and the 1910 Revolution, with Karl Marx pointing towards the future.

On the night of September 15, the president of Mexico appears on the main balcony of the Palacio to ring the bell with which Father Hidalgo summoned the people of his congregation in Dolores (*see page 244*), thus starting the War of Independence. *El Grito* (The Shout) is a short but emotional ceremony; the president proclaims once again the Independence of Mexico and the crowd in the Zócalo shouts: "¡Viva México! ¡Viva la Independencia!" (Many people prefer to take part in *El Grito* in Coyoacán's Plaza Hidalgo, which is just as lively but considered somewhat safer than the milling, often overly enthusiastic throngs in the Zócalo.)

The **Museo Nacional de Las Culturas** ❾ (open Tues–Sun; entrance free), in the same block as the Palacio Nacional, is housed in an impressive 18th-century structure whose patio is filled with trees, flowers and a fountain. The museum has exhibits on the history of cultures from all over the world, and free cultural videos are shown at weekends on the second floor. At the northwest corner of the Zócalo the **Monte de Piedad** ❿ is an enormous pawnshop which was founded in 1775 and has since become an important part of Mexico City

BELOW: a shoe-shine dreams while he cleans.

Danzón in the street.

life, especially at holiday time, when people queue up all along the street to hock their cherished family possessions.

One block south of the Zócalo, on Calle 20 de Noviembre, the **Palacio de Hierro** department store is worth visiting, if only to see one of the most gorgeous stained-glass ceilings in existence. On the parallel street of Pino Suárez, the **Museo de la Ciudad de México** ⓫ (open Tues–Sun; entrance free), housed in the magnificent former palace of the Counts of Santiago de Calimaya, provides a good overview of the history of the city from prehistoric to modern times. Across the street is the fort-like **Hospital de Jesús** ⓬, a hospital and church which was established in 1524 by Hernán Cortés himself. It is the oldest hospital built in the New World and is said to be located at the very spot where Cortés met Moctezuma for the first time. The conquistador's remains are in a tomb beside the altar of the church, whose vaulted ceiling is decorated with a mural by José Clemente Orozco (*see pages 108–111*).

Street markets

One of Mexico City's largest wholesale food markets, the **Mercado de la Merced** ⓭, near the metro station of the same name, is an immense warren of activity with an almost overpowering variety of sounds and smells: chickens frying, radios blaring and men with loudspeakers peddling their unusual remedies alongside girls pressing, heating and filling *tortillas* from brightly colored plastic bowls. A couple of blocks away, on Fray Servando Teresa de Mier, is the **Mercado de Sonora**, famed for its wide array of medicinal herbs and the alleged witch doctors who sell some of them. The atmosphere in Sonora market is subdued, almost reverent after the bustle of La Merced. At one end, past the

BELOW: Diego Rivera's *The Great Tenochtitlán*, at the Palacio Nacional.

shelves of garish religious figurines, is the animal market with tanks of frogs, turtles and snakes, and cage after stacked cage of rabbits, pigeons, doves, parrots, parakeets, canaries and puppies.

Map on page 152

North of the Zócalo

Founded by one of México's best known modern artists, the **Museo José Luis Cuevas** ⑭ (open Tues–Sun; entrance fee) with, among other halls, its controversial Sala de Erótica, is located to the northeast of the Zócalo.

This used to be the university area, although it has long been superseded by the vast campus in the southern part of the city. Behind the Templo Mayor, in the **Colegio de San Ildefonso** ⑮, murals cover the walls around the patios on three floors of the former Jesuit college, also known as the **Escuela Nacional Preparatoria** (National Preparatory School). The main work here is by Orozco, although Siqueiros and Rivera and others also feature.

The very best of Diego Rivera's work can be seen around the corner in the twin patios of the **Secretaría de Educación Pública** ⑯ (open Mon–Fri; entrance free). Outside stands an immense statue of José Vasconcelos, the radical education minister after the Revolution who was responsible for commissioning the murals. Just inside this magnificent old building, which now houses the **Librería Justo Sierra**, is a small (free) cinema (its schedule is listed on a nearby board).

The delightful **Plaza Santo Domingo** ⑰ is one of the most traditional in Mexico. Under the colonnade on the west side of the square, public scribes, known as *evangelistas,* still write letters and fill out forms for the illiterate on ancient typewriters. Street printers with old-fashioned hand presses also vie for trade. The beautiful baroque **Iglesia de Santo Domingo**, at the north end of the plaza, is the city's main Dominican church. Just across the road stands the **Palacio de la Inquisición**, the headquarters of the dreaded and oppressive Inquisition which was administered by the Dominicans.

Markets and mariachis

During the week, **La Lagunilla** ⑱ is just another of the city's markets. On one side of the road is the food section where men with knives, choppers, and hatchets slash, cut and scrape the countless pineapples, cactus leaves, carrots, and slabs of meat and fish; scrawny heads of skinned ducks hang over the edge of a nearby counter; chickens are eviscerated, their livers laid out in bloody lines; the manicured pink toes of the pigs' trotters stand in neatly arranged lines; soup is ladled from giant enamel pots, and a woman gurgles lovingly to her infant as she places him carefully on the potato-weighing scales.

The other section of the market resembles a Haberdashers' Hall of Fame: embroidered *charro* hats, children's party dresses and scores of mannequins, gaudily draped with sequined dresses or polyester suits. On Sundays, the Lagunilla spills out onto the surrounding streets and is transformed into a massive **flea market** with hundreds of stalls selling treasures, trash and anything in between.

BELOW: miraculous remedies for all ailments at the Mercado de Sonora.

The famous **Plaza Garibaldi**  is a few blocks south of La Lagunilla. It is best visited at night, when costumed *mariachi* bands stand around with their instruments until someone pays them for a song, and the lively bars, nightspots and burlesque theaters are in full swing. Meanwhile, *tacos* and other indigenous fast food are on offer in the nearby **Mercado de Alimentos San Camilito**.

Once the site for the burning of heretics, **La Alameda** ⑳ was transformed in the 19th century into a romantic park full of trees, fountains, sculptures, and the inevitable music kiosk. It is a welcome refuge in the middle of the noisy and chaotic capital. Among the park's monuments is the Hemiciclo, a tribute to **Benito Juárez** in white Italian marble, a statue of Beethoven, and two charmingly erotic girls, also in marble, called *Malgré Tout* (In Spite of Everything) and *Désespoir* (Despair).

Bellas Artes

At the east end of the Alameda is the huge and extravagant **Palacio de Bellas Artes** ㉑ (Palace of Fine Arts; open Tues–Sun; entrance free), commissioned by President Porfirio Díaz at the beginning of the 20th century. Although the original design was by the Italian architect Adamo Boari, building was interrupted by the Revolution and was finished 30 years later by the Mexican architect Federico Mariscal.

This time-lapse helps to explain the blend of styles: the white Italian marble exterior is a combination of neoclassical with art nouveau, full of flying sculpture and floral decoration, while the interior is a sort of Aztec art deco. The structure is so massive and heavy that it has sunk noticeably more than any other building in the area.

BELOW: a scribe in the Plaza Santo Domingo.

The theater is used for concerts, traditional dance performances by the **Ballet Folklórico**, and art exhibitions, including a permanent show of modern Mexican painting and some of the country's best murals. Most notable is Diego Rivera's own replica of a controversial painting commissioned in 1934 for the Rockefeller Center in New York. However, the anticapitalist subject matter was deemed as being too left wing and the original mural was destroyed. There are other works by Rivera in addition to murals by Orozco, Siqueiros, O'Gorman and Tamayo.

The well-publicized stained-glass curtain, based on a painting by Gerardo Murillo, "*Dr Atl*", was made by Tiffany of New York. Showing the volcanoes Popocatépetl and Iztaccíhuatl, it is a masterpiece of high-class kitsch and is lit up for public viewing on Sunday mornings and before evening performances.

Map on page 152

Beloved monument

Across the street, only a few steps from the elaborate Venetian-style **Correo Central** (Central Post Office), also designed in the early 20th century by Adamo Boari, is Mexico's most beloved monument, **El Caballito** (The Little Horse). The sculpture, which is not little at all, but huge and formal, depicts the Spanish king Charles IV riding a horse.

Sculpted by Manuel Tolsá in 1803, El Caballito has galloped all over Mexico City in search of a permanent site; at different times it has adorned the Zócalo, the University patio, and the busy Reforma, Juárez and Bucareli crossroads. But increasingly heavy traffic meant the statue became a nuisance and, in 1981, it had to be moved yet again.

One of its current neighbors is the elegant **Palacio de Minería** ㉒ (open

Charles IV on the well-travelled El Caballito statue.

BELOW: Palacio de Bellas Artes, downtown Mexico City.

Mon–Fri; entrance free), also designed by Manuel Tolsá and one of the best examples of neoclassical architecture in the country.

La Alameda is flanked by **Avenida Hidalgo** along the north, while on the south side is **Avenida Juárez,** with its restaurants, shops and still-abandoned buildings that were badly damaged in the 1985 earthquake. At the western end of the Alameda, the former church of San Diego houses the **Pinacoteca Virreinal** (open Tues–Sun; entrance fee), a museum of beautifully displayed colonial painting with works by masters such as Echave, Juárez, Cabera and López de Herrera. Mexican colonial painting, strongly influenced by Spanish and Italian models, is predominantly religious, and tends to be somewhat somber.

Nearby, the **Museo Mural Diego Rivera** ❷ (open Tues–Sun; entrance fee), houses Rivera's famous mural *Sueño de una Tarde Dominical en la Alameda* (Dream of a Sunday Afternoon in the Alameda), which portrays over 100 historical characters – including the artist himself, his wife, Frida Kahlo and the engraver, José Guadalupe Posada – under the trees of the Alameda park. After the earthquake of 1985, when the Hotel del Prado – the original location of the mural – tragically collapsed, a mammoth operation was mounted to transport the entire wall with the mural along Avenida Juárez to its present site.

Tilting churches

On Avenida Hidalgo, two small colonial churches face the tiny, peaceful **Plaza de la Santa Veracruz,** which preserves some of the atmosphere of old Mexico City. Next door to the severely tilting baroque Templo de San Juan de Dios, in a beautifully restored 16th-century hospital, is the **Museo Franz Mayer** ❷ (open Tues-Sun; entrance fee).

A German-born financier who later became a Mexican citizen, Mayer assembled a fantastically rich collection of period furniture, stylish pottery, tapestry, rugs, silver objects and paintings. The collection is beautifully exhibited in rooms around a delightful garden courtyard and the Cafetería del Claustro adds to the charm too.

The **Museo Nacional de la Estampa** (open Tues–Sun; entrance fee), also on the little plaza, specializes in 19th-century engravings and prints by well known Mexican artists such as José Guadalupe Posada. Another leaning church next door, the 18th-century **Iglesia de la Santa Veracruz,** has a fine churrigueresque façade.

On the corner of Avenida Hidalgo and Paseo de la Reforma, the small church of **San Hipólito** stands on the spot where the Spaniards were defeated by the Aztecs in July 1520 on the occasion known as the *Noche Triste* (Sad Night – *see page 43*). The church was built by the Spanish soon after to celebrate their eventual victory and to commemorate the events of the *Noche Triste*; it is in fact the only landmark commemorating the Spanish conquest of Mexico.

Art deco monument

At the hectic intersection of Reforma, Juárez and Bucareli is the tall tower of the **Loteriá Nacional** (Na-

BELOW:
"Eco taxis" run on unleaded fuel.

tional Lottery Building), where public draws take place two nights each week. From the crossroads, Reforma marches grandly along towards Chapultepec castle, while Avenida Juárez heads up to the massive **Monumento a la Revolución ㉖**. Some consider this Monument to be the biggest art deco building in the world.

Map on page 152

The Monument began as the huge central dome of the never-completed legislative palace, part of Porfirio Díaz's plan to transform Mexico City into a sort of Latin American Paris. But the Revolution interrupted that grand scheme and the gigantic, empty, iron structure was left to rust for years until an enterprising architect transformed it into the imposing, if ugly, monument it is today. The **Museo Nacional de la Revolución** (open Tues–Sun; entrance free), in the basement of the monument, has fascinating exhibits on the history of the Revolution as well as a collection of cartoons in which the building assumes many amusing forms.

Three blocks northeast on Puente de Alvarado, the **Museo de San Carlos** (open Wed–Sun; entrance fee), in an 18th-century mansion, was the first art academy in Mexico; now it houses fine Mexican colonial art and a first-class collection of European paintings with works by Rubens, Rembrandt and Goya.

Shoeshine and the daily news.

Seine in cement

From the days of the Emperor Maximilian, the **Paseo de la Reforma** was a grand promenade, full of shade trees and monuments, which culminated in Chapultepec Park and its romantic castle. The Mexican writer, Octavio Paz, said the Paseo was Mexico City's river, a sort of Seine in cement, majestically crossing the best part of town. But, alas, the horses and carriages were replaced

BELOW: handicrafts on sale from all over Mexico.

by automobiles, and many of the French-looking mansions were torn down and replaced by skyscrapers.

Even today the Paseo is a beautiful street with trees, gardens and monuments. The **Glorieta Cristóbal Colón** has a large statue of Christopher Columbus. Further south, at the Reforma and Insurgentes crossing, is the monument to **Cuauhtémoc**, the last Aztec emperor and first Mexican hero. Cuauhtémoc, who ruled after Moctezuma and during Cortés's siege of Tenochtitlán, became the perfect romantic figure, valiant and doomed; he stands erect and proud like a Roman senator wearing a feather headdress at one of Mexico City's busiest intersections.

The **Angel de la Independencia** is perhaps the most beautiful and best loved of all the monuments. Poised gracefully atop a tall and elegant column, the golden Angel commemorates Mexico's Independence. Nearby are such grand buildings as the **Sheraton Hotel** and the **American Embassy**.

The Zona Rosa

South of Reforma and between Cuauhtémoc and the Angel is the famous **Zona Rosa** ㉗, or Pink Zone, a colorful neighborhood crowded with fancy boutiques and galleries, expensive restaurants, sidewalk cafés hotels and stores. It is a perfect area for eating, shopping and people-watching.

Amberes has been a chic shopping street since the 1960s and it is known for its exclusive goods. In particular, look out for the whimsical, tinted sculptures and jewelry of **Sergio Bustamante**. **Gucci** is at the corner of Hamburgo, and **Los Castillo** has intriguing silver inlay chinaware. The entrance to the glitzy **Plaza Rosa** mall is across the street. **Plaza Angel**, a mall on Calle Lon-

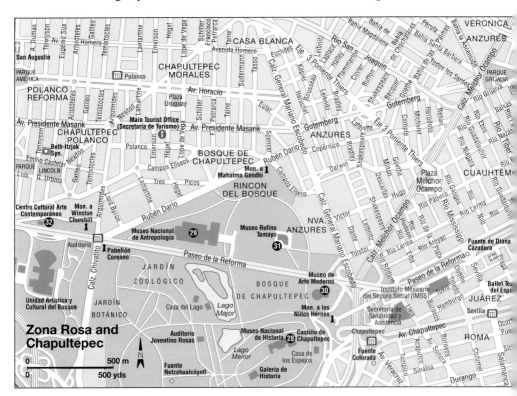

Zona Rosa and Chapultepec

dres, specializes in antiques such as sculpted colonial furniture and quaint pictures of saints and miracles on tin.

Its central patio and walkways are filled on Saturday mornings with a popular flea market. Across the street is the **Mercado Insurgentes**, with its extensive array of silver, serapes, embroidered clothing and all kinds of souvenirs. One side is lined with cheap but clean food counters.

The **Metro Insurgentes** station is located on a huge circle packed with stalls of every type. In other cities, subway stations are just subway stations; no more, no less. In Mexico, they are grand exhibition spaces.

Grasshopper Hill

Six vast columns, the **Monumento a los Niños Héroes**, commemorate the "Boy Heroes", the six young cadets who died defending the castle (then a military academy), against the invading US army during the Mexican-American war in 1847. The huge monument also marks the entrance to the **Bosque de Chapultepec**, the largest green area in Mexico City, and one of the few places in the capital where you can relax in the open air. It is also a place of great historical importance. Mexico's rulers lived here for centuries, and it is believed that even the famous king Netzahualcóyotl had a palace there. In pre-Hispanic times, the city's drinking water came from the springs of Chapultepec, which means "hill of the grasshopper" in Náhuatl.

Ghosts of the Hapsburgs

El Castillo de Chapultepec ㉘, which was built as a residence for the Spanish viceroy, is said to be inhabited by the ghosts of Maximilian of Austria and his

Map on pages 162–3

TIP

Long lunches are a Mexican institution, so take your time and unwind at one of the Zona Rosa's many restaurants or cafés. The ones on Copenhagen or Genova are the most interesting.

BELOW: the Angel of Independence.

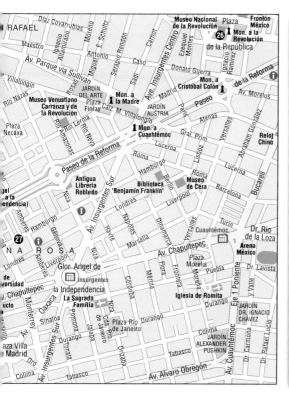

Fine Huastec figure, believed to be of the young Quetzalcóatl, at the National Anthropological Museum.

BELOW: there are boats to hire on the Bosque de Chapultepec's lake.

wife Charlotte, who lived here during their short reign as Emperor and Empress of Mexico. Nowadays the castle – a steep 20-minute hike up from the park – houses the **Museo Nacional de Historia** (open Tues–Sun; entrance fee). where exhibits chronicle Mexican history from the Spanish conquest up to the Revolution. Many of rooms are decorated in period furniture and artefacts include the carriage belonging to Maximilian. Several rooms contain impressive historical murals by well known 20th-century artists such as Siqueiros, O'Gorman and Orozco. Smog permitting, there is a fantastic view over the city from the upper level of the castle.

Just down the hill from the castle, the so-called **Museo del Caracol** (open Tues–Sun; entrance free) concentrates its exhibits on Mexico's fight for independence from the late colonial period to the 1917 Constitution. Apart from these history museums, the park has theaters, botanical gardens, a zoo and a lake.

Anthropology Museum

But most of all Chapultepec Park is home to one of the most outstanding museums in the world, the **Museo Nacional de Antropología** ❷ (open Tues–Sun; entrance fee). The entrance to the Anthropology Museum on Reforma is marked by a vast stone statue supposedly representing the rain god Tlaloc, although some studies suggest it may be Chalchiuhtlicue, the Aztec goddess of water. The 7.5-meter (25-ft) tall monolith was brought here in the 1960s, when the museum opened, amid continuous heavy downpours which were interpreted by some to be the god's protest at being moved.

Pedro Ramírez Vásquez, the architect, found his inspiration for the museum building in the Mayan ruins at Uxmal (*see page 322*). All the exhibition halls

open onto a large central patio which is shaded by an immense rectangular roof-fountain, held up, amazingly, by a single central pillar.

The halls are organized anticlockwise around the central patio as follows: Introduction to Anthropology; Introduction to Mesoamérica; Origins of Man in Mesoamérica; Preclassical Cultures; Teotihuacán; Toltecs; Mexicas (Aztecs); Oaxaca (Mixtecs and Zapotecs); Gulf of Mexico (Olmecs, Totonacs and Huastecs); Mayas; Northern and Western Mexico.

The marvelous **Sala Mexica**, dedicated to Aztec art and history, is one of the museum's highlights. Its exhibits include the famous Sun Stone, also known as the **Aztec Calendar**, and the wonderful sculpture of **Coatlicue** (*see photo page 29*), the goddess of Earth and Death. The **Sala Maya** has a model of the tomb of the deified king Pakal, discovered in the depths of Palenque's Templo de las Inscripciones. There is also a reproduction of the famous murals of Bonampak. Upstairs, there are ethnographic exhibitions on the many different indian groups that still exist in Mexico today.

Art museums

The **Museo de Arte Moderno** ㉚ (Tues–Sun; admission fee), housed in two rounded glass buildings, exhibits a permanent collection of paintings by some of Mexico's best known 20th-century artists, including Frida Kahlo, Rufino Tamayo and *los tres grandes*, Orozco, Rivera and Siqueiros. One room is dedicated to the great Mexican photographer Manuel Alvarez Bravo, and a series of landscape paintings by the 19th-century José María Velasco is also well worth seeing. There is usually at least one interesting temporary show, so be sure to check.

Maps on pages 162–3

TIP

There's a lot to see in the Anthropological Museum. If you don't have much time, head straight for the rooms dealing with the pars of Mexico you are planning to visit. The English guidebook is worth buying as labels are in Spanish only.

BELOW: the National Anthropological Museum.

The **Museo Rufino Tamayo** (open Tues–Sun; entrance fee), just east of the Anthropology Museum, has a fine collection of contemporary art donated by Rufino Tamayo and housed in an ingenious building conceived by designers Zabludosky and González de León. The museum contains some vibrant works by Tamayo himself, including a splendid portrait of the artist's wife, Olga.

The Paseo de la Reforma continues west towards some well-to-do residential areas. One of these, **Polanco**, has excellent shopping, some fine upscale restaurants and expensive hotels.

At the impressive **Centro Cultural Arte Contemporáneo** ❷ (open Tues–Sun; entrance fee) shows tend to focus on more progressive art than either of the previous museums. The three floors include the Center's permanent collections and some of the city's best traveling exhibitions, with work by artists from all over the world. The excellent museum shop is well worth a browse.

Mexican Madonna

The image of **La Virgen de Guadalupe** (*see pages 118–19*) is everywhere in Mexico: in homes, stores, places of work, and even buses, trucks and taxicabs. On December 12, tens of thousands of penitents make the pilgrimage to the **Basílica de Nuestra Señora de Guadalupe** Ⓐ, in the north of the city, for the anniversary of her 16th-century apparition.

When the beautiful 18th-century basilica became too small to accommodate the enormous crowds (besides, it was beginning to list noticeably and gradually sink into the ground), a new one was built next door on the vast plaza. Designed by top architect, Pedro Ramírez Vásquez (who was responsible for the acclaimed Museo de Antropología), the massive concrete Basílica was completed in 1976 with a rounded, open-plan interior which can accommodate as many as 10,000 worshippers at a time.

There is almost always a service taking place in the Basílica, but people are constantly wandering in and out, admiring the stained-glass windows, the marble stairs, latter-day chandeliers and fluted ceiling of burnished wood. A slow-moving, mechanical walkway carries an endless stream of admirers past the much-revered image of the Virgin, high up on one wall.

The old church serves as a museum, with a fine collection of colonial paintings. Behind the Basílica a path winds uphill past the **Iglesia del Cerrito** to the **Capilla del Pocito**, a small circular chapel with a well; in front is a string of shops and stalls selling religious images, incense, food, toys and lottery tickets.

Plaza de las Tres Culturas

The **Plaza de las Tres Culturas** Ⓑ (toward La Villa de Guadalupe, in Tlatelolco) is hailed as a symbol of modern Mexico, whose culture was born of the fusion of two previous cultures (pre-Hispanic and colonial). In the center of the square are the ruins of **Tlatelolco**, site of the biggest marketplace in the Valley of Mexico and the final stronghold of the Aztecs in their battle against the Spanish conquistadores.

According to a plaque in the square "it was neither a victory nor a defeat, but the painful birth of the

TIP

If you're going to the Basílica, de Nuestra Señora de Guadalupe, get off at La Villa metro station as it's closer than the station called Basílica.

BELOW: every neighborhood has a weekly *tianguis* (street market).

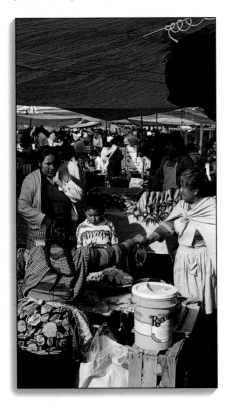

mixed race that is Mexico today." Overlooking the ruins, the **Iglesia de Santiago** dates from 1524 although it was later rebuilt in the 17th century. The modern buildings lining the square, including the rather bland **Ministry of Foreign Affairs** building, are not the best examples of contemporary Mexican architecture, but there they are, nevertheless.

Today, the square is remembered mainly for the hundreds of people who were massacred here on October 2, 1968, when police and army troops were ordered to open fire on the thousands of students who were protesting over the government's social and educational policies.

South along Insurgentes

Avenida Insurgentes, the city's longest artery, provides a 25-km (15-mile) link between the industrial north and the less-congested south, where the colonial suburbs of San Angel and Coyoacán offer a very different and more tranquil side of Mexico City.

The first landmark to look out for on Insurgentes Sur is the 50-storey **World Trade Center ⊙**, which has a revolving restaurant and a nightclub on the top floor. In front of the Center stands the unusual and seemingly haphazard **Poliforum Cultural Siquieros ⊙** (open daily; entrance free), a multi-faceted building designed and decorated by the artist David Alfaro Siqueiros (*see pages 108–11*). Inside, a huge three-dimensional mural entitled *The March of Humanity on Earth and Towards the Cosmos* combines painting and sculpture, and is said to be the world's largest mural.

Another record breaker, just a few block further south, is the Plaza México, reputedly the largest bullring in the world with seating for some 64,000 spectators.

Maps
on pages
162 & 168

BELOW: *gorditas*, a specialty from La Villa de Guadalupe.

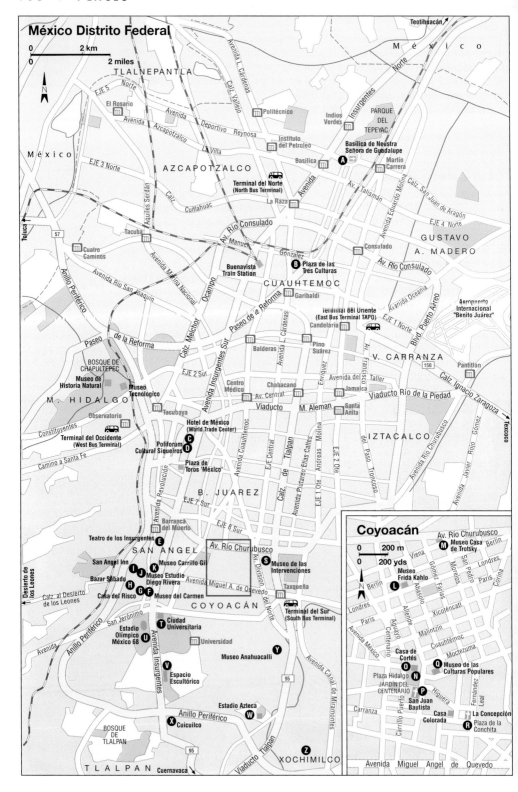

México Distrito Federal

0 ——— 2 km
0 ——— 2 miles

M é x i c o

Teotihuacán

México Norte

TLALNEPANTLA

EJE 5 Norte

El Rosario

Avenida

Avenida Azcapotzalco

Deportivo Reynosa

Politécnico

Indios Verdes

Insurgentes

PARQUE DEL TEPEYAC

AZCAPOTZALCO

Instituto del Petroleo

La Villa

Basílica de Neustra Señora de Guadalupe

Basílica Ⓐ

Martín Carrera

México

EJE 3 Norte

Aquiles Serdán

Calz.

Cuitlahuac

Terminal del Norte (North Bus Terminal)

La Raza

Av. Talismán

Av. San Juan de Aragón

Calz. Eduardo Molina

GUSTAVO A. MADERO

Toluca

57

Tacuba

Cuatro Caminos

Anillo Periférico

Avenida Río San Joaquín

Avenida Marina Nacional

Ocampo

Av. Río Consulado

Av. Manuel González

Consulado

Av. Río Consulado

EJE 4 Norte

Buenavista Train Station

Ⓑ Plaza de las Tres Culturas

CUAUHTEMOC

Garibaldi

Avenida Oceania

Aeropuerto Internacional "Benito Juárez"

Paseo de la Reforma

Calz. Melchor Ocampo

Terminal del Oriente (East Bus Terminal TAPO)

Candelária

EJE 1 Norte

Blvd. Puerto Aéreo

BOSQUE DE CHAPULTEPEC

Museo de Historia Natural

Museo Tecnológico

Paseo de la Reforma

EJE 2 Sur

Avenida Insurgentes Sur

Balderas

Av. Cárdenas

Pino Suárez

Centro Médico

Chabacano

Av. Central

Enriquez

Av. Francisco Morazán

V. CARRANZA

Pantitlán

150

Calz. Ignacio Zaragoza

Texcoco

M. HIDALGO

Observatorio

Terminal del Occidente (West Bus Terminal)

Constituyentes

Camino a Santa Fe

Tacubaya

Hotel de México (World Trade Center)

Ⓒ

Poliforum Cultural Siqueiros Ⓓ

Plaza de Toros 'México'

Viaducto

M. Aleman

Santa Anita

Avenida del Taller

Jamaica

Viaducto Río de la Piedad

IZTACALCO

Avenida Río Churubusco

Av. del Paso Troncoso

Avenida Javier Rojo Gómez

B. JUAREZ

EJE 7 Sur

Avenida Revolución

Barranca del Muerto

EJE 8 Sur

Teatro de los Insurgentes Ⓔ

SAN ANGEL

San Angel Inn

Bazar Sábado

Desierto de los Leones

Catz. at Desierto de los Leones

Museo Carrillo Gil Ⓚ

ⒾⒿ

Museo Estudio Diego Rivera

Ⓗ

ⒼⒻ

Casa del Risco

Museo del Carmen

Av. Río Churubusco

Ⓢ Museo de las Intervenciones

Av. División del Norte

Av. Miguel A. de Quevedo

COYOACÁN

Taxqueña

Terminal del Sur (South Bus Terminal)

San Jerónimo

Ⓣ Ciudad Universitaria

Estadio Olímpico México 68 Ⓤ

Avenida Insurgentes

Universidad

Anillo Periférico

Avenida

Museo Anahuacalli Ⓨ

Ⓥ Espacio Escultórico

95

Estadio Azteca Ⓦ

Anillo Periférico

Ⓧ Cuicuilco

BOSQUE DE TLALPAN

95

Ⓩ

TLALPAN

Cuernavaca

Avenida Canal de Miramontes

Viaducto Tlalpan

XOCHIMILCO

Coyoacán

0 ——— 200 m
0 ——— 200 yds

Av. Río Churubusco

Ⓜ Museo Casa de Trotsky

Berlín

Viena

Gomez Farias

San Pedro

Paris

Colima

Museo Frida Kahlo

Ⓛ

Morelos

Berlín

Londres

Adadelo

Xicotencatl

Allende

Aguayo

Centenario

Avenida México

Malintzin

Cuauhtémoc

Moctezuma

Londres

Paris

Casa de Cortés

Ⓞ

Ⓠ Museo de las Culturas Populares

Plaza Hidalgo

JARDÍN DEL CENTENARIO

Ⓝ

Ⓟ

San Juan Bautista

Carranza

Carrillo Puerto

Higuera

Casa Colorada

Fernández Leal

Ⓡ La Concepción

Plaza de la Conchita

Avenida   Miguel   Angel   de   Quevedo

The huge mosaic covering the front of the **Teatro de los Insurgentes** ❺ (on the right-hand side, ten blocks before San Angel) is the work of Diego Rivera (see photo pages 106–7). The mosaic includes many characters from the Mexican history books; but pride of place goes to Cantinflas, the national hero of popular comedy, who is portrayed christ-like in the center, with outstretched arms, taking from the rich and giving to the poor.

Map on page 168

San Angel

The fashionable "village" of **San Angel**, once some distance from the city and now encompassed by its sprawl, has managed to retain much of its charm. The delightful Carmelite **Iglesia del Carmen**, with its tiled domes, serene cloister and flamboyant churrigueresque altar, was one of the wealthiest in the area when it was built at the beginning of the 17th century. The adjacent **Museo del Carmen** ❻ (open Tues–Sun; entrance fee), housed in the convent building, has frescoed walls, fine furniture and religious paintings. However, most people head for the basement crypt to glimpse the extraordinarily eerie group of naturally mummified bodies in glass-topped cases.

Up the hill, in the patio of the 18th-century **Casa del Risco** ❼ (open Tues–Sun; entrance free) is a wonderful fountain composed of hundreds of gaily colored plates, cups, saucers and vases, most of them centuries old.

You can still escape the city's hustle along these quiet cobblestone streets where bougainvillea cascades riotously down high stone walls which hide wonderful and secluded mansions. Time seems to stand still here, except on Saturdays, that is, when droves of tourists from all over descend upon San Angel for the famous **Bazar Sábado** ❽, an indoor market with crafts from all over the

The watchful presence of the Church.

BELOW: the Plaza de las Tres Culturas was the setting for several historic catastrophes.

The coyotes of Coyoacán in the Jardín Centenario.

country and brightly colored stalls which spill out onto the normally sleepy Plaza San Jacinto. The late 16th-century **Iglesia de San Jacinto**, housed in an enchanting courtyard just off the square, has a renaissance façade with beautifully carved wooden doors.

A short walk away on Altavista, the **San Angel Inn** is one of Mexico's most exclusive traditional restaurants; a former 18th-century hacienda, it is set in stunning colonial grounds. The modernist, somewhat box-like building just across the road is the **Museo Estudio Diego Rivera** (open Tues–Sun; entrance fee), where the controversial artist worked for many years, and indeed where he died in 1957.

The house will delight any Rivera admirer. On show are some of his later portraits and a medley of objects including the characteristic denim jacket, painting materials, newspaper cuttings and his collection of masks and pre-Hispanic art. It is a five-minute walk back to Avenida Revolución and the **Museo Carrillo Gil** (open Tues–Sun; entrance fee), which houses one of Mexico City's best collections of modern art.

Coyoacán

After the fall of Tenochtitlán, Cortés set up his government in Coyoacán, south of San Angel and still a town apart in the 1940s when it was home to many celebrities – Frida Kahlo, Diego Rivera, Leon Trotsky, actress Dolores del Río. It is still a desirable neighborhood for artists, intellectuals and bohemians. On the corner of Londres and Allende, the **Museo Frida Kahlo** (open Tues–Sun; entrance fee), is the bright blue house where Frida was born and where she later lived with Diego Rivera. It contains some of her work, an inspirational

BELOW: cool drinks in the shade; wedding pose (below right).

kitchen and all kinds of memorabilia, including the couple's love letters and Frida's indian dresses.

Six blocks away, in a far more somber setting, the **Museo Casa de León Trotsky** (open Tues–Sun; entrance fee), home of the exiled communist leader, has bricked-up windows, a high wall and watchtowers. Bullet holes remain from a failed assassination attempt in 1940 (led allegedly by the muralist David Siqueiros). Three months later, Trotsky was assassinated with an iceaxe by a Spanish Stalinist agent as he sat at his desk in this house. His small tomb stands in the gardens.

In the center of Coyoacán, the attractive **Plaza Hidalgo** ⓝ and adjoining **Jardín Centenario**, buzzes with activity at weekends (it is worth standing in line at the shop on the corner which sells some of the best ice-creams in Mexico City.) The 16th-century **Casa de Cortés** ⓞ, now government offices, lines the north side of the plaza. This is said to be the spot where the Spanish tortured the defeated Aztec emperor, Cuauhtémoc – by burning his feet – to persuade him to reveal the whereabouts of treasure. Occupying the south side of the plaza is the parish church of **San Juan Bautista** ⓟ, also dating from the 16th-century. One block away, is the **Museo de Culturas Populares** ⓠ (open Tues–Sun; entrance free), a low-budget museum with highly imaginative exhibits focusing on different aspects of Mexican culture.

Baroque weddings

Two blocks east of Plaza Hidalgo is the picturesque **Plaza de la Conchita** ⓡ, where the baroque façaded Capilla de la Concepción is a favorite for weddings. Overlooking the square is the Casa Colorada, which was built for La Malinche,

Map on page 168

TIP

Most public museums and galleries throughout Mexico are free on Sundays (although this often means they are also more crowded); and most are closed on Mondays.

BELOW: escape the downtown bustle in beautiful Coyoacán.

Cortés's native interpreter and mistress, and where the conquistador allegedly murdered his wife shortly after her arrival from Spain. The **Museo de las Intervenciones ⑤** (open Tues–Sun; entrance fee) set in the fortified Ex-Convento de Churubusco – in the northeast of Coyoacán – traces the history of the many foreign interventions into Mexico. It was here that General Anaya surrendered after defeat in the Mexican-American War in 1847. Special tribute is paid to a group of Irish soldiers, who deserted from the US army to fight with the Mexicans but were captured during the battle and condemned to death.

TIP

A good place for a drink is La Guadalupana, a well known cantina near the center of Coyoacán.

Ciudad Universitaria

Further south still, Insurgentes Sur crosses the vast campus of Mexico's National University (UNAM). **Ciudad Universitaria ⑦**, with its bold use of color, murals and sculpture, was a progressive campus when it was constructed in the 1950s and the university moved here from downtown Mexico City. The **Biblioteca Central** (Central Library), Mexico's most photographed modern building, is an extraordinary 10-story block whose walls are entirely covered by a Juan O'Gorman stone mosaic.

Also worth seeing is the Siqueiros mural behind the nearby **Rectoría** building, and another by the lesser-known José Chávez Morado on the old science faculty. Across the road, a mural by the prolific Diego Rivera adorns the **Estadio Olímpico México 68 ⓪**. The stadium, which was built for the 1968 Olympics and was designed to resemble a volcano, holds up to 80,000 people.

The huge campus is built on a vast area known as **El Pedregal**, the result of the Xitle volcano erupting almost 2,000 years ago. Tucked away behind the theaters, cinemas, café and bookshop of the **Centro Cultural Univer-**

BELOW: Frida Kahlo, self-portrait.

FRIDA KAHLO

Long overshadowed by her husband, the famous muralist Diego Rivera, Frida Kahlo (1907–1954) became considered a serious artist in her own right in the 1980s, 30 years after her death. Now she is an international cult figure and is probably even better known than the great Diego himself.

Frida's traditional embroidered costumes, elaborate hairstyles, exotic jewelry and thick, connected eyebrows – exaggerated in her paintings – became her trademark. Although she and the flamboyant Rivera were central figures of the left-wing, nationalist movement, Frida's art was surrealist, highly symbolical and never overtly political. She took to painting after the injuries suffered in an almost fatal tramway accident in her late teens left her confined to a wheelchair.

Frida's best-known works are her self-portraits, many of which were nightmarish and gory references to her accident. Perhaps serving as therapy to the artist, these intimate studies express the anxiety of a woman whose life was stricken with physical suffering and mental anguish caused by, among other things, many painful operations, two miscarriages and her stormy and much-commented marriage to Diego.

sitario, is the **Espacio Escultórico** , executed by six sculptors in the 1980s, who engulfed a large expanse of the craggy, black volcanic rock in a huge circle of uniform cement pyramids giving the arena a strange, almost unearthly atmosphere. There are also monumental sculptures created by each of the participating artists. Not far from the **Estadio Azteca** , one of the biggest soccer stadiums in the world, is the oldest ceremonial center in the Valley of Mexico: the round pyramid of **Cuicuilco** (open daily; entrance free), built as early as 1000 BC but buried when the Xitle volcano erupted around AD 100.

The very unusual and little-visited **Museo Anahuacalli** (open Tues–Sun; entrance free) was designed by Diego Rivera and houses his personal collection of pre-Hispanic art. The somber building of dark volcanic rock is reminiscent of an Aztec or Mayan temple. Apart from the ancient treasures (mostly from West and Central Mexican cultures), there is a replica of his studio with some of his work and possessions, and a superb view of the city and volcanoes.

Floating gardens

The famous floating gardens of **Xochimilco** (take the light rail from Tasqueña metro station) is the only remnant of the pre-Hispanic lake cities. They are a favorite place for a Sunday outing for local residents, who come to eat, drink and be serenaded by *mariachis* on the flowery *trajineras* (boats). Weekdays are not half as jolly but they can be cheaper (the hourly rate for a *trajinera* is posted, but there's room for negotiation). A nearby market on Nuevo León sells exotic fruit, such as tamarinds, persimmons, guavas and papayas, all impeccably arranged. Further along, just off the main plaza, is the lovely 16th-century church of **San Bernardino.** ❑

Map on page 168

The famous "Mexican wave" originated in the Estadio Azteca during the 1986 World Cup.

BELOW: go for a ride in a *trajinera* at Xochimilco.

AROUND MEXICO CITY

Massive pyramids, ornate colonial baroque, snow-capped volcanoes, sub-tropical gardens; whoever chooses Mexico City as a base will find interesting excursions in every direction

Map on page 178

México City

Although sprawling suburbs have engulfed much of the area around Mexico City, just an hour or two's drive in almost any direction will introduce you to the heart of the country. East, north and west of the city is the State of Mexico; to the south is Morelos. Also within easy reach are Hidalgo to the north, Puebla and Tlaxcala to the east. This is the heart of Mexico, comprising a mosaic of peoples and offering a geography ranging from cool, stately pine forests and snow-capped volcanoes to hot and humid valleys bursting with plant life.

North to Tepotzotlán

The town of Tepotzotlán is about 35 km (22 miles) north of central Mexico City, by the toll gates on the Querétaro road (Mexico 57), which starts near the Cuatro Caminos bullring. The road passes the **Torres de Satélite**, a giant sculptural group of brightly colored modern towers designed by German-born artist Mathías Goeritz, and crosses the endless industrial and middle-class northern surburbs.

The magnificent Jesuit church and monastery of **Tepotzotlán** ❶ are one of the jewels of Mexican colonial art. The monastery was designed in the 16th century as a school for indian converts; later it became a Jesuit seminary before being converted into a museum in the 1960s.

The church of **San Francisco Javier**, is one of the three best examples of churrigueresque architecture in Mexico (the other two are in Taxco and Tlaxcala, see pages 193 and 189). Completed in 1762, it has a lavishly decorated stone façade and a single, deliciously carved and graceful belfry. The door and central window are flanked by four richly adorned columns framing niches which contain sculptures of saints. The interior is a medley of golden altarpieces which appear to grow and multiply like an exotic tropical plant, covering the walls and transforming them into a mysterious, glittering curlicued mass; at times the gilt decor is a meter thick. It provides an inspiring frame to sculpture and paintings by masters of the colonial era, such as Miguel Cabrera's retable of Our Lady of Guadalupe.

The baroque ornamentation reaches its dazzling extreme in the **Camarín de la Virgen**, where every inch is covered in a riot of archangels, cherubim, fruit, flowers and shells. This small octagonal room, used to dress the statue of the virgin, is reached through the Capilla de la Virgen de Loreto. The little chapel contains a replica of the house in Nazareth where the Virgin Mary is supposed to have lived. Baroque style, it has been suggested, goes hand in hand with

PRECEDING PAGES: Iztaccíhuatl and Popocatépetl. **LEFT:** gilded interior, Tepotzotlán. **BELOW:** the Atlantes of Tula once supported the roof of the Temple of the Morning Star.

Mexican sensitivity; the lavish use of color and movement, the excesses and unbounded imagination are said to be the soul of Mexican art. Perhaps Mexicans are a baroque people at heart, helplessly in love with color, with murals, with ornament.

The adjacent monastery, with its graceful cloisters and gardens, houses the **Museo Nacional del Virreinato** (National Museum of the Viceroyalty; open Tues–Sun). Exhibits include paintings depicting scenes from the life of San Ignacio Loyola, founder of the Jesuit order, and a varied collection of ornaments, jewelry and other objets d'art from the Colonial period.

Space-fiction author Erich von Däniken claims the Atlantes are carrying laser-beam throwers, brought from another planet.

Tula and the Toltecs

The ancient city of **Tula ②** (open daily; entrance fee), capital of the Toltecs, is situated about 50 km (31 miles) north of Tepotztlán. The city played a major role in Mesoamerican history and provides an important link in the chain of civilizations that dominated the central highlands. It was founded at the beginning of the 10th century, after Teotihuacán had been destroyed and before the rise of Tenochtitlán. Topiltzin, the city's legendary founder, was expelled by a warrior faction which was to dominate the culture and indeed the art of Tula, until the site was destroyed over 300 years later.

The main pyramid here is the **Tlahuizcalpantecuhtli**, Temple of the Morning Star, on top of which stand, 4.6 meters (15 ft) tall, the famous **Atlantes**. These basalt telamones, which would once have supported the wooden roof of a temple, are considered Tula's most important contribution to Mexican art. They represent Quetzalcóatl as the morning star, the planet Venus. He is armed with javelins and dressed in warrior garb, wearing a pectoral in the form of a

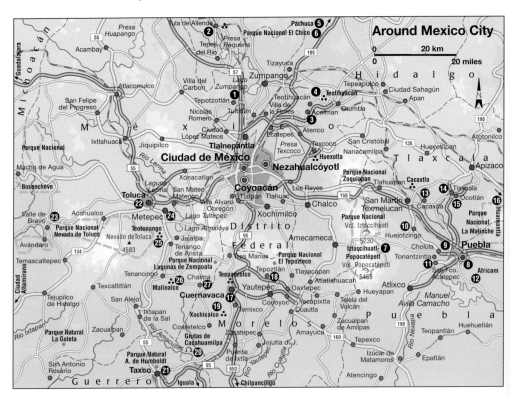

butterfly. On his back he carries a round shield in the form of the setting sun and in the center of the shield is a human face. The box-like headdresses are decorated with vertical feathers.

Of the other structures in Tula that have survived the centuries, perhaps the most interesting is the **Coatepantli**, or Wall of Serpents, raised along the north side of the pyramid; 40 meters (130 ft) long and over 2 meters (6.5 ft) high, the reliefs show a series of snakes devouring human bodies. Nearby, in front of the **Palacio Quemado** (Burnt Palace), is the chacmool, the reclining figure of a priest; on his chest sits a receptacle into which offerings to the gods were placed.

Place of the gods

Head out of Mexico City along Insurgentes Norte and Highway 132 to reach Acolman and the ancient city of Teotihuacán, about 50 km (31 miles) northeast of the capital. A few minutes before the Teotihuacán turn-off, keep your eyes peeled on the left for the fortress-like **San Agustín Acolman** ❸ (open Tues–Sun; entrance fee), an imposing 16th-century church and monastery with a fine plateresque façade and Gothic interior. There is a large open chapel, built to accommodate the crowds of indian converts, and original frescoes adorn the cloisters. In the center is a remarkable mission cross, carved by an anonymous indian sculptor who interpreted the symbols of Christ's Passion.

Teotihuacán ❹ (open daily; entrance fee), the City of Quetzalcóatl, "the place where men became gods," is a major archeological center and one of the best preserved in the country. It is not as exotic as the more remote Mayan cities, which are lost in tropical green, for its beauty is subdued, even sober.

Map on page 178

TIP

Buses go to Acolman from the Metro Indios Verdes; the pyramid bus does not stop here. You can take a local bus or a taxi from here to Teotihuacán.

BELOW: the Avenue of the Dead and the Pyramid of the Moon, Teotihuacán.

TIP

Be prepared for a lot of walking when visiting the pyramids. Take something to eat, a hat, and plenty of bottled water; the sun can be fierce and there's not much shade. Don't be caught out by afternoon thunderstorms in the summer months.

BELOW:
feather-collared serpents' heads on the Templo de Quetzalcóatl.

Beginning as an agricultural settlement several hundred years before the Christian era, Teotihuacán became one of the biggest cities in the world with a population of around 200,000. At its zenith the ancient city, set in a rather bare not too fertile valley, covered an area of 20 sq. km (8 sq. miles), more extensive even than its contemporary, Imperial Rome.

Around AD 600 the great city began to decline and was virtually abandoned soon after. The exact reasons for the collapse are unknown, but shockwaves were felt throughout ancient Mexico. When the Aztecs arrived in the 14th century Teotihuacán had long been deserted.

Temple tour

The bus (which takes about an hour from the Terminal del Norte in Mexico City) drops you at Gate 1, where you pay the admission charge and a fee for any cameras you are seen to be carrying. Walk up past the multitudinous stalls selling clothing and souvenirs to the **museum** which contains a scale model of the site, explanatory maps and diagrams, and some reproductions of items found here (the originals are in the Museum of Anthropology in Mexico City). Upstairs is a small café and an exorbitantly expensive restaurant. There are other restaurants in the area but virtually none of them can be reached without a car. The site itself is huge, so it becomes crowded only in a relative sense. In fact, it sometimes feels as if there are as many hawkers selling things as there are visitors.

The entrance emerges at the south end of the of the **Avenida de los Muertos** (Avenue of the Dead), the main axis, which stretches 3 km (2 miles) north, past the Pyramid of the Sun to the Pyramid of the Moon. Near the entrance, in a sunken square known as the **Ciudadela** (Citadel), is the **Templo de Quetzal-**

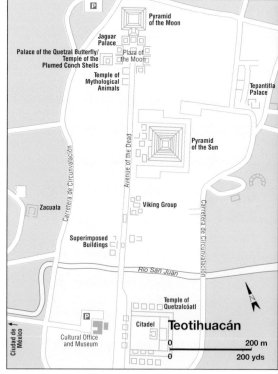

Teotihuacán

cóatl. Noted for its sculpted façade, the tiered temple is decorated in relief with alternating motifs of the serpent deity emerging from a collar of plumes, and the typical goggle eyes of the rain god Tlaloc. The temple was discovered, hidden beneath a later structure, during excavations at the beginning of the century.

Just over halfway along the avenue, stands the gigantic **Pirámide del Sol** (Pyramid of the Sun), Teotihuacán's main landmark. Built around AD 100, the entire structure, with a base measuring almost 225 meters (738 ft) square would once have been covered in stucco and brightly painted. For an impressive overview of the city, a steep 248-step climb will take you up the 64 meters (210 ft) to the top, where a temple once stood. Behind the pyramid, the **Palacio de Tepantitla** contains the remains of the famous *Paradise of Tlaloc* mural (reproduced in the Museum of Anthropology in Mexico City).

The **Pirámide de la Luna** (Pyramid of the Moon) though smaller than the Sun pyramid is built on higher ground and so their tops stand at the same level. It is also easier to climb. Overlooking a plaza at the northern end of the avenue, the Moon pyramid is surrounded by a dozen small temples. Nearby, in the **Palacio del Quetzalpapalotl** (Palace of the Quetzal Butterfly) there are well-preserved murals and highly symbolized bas-reliefs of creatures that are part bird and part butterfly.

Also noteworthy is the **Palacio de los Jaguares** (Palace of the Jaguars), named after its feline mural painting, and the **Templo de las Conchas Emplumadas** (Temple of the Plumed Conch Shells) which still bears traces of the red, green, yellow and white symbols representing birds, maize and water.

You could spend a whole day wandering around the complex, but you'll probably find a couple of hours is enough. Although most guidebooks advise you to

Map on page 178

The world's third largest pyramid, the Pyramid of the Sun at Teotihuacán, is less than half the height of the great Pyramid of Cheops in Egypt, although their base sizes are the same.

BELOW: well-preserved fresco in the Palacio de los Jaguares.

arrive early to avoid the crowds, the pyramids actually look their most impressive at sunset. The grounds close at 6pm.

Don't fail to explore the surrounding countryside. Nearby is Otumba, where the Aztecs were defeated by Hernán Cortés in one of the decisive battles of the Spanish Conquest. Farther to the northeast is Ciudad Sahagún, one of Mexico's industrial experiments.

When the Aztecs came to Teotihuacán in the 14th century AD, it had been abandoned for about 700 years.

The region is typical of central Mexico; desert plains and hills, in which the main vegetation is the maguey cactus plant from which *pulque*, a national beverage, is extracted. Peculiar-tasting, frothy, beerish and loaded with vitamins, pulque is said to be very nourishing (the best excuse in the world for a favorite drink). During colonial times and in the 19th century, big pulque plantations were developed. The manor houses of such plantations were magnificent. Some survive – such as Xala, near Ciudad Sahagún, which has been transformed into a hotel and preserves something of its earlier grandeur.

Hidalgo

Tucked-away Hidalgo is one of Mexico's least visited yet most beautiful states. For a weekend escape, the state capital **Pachuca ❺**, 90 km (56 miles) northeast of Mexico City, makes a good base. The city's history is closely linked to the local silver mines which have been run by Spanish, English, Mexican and US firms since the 16th century. A few blocks southeast of the Plaza de la Independencia, the 16th-century Ex Convento de San Francisco now houses the **Hidalgo Cultural Center** (open Tues–Sun; entrance free). Inside, the Museo Nacional de Fotografía (National Photography Museum) has pictures from the famous Casasola Archives and a large collection by controversial 20th-century

BELOW:
open for business.

photographer, Tina Modotti. The Regional Museum is in the same complex, while next door is the church of **La Asunción**. Lying on an altar inside the church is the mummified body of Santa Columba, who was martyred in France in the 3rd century.

Just over 20 km (12 miles) north of Pachuca, the pine forests, lakes and spectacular rock formations in the **Parque Nacional El Chico ❻** provide great hiking terrain. Nearby, is the picturesque old mining town of **Mineral El Chico**.

Monday is market day in the town of **Ixmiquilpan**, 75 km (47 miles) northwest of Pachuca along Highway 85. This is the best day to see the beautiful textiles and fine inlaid wooden objects brought to market by the local Otomi indians. On the way, stop off at Actopan to see the 16th-century fortified monastery and, further on, the waterfalls, hot springs and caves of the **Barranca de Tolatongo** (Tolatongo Canyon).

East of Mexico City

The road to Puebla and the east coast is a continuation of the great avenue called **Calzada Ignacio Zaragoza**, the backbone of proletarian Mexico City. It begins near the airport and runs by the sprawling dormitory suburb of **Ciudad Netzahualcóyotl**, which has a working-class population of more than 2 million, and is sometimes called "Mexico's third largest city."

Once the calzada leaves the urban area behind, the road to Puebla enters the beautiful pine-forested mountains near the **Parque Nacional Iztaccíhuatl-Popocatépetl ❼**. The volcanoes loom very close and the climate becomes cooler. The route to these magnificent snow-capped wonders is via the **Amecameca** road through a pleasantly pastoral land.

Map
on page
178

*Soccer was introduced into Mexico in the 19th century by miners from Cornwall in England. These immigrant workers were also responsible for the local meat-pie specialty: Cornish pasties (*pastes*).*

BELOW: Jaguar Warrior, from mural in Cacaxtla, near Tlaxcala.

THE VOLCANOES

Built in an area of frequent earthquakes, Mexico City is surrounded by volcanic peaks such as the majestic Popocatépetl (5,452 meters/17,886 ft) and Iztaccíhuatl, (5,286 meters/17,342 ft), affectionately known as Popo and Izta. In the past, the enormous snow-capped volcanoes were a backdrop to the Mexican capital, some 60km (40 miles) away. Nowadays it's a talking point if the pair are not obscured by smog; however, they still make an impressive sight for anyone traveling west of Mexico City towards Puebla or the Gulf coast. According to the legend, Popocatépetl (Náhuatl for "smoking mountain") was a warrior in love with Iztaccíhuatl ("white lady"), the beautiful Aztec princess. Fearing her lover had been killed in battle, Iztaccíhuatl died of grief, and when Popo returned alive, he laid her body on the hill where he stands, the eternal sentinel, beside her. Recent volcanic activity have led the Mexican authorities to close access to Popocatépetl. The road is open as far as the Paso de Cortés, where the conquistadores crossed into Tenochtitlán from Veracruz in 1519. Izta no longer even has a crater and is a challenging alternative, although mainly for experienced climbers, as is Mexico's highest mountain, the Pico de Orizaba (5,760 meters/18,900 ft), which is also known as Citlaltépetl.

Between 11am and 12pm you can climb one of the cathedral belltowers for a superb view of the city and nearby volcanoes. They only let you up, however, if you're accompanied.

Puebla: City of the Angels

After crossing the mountains, the road descends into the ample valley of **Puebla ❽**, a city founded during colonial times and capital of the state with the same name. In spite of being a growing industrial center, famous for its enormous Volkswagon car plant, Puebla has managed to preserve part of its old character and possesses some of the most important colonial works of art in Mexico.

One such gem is the elegant and majestic **Cathedral Ⓐ**, the second largest in the country, with the highest belltowers, and regarded by some as the finest in Mexico. It was consecrated in 1649 and combines early Baroque with the most refined architectural style of the Spanish Renaissance, the Herreriano (named after Juan de Herrera, the architect of the Escorial, in Spain,). The exterior is severe and somber while inside, the fine main altar, the work of the famous neoclassical artist, Manuel Tolsá, is like a miniature Roman temple. The angel statues all round the atrium are symbols of the town which is, in fact, called Puebla de los Angeles.

The tourist office is beside the cathedral on Calle 5 Oriente, almost next door to the **Casa de la Cultura**. Founded as a seminary in 1646, the cultural center now has a sculpture garden, a tiny coffee shop, and an open-air theater. Up the stone stairs is the splendid **Biblioteca Palafoxiana ❸**, the oldest library in America, with its 50,000 volumes on ornately carved wooden shelves.

Two blocks west, the **Museo Bello ❻** (open Tues–Sun; entrance fee) contains a fascinating and eclectic collection of decorative art amassed by a local industrialist in the 19th century. Puebla's best museum, the untypically high-tech **Museo Amparo ❹** (open Wed–Mon; free on Tues) was inaugurated in 1991 in an 18th-

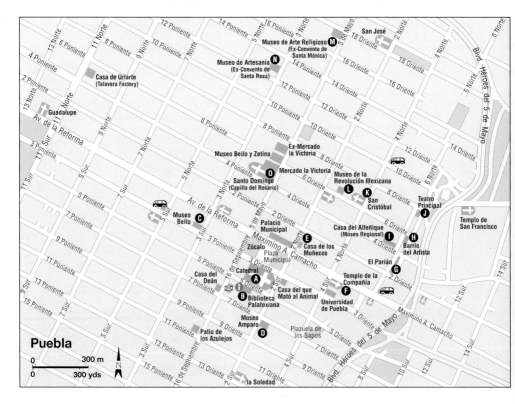

Puebla

century hospital building. There are interactive videos providing information on the extensive and beautifully displayed collection of pre-Hispanic artefacts. The second section of the museum houses art and furniture from the Colonial period.

The 18th-century **Casa de los Muñecos** **E** (House of Puppets) which contains the University Museum (open Tues–Sun; entrance fee) has probably the most amusing tiled façade in Puebla; the characters portrayed are allegedly caricatures of the original owner's enemies.

One block away, the distinctive **Templo de la Compañía** **F**, with its elaborate façade, is said to be the last resting place of the famous **China Poblana**, a 17th-century Asian princess whose statue surmounts a fountain at the east side of town. Her costume of frilly blouse atop embroidered and sequined skirt has become a characteristic cliché of Mexican peasant garb. Adjoining the church, bordering a pleasant, cobbled alley, is the 16th-century **Puebla University** building which once served as a Jesuit college.

The stalls of Puebla's main tourist market, **El Parián** **G**, sell everything that is Mexican, from serapes to sombreros. However, if it's pictures you're after, cross over the road and wander through the open studios of the **Barrio del Artista** **H**.

Much of the architecture of Puebla might be regarded as a Mexican version of Spanish Baroque, interpreted through a great profusion of tiles and plaster decoration. The sugar-icing stucco of the **Casa del Alfeñique** **I** is perhaps the best example. Now the **Regional Museum** (open Tues–Sun; entrance fee), it contains good examples of ceramics produced in the state, and memorabilia from the Cinco de Mayo (May 5) battle, in 1862. Just beyond the "artists' quarter" is the **Teatro Principal** **J** which was almost 150 years old – one of the old-

Maps
Area 178
City 184

The Fonda Santa Clara, almost directly opposite the Museo Bello, specializes in typical Puebla dishes. Try a chile en nogada: *green chili stuffed with meat, white walnut sauce and red pomegranate seeds – the colors of the Mexican flag.*

BELOW: beetling through the streets of Puebla

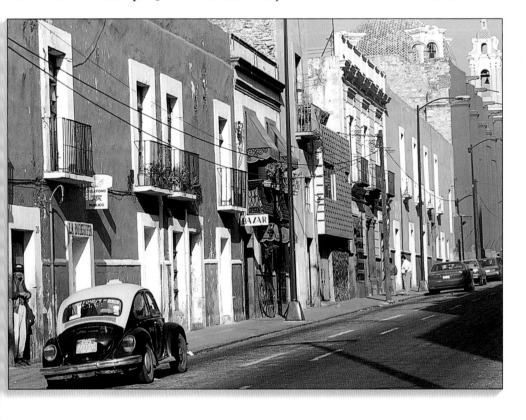

On May 5, 1862, a Mexican army, led by General Ignacio Zaragoza and including a battalion of barely armed indians, defeated a large French army. The victory boosted Mexican morale, but was unable to prevent French occupation a year later.

est in the Americas – when it suffered a disastrous fire in 1902, after which it had to be rebuilt.

Calle 6 Oriente is a fascinating street, renowned mainly for its numerous *dulcerías*, sweet shops with beautiful old-fashioned diplays of exquisite hand-made confections. There are *camotes* (sweet potatoes prepared with fruit and sugar), fudge-like *dulce de leche*, limes filled with sweet coconut, and *rompope*, a sort of eggnog, said to be a child's introduction to alcohol.

The church of **San Cristóbal ⓚ**, with its onyx windows and carved ceiling vault is also on this street. The first battle of the 1910 revolution was fought next door; the house used to belong to a family of liberal activists who opposed the dictatorship of Porfirio Díaz; now it houses the **Museo de la Revolución Mexicana ⓛ** (open Tues–Sun; entrance fee). Looking west up 6 Oriente you can see the cast-iron structure of the old **Mercado la Victoria**, recently trans-formed into a modern shopping mall. It was one of the last of the grand old markets, built by Porfirio Díaz who sought to transform Mexico into a carbon copy of France.

The people of Puebla have a reputation for being the most traditional and staunchest Catholics in all Mexico. Two ex-convents are well worth visit-ing. **Santa Mónica ⓜ** (open Tues–Sun; entrance fee), now a museum of reli-gious art, operated secretly during the years of clerical persecution after the 1857 Reform Laws; it was only discovered, or acknowledged, by the secular authorities in 1933. Seventeenth century **Santa Rosa ⓝ** (open Tues–Sun; entrance fee) has a mottled history, but is now a craft museum with a won-derful collection of the many crafts produced in the State of Puebla. Every inch of the beautiful vaulted kitchen downstairs is covered with *azulejo* tiles;

BELOW: kitchen of former convent of Santa Rosa, Puebla.

Mexico's famous *mole* sauce is said to have been invented by the nuns in this very room.

The pride of Puebla's religious architecture is tucked away inside the 16th-century **Santo Domingo** church: the breathtaking **Capilla del Rosario ❶**, to the left of the main altar, is a dazzling mass of baroque gilt decoration.

Maps
Area 178
City 184

City of churches

Cholula **❾** has become a suburb of Puebla, although in pre-Hispanic times it was a major center of religious cult. During the Conquest, Cortés, fearing an ambush at Cholula, set up an effective counter-blow which resulted in the killing of some 3,000 people. Then, after decimation by plague, Cholula, once a city of great importance, became an impoverished village.

Nowadays, Cholula is an attractive town, home to the **University of the Americas** campus, and famous for its many churches; according to tradition, the conquistadores vowed to build one for every pagan temple they found or, if you prefer the other version, one for each day of the year. The16th-century fortified **Convento de San Gabriel** is the most impressive; its massive atrium, which lines the east side of the zócalo, leads to three fine churches, including the **Capilla Real**, which was inspired by the great mosque of Córdoba, in Spain. Originally an open chapel for indian converts, the roof with its 49 little domes was added in the 18th century.

Most people come to Cholula to see what looks like an ordinary hill with a church on top. In fact, it is the **Gran Pirámide** (open daily; entrance fee), the biggest pyramid ever built in Mesoamerica. During the final phase of its construction, the entire pyramid was covered with a thick layer of adobe which

A shapely example of fine Talavera pottery.

BELOW: you name it, we bottle it.

TALAVERA POTTERY

Talavera pottery is everywhere in Puebla: there are tiles, bowls, vases, flowerpots, jugs and sculptures. The technique was introduced into Mexico in the 16th century by Dominican monks from Talavera de la Reyna, in Spain. The original pottery was cobalt blue and white, with strongly Moorish motifs, but the Mexican potters added their own touch and also received influences from China and Renaissance Italy. This led to the introduction of new designs and colors, particularly greens, yellows and oranges.

Using the original technique, it takes six months to produce one piece of authentic Talavera pottery, and it is fairly easy to distinguish the earthy mineral colours of the originals from the bolder, harsher hues of mass-produced copies (there is also a significant difference in price).

Some workshops in and around Puebla, such as the historic Taller Uriarte, give tours which explain the process from beginning to end. First the clay is left to stand for three months, it is then wedged underfoot until it is well kneaded. After another month, the piece of pottery is made and left to dry before it is fired, painted, glazed, and fired again.

became overgrown and prompted the Náhuatl title of Tlachihualtépetl, or "hand-made mountain."

A masked carnival

Huejotzingo , about 17 km (11 miles) northwest of Cholula, is a small town known mainly for its cider, woolen serapes and its masked carnival dance in February, which re-enacts a battle between French and Mexicans. Just off the main square is an impressive 16th-century **Franciscan monastery** (open Tues–Sun; entrance fee). Heavily fortified, with crenellated walls and a stern exterior, the monastery exhibits artefacts relating to the Spanish missions and the monastic way of life.

Santa María Tonantzintla ⓫, a village just south of Cholula on the old road to Oaxaca, has a remarkable folk-baroque church whose interior is entirely covered with colorful and vibrant carvings. The decor took 200 years to complete and is a splendid example of how indian artisans adopted Spanish iconography. The spectacular tiled façade of the church of **San Francisco Acatepec**, a couple of miles further south, is also well worth seeing, although it was destroyed by fire in 1941 and had to be rebuilt.

For those who love zoos, **Africam** ⓬, 16 km southeast of Puebla on the Valsequillo road, is Mexico's first safari park where you can drive among the 250 bird and animal species.

In the neighboring state of Tlaxcala, and 18 km (11 miles) southwest of the state capital, is **Cacaxtla** ⓭ (open daily; entrance fee), "the place where the rain dies in the earth." Once the center of a people from the Gulf coast called the Olmeca-Xicalanca, this archeological site dates from the 7th century. In 1974,

TIP

You can walk inside the pyramid in Cholula along warren-like – though well-lit – tunnels. But first, have a look at the large cut-away model in the museum opposite the entrance.

BELOW: the Cholula pyramid towers in the background behind the domes of the Capilla Real.

Map
on page
178

archeologists discovered here some of the best-preserved murals in Mexico, notably the 22-meter long *Mural de la Batalla*, which colorfully depicts a violent battle between jaguar and eagle warriors.

The town of **Tlaxcala** ⓮, capital of Mexico's smallest state, is one of the country's hidden-away Colonial treasures. The town center has been beautifully restored and a traffic control scheme means you can wander through the streets or sit at outdoor cafés on the plazas without the fumes and noise of passing buses – a rare treat in Mexican cities these days.

Although they lived only 115 km (70 miles) from the Aztec capital, the Tlaxcalans had always managed, through constant battles, to maintain their independence. When Hernán Cortés arrived in 1519, they became his most crucial allies in the conquest of Tenochtitlán. A mural painted by local artist Desiderio Hernández Xochitiotzin, which hangs in the **Palacio de Gobierno**, tells the story.

Up the hill, with a beautiful view over the city and into the bullring, the **Convento de San Francisco**, has a Moorish-style wooden ceiling and the font used to baptise the four Tlaxcalan indian chiefs. Next door, in the **Museo Regional**, you can see a fascinating collection of local pre-Hispanic pieces, including a stone statue of Camaxtli, the god of war and hunting.

Also worthwhile is the **Museo de Artes y Tradiciones Populares** (open Tues–Sun; entrance fee), a so-called living museum where local craftsmen and women demonstrate the intricate work involved in producing some of Tlaxcala's wonderful handicrafts.

Perched on a hill above the town, in the village of Ocotlán, is a twin-towered church which seems as lightly spun as sugar candy. This is the 18th-century **Basílica de Ocotlán**, another of Mexico's most ornate churrigueresque churches (*see page 177*). The explosion of baroque giltwork inside is quite dazzling and not to be missed.

Other historical landmarks in this little state are the pulque haciendas that prospered until the Revolution; among the best are San Bartolomé del Monte, San Cristóbal Zacacalo and San Blas. The town of **Huamantla** is famed for its celebration, in August, of the feast of the Assumption and the following *huamantlada*, when bulls run through the streets Pamplona-style. Many of Mexico's fighting bulls are bred in nearby haciendas. The **Museo Nacional del Títere** on the main square houses an interesting collection of puppets.

When Mexico City's Insurgentes Sur joins the highway to **Cuernavaca** ⓱, it becomes one of the busiest thoroughfares in Mexico. After an initial climb, the road descends, 75 km (47 miles) later, to an altitude substantially lower than that of the capital. Cuernavaca is *the* weekend resort, where the *capitalinos* go for clean air, pleasant climate and relaxation. It has always attracted the capital's élite: Aztec emperors built temples here and Cortés built a palace; wealthy citizens, artists, retired Americans and even the fugitive Shah of Persia have also chosen to settle in this flower-filled "city of eternal spring." In spite of rapid growth over the last two decades and mounting pol-

Although Tlaxcala is Mexico's tiniest state, covering only 2 percent of its territory, it is comparable in size with Belgium, Switzerland, Holland or Israel.

BELOW: the richly decorated San Francisco Acatepec.

lution and traffic congestion, a weekend here still comes as a welcome escape from the cacophony of the metropolis.

In the center of town the main square, or **Plaza de Armas**, is flanked on the east side by the **Palacio de Cortés** (open Tues–Sun; entrance fee), which the Conqueror built on the ruins of a pre-Hispanic temple. The palace now houses the **Museo Cuauhnáhuac** (the indian name for Cuernavaca) which has a substantial collection of colonial art. There is also a series of murals by Diego Rivera (*see pages 108–11*) depicting almost 400 years of Mexican history (from the Conquest to the 1910 Revolution). For decades, long before the *Where's Wally?* concept caught on, the murals have been challenging Mexican children to identify the famous heroes and villains of their national saga.

Kiosk by Eiffel

The adjacent **Jardín Juárez**, at the northwest corner of the main square, has a central kiosk, designed by Gustav Eiffel, of tower fame, where you can buy fresh fruit juice or *licuados* (milk shakes) to sip in the shade of the raucous flame trees.

Two blocks west up Calle Hidalgo, the imposing 16th-century fortified **cathedral** compound stands in a high-walled garden. Some curiously Oriental frescoes were discovered here during renovation work in 1959. They seem to depict the mass crucifixion of missionaries in Japan, and are believed to have been painted in the 17th century by a Japanese convert to Christianity. The Sunday mass (11am) with mariachi musicians is famous all over Mexico.

Also within the compound is the **Museo Casa Robert Brady** (open Thurs–Sat; admission fee). Brady, a wealthy American artist and collector, lived

On 14 August, known as "the night when nobody sleeps", the people of Huamantla create beautiful carpets of flowers and colored sawdust along 12 km (7 miles) of streets.

BELOW: detail from Rivera mural in the Palacio de Cortés, Cuernavaca.

and worked in Mexico until his death in 1986. The museum exhibits his extraordinary collection of art, antiques and crafts from Mexico and other parts of the world. Nearby, in the **Palacio Municipal** (open Mon–Fri; entrance free), a colorful series of paintings displayed around the courtyard gives a romantic vision of indian life in pre-Colonial times.

Because so much of Cuernavaca's beauty lies behind the high walls of private gardens, the town can be disappointing for the visitor. However, the nicest of all its gardens, the **Jardín Borda** (open Tues–Sun; entrance fee), which once surrounded the 18th-century home of Taxco's richest silver magnate, happens to be public. It was restored a few years ago and is exceptionally pleasant with fountains, terraces, artificial lake and outdoor theater. The museum, in one wing of the house, has exhibits from the 19th century, when the house was the summer residence of Emperor Maximilian and his wife Charlotte.

Apart from the **market** (across the ravine to the east) and the not especially impressive **Teopanzolco Pyramid** (Tues–Sun; entrance fee), in a park even further east (you'll need to take a bus or taxi), that's about it for Cuernavaca. It does have some excellent hotels, though; the most famous is possibly **Las Mañanitas**. If you've ever dreamed of staying in a beautiful, flower-filled garden where fountains tinkle and peacocks strut; of sleeping in a room filled with period furniture and eating first-rate food, now is the time to indulge.

Cuernavaca is the capital of the state of **Morelos**, the sugar-bowl of Mexico. The conquistadores brought sugar cane here, along with black slaves who worked in appalling conditions and planted not only sugar, but also the seed for the agrarian movement in Morelos. The revolutionary leader Emiliano Zapata was from nearby **Cuautla**, and the local villages still display his portrait: the

Map on page 178

Spiritual support, statue in colonial church niche.

BELOW: girls' talk.

huge bristling mustache, the *charro* attire, the sombrero, and the deep, sad look in his eyes.

Tepoztlán  – not to be confused with Tepotzotlán (*see page 177*) – is an attractive town nestling at the foot of the Tepozteco hill, 26 km (16 miles) northeast of Cuernavaca. The center of town is dominated by a massive fortified **Dominican monastery** and church which date from the 16th century. Behind the church, a small **archeological museum** (open Tues–Sun; entrance fee) has a remarkably good collection of pieces from this and other parts of Mexico. It is a strenuous one-hour hike up to the **Tepozteco Pyramid** (open daily; entrance fee), a pre-Hispanic temple dedicated to Tepoztécatl, Aztec god of fertility and pulque (an alcoholic drink made from fermented juice of the maguey plant); the climb is further rewarded with the awe-inspiring view of the Tepoztlán valley. Easily reached from Mexico City, the Sunday craft market in Tepoztlán draws the crowds, as does the Tepoztán pulque festival in September.

Heading south from Cuernavaca on the old road to Taxco, a short detour leads to the spectacular yet little-visited archeological site of **Xochicalco** ⓳ (open daily; entrance fee), meaning "place of the house of flowers" in Náhuatl. This important commercial and ceremonial center flourished between the 7th and the 10th centuries, bridging the gap between the decline of Teotihuacán and the rise of the Toltec civilization in Tula. Xochicalco is sometimes called the crossroads of Ancient Mexico, and is considered one of the most significant sites of the central region. Although the whole site covers over 25 hectares (62 acres), much of it has yet to be excavated. The most striking monument to see is the **Pyramid of the Plumed Serpent**, with its superb bas-reliefs, situated at the very summit of the terraced platforms.

Oscar Lewis based his study of Life in a Mexican Village *on* Tepoztlán, and part *of the film* Butch Cassidy and the Sundance Kid *was set near here.*

BELOW: the cobble-stoned back streets of Taxco.

Map on page 178

If you like caves, the **Grutas de Cacahuamilpa** ❷⓿ (open daily; entrance fee) are enormous, intriguing and frightening for the claustrophobic; several kilometers of well-lit paths pass vast chambers with stalagmites, stalactites and extraordinary rock formations.

Silver town

Taxco ❷❶, Mexico's famous silver-working town, is some 72 km (45 miles) south of Cuernavaca and about a third of the way between Mexico City and Acapulco. It is a truly picturesque town, one of the few in Mexico to have been declared a national monument: red-roofed whitewashed houses, pretty plazas, cascading bougainvillea and narrow, cobblestone streets twisting up and down the steep hills. All will eventually lead you to the zócalo (main square), which is overlooked by the pink stone colonial church of **Santa Prisca**. Completed in 1758, and dominated by twin, 40-meter (130-ft) baroque towers, its elaborate churrigueresque façade and tiled dome are more than matched by the dazzling gilded interior. Take special notice of the fine German organ, the delicately carved wooden pulpit and the paintings by the well-known 18th-century artist, Miguel Cabrera. This church was paid for by José de la Borda, the French silver miner who became one of the richest men in Mexico.

To the right as you leave the church, still in the plaza, a plaque marks the **Casa Borda**, where the town's rich patron once lived; through the adjoining arcade and downstairs is the **Museo de Plata** (Silver Museum) (open Tues–Sun; entrance fee), which contains a rich selection of work, including a chess set with pieces matching the indians against the conquistadores. It was William (Guillermo) Spratling, an architecture professor from New Orleans, who sparked off the jewelry boom when he opened the first silver workshop here in the early 1930s. Soon Spratling's apprentices began to go solo, and today there are over 300 hundred shops in Taxco, selling an enormous variety of silverwork, including some of the finest in the world.

The **Museo de Taxco Guillermo Spratling** (open Tues–Sat; entrance fee), Spratling's home until his death in a car accident in 1967, houses his private collection of pre-Hispanic art and antiquities. There is also a small section devoted to local history. Down a flight of narrow steps behind the cathedral is the **Mercado de las Artesanías**, where scores of market stalls sell all kinds of crafts.

The **Casa Humboldt**, on Juan Ruiz de Alarcón, is one of Taxco's oldest colonial houses. It was so-named after the noted German explorer-scientist Baron Alexander von Humboldt (1769–1859) stayed a night there in 1803, during his travels in Central and South America. Convent, hospital and later a guesthouse, this beautiful Moorish-style house now contains the **Museo de Arte Virreinal** (Museum of Colonial Art; open Tues–Sat; entrance fee) with a miscellaneous collection of religious artefacts and other items.

During Easter, when people flock to Taxco to see the processions, penitents and a re-enactment of

Although some silverware prices are similar to those in Mexico City, excellent bargains can be found and many people come to Taxco for that purpose alone. The silver is usually 925 sterling, with copper alloy. However, a word of warning: alpaca, or nickel silver, contains no silver at all.

BELOW: silver souvenirs fill Taxco's gift shops.

Christ's last hours, it is a good idea to have confirmed hotel reservations as rooms will be extremely hard to come by. From Taxco, you can either continue south to the coast and the famous resort of Acapulco, or return to Cuernavaca and Mexico City.

West to Toluca

Several roads connect Mexico City with **Toluca** , capital of the state of Mexico and an hour's bus journey due west of the capital. A direct road leaves from Mexico City's Chapultepec Park via Avenida Constituyentes. The road climbs through surprising countryside with tall pine forests reminiscent of Germany. But typical Mexican landscapes soon reassert themselves in dry, golden fields, cacti and adobe houses.

Toluca's proximity to the capital has influenced its rapid industrial growth and it has long been a busy commercial center. Its Friday **open-air market** (on the ourskirts of town, near the bus station), reputedly the largest in Mexico, draws huge crowds.

The center of Toluca is typically provincial with colonial churches, 19th-century buildings, a large **zócalo** (Plaza de los Mártires) and 120 *portales* (arcades): the bustling hub of town. Toluca's food and drink specialties are all sold here. Keep your eyes open for the locally-made fruit jam, excellent candy, spicy *chorizos*, (Spanish chili sausage) and the famous *moscos* which come in bottles with long spouts and, like all street liquor, are *muy traidores* (very treacherous).

One block north of the zócalo, in the old market building on Plaza Garibay, is the **Cosmovitral** (Tues–Sun; entrance fee), an attractive botanical garden

TIP

Although some stalls do sell local handicrafts – mainly woven goods and pottery – you may find the state-run Casart in Paseo Tollocán 700 offers a wider range.

BELOW: detail from a Tree of Life, ceramic sculpture.

Map on page 178

surrounded by the most brilliantly colored stained-glass panels. The best examples of traditional arts and crafts of the region are to be found in the **Museo de Culturas Populares** (Tues–Sun; entrance fee), which is one of three museums in the Centro Cultural Mexiquense, 8 km (5 miles) west of the city center.

Out of Toluca you have several options. One is to head west over a newly constructed road to **Valle de Bravo** ㉓, a picturesque mountain settlement 80 km (50 miles) from Toluca. Wealthy weekend visitors from the capital, including a fairly large British community, enjoy the idyllic surroundings of thatched houses with white walls and stone chimneys overlooking the lake and wooded mountain scenery. Watersport enthusiasts are well catered for, while other popular activities in the area include riding, golf and hiking.

Another possibility is to head south from Toluca through **Metepec** ㉔, famed for its colorful ceramic trees of life, which offer an indian interpretation of the story of Adam and Eve. Further south, above the town of Tenango del Valle, are the hilltop ruins of **Teotenango** ㉕ (open Tues–Sun; entrance fee) a fortified Matlazinca ceremonial center thought to date from the 7th century.

Further south on the main road (Mexico 55) is the spa resort of **Ixtapan de la Sal**, semi-tropical and flowery, whose mineral waters are said to have rejuvinating and curative properties. On the outskirts of town is the **Parque de los Trece Lagos** (open daily; entrance fee and charges for separate activities). Here you can either head for the slides and wave machines, swim in the Olympic-sized pool or relax in Roman-style baths with massage, mud and beauty treatments. The park is a family attraction, with a monorail running around the grounds and pleasant grassy picnicking areas. Alternatively there is a municipal spa in the town itself (daily; entrance fee). From Ixtapan, the road continues south to the Cacahuamilpa caverns and the silver town of Taxco.

Aztec and Christian shrines

Not too far from Ixtapan de la Sal is the site of **Malinalco** ㉖ (open Tues–Sun; entrance fee) built by the Matlazinca culture and subsequently absorbed into the Aztec empire. The main temple, the **Cuauhcalli** (House of the Eagle Warriors), is carved into the rock face of the mountain. This was the site of sacred initiation ceremonies of young Aztec nobles into the warrior elite. The entrance is over the tongue and through the giant mouth of a fanged serpent. Inside, there is a circular chamber with an eagle marking the center of the floor. Images of sacred animals, such as eagles, serpents and jaguars abound throughout this site, which must have been of great religious significance to the Aztecs. The nearby town of Malinalco has become a fashionable weekend getaway for wealthy Mexicans; there is a new golf club and some worthwhile shops and a restaurant.

Several times a year, thousands of pilgrims swarm to the village of **Chalma** ㉗, 12 km (7 miles) further east, to worship the "Santo Señor de Chalma," an image of Christ which "miraculously" appeared in 1533, soon after the arrival of the missionaries. From here, you can return directly by bus to Mexico City, and back to the present. ❏

BELOW: sailing at Valle de Bravo.

THE NORTH

*South of the border is not just a buffer zone, this often
bypassed region has natural and cultural gems all of its own*

The fact that most of northern Mexico is not tourist country, is one of its main attractions. This rugged, lonely and often inhospitable land is a region of desert landscapes with huge and varied cacti, lofty mountains and high plateaus. It is Mexico's Wild West, renowned for its vast cattle ranches – indeed many westerns have been filmed around the Durango area – and it also contains some of Mexico's most fertile agricultural land.

The Sierra Madre Oriental and the Sierra Madre Occidental run parallel to the east and west coasts; to the east is the Gulf of Mexico, to the west the Gulf of California and the Pacific Ocean. Seismic activity along the notorious San Andrés fault caused the 40,000 sq. km (15,440 sq. miles) of Baja California to peel away from the mainland some 20 million years ago.

For an increasing number of visitors, Baja California is becoming a destination in its own right. Away from brassy Tijuana (which receives more US visitors per year than any other foreign city in the world), the Baja Peninsula is a combination of deserts, pine-forested mountains, idyllic hidden-away beaches and glitzy new tourist developments. Hundreds of miles of coastline are accessible only by sea, and four-wheel-drive vehicles are the only way to negotiate many of the rough inland trails. Much of Baja's fame rests upon its reputation as a sports fishing paradise. Nowadays, however, more and more visitors come to the beaches and to witness the massive Californian gray whales cavorting in their breeding waters at Scammon's Lagoon.

The far north of mainland Mexico – the vast and monotonous Sonora Desert, the imposing Sierra Madre, or the sprawling industrialized cities – is usually visited in transit; en route to somewhere else. But the interminable, barren landscape also conceals some outstanding surprises: the pre-Hispanic Paquimé ruins at Casas Grandes or – the highlight of any trip to northern Mexico – the world's most spectacular train-journey, from Chihuahua to Los Mochis, through the breathtaking scenery of the Barranca del Cobre.

South of the Tropic of Cancer the country becomes gentler, the climate less extreme and, for many visitors, the Pacific resort of Mazatlán or the beaches at San Blas mark the end of the journey. ❑

PRECEDING PAGES: the crumbled landscape of Bahía de los Angeles, Baja California.
LEFT: taking the long way up.

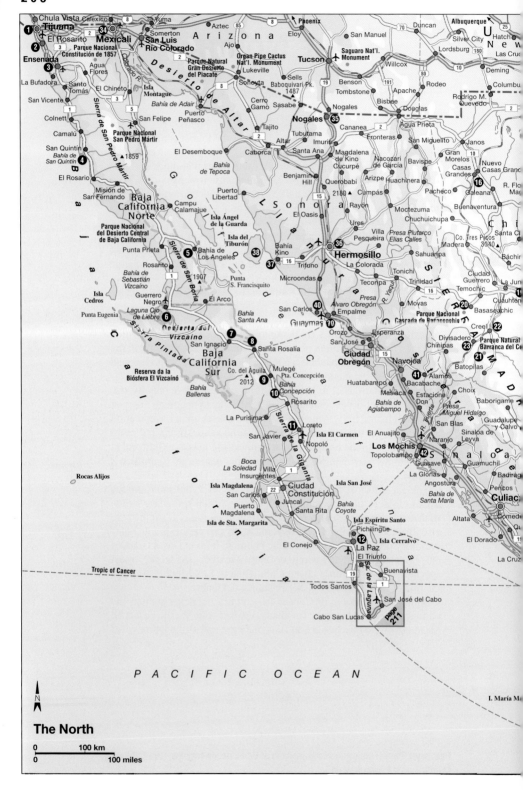

The North

N

0   100 km
0   100 miles

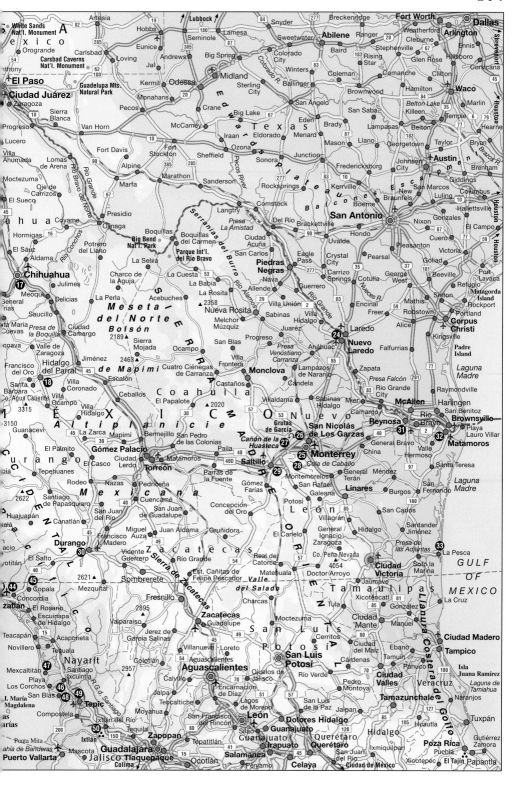

BAJA CALIFORNIA

Mountains, deserts and thousands of kilometers
of coastline for exploring, snorkeling, whale-watching, diving,
and some of the best deep-sea fishing in the world

Map
on pages
200–1

México City

Highway 1, the 1,690-km (1,050-mile) road that spans the peninsula from Tijuana to Los Cabos, didn't even exist until 1973 and although there are half a dozen shorter subsidiary routes, hundreds of kilometers of Baja's coastline and almost all the interior can be comfortably reached only by 4-WD vehicles. While some people deplore this inaccessibility, the majority of Baja fans rejoice in their knowledge of a land that – though a very close neighbor to California and its teeming millions – remains largely unexplored.

The peninsula was opened, Christianized and depopulated by the Spaniards; of the 40,000 indigenous inhabitants of Baja, there are less than 500 left. Those few survivors live in the north, whereas in the south all that is left of the indians' ancestors are the 400 or so sites of cave paintings which date back between 500 and 1,000 years.

Baja's population and its economy are both concentrated in the north. Bumper crops are produced in the irrigated lands around Mexicali: cotton, alfalfa, wheat, tomatoes and grapes. Workers in northern Baja get the highest minimum wage in the country.

There are three major crossings into Baja at the California border – **Tijuana**, **Tecate** and **Mexicali** – all connected by Highway 2.

LEFT: huge natural arch at Cabo San Lucas in southern Baja California.
BELOW: crafts for sale in El Rosario.

A shopper's paradise

Once a rip-roaring, shoot 'em up, anything-goes border town, **Tijuana ❶** is now one of Mexico's busiest and most prosperous cities. It also claims to be the most-visited border city in the world.

Because Tijuana is a duty-free zone, imported goods can be surprisingly cheap and there are bargains to be found in Russian caviar, Spanish leather, French perfume and even Cuban cigars. The city's main drag, Avenida Revolución, is lined with popular bars, nightclubs, craft stores and clothing and jewelry stores mixed among the serapes and sandals, but shoppers will find even more variety in the Plaza Río Tijuana near the river, the largest shopping center in northwestern Mexico. For a massive selection of footwear, head for the Plaza del Zapato, within the Plaza Fiesta.

The distinctive red **Tijuana Trolley** runs continuously between the city's main sightseeing attractions from 10am to 5pm every day, but it's a pleasant stroll back northwards along Via Poniente along the river. It will bring you to an older, funkier shopping center, **Pueblo Amigo**, which comes alive at night.

Things to see

Topped with a glass *piñata* that's visible from the pedestrian bridge, is **Mexitlán** (open daily; entrance

TIP

Don't forget to get your passport stamped at the border if you plan to travel south beyond the "free zone".

fee), an intriguing $23 million cultural theme park. One of its most important attractions is a series of enormous relief maps of the whole of Mexico, which contain 150 of its major landmarks reproduced to scale.

Behind the Plaza Revolución is the **Museo de Cera** (open Mon and Wed–Sat; entrance fee), the wax museum whose motley inhabitants range from Madonna, Gandhi and the Pope, to Mexican revolutionary heroes and a grey-haired lady known as **Tía Juana** ("Aunt Jane"), the legendary *cantina* owner after whom the city was named.

The ultra-modern **Centro Cultural** (Cultural Center), with its comprehensive survey of Mexican history, adjoins a building that resembles a giant golfball. This is the concert hall and 26 meter (85 ft) high **Omnimax Theater** where a film about Mexico's history and culture is shown at 2pm daily.

There are well-attended games of *jai alai* at the **Palacio Frontón**, on Avenida Revolución. Said to be the fastest game in the world, players use a curved wicker basket attached to the forearm to propel the ball at speeds of up to 290 kph (180 mph). Games are held Mon–Sat at 8pm.

The highway west of Tijuana leads to the **Plaza Monumental** bullring, 10 km (6 miles) away, beside the sea. Bullfights take place (either here or at the older bullring downtown) on Sundays during the season, which runs from May to September. There are inexpensive motels along the seashore road and stalls selling coconut drinks and seafood.

Heading South

The expensive *cuota* toll road to Ensenada includes stretches of fine ocean scenery (the *libre*, or free road, runs parallel most of the way). About 27 km

BELOW: "craft" market in Tijuana.

BORDER TOWNS

During the years of Prohibition in the United States the border towns of Mexico, and particularly Tijuana, became havens of sex, drink and gambling, attracting ordinary Americans and Hollywood stars in droves. The Sin-City reputation still lingers even though Tijuana has done a lot to clean up its act.

Today, most of Mexico's border towns are grimy, noisy industrial centers surrounded by shanty town sprawl that seem to absorb the worst of the cultures on both sides. Cross-cultural influence is indeed strong and Tex-Mex, no longer used merely to describe food or music, has rapidly become a way of life. The southern US relies on cheap Mexican labor, while North American investment thrives in the thousands of *maquiladoras* (assembly plants) along the south side of the border. Some 518,000 workers are employed in these plants, which use cheap Mexican labor and re-export the goods with duty levied only on the value added.

The US is an economic magnet, notoriously for the thousands of undocumented *mojados* (wetbacks) and the influential drug cartels. But millions more cross the border each year, in both directions; over 35 million people a year cross the border into Tijuana alone.

Map
on pages
200–1

(17 miles) south of the border is **Rosarito ❷**, an over-commercialized beach town which gained celebrity after 1927, when the newly opened Rosarito Beach Hotel began to attract the movie crowd and other famous faces. Lobster is a favorite in the town's numerous restaurants and there is even a so-called "Lobster Village" – **Puerto Nuevo** – 10 km (6 miles) to the south, where this dish is widely available and uniformly overpriced.

Yellowtail capital of the world

As you enter the big city of **Ensenada ❸** (population 230,000), almost 113 km (70 miles) south of the border, turn right off Highway 1 and drive up Avenida Alemán into the Chapultepec Hills, a high-rent district which offers a magnificent view of the city set around Todos Santos Bay.

A busy port, Ensenada is a regular stop for cruise ships and the furthest south that the vast majority of tourists penetrate. It stages bike rides, regattas and, in November, a noted off-road race. A favorite haunt for fishermen, it tags itself "the yellowtail capital of the world," with surf fishing along the rocky shoreline and organized trips from the sport-fishing piers off Boulevard Lázaro Cárdenas. In winter, whale-watching trips are also popular.

Ensenada is the center of the area's wine industry, and there are winery tours every day except Monday at the **Bodegas de Santo Tomás** (Miramar 666). The main tourist shopping zone is along **Avenida López Mateos**, a few blocks from the bay, but prices are lower around Avenida Ruiz and Calle 11, where every other store or bar seems to bear the name Hussong. The original Hussong's *cantina*, with its sawdust floor, is a popular drinking place, and visitors from all over the world have been pinning samples of their currency to the walls for a century.

Robert Louis Stevenson penned part of his book Treasure Island *while in the port of Ensenada.*

BELOW: Rockodile Bar, San Felipe.

The national observatory was built here because Baja, along with the west coasts of Africa and Chile, has some of the clearest skies in the world.

BELOW: a gray whale surfaces at Laguna San Ignacio.

South of town take the turnoff to **La Bufadora**, where incoming waves are forced into narrow vents, causing great jets of sea water to spout over 18 meters (60 ft) into the air, spraying amused spectators. Incoming tides are best, and it is a good idea to consult the *Baja Sun* for the tide timetable.

The devil's peak

Back on Highway 1, at **San Telmo de Abajo**, just south of Colonet, a reasonably good road (in the dry season) heads east to the sprawling Meling Ranch. You can stay here in comfortable quarters, swim in the pool and ride horses into the mountainous **San Pedro Mártir** national park, with its beautiful oak and pine forests. The National Observatory is located near the highest peak, the **Picacho del Diablo** (3,090 meters/10,150 ft).

Productive agricultural land surrounds **San Quintín,** a small town strung out along the highway. To reach the best place for an overnight stop, turn right off the highway just south of the military camp at Lázaro Cárdenas and drive 5 km (3 miles) along the unpaved road to the **Old Mill**, a reminder that this area was once colonized by an English land company that went bankrupt; the names of the almost forgotten pioneers are recorded on a group of lonely graves by the shore. The wild peninsula along **Bahía de San Quintín** ❹ is a well-loved camping area for the cognoscenti whose favorite pastimes include fishing and digging for "chocolate-tipped" clams.

Boulders, cacti and boojum trees

South of San Quintín the road veers inland and you will begin to see the spidery *cirio* trees (*Idria columnaris*) which bear tiny yellow flowers and are some-

Map
on pages
200–1

times referred to as **boojum** after the mythical species described by Lewis Carroll in *The Hunting of the Snark*.

Gigantic boulders carpet the landscape here. Heading southeast, past **Cataviña** (an unexpected oasis with a Pemex station) the road climbs over the summit of the sierra, then drops into the arid bed of **Laguna Chapala**.

Near the south end of the boojum area, a paved side road branches east to **Bahía de Los Angeles ❺**, on the calm waters of the Gulf of California. Protected by the aptly-named **Isla Angel de la Guarda** (Guardian Angel Island), the fishing and shelling here are great; dolphins can often be seen in the bay, and the waters teem with fish; the tiny island of **Isla de la Raza** is a wildlife refuge. The town itself still has few facilities: a minuscule museum, a store and a couple of hotels and trailer parks, but the views are splendid and the setting idyllic.

As many as 80 species of edible plants manage to grow in the windswept wastes of the Vizcaíno Desert. Try the juicy pitahaya fruit, similar to the prickly pear, but dark red in color.

A sanctuary for whales

Back on the main road, going south, you reach the 28th parallel, where a looming metal sculpture marks the boundary between Baja California Norte and Baja California Sur. Acres of shallow saltwater ponds lie just beyond this border, at **Guerrero Negro**, the largest salt plant of its kind, producing one-third of the world's supply. The town has hotels, restaurants, stores and gas, although only from January to March is it of much interest to the many tourists who come to watch the whales in the **Laguna Ojo de Liebre ❻**. Scammon's Lagoon, as it is also known, is at the end of a dirt road several kilometers south of town, past the salt-evaporating ponds.

From Guerrero Negro, the highway cuts across the peninsula to the Sea of Cortés. A mandatory stop should be made at tiny **San Ignacio ❼**, whose plaza,

BELOW:
whale-boat guide
in Guerrero Negro.

WHALE WATCHING

For centuries, gray whales have travelled from Alaska's icy Bering Sea to mate and spawn in the warm, shallow waters off the coast of Baja California. It takes these gentle giants two or three months to complete the 9,500-km (5,900-mile) journey, the longest migration of any mammal. They arrive between December and January and stay until March, or sometime as late as June.

In 1857 the breeding ground was discovered by a rapacious whaling captain from Maine, Charles M. Scammon – hence Scammon's Lagoon. For the next hundred years the whales were hunted almost to extinction until, in 1972, the area became the world's first whale sanctuary, the Parque Natural de Ballena Gris. Nearby Guerrero Negro (Black Warrior) is named after a British whaling boat that was wrecked off the coast soon after.

Today's hunters come armed only with binoculars and cameras and the gray whale population has almost fully recovered. Early morning or late in the day are the best times for whale-watching, either from the shore (or observation tower by Scammon's Lagoon), or else from locally hired boats, which provide an even closer view of these magnificent, 15-meter (49-ft) long leviathans.

Abandoned trolley from the El Boleo copper mine.

lined with shady laurel trees, is dominated by the San Ignacio mission. Built by the Dominicans in 1786, with 1.2 meter (4 ft) thick walls and vaulted ceiling, it replaced an earlier (1728) Jesuit mission. The church, with its perfect symmetry and baroque façade, is a charming example of what is left of colonial architecture in Baja California. An oasis of almost 100,000 date palms, sustained by an underground spring which surfaces here, has become the basis of the town's economy.

The Sea of Cortés

After many dramatic curves, Highway 1 reaches the coast, 73 km (45 miles) beyond San Ignacio, at **Santa Rosalía ❽**. In 1887, a French company opened the El Boleo copper mine here. The company left in 1954, but the small wooden houses from the French era still give the town a curiously anomalous look; indeed author John Steinbeck called it the "least Mexican-style city" he had seen. Unexpectedly, the church behind the plaza was built by **Eiffel,** the French engineer responsible for the famous Parisien tower. This prefabricated metal structure won second prize at the 1889 Universal Exposition in Paris; it was later acquired by the El Boleo company, shipped over from France and assembled here.

From Santa Rosalía, an overnight ferry crosses the Gulf to **Guaymas** on the Sonora coast. Otherwise you can follow the Transpeninsular Highway down the dry Gulf coast to **Mulegé ❾**. Threatening US warships were frightened away from here by a locally orchestrated subterfuge during the Mexican-American war in 1847. In July and August the town is stiflingly hot, but usually the palm trees and plantings along the Santa Rosalía river make Mulegé a pleasant oasis. There's a wonderfully situated 1766 mission church on the outskirts

BELOW: view from the Old Mill Hotel, San Quintín.

of town, and a fortress-like museum – a jail until 1975 – up the hill. Snorkeling, diving and, of course, fishing are all popular activities, although some people just come to tour the ancient **cave paintings** in the sierra.

South of Mulegé the highway skirts the shore, offering tantalizing glimpses of delightful coves and bays which are only accessible with a four-wheel-drive vehicle. Framed to the east by a northward-pointing peninsula, the 40-km (25-mile) long **Bahía Concepción ⓰** is particularly renowned for its enticing camping beaches, all with at least a few facilities such as toilets, trash cans and sheltering *palapas*. Most of the rocks between the beaches are occupied by morose pelicans gazing silently at the sea.

Old capital

Loreto ⓫, about 136 km (85 miles) further south, was the site of the first permanent mission and for 130 years the capital of Baja. After it was leveled by a storm in 1828, the capital was moved to the pearling center at La Paz. The twin towers on the restored mission were replaced with money won by the local priest in the national lottery. The town's main street is named after the Jesuit priest Juan María Salvatierra, who established and ran the mission here for 20 years. The government-planned tourist complex at **Nopoló**, 25 km (15 miles) south of Loreto, expects to attract up to 8,000 boats a year to its pleasant marina by the end of the decade.

En route to La Paz

The scenery south of Loreto is spectacular; lovely beaches and the reddish-brown slopes of the Sierra de la Giganta sometimes distract attention from the

Map
on pages
200–1

TIP

Call Oscar Fischer at La Posada Motel (tel: 685-40013) in San Ignacio to arrange an excursion to see the pre-Hispanic cave paintings in the area.

BELOW: San José church in San José del Cabo.

Baja California is twice as long as Florida, but much skinnier. A great crack in the San Andreas fault created the Gulf of California millions of years ago; the water is 3,290 meters (1,800 fathoms) deep off La Paz.

dangerous curves and steep switchbacks on the highway. In the fertile Santo Domingo valley, **Ciudad Constitución** is a fast-growing, busy agricultural center with some of the ambience of the old American West. Highway 22 heads west from here 57 km (36 miles) to the Pacific port of **San Carlos**, a small town overlooking Bahía Magdalena, the largest bay in Baja, which shelters a commercial fishing fleet and, during the spawning season, Californian gray whales (*see page 277*).

Early this century there were steamboat connections from **La Paz** ⓬ to other Baja ports; now there are daily ferries to Mazatlán and Topolobampo on the Sonora coast. La Paz, the capital of Baja California Sur, is a delightful city with a population of about 180,000. Its streets, with their old colonial buildings, are shaded by coconut palms and laurel trees and, in the spring, blossoming jacaranda, acacia and flame trees add to the splendor.

Apart from its celebrated sports fishing, La Paz is famous for its spectacular sunsets – best viewed from the terrace café of the popular Hotel Perla, on Paseo Alvaro Obregón; the local **tourist office**, also on the seafront, is about one block away.

If you have the time, it is worth visiting the **Biblioteca** opposite the cathedral on the zócalo and the **Museo de Antropología** (open Tues–Sat; donation), on Altamirano, for information and exhibitions on Baja's history.

Northwards out of La Paz, the road goes up the **Pichilingue** peninsula, past the ferry terminal (bus every hour) to lovely bays and beaches at **Balandra** and **Tecolote**. Another popular destination is the island of **Espíritu Santo** (8 km/ 5 miles offshore), uninhabited today, but once known as the "isla de perlas" after Cortés harvested black pearls here in the 16th century. After centuries of

BELOW: Hotel Presidente beach in San José del Cabo.

exploitation, the pearl trade finally came to an end in the 1940s when a mysterious disease wiped out the oyster beds of La Paz.

Los Cabos

Of the two famous *cabos* (capes) at Baja's southern tip, **San José del Cabo** ⓭ is by far the less glitzy and more typically picturesque. The 32-km (20-mile) strip of highway between the two is filling up with resorts, golf courses and all the trappings of a developing tourist region, but San José itself, at the eastern end of the "corridor", remains relatively unspoiled. Rent a bicycle or car, or walk to the beach at **La Playita**, where you can dine on freshly caught seafood, go fishing in a *panga* or just admire the estuary, home to thousands of birds.

The highway continues on down to the tip of Baja at **Cabo San Lucas** ⓮, a former supply station for the Spanish treasure galleons from Manila and now a major tourist center bulging with bars, cafés, nightspots and dozens of luxury hotels; some have private beaches and their own landing strips for small aircraft.

The tides in the Gulf are powerful and tricky, and the wind is strong. This means small boats are hard to handle and it can be very dangerous. You can rent a boat with an experienced local crew at the marina; this is also the place to take glass-bottomed boat trips to **El Arco**, the famous natural stone arch at the southernmost point of the peninsula.

From the town of Cabo San Lucas you can make your way back to La Paz along the Pacific coast on a good but partially unpaved road past some lovely lonely beaches, though the ocean is rough. The road leaves the coast near **Todos Santos**, which stands exactly on the Tropic of Cancer, and heads back across the peninsula to La Paz. ❑

Map on page 211

Sailfish, marlin, roosterfish, swordfish, yellowtail, dolphin fish, cabrilla, tuna and sierra are among the many fish living in the waters off La Paz.

BELOW: fishermen's rack, Bahía de los Angeles.

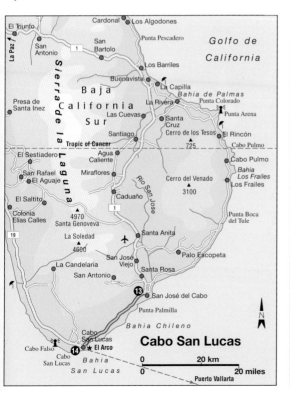

THROUGH THE SIERRAS

*The mountainous north is different
from the rest of the country; this is Mexico's Wild West,
where men wear stetsons not sombreros*

Map
on pages
200–1

México City

Heading south from the Texas border, you will be confronted by two great mountain ranges, the Sierra Madre Occidental in the west and the Sierra Madre Oriental in the east. The former is by far the more rugged of the two. Between Ciudad Juárez, on the US border, and Guadalajara, 1,600 km (1,000 miles) further south, there are only two ways to cross the mountains to the Pacific coast: the railroad from Chihuahua City to Los Mochis or, much further south, the road from Durango to Mazatlán.

Ciudad Juárez ⑮ lies just across the border from El Paso, in Texas. It's an interesting town, the biggest in the state of Chihuahua, where you can watch the bullfights, go to the greyhound races or even to the dentist (dental work is cheaper here than in the United States). However, most travellers move on fairly quickly.

About 300 km (186 miles) south of Ciudad Juárez, **Casas Grandes ⑯** (open daily; entrance fee) is the most important archeological site in northern Mexico. The Paquimé people, who lived here from around AD 900, knew how to irrigate the land and build three-story adobe houses. Once an important trading center, Casas Grandes combines elements of the Pueblo indian civilization from the southwestern United States and Mesoamerican influences. The town was abandoned around the year 1300, possibly after attacks by Apache indians. Most of the pottery found here can be seen at the Museum of Anthropology in Mexico City (*see page 164*).

LEFT: paper flower vendor.
BELOW: García Caves, Monterrey.

Chihuahua

Founded in 1709, **Chihuahua City ⑰**, with a population of over 1.2 million and some fine colonial buildings, is worth more than a casual look. Quinta Luz, the 30-room mansion belonging to Pancho Villa is now the **Museo de la Revolución** (open daily; entrance fee). Among the assorted memorabilia is the bullet-riddled Dodge car in which the bandit-turned-hero of the Revolution was gunned down in 1923. Señora Luz Corral de Villa, one of his many *compañeras*, lived here until her death in 1981.

On the main plaza, the twin-towered baroque **cathedral** is one of the few outstanding gems of colonial architecture to be found in the north of Mexico. It was financed by voluntary contributions from miners working in the nearby silver mines.

An aqueduct and the church of **San Francisco** also date from colonial times. Murals inside the **Palacio de Gobierno** tell the history of Chihuahua, while in the inner courtyard stands a monument to Father Miguel Hidalgo, hero of the War of Independence, who was executed here. You can visit the grim dungeon in the Palacio Federal where he was imprisoned while await-

ing his fate. Another mansion, **Quinta Gameros**, dates from the turn of the century and now houses the **Museo Regional** (open Tues–Sun; entrance fee), with elaborate Art Nouveau exhibits and a display of Paquimé artefacts from Casas Grandes.

The little Chihuahua dogs so loved and loathed all over the world originate from this, the largest state in Mexico.

Hidalgo del Parral and Pancho Villa

Driving south from Chihuahua City you will see the state's richest agricultural regions. It is here that they grow many of Mexico's famous chili peppers. Silver was once the main support of the economy in the prosperous old mining town of **Hidalgo del Parral** ⓲. Nearby mines are still active although lumbering and commerce are now equally important.

The fine 18th-century church of **Nuestra Señora del Rayo** (Our Lady of the Lightning) is said to have been paid for in ingots by a local indian who had struck gold but refused to reveal the location of the mine, even when beaten and tortured to death. Another fine church, **Nuestra Señora de Fátima**, is built entirely out of ore-bearing rock – gold, silver, copper, lead, zinc – right down to the pews inside.

Parral, as it is often called, is notorious as the town where General Francisco "Pancho" Villa was assassinated in 1923. There's a small museum near the center which contains old photos and a number of mementoes. Some years ago the government decided to rank Villa in with the country's other revolutionary heroes, and his grave was dug up, then the body reburied in the Monument to the Revolution in Mexico City.

BELOW: Chihuahua landscape.

The villages around the town of **Cuauhtémoc** ⓳, 95 km (60 miles) southwest of Chihuahua City, are home to 15,000 members of the Mennonite sect, whose

Map
on pages
200–1

families moved here in the 1920s. Speaking their own dialect of old German, the Mennonites are farmers, best known for the cheese they produce (*queso menon-ito*). They do not mix much and few speak Spanish. It is their custom to shun luxury and modernization, and most still drive around in horse-drawn carts (although nowadays you may see a pickup truck or two).

Yet television is still taboo in most of the homes, and 10-children families are not uncommon. Some tours from Creel include sharing a simple lunch in a Mennonite household. Cuauhtémoc is the Mennonite center for commercial activity, though the people do not live here. During the day you will see them: overall-clad men, married women dressed in dark colors, and girls in bright floral dresses.

From Cuauhtémoc a paved road leads to the **Parque Nacional Cascada de Basaseachi ⑳** and Mexico's highest waterfall. Be sure to enquire about road conditions before venturing along this route as access to the waterfall is diffi-cult, especially during the rainy season. The falls plunge over 300 meters (1,000 ft), but it's an easy walk up the road to the top. If you are in good shape, walk about halfway down for a spectacular view. It is best to hire a local guide as the path is not clearly marked.

The Sierra Tarahumara

The **Barranca del Cobre ㉑** (Copper Canyon; see pages 220–221), one of many canyons in the Sierra Tarahumara, southwest of Chihuahua City, is even deeper than the famous Grand Canyon of Colorado. This is Tarahumara indian country. Some 50,000 of them live in this region, often in caves or wooden huts in the mountains. Although they are one of the largest indian groups left in

BELOW: Mennonite gathering.

Carta Blanca is one of the beers produced in a huge brewery in the city of Monterrey.

Mexico, the Tarahumara are also one of the most isolated, a condition that has exacerbated their dire poverty while at the same time enabling them to maintain many of their traditions. You'll probably see them in the towns and cities in the vicinity with long, black hair and colored headband, white *tapote* (loin cloth) and rough cloth shirt. The mission store in **Creel** ㉒ has moderately priced Tarahumara craftware and the indians benefit from all sales. There are tours of the Copper Canyon, particularly those operated by Ecogrupos de México (based in Mexico City; tel: 661 9121), which devote some time to exploring San Ignacio, with its valleys of towering rocks and caves in which the Tarahumaras still live. These tours include a visit to the school to which the indian children come from miles around.

The Chihuahua–Pacífico train ride, which has been called "the world's most scenic railroad," winds up, over, around, under and through the Sierra Madre mountains. You can stop off at Creel or **Divisadero** ㉓ and explore some of the canyon on foot (there are special trails to follow).

Northeast Mexico

Most foreign tourists cross the border into the northeast of Mexico at **Nuevo Laredo** ㉔. From here, it is under a two-hour drive on the *cuota* (toll road) south to **Monterrey** ㉕, the third-largest city in the country and a center for industry and commerce. Old guidebooks refer to Monterrey as the "Pittsburgh of Mexico," but that description is outdated, for its huge steel industry was shut down years ago. *Regiomontanos* (natives of Monterrey) have an uneasy relationship with the government in Mexico City, and local businessmen often seem to have closer cultural ties with the US than with the rest of Mexico.

BELOW: Basaseachi Falls.

Monterrey, capital of the state of Nuevo León, produces 25 percent of Mexico's manufactured goods, including half of the country's manufactured exports. Dynamic Monterrey is Mexico's center of private enterprise; the Cintermex is one of the largest exhibition and trade show areas in the country. In addition to this, the Monterrey Institute of Technology, patterned after the United States' Massachusetts Institute of Technology, is probably Mexico's most outstanding university. Credit for this industrial development is often given to the Garza-Sada family, a group of free-enterprisers who emigrated to Mexico from Spain in the 19th century.

In the center of town, at the south end of the vast Macro Plaza, is the busy **Plaza Zaragoza**, with a baroque-façaded **cathedral** on its east side and the modern Palacio Municipal to the south. In between the two is the **Contemporary Art Museum**, MARCO (open Tues–Sun; entrance fee), with its Latin American collection, while nearby stands a large free-form sculpture by Rufino Tamayo, one of Mexico's best-known 20th-century artists (*see page 111*). Dominating the plaza is the Faro del Comercio, a concrete "beacon of commerce" designed by architect Luis Barragán, with a laser beam that sweeps the city every evening.

The church of the **Purísima Concepción**, 13 blocks west, designed by Enrique de la Mora, is a prize-winning example of Mexican architecture of the 1940s. Inside, a small wooden statue of the Virgin is said to have miraculously prevented the Santa Catarina river from flooding the city in 1756. Hurricane Gilbert, however, turned this normally dry river into a raging torrent in 1988, killing hundreds.

Strategically situated on a hill 2.5 km (1½ miles) west of the center, the 18th-century **Obispado** (bishop's palace), now a **museum** (open Tues–Sun; entrance fee), affords an excellent overview of the city and an impressive mountain backdrop called **Cerro de la Silla** (Saddle Peak). The bullet holes and shellfire scars are souvenirs of the American invasion of September 22nd, 1846; it was also attacked by French forces in the 1860s and witnessed clashes between Villa's troops and the Constitutionalists during the Revolution half a century later.

A cheerful way to start or finish a tour of Monterrey, especially if you are thirsty, is with a visit to the **Cervecería Cuauhtémoc,** Mexico's biggest and oldest brewery which produces Carta Blanca and Bohemia brands, fine Pilsner-type beer. The original brewery, also within the complex, has been converted into the **Museo de Monterrey** (open Tues–Sun; entrance free), one of the best museums of contemporary art in Mexico, with work by Murillo, Siqueiros, Orozco, Rivera and Tamayo, among others (*see pages 108-11*), and some excellent visiting exhibitions too.

Out of town

It's worth spending some time exploring the area around Monterrey. A short drive up the pine-covered slope to the southwest of the city leads to **Chipinique Mesa,** Monterrey's most exclusive suburb which also offers a restaurant, hotel,

Map on pages 200–1

BELOW: Copper Canyon, Sierra Madre mountains.

Popular local foods include cabrito al pastor *(charcoal grilled young goat),* pan de pulque *(a delicious sweet bread made with the fermented sap of the maguey plant) and* huevos con machaca *(scrambled egg with Mexican-style dried beef).*

picnic facilities and stunning views over the city and surrounding area. The **Grutas de García**  (open daily; entrance fee), about 35 km (21 miles) northwest of town, near Villa de García, are a spectacular series of caverns set high inside a mountain with astounding rock formations, stalactites and stalagmites. The drive from Monterrey is beautiful, but winding and narrow. A little cable car will then take you up to the cave entrance.

Only a 15-minute drive from downtown Monterrey, outside suburban Santa Catarina, the **Cañón de la Huasteca** is a dramatic 300-meter (1,000-ft) deep canyon (the road is good only as far as the Gruta de la Virgen). The **Cola de Caballo** waterfall is a 35-km (22-mile) drive south of Monterrey. The area around the triple cascade called the **Tres Gracias** is an ideal picnic spot. En route you pass **La Boca** dam, where there is good fishing and water sports.

Mile-high city

The state of Coahuila is almost as big as neighboring Chihuahua. **Saltillo** , at 1,598 meters (5,245 ft) above sea level, is the state capital with a population of 650,000. This mile-high altitude with its sunny, dry climate has made Saltillo a favorite summer vacation spot, especially for visitors from the United States, for many years. There is also a fine university which runs Spanish courses for foreign students in summer.

Founded in 1575 by Captain Francisco Urdiñola, Saltillo became the Spanish headquarters for exploring and colonizing land to its north, and in the early 19th century it was the capital of a large area which included Texas. In 1847 one of the bloodiest and most decisive battles of the Mexican-American War took place at **Buena Vista** (half an hour south on Highway 54). A small monument

BELOW: Coahuila vineyards.

Map on pages 200–1

marks the site. Soon after this battle the war ended and Mexico lost half of its territory to the USA. Nowadays, Saltillo is an interesting blend of colonial and modern; the city manages to maintain its charm despite being an important industrial center. The elaborate façade of the late 18th-century **Catedral de Santiago** on the main plaza is one of the finest and northernmost examples of churrigueresque architecture in Mexico.

The elegant **Palacio de Gobierno** on the opposite side of the square is also worth visiting. Among the museums of Saltillo are the **Archivos Juárez**, where much of the early history of Texas is recorded, and the **Museo de las Aves** (open Tues–Sun; entrance fee), a new and interesting museum which is devoted to the many birds of Mexico.

Parras, a small town about 160 km (100 miles) west of Saltillo, is an oasis in the Coahuilan desert and is also the birthplace of revolutionary leader Francisco Madero. An excellent local wine is bottled at nearby San Lorenzo. This is Mexico's oldest winery, founded in 1626 (tours are conducted). Another speciality of the famous Saltillo vineyards is Brandy Madero, said to be the world's best-selling brand.

South of Chihuahua and Coahuila, but still considered the North, the state of Durango is a cattle and lumber center which has gained fame as a popular location for Hollywood westerns. Excursions to the film sets at **Chupaderos** and **Villa del Oeste** can be arranged by the local tourist office. The industrial city of **Durango** 🔟,with an attractive plaza, baroque cathedral and other fine colonial buildings, is situated at a crossroads: to the southeast lies Zacatecas and the colonial heartland (*see pages 235-47*); to the southwest is Sinaloa and the Pacific coast at Mazatlán.

Saltillo is famous for its colorful hand-woven serapes which can be bought at the market on Plaza Acuña.

BELOW: knocking it down at the Coahuila Wine Fest.

The Gulf Coast

People who cross the border at Brownsville or McAllen, in the east of Texas, enter Mexico through the towns of **Reynosa** 🔟 or **Matamoros** 🔟, in the state of Tamaulipas. The Gulf Coast of Mexico between the border and Tampico, 619 km (384 miles) further south, has little to offer tourists except a scattering of hunting lodges and fishing camps, the roads are often poor and the coast is littered with oil refineries and tankers.

Most visitors choose to drive south through Monterrey and down to the colonial heartland of the central states. If you do choose the east coast route, the little town of San Fernando is a popular spot for a break, with good restaurants and hotels. It is also the center for hunting in the area.

About three hours southeast of Soto La Marina, **La Pesca** 🔟 is a sleepy little fishing village that was saved from being another tourist-trap like Cancún only by its lack of resources. In 1991 the government designated it as a megaproject; a small airport was built, plans were laid for building five-star hotels and land speculation became frantic. Fortunately the project eventually fizzled out and the village, with its hotels, hunting lodges and an RV park, retains much of its charm. From Soto La Marina to Tampico it's about a three-hour drive. ❏

THE WORLD'S MOST SCENIC RAILROAD

Riding on bridges over yawning chasms, viewing awesome scenery and age-old indian settlements – welcome aboard the Copper Canyon Railroad

Some of Mexico's most spectacular scenery is found in Chihuahua -- the massive canyons and gorges in the Sierra Madre known as the Barranca del Cobre. It has taken millions of years for rivers and wind to mold what is actually a series of five interconneted canyons, covering 25,000 square miles of rugged land, that ranges from below sea level to more than 3,046 meters (10,000 ft) at its peak. Mexico's tallest waterfall, the 300-meter (984-ft) Cascada de Basaseachi, is found here, as well as a variety of plant life and one of the world's most interesting indian tribes. It is a living museum of natural history – except for animals. Although you may see buzzards and bald eagles flying overhead, most animal life has disappeared.

SPECTACULAR VIEWS

The Ferrocarril Chihuahua al Pacífico, called "the world's most scenic railroad," hauls timber and tourists through this spectacular setting. This extraordinary feat of engineering – 661 km (410 miles) in all – was begun in 1881 and not completed until 1961, at a total cost of more than US$100 million. It passes through 87 tunnels (one almost a mile long) and crosses 35 bridges. The train ride from Chihuahua to Los Mochis takes about 12 hours with short stops along the way to enjoy the splendid views – from alpine forests and rushing rivers, to dusty gorges studded with Tarahumara indian settle- ments and the remains of old missions and mining towns.

▷ **LOCAL COSTUME**
Clothing for Tarahumara women and girls is usually a sack-shaped tunic. Sometimes a woolen skirt is wound around their waist and held by a belt.

▷ **LOCAL CRAFTS**
A Tarahumara mother and her daughter sell their homemade handicrafts by the railroad line at the edge of the canyon.

△ **A TASTY TORTILLA**
The Chihuahua-Pacífico Railroad is renowned for big vistas and small lunches. Local snacks fill a gap in the market.

△ **TAKE THE TRAIN**
The railroad project was conceived by US idealist Albert Owen, who came to Mexico to form a utopian colony on the Pacific coast.

▷ **HEAD FOR HEIGHTS**
If you prefer your views from the comfort of your own hotel room, try the Posada Barrancas Mirador in Divisadero, where everyone gets a look in.

THE TARAHUMARAS

△ QUIET REFLECTION
A Mennonite community from Canada purchased 230,000 acres of land in Cuauhtémoc and migrated here in 1921.

▽ VIEW FROM THE BRIM
The best way to explore the canyon is on foot, but the local *rancheros* are seldom parted from their horses.

Long before the advent of the railroad, the highlands and deep gorges of the Copper Canyon have been inhabited by the Tarahumara indians. Exploited for centuries by the Spanish colonists and the mestizos, the 60,000 or so descendants keep to themselves and avoid modernization. "Home" is a cave or a simple wood cabin and their meager diet consists of corn tortillas, potatoes, beans and squash. In church their ancient gods *Raiénari* (Sun) and *Mechá* (Moon) happily exist side by side with images of Christ and the Catholic saints.

Map
on pages
200–1

México City

THE NORTHWEST COAST

From the great desert of Sonora to the tropics of Nayarit,
the northwest of Mexico offers fantastic beaches,
good fishing, delicious seafood and spectacular birdlife

Northwest Mexico was neglected until the missionaries started to work among the tribes in the 17th century. The Jesuits were most successful; the priests introduced domestic animals, showed the indians new crops and taught them farming and building techniques. Problems arose when Spanish colonists arrived and tried to take the most fertile lands and force the indians into hard labor. The indians resisted and, as they were split into many tribes and spread out over great distances, they could not be conquered in one blow. Rebellion flared, on and off, for many years.

When the Jesuits were expelled from Mexico in 1767, the missions disintegrated and the colonists brazenly encroached on tribal lands. The Yaquis, a fighting race, reacted angrily and the Spanish dealt with them harshly.

For centuries the tribes of the northwest were isolated in a remote corner of Mexico. They took little part in the life of the nation and were marginal to the Independence movement of the 1810s. The region was weak and unprotected and practically invited invasion. The French, led by Gaston Raousset de Bourbon, captured Hermosillo in 1852, and in 1857 Henry Crabb, an American from California, tried to capture northern Sonora. In both instances, the Mexicans reacted vigorously, defeating the invaders and executing the leaders.

BELOW: pelicans
waiting for supper,
La Paz.

La Familia Revolucionaria

By the time the Revolution broke out in 1910 , the Northwest had developed muscle and conscience and was ready to take part wholeheartedly, providing troops and the general (Alvaro Obregón) who emerged after the inevitable internal power struggle. For a decade, Mexico was ruled directly or indirectly by Sonora's *Familia Revolucionaria,* first Obregón, then General Plutarco Elías Calles.

The Yaqui deal

The Yaquis, who had joined General Obregón's forces, wanted their tribal lands back, and when Cárdenas became president in the 1930s, he ordered a dam to be built on the upper Yaqui river for irrigation, setting aside 4.5 million hectares (1 million acres) for the Yaqui tribes. It included the whole north bank of the river and part of the south. Setting up a reservation, the Yaquis took over their own tribal lands, which they control to this day. Other northwest indians did not fare so well. The Seris, for example, were either killed or died of disease and their population dropped from 5,000 to less than 200. The Opatas, on the other hand, assimilated readily: they learned Spanish, intermarried and cooperated in the battles against the Apaches.

Carved coconut head, a truly original souvenir.

The Northwest is a highly productive region: Sonora leads the nation in cotton, wheat and soybean production; Sinaloa tops the other states in tomatoes – most of which go to the US – and also raises a hefty crop of wheat, cotton, sugar cane and chickpeas, which are exported chiefly to Spain and Cuba. Although the silver mines of the Northwest are practically exhausted, the mines of Cananea make Sonora the country's leading producer of copper. (The 1906 miners' strike at Cananea was critical in the lead up to the Revolution.)

BELOW: a tranquil walk above the seashore.

Mexicali to Mazatlán

The Pacific beaches are the main attraction of the route from the Arizona border to Mazatlán, but there are also interesting mountain towns and historical sights along the way. An excellent, though expensive super-highway stretches down most of the coast. The alternative *libre* (free) route is longer and the traffic is predictably heavier.

Many people who come south from the US, either through **Mexicali** ❹ or **Nogales** ❺ begin with a jaunt to **Puerto Peñasco** in the far northwest corner of Sonora. This is a funky fishing village that is now a popular weekend retreat for Arizonans. Fishing and beaching are the main reasons for going there. If you are thinking of taking a boat out, be extremely careful as tides are hazardous and winds are strong in the shallow waters at the head of the Gulf of California. Like most of the resorts in the north, Puerto Peñasco offers good trailer facilities, with water and power hook-ups.

El Gran Desierto

There is precious little to break the barren monotony between the border and Hermosillo. In the small town of **Magdalena**, 20 km (12 miles) northeast of the junction at Santa Ana, a glass shrine contains the mortal remains of Padre Eusebio Kino, the Jesuit priest

Waiting for a wave?

who helped establish missions along the coast, and later in Arizona and California. Often crippled with arthritis, Kino, a mathematician, astrologer, architect and economist, died in 1711 but his grave was only discovered in 1966. Gold is mined in the hills around Santa Ana but neither it nor Sonora's capital **Hermosillo ㊱**, a thriving city with a Ford plant, have much of interest to tourists.

Seri ironwood carvings

The next worthwhile stop is **Bahía Kino ㊲** which still manages to maintain its unsophisticated fishing-village atmosphere, despite the many *norteamericanos* who choose to spend the winter months there. The local Seri indians sell wonderful handicrafts such as baskets and ironwood carvings, so-called because they are made out of an exceptionally hard local wood. The Seris, a nomadic people, were moved to this part of Sonora from nearby **Isla del Tiburón ㊳** (Shark Island), which is now a wildlife sanctuary.

Cool winter nights

You can rent a boat for fishing in most of the resort towns along the coast. It is easy to acquire a permit, and most come complete with tackle, crew and cold beer, though prices do vary, so you would be wise to shop around. Winter nights can get chilly along the coast of Sonora, and although it is sunny during the day, the water is cold for swimming. The ocean can get rough and swimmers should be careful of the big waves and powerful undertow, except in protected bays. There are ocean breezes even when it does warm up, and the Pacific beaches seldom gets as muggy as the Gulf coast.

BELOW:
fishing harbor at
sunrise, Guaymas.

A gringo oasis

Though many people call **Guaymas** ❸ a beach resort, it is not. It is a fishing town and Sonora's main port, with ferries to Santa Rosalía in Baja California. While you won't save any money by taking the ferry to Baja, you will save time, and the cost per passenger is still very reasonable. But don't plan your trip too closely as the ferry times and days change often.

Nearby **San Carlos** ❹ is the beach resort; it is a gringo oasis inhabited by many retired Americans and Canadians. There are dozens of hotels and restaurants, and it has one of Mexico's largest marinas, with sailing vessels from all around the world. The 1970 movie *Catch 22* was shot nearby.

Navojoa, south of **Cuidad Obregón**, is the center of a major cotton-producing area and the home of the Mayo indians. A detour from Navojoa takes you 53 km (33 miles) inland to the beautiful old town of **Alamos** ❹ in the foothills of the Sierras. This was a rich mining center in the 18th century, with dozens of fabulous residences lining its cobblestone streets. After the Revolution the mines were closed down and the town was practically abandoned. In the late 1940s, Alamos was rediscovered by wealthy Americans who bought up many of the colonial mansions and restored them. The beautiful central plaza is dominated by the baroque-façaded church of **Nuestra Señora de la Concepción**. The town of Alamos, which has some of the best examples of colonial architecture on the West Coast, is a national monument, and to visit it is like stepping back in time.

Los Mochis

From Navojoa, the main highway continues through some of the richest farmland in Mexico to **Los Mochis** ❹, a pleasant and friendly town. Most people

Map on pages 200–1

Alamos is the capital of the Mexican jumping bean, which is in fact a seed pod whose restlessness is due to the tiny larva of a moth growing inside it.

BELOW: the marina, San Carlos Bay.

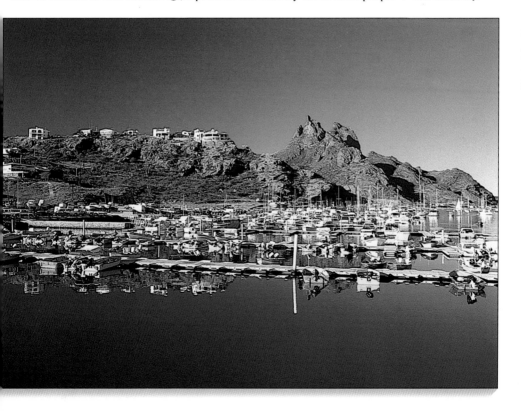

spend a day or two here while waiting for the **Copper Canyon train** (*see pages 220–21*), which traverses the rugged mountains of the Sierra Madre to Chihuahua, offering one of the most spectacular train rides in the world. It leaves early in the morning and arrives in Chihuahua in the early evening. Los Mochis has become a boom town with rice, cotton, winter vegetables, sugar cane, and marigolds all produced neaby. What you may not know is that when marigolds are fed to chickens, it makes the yolks of their eggs bright yellow.

The ferry from La Paz in Baja California docks south of Los Mochis in **Topolobampo.** Just off the coast, the rocky island of **Farallón** (sometimes called Isla las Animas) is a breeding ground for sea lions and attracts flocks of seabirds. The underwater marine life around the island is colorful.

El Fuerte, an important Spanish settlement during colonial times, and once capital of the state of Sinaloa, is a picturesque town 78 km (48 miles) northeast of Los Mochis. Apart from the plaza, the museum and the church it is worth visiting the Posada del Hidalgo, a 19th-century mansion which has been converted into a beautiful hotel. Fishing for catfish and carp is possible in the nearby Presa Miguel Hidalgo, one of the best bass-fishing lakes in the country.

From Los Mochis to Mazatlán, the highway cuts through **Culiacán**, capital of Sinaloa, known for its bumper crops of tomatoes and opium, both destined for the US (some opium is legally exported for medicinal purposes). Marijuana is also grown amongst the hemp plantations in the complex landscape of the Sierra Madre Occidental. Culiacán is the center of the Mexican drug trade, and visitors must be warned against both using and dealing; the Mexican anti-drug laws are strict.

The toll road from Culiacán to Mazatlán, the most expensive stretch, saves

BELOW: Mazatlán, Mexico's biggest Pacific port.

about 1.5 hours on the drive. Traffic on the old free route is congested, although the road surface is usually quite good. About halfway between the two, you can make a detour to **Cosalá**, an old mining town with hot springs nearby.

Map on pages 200–1

The Pearl of the Pacific

Mazatlán ❸ (meaning "Place of the Deer" in Náhuatl) is a booming resort town about 15 km (9 miles) south of the Tropic of Cancer. It is also one of the most important ports on Mexico's west coast and home to the country's largest shrimp fleet. Most of the local shrimp is exported to the USA and what little remains tends to fetch a premium price; so if your budget is tight, stick to fish, which is prepared in many mouth-watering ways. Restaurants on the beach or in beach hotels usually have the best-quality seafood, but it tends to be the most expensive; the further you are from the beach, the lower the prices.

The old part of the city, situated on a peninsula, centers around the Plaza Principal and the 19th-century twin-towered cathedral, whose unusual façade is decorated with intricately carved volcanic rock. Towering over this old part of town, the **Cerro de la Nevería** (Icebox Hill) has panoramic sea views. Most tourists spend their time in the so-called **Zona Dorada** (Golden Zone), a long stretch of hotels, restaurants and shops about 3 km (2 miles) north of the old town. Here, close to the biggest hotels, is the well-stocked **Centro de Artesanías** (arts and crafts center), where there are frequent breathtaking performances by a group of *Voladores de Papantla* (Papantla flyers – *see page 281*). A little further south, near Playa del Norte, the **Acuario Mazatlán**, with over 200 species of fish, is worth a visit. Local travel agencies organize city and jungle tours, and there are also boat trips around the harbor and to the nearby islands.

Winter is the most popular season here, though any time of the year is pleasant. Summer is the "rainy" season, but unless there is a hurricane nearby it will not greatly inconvenience you. *Carnaval* in Mazatlán (the week before Ash Wednesday) is one of Mexico's liveliest fiestas; hotel reservations are essential then as they are between Christmas and New Year, and for the week before Easter, when all beach resorts are jam-packed. At any other time, you will find hotels in all price ranges.

A short detour east up highway 40 into the foothills of the Sierra Madre makes a pleasant day-trip from Mazatlán. The colonial town of **Concordia** ❹, set in lush, tropical vegetation with hot springs nearby, is known for its pottery and hand-carved furniture. Picture-postcard **Copala** ❺, 25 km (16 miles) further on, with its cobblestone streets, red-tiled roofs and wrought-iron balconies, is an old silver-mining town.

The Huichol indians

Craftwork from all over the Republic can be found in Mazatlán, but particularly beautiful is the beaded artwork and weavings of the Huichol indians. However, if you are on your way south, it is more helpful to them – and more interesting for you – if you wait until you reach **Santiago Ixcuintla** ❻. Here there is a Huichol Center for Cultural Survival, where you can watch Huichol families making their crafts; any

The best views in Mazatlán are from El Faro, a lighthouse at the southern tip of the peninsula; at 157 meters (515 ft) above sea-level, it is said to be the world's second highest (after Gibraltar).

BELOW: gentle sunset over the water

Map on pages 200–1

Mexico's national symbol originated from an Aztec legend.

money you spend here goes directly to the tribe, and much of it to the nearby hospital (tuberculosis, malnutrition and other ailments mean Huichol children suffer a 50 percent infant mortality rate).

The Venice of Mexico

The small island village of **Mexcaltitán** ❹ was nicknamed the "Venice of Mexico," because, during heavy rains the streets are flooded and you have to pole your way around in a canoe. More and more of the streets have been filled in, so its waterlogged days are probably limited. The seafood here is excellent, but don't look for luxury hotels; the town is a bit run down. Some historians believe that Mexcaltitán is the legendary island of Aztlán, the original home of the Aztec people and the place where they first had the vision of the eagle perched on a cactus with a serpent in its claws; this symbol of their promised land was eventually found in Tenochtitlán, now Mexico City.

Surf City

San Blas ❹ is a quiet fishing town and low-key resort noted for the ferocity of its gnats, known as *jejenes*. The insects are at their worst early in the morning, in the evenings and during a full moon, so be sure to stock up on insect repellent. Surfers flock to San Blas to ride its famous long waves, and ornithologists come to watch the many species of migrating and native birds that take refuge here. Bird-watching trips to the **Santuario de Aves** (bird sanctuary) can be arranged. Another popular pastime is to take the jungle boat-ride up the San Cristóbal estuary, through a green tunnel of vegetation to **La Tovara** springs, where you can swim in crystal-clear water, picnic, or eat at one of the *palapa* restaurants.

BELOW: offshore parasailing.
RIGHT: dressed for a fiesta.

Although it is hard to believe now, San Blas was once a ship-building center and the point of departure for Spanish exploration of the Pacific Northwest. Vestiges of this period include the old **Aduana** (customs house) by the port and the **Fuerte de Basilio**, a counting house built in 1768. It was the church here that inspired 19th-century US poet Henry Wadsworth Longfellow to write the poem entitled *The Bells of San Blas*.

The journey to Ixtlán

About 70 km (44 miles) inland, **Tepic** ❹, the capital of the state of Nayarit, has a pleasant zócalo, flanked by a cathedral with impressive neo-Gothic towers. The **Museo Regional** (open Mon–Sat; entrance fee) houses a collection of pre-Hispanic ceramics and the **Museo de Artes Populares** (open daily; entrance free) exhibits handicrafts by Huichol, Cora, Nahuatl and Tepehuano indians which can be bought far cheaper here than in the resort boutiques.

Just ouside the town of **Ixtlán del Río** ❺ – made famous by Carlos Castaneda's *Journey to Ixtlán* – is an extensive and largely restored archeological site, **Los Toriles**, which flourished in the 2nd century AD. (open daily; entrance fee). The main structure is an unusual circular stone temple with cruciform windows dedicated to **Quetzalcóatl**. ❑

CENTRAL MEXICO

Famous for its Pacific beaches, tequila and the hat dance,
but above all this is the heartland of colonial Mexico

The Central Highlands were a source of enormous wealth for the Spanish colonists. The silver route from Zacatecas to Mexico City passed through the magnificent towns of the so-called Colonial Heartland. The cathedrals, monasteries, chapels and mansions that can be visited today are the exquisite legacy of Spanish prosperity, on the one hand, and of the extreme exploitation of indian labor, on the other. It is no coincidence that the 19th-century Independence movement was ignited in El Bajío – the triangle formed by the towns of Querétaro, San Luis Potosí and Aguascalientes.

South of El Bajío are the verdant rolling hills of Michoacán, one of the most beautiful and fascinating states in the Republic. Visitors can ride up to the crater of a smoldering volcano or else witness the spectacular sight of the Monarch butterflies, that arrive from Canada in their millions each year. Michoacán craftsmen are particularly renowned for their skill and the variety of their work; and for anyone travelling in November, nowhere is Mexico's unique Day of the Dead celebrated more fervently than in the delightful town of Pátzcuaro and on the nearby island of Janitzio.

Endless fields of blue-green agave surround the small but world-famous town of Tequila, in the neighboring state of Jalisco, home to many clichés about Mexico and its inhabitants: *charros, mariachis,* the Mexican hat dance and, of course, tequila all originate from this important state. But Jalisco, and its capital Guadalajara (Mexico's second largest city), go far beyond the strereotype. Among other things, Jalisco is home to the Cora and Huichol indians who live in the sierra and make yearly pilgrimages to San Luis Potosí – a 1,600-kilometer round trip – to collect the hallucinogenic peyote cactus that is central to their ancient rituals.

Jalisco is also the gateway to the Pacific coast, where mega-resorts attract sunseekers by their thousands. The palm-fringed beaches and azure lagoons are set against the craggy mountains of the Sierra Madre Occidental and the Sierra Madre del Sur. The major resorts are geared towards sun-worshipping, fishing and every imaginable water sport. But for anyone who wants to get away from the crowds, there are still hundreds of kilometers of deserted coast fringed with vast plantations of bananas, mangoes and coconuts. ❑

PRECEDING PAGES: rowing across a tranquil Lake Pátzcuaro.
LEFT: offerings to Christ from Day of the Dead ceremony.

EL BAJÍO AND
THE COLONIAL HEARTLAND

*For centuries, the mines of central Mexico produced much
of the world's silver; their legacy today is reflected in some of the
country's finest colonial architecture*

Map
on pages
236–7

L ess visited than the coastal resorts and some parts of southern Mexico, the five states of the central highlands, to the north of Mexico City, have much to offer any traveler who has the time, patience and curiosity to explore. Zacatecas, Aguascalientes, San Luis Potosí, Guanajuato and Querétaro are the Colonial Heartland of Mexico. Some of the most impressive colonial architecture can be seen in the cities of this region, which grew and flourished under Spanish rule as a result of the huge quantities of silver and other metals extracted from the local mines.

Zacatecas, the pink city

The state of **Zacatecas** is the gateway between the huge, barren and empty north and the richer, more fertile and more densely populated highland region of Central Mexico. The fortified archeological site at **Chalchihuites ❶**, in the northwest of the state, which flourished from AD 900 to 1200, has yielded ceramic treasures that suggest contact between the Mesoamerican style of the central highlands and the simpler geometric art style of the American West.

The city of **Zacatecas ❷**, spectacularly sited between arid hills at an altitude of 2,500 meters (8,200 ft), was declared property of the Spanish Crown in 1546. Soon after, enormous quantities of silver were being mined and shipped off to Spain. Fortunes were rapidly amassed and Zacatecas, as a result of this prosperity, has some of the finest colonial architecture in Mexico. The town, which is one of the cleanest and friendliest cities in Mexico, has a curious atmosphere, combining the vigor and roughness of the north with the architectural refinement of the central highlands. The elegant stone mansions have fancy wrought-iron balconies and window grilles. The city's main sights are mostly concentrated in a small area of 12 blocks, best explored on foot. To the north of this area, on the Plaza de Armas, the **cathedral**, with its delicately carved pink *cantera* – stone façade, is considered one of the masterpieces of Mexican baroque. Also on the plaza are two colonial mansions: the **Palacio de la Mala Noche** and the **Palacio de Gobierno**.

Just south of the cathedral are the 19th-century **Teatro Calderón** and the **Mercado González Ortega**, a turn-of-the-century cast-iron structure that has been converted into a shopping center. Uphill from the Plaza de Armas, behind a sober façade, the 18th-century **Santo Domingo** church holds some fine gilded altarpieces. The 17th-century monastery next door, now the **Museo Pedro Coronel** (open Fri-Wed; entrance

LEFT: rooftop view of Pátzcuaro.
BELOW: Jaguar Dance mask in the Museo Rafael Coronel, Zacatecas.

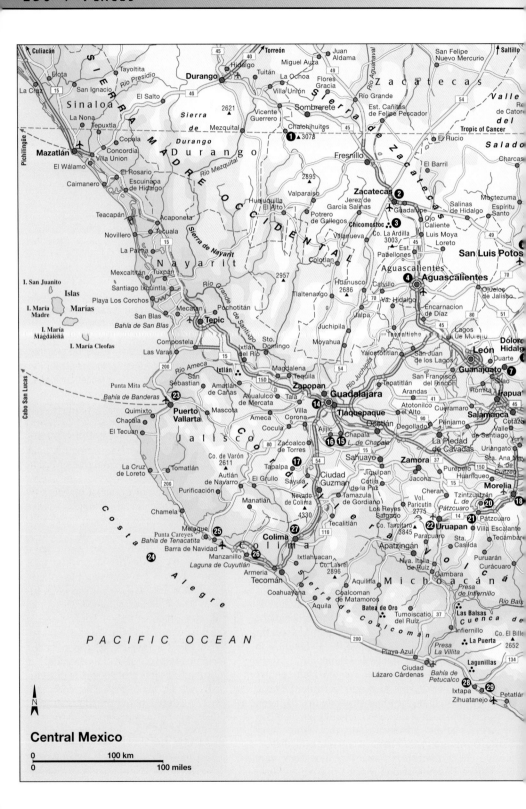

Central Mexico

0 _____ 100 km

0 _____ 100 miles

fee), exhibits an enviable collection of both ancient and modern art and artefacts from all over the world (including works by Picasso, Braque, Chagall and Miró), which this noted Zacatecan artist bequeathed to his home town. The artist's brother also donated a collection, this time of masks, 19th-century marionettes and some pre-Hispanic pottery. These are displayed in the magnificently restored Convento de San Francisco, now the **Museo Rafael Coronel** (open Thurs–Tues; entrance fee).

Perhaps the most fascinating local attraction is a trip into the heart of the **Mina El Eden** (Tues–Sun; entrance fee), one of Mexico's richest mines, which was worked from 1586 until the 1950s. As the tour passes dramatically lit shafts, subterranean pools and chasms, the guides describe the deplorable working conditions that existed for the miners in the colonial era. For a thrilling view of the city, a cable car will take you from the entrance to the mine up to the top of the **Cerro de la Bufa**. On weekends there's dancing in a discotheque that has been installed near the entrance of the mine.

The early 18th-century **Convento de Guadalupe** (open Tues–Sun; entrance fee), 10 km (6 miles) southeast of Zacatecas, is a remarkable museum and monastery with one of the most elaborately decorated chapels and an impressive collection of colonial paintings.

About 45 km (28 miles) to the west of Zacatecas, through the best cattle-raising country in Mexico, in the attractive colonial town of **Jerez**, is the horseshoe-shaped **Teatro Hinojosa**, a replica of Ford's theater in Washington, DC.

Just off the road to Guadalajara, about 50 km (30 miles) south of Zacatecas, the ruins of **Chicomostoc ❸** (open daily; entrance fee) spread over the hillside. La Quemada, as it is also known, is thought to have been part of a trade network, and was inhabited between AD 300 and 1300, when it was destroyed by fire.

Aguascalientes

The city of **Aguascalientes ❹** regards itself as Mexico's grape capital. Until

Large quantities of grapes are harvested in Zacatecas, most of which go to make a local brandy .

recently the small state of Aguascalientes, south of Zacatecas, was an important wine-producing region but the local vintners could not compete with imported wines, either on price or quality. Today most of the grapes wind up as Mexican brandy, which bears only slight resemblance to Spanish brandy or French cognac. The **San Marcos Winery** north of the city, conducts tours. Also north of town are the hot springs from which the town takes its name.

Aguascalientes is a pleasant city whose celebrated **Jardín San Marcos**, west of the town center, hosts one of Mexico's biggest annual festivals. During the end of April and early May, thousands of visitors flock to the **Feria de San Marcos** for the parades, exhibitions, bullfights, song, dance and brandy drinking.

On the main Plaza de la Patria is the impressive 18th-century **Palacio de Gobierno**; brightly colored murals by Chilean artist Oswaldo Barra Cunningham decorate the patio walls inside. The 18th-century baroque **cathedral** and the religious picture gallery next door, both contain paintings by colonial artist Miguel Cabrera. There are several museums in Aguascalientes, but the highlight is the **Museo José Guadalupe Posada** (open Tues–Sun; entrance free), next door to the Templo del Encino. Posada, most famous for his satirical *calavera* (skeleton) prints (*see pages 262–3*) and a great social and political critic during the Porfiriato, inspired many later artists, including Diego Rivera and José Clemente Orozco (*see pages 108–11*). The museum houses over 200 works by this local artist.

San Luis Potosí

BELOW: a horse takes a well-earned break.

The state of San Luis Potosí is large and diverse: the east is hot and tropical; dry plains stretch across the center; while the west, like neighboring Zacatecas, is mountainous and rugged. The industrial city of **San Luis Potosí ❺** is the state

capital and was the seat of Juárez's government before the defeat of Maximilian.

The attractive city center has many plazas and elegant mansions. The city's pre-eminent jewel is the **Templo del Carmen**, a churrigueresque church completed in 1764 and adorned with shells on the façade, multicolored tiles on the dome and a wonderfully intricate *retablo* inside. The adjacent **Teatro de la Paz** was built in the 19th century, during the dictatorship of Don Porfirio Díaz. Across the street the **Museo Nacional de la Máscara** (open Tues–Sun; entrance free) displays about 1,500 ceremonial masks, both pre-Hispanic and modern, from all over Mexico. The **Museo Regional de Arte Popular** (open Tues–Sun; admission fee), is a regional handicrafts museum housed in a former Franciscan monastery; upstairs is the richly decorated 18th-century Capilla de Aranzazú.

La Posada de la Virreina, former home of Spanish viceroys, is one of Mexico's best restaurants.

Ghost town

Once a thriving silver-mining center housing a royal mint and 40,000 inhabitants, **Real de Catorce ❻** is practically a ghost town today. It is located in the mountains west of Matehuala. You have to go through a 2.5 km (1½ mile) tunnel – a former mine shaft – to reach this extraordinary town where street after street of once sumptuous mansions stand eerily in ruins. However, the 800-strong population provides rooms to rent, as well as stores, restaurants, silversmiths and mystics. Once a year, on October 4th, Real de Catorce comes back to life when thousands of pilgrims arrive to celebrate the feast of Saint Francis.

Guanajuato

The city of **Guanajuato ❼**, capital of the state, is one of Mexico's most famous tourist spots and in colonial days it was the center of a rich mining area and one

BELOW: collecting peyote in Real de Catorce.

PEYOTE RITUAL

Offerings are made to the gods and other elaborate preparations go on for a day and a night before the Huichol indians set out on their annual pilgrimage to the sacred peyote grounds near Real de Catorce, in San Luis Potosí. Every year they make a 1,000-km (620-mile) round trip to fetch the thornless, spineless and hallucinogenic cactus that is central to their ritual. This used to be a 20-day walk but nowadays the pilgrims walk for a few days then take a bus or a truck, stopping off to pay tribute at sacred places along the way.

It is not easy to find the elusive plant; only its tip peeps up from the ground and its color blends with that of the earth. It takes two or three days to gather some 10 or 15 kgs (22–33 pounds) of peyote. A little is eaten at the site to communicate with the gods; the remainder is dried and taken home.

Before they return to their families, the Huicholes pay tribute to the gods so that crops will bloom the following year and life will be good. Everyone eats peyote at the homecoming – even the children, who wash it down with a chocolate drink. Shamans take peyote for wisdom to diagnose illness and it is connected with the ceremonies of planting and harvesting, the deer-hunt and the rain god.

Statues of Don Quixote and Sancho Panza at the Museo Iconográfico del Quijote in Guanajuato.

of the greatest producers of silver in the world. The mines were flooded during the wars for Independence, but reopened again under Porfirio Díaz. Abandoned again in the Revolution, they reopened recently as the price of silver escalated.

Classed as a national monument, Guanajuato is charming, romantic and sometimes eerie. This well-preserved city is built in a ravine and on the banks of a river; no street runs in a straight line; all go their crooked ways, up and down steep hills, some falling into an abyss; in some houses the entrance is through the roof. Tunnels and streets wind their way along the basements of the town's old buildings, with steps intermittently leading to a square or winding alley.

The heart of the city

At the heart of Guanajuato and a good place to start a tour is the **Jardín de la Unión Ⓐ**, a cool, shady wedge-shaped plaza surrounded by cafés. Across the road is the churrigueresque church of **San Diego Ⓑ**, next door to the magnificent **Teatro Juárez Ⓒ** (open Tues–Sun; entrance fee), inaugurated in 1903 by the dictator Porfirio Díaz himself, and with a "French-Moorish" interior.

Almost all of Guanajuato's sights are to the west of the Jardín de la Unión, with the exception of the **Museo Iconográfico del Quijote Ⓓ** (open Tues–Sun; entrance free), a few blocks to the east. Dedicated to Cervantes's *Don Quixote de la Mancha*, the collection – ranging from dime-store junk to works by Picasso and Dalí – was donated by a rich advertising executive and avid Quixote-phile.

Two blocks west of Jardín de la Unión, near **Plaza de la Paz Ⓔ**, are some of Guanajuato's richest colonial buildings. The Supreme Court, which was designed by the 18th-century architect Eduardo de Tresguerras, was the home of the **Condes de Rul y Valenciana**, owners of Mexico's richest silver mine. On

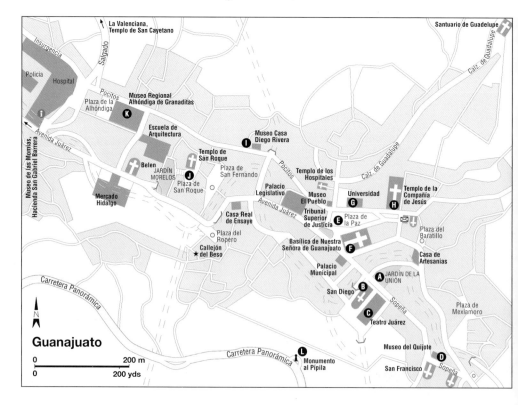

Guanajuato

0 _____ 200 m
0 _____ 200 yds

Maps
Area 236
City 240

the east side of the plaza is the **Basílica de Nuestra Señora de Guanajuato** , which houses the image of the city's patroness, a gift in 1557 from King Philip II of Spain and said to date from the 7th century.

The **University** , a huge white building, is an outstanding example of Moorish-inspired architecture only half a century old. It is the pride of Guanajuato and the centerpiece of the **Festival Cervantino**, an important international arts festival which is celebrated in Guanajuato every October. Its neighbor, the pink-stone baroque **Templo de la Compañía** , is the grandest church in town with an impressive 19th-century dome and paintings by Miguel Cabrera inside. One block west of the university, the **Museo Casa Diego Rivera**  (open Tues–Sun; entrance fee) exhibits a collection of works by the famous muralist, who was born in this house in 1886. Nearby, in a French wrought-iron structure, Guanajuato's **market** is large, noisy and full of good and bad smells.

Plaza San Roque  is renowned for its presentations of *Entremeses Cervantinos*. These light-hearted theatrical sketches by 16th-century Spanish writer Miguel de Cervantes have become a tradition in Guanajuato and are central to the Festival Cervantino.

The Pípila and beyond

Originally a granary, the impressive **Alhóndiga de Granaditas**  (open Tues–Sun; entrance fee) was used as a fortress for the Spanish and Royalists during the War of Independence before being captured by the rebels after the famous Pípila incident. Carrying a slab of stone on his back for protection, a local miner known as the Pípila rushed the door of the Alhóndiga, set it on fire, and the rebels poured in. Today the building houses a museum with murals by Chávez

BELOW: overview of Guanajuato, from the Pípila monument.

The Callejón del Beso, Guanajuato's most famous alley, is said to have acquired its name (Kissing Alley) when two lovers, kept apart by their families, were able to exchange kisses from their balconies on opposite sides of the narrow callejón.

Morado and a collection of paintings by the 19th-century Guanajuato artist, Hermenegildo Bustos. A grandiose monument to **Pípila** ❶ stands on a ridge overlooking the city; it's a steep climb, but the view from the top is superb.

The best panoramic view of Guanajuato is from **La Valenciana** (open daily; entrance free), the mine which under its Spanish colonial masters produced a large quantity of the world's silver. The elaborate church of **San Cayetano**, next to the mine, is a masterpiece of churrigueresque style and the interior is quite dazzling. On the way you may (or may not) want to stop at Guanajuato's most famous attraction, the **Museo de las Momias** (open daily; entrance fee). The museum exhibits over 100 grotesque mummified corpses mostly found when the public cemetery was extended in 1865 (the combination of mineral-rich soil and exceptionally dry air can mummify bodies in as little as five years).

The beautiful 17th-century **Hacienda San Gabriel Barrera** (open daily; entrance fee), about 2 km (1 mile) out of town on the road to Marfil, may not be completely authentic, but it does give visitors an idea of the opulence of the wealthy during the colonial era.

The Cradle of Independence

Dolores Hidalgo ❽, 45 km (28 miles) northeast of Guanajuato, is known as the cradle of Mexican Independence. The beautiful 18th-century **Parroquia** on the main square, where Hidalgo uttered his famous *Grito,* is lovingly preserved. The **Museo–Casa de Hidalgo** (open Tues–Sun; entrance fee), at the corner of Hidalgo and Morelos, is where Hidalgo lived and plotted the uprising with Ignacio Allende and Juan de Aldama. The museum displays personal items and documents related to the life of the padre. Dolores is a typical Mexican town:

BELOW: scenic view of San Cayetano Church in Guanajuato.

the houses are solid and secretive, and there are many simple churches. Several workshops in town produce Talavera-type pottery and the ice-cream stands round the zócalo are famous for the unusual variety of flavors they offer.

San Miguel de Allende

The pretty colonial streets and buildings of **San Miguel de Allende ❾** have been protected since 1926, when the whole town was declared a National Monument. In 1938, US artist Stirling Dickinson founded an art school here. Soon after, the town began to attract foreign artists, writers and, eventually, tourists. The **Instituto Allende**, as it is called, is still a popular art and language center and one of the town's chief attractions. It is housed in what was the 18th-century home of the Conde de Canal, to the south of the town. San Miguel de Allende now has a large community of US expatriates, including many artists and writers, some of whom only spend the winter months here.

On the main plaza and dominating the entire town, the neo-Gothic **Parroquia** was designed in the late 19th century by self-taught indian stonemason, Zeferino Gutiérrez who found his inspiration looking at postcards of French churches.

Across the road from the Parroquia, the **Museo Histórico de San Miguel de Allende** (open Tues–Sun; entrance free) occupies the elegant house where Independence hero Ignacio Allende was born. Exhibits relate to local history, particularly that of the Independence movement and its heroes. Also on the plaza is the **Casa de los Condes de Canal** (open Tues–Sun; entrance free), one of the palatial *mansions* of the aristocratic Canal family, the devout "Medici" of San Miguel. It was Canal money in the 1730s that paid for the **Santa Casa de Loreto**, part of the multi-towered, 18th-century **Oratorio de San Felipe Neri**,

Map on pages 236–7

For information on the variety of arts, crafts and Spanish language courses running at the Instituto Allende, call (415) 2 01 90.

BELOW:
campesinos chew the fat in Atotonilco.

The Cerro de Cubilete, a mountain between Guanajuato and León, marks the geographical center of Mexico. On the summit stands a 20-meter (65-ft) statue of Christ with open arms, blessing the valley below.

a few blocks northeast. Dedicated to the Virgin Mary, the chapel is a replica of one in Loreto, Italy, and contains a lavish and whimsical *camerino,* or dressing chapel. The main church contains over 30 oil paintings depicting the life of San Felipe, some by Miguel Cabrera.

Two blocks west of the *Jardín* on Calle Canal, is the church and monastery of **La Concepción** whose huge dome (added in the late 19th century, again by Zeferino Gutiérrez) was inspired by that of Les Invalides in Paris. The former monastery now houses **Bellas Artes**, a state-run fine arts education and - cultural center. Like the Instituto Allende, Bellas Artes runs arts and crafts courses, although usually only in Spanish. One room contains an unfinished mural by David Alfaro Siqueiros (*see pages 108–11*) who taught at the Institute in the 1940s.

One of San Miguel's major attractions is the excellent shopping. Galleries and handicraft shops line the streets around the main square. Many of them sell beautiful handmade items, including the fine woven tablecloths and the tin and brass ware produced in the region.

El Charco del Ingenio is a 65-hectare (160-acre) botanical garden mainly devoted to the cultivation of cacti and other plants native to this semi-arid region of Mexico. Situated on a hill just 1.5 km (1 mile) northeast of San Miguel, the view of the town in the valley below is spectacular.

There are several resorts with hot springs and mineral waters in the area surrounding San Miguel. **Taboada,** 10 km (6 miles) northwest, is probably the most popular. A little further on, in the village of **Atotonilco** ❿, is a baroque pilgrimage church filled with a huge variety of artwork including frescoes by the colonial artist Miguel Antonio Martínez de Pocasangre.

BELOW: a Mexican bride arrives at church.

THE CRY OF INDEPENDENCE

On the morning of September 16, 1810, in the town of Dolores, the parish priest Padre Miguel Hidalgo rang the church bells. He addressed the congregation with an impassioned speech and ended with his famous *Grito de Dolores*: "Death to the Spaniards" (*Que mueran los gachupines*) – the "shout" for independence from Spanish rule, and the most famous outcry in Mexican history.

Hidalgo, a creole, soon became the moral and political leader of the Independence movement. He had no military training but with the help of men like Ignacio Allende, his forces – creoles, mestizos and indians – took control of a large part of western central Mexico and came close to taking the capital itself. Ten months later Hidalgo was imprisoned and executed by firing squad in Chihuahua. After Independence was finally won 11 years later the town was renamed Dolores Hidalgo.

Every year, on the night of September 15, enormous crowds gather to hear the president and politicians in zócalos of every town across the whole country repeat *El Grito*: "¡Viva Mexico!" marking the beginning of Independence Day celebrations; and that is the one night of the year when the church bell still rings out in the town of Dolores Hidalgo.

Cities of El Bajío

The colonial cities of **León**, **Irapuato**, **Salamanca** and **Celaya**, also in the state of Guanajuato, are growing rapidly and not much favored by tourists. Lively **León** is an important industrial and commercial center; it is Mexico's shoe-making capital and a good place to buy leather goods of any kind.

Salamanca, once a sleepy agricultural town, has become prosperous and chaotic since it became the site of a huge oil refinery. A redeeming feature is the church of **San Agustín**, which possesses some of the most beautiful *retablos* in Mexico. South of Salamanca, the farming village of **Yuriria** is the site of a 16th-century Augustinian monastery with an ornate plateresque façade.

Celaya has some late-colonial architecture and the neoclassical **Templo del Carmen**, designed by 18th-century architect Eduardo de Tresguerras.

Querétaro

Alongside Guanajuato is the state of Querétaro whose capital, also called **Querétaro ⓫**, is known for its colonial art. It also has a good bullring and its festival attracts famous *toreros* and enthusiastic fans from afar. Querétaro has staged some of the greatest episodes in Mexican history, including the events that accelerated the proclamation of Independence. The Treaty of Guadalupe Hidalgo, which ended the Mexican-American war and handed over half of Mexico's national territory, was signed in Querétaro in 1848. It was here that Maximilian was executed in 1867 and that the Constitution was signed in 1917.

The outskirts of Querétaro are sprawling and industrial, but the historic center has been well preserved. The main plaza, or Jardín Obregón, at the heart of the city is dominated by the church of **San Francisco**, one of the city's earliest. The

Nopal cactus leaves are tasty grilled, boiled and in tacos – but don't forget to remove the spines!

BELOW: throwing a bull by its tail.

TIP

To get an overview of
the town, join the
guided walking tour
that leaves from the
tourist office (Pasteur
17) at 10.30 every
morning.

dome's colored tiles were imported from Spain in 1540. The cloister of the adjoining monastery now houses the **Museo Regional** (open Tues–Sun; entrance fee) with exhibits relating to local archeology as well as some fine colonial paintings.

One block north of the Jardín, is the 19th-century **Teatro de la República** (open Mon–Sat; entrance free). This was where a tribunal decided the fate of Emperor Maximilian in 1867 and it also witnessed the signing of the Mexican Constitution in 1917.

Facing the charming Plaza de la Independencia, the **Casa de la Corregidora** (now the Palacio de Gobierno) was once the elegant residence of Doña Josefa Ortiz de Domínguez, wife of the local governor. In 1810 Doña Josefa, *la Corregidora*, sent a secret message from this house to the Independence conspirators, alerting them that her husband had discovered their plot; her action triggered Father Hidalgo's *Grito de la Independencia* (*see page 243*).

Aristocratic monuments and leering gargoyles

Curiously enough, the monument in the square is not dedicated to Father Hidalgo or Ignacio Allende, but rather to a colonial aristocrat, Don Juan Antonio Urrutia y Aranda, who built the magnificent 1,170-meter (3,840-ft) **aqueduct** with its 74 towering arches more than 250 years ago. The aqueduct, which can be seen from the mirador in the east of Querétaro, still carries water into the city.

The **Museo de Arte de Querétaro** (open Tues–Sun; entrance fee) is housed in a late-baroque Augustinian monastery with fantastically carved columns and arches. The leering gargoyles are said to be uttering the Ave Maria in sign language. The museum also exhibits a fine collection of 16th- to the 20th-century paintings.

BELOW: ploughing in the highlands.

Map on pages 236–7

Religious baroque

Behind a deceptively austere façade, the church of **Santa Clara**, one block north on the corner of Madero and Allende, is wildly baroque: the interior walls are covered with overflowing gilt *retablos*, and the grille separating the choir from the congregation is certainly a masterpiece. Outside, the fountain dedicated to Neptune was designed in 1797 by one of Mexico's greatest architects, Francisco Eduardo Tresguerras. **Santa Rosa de Viterbo**, southwest of the center at Arteaga and Montes, contains grand altarpieces and a splendid organ. It has a more flamboyant exterior with buttresses that seem more Chinese than European in style.

East of the center, the **Convento de la Santa Cruz** (open daily; donation requested) is built on the site of the Otomí defeat in 1531, and is said to be inhabited by the ghost of Emperor Maximilian, who was imprisoned here before his execution.

To the west of Querétaro, the **Cerro de las Campanas** is a low, barren hill where Maximilian went before the firing squad. Nearby is a humble chapel dedicated to the emperor and a huge statue of Benito Juárez.

Eyewitness accounts inspired the French Impressionist Edouard Manet to produce his famous painting of the execution of Emperor Maximilian.

Provincial Querétaro

About 61 kms (38 miles) south of Querétaro, **San Juan del Río ⓬** is a popular weekend outing from the capital. A white market town with narrow streets and solid provincial houses, it is not as aristocratic as Querétaro, but offers the atmosphere of rural Mexico. Some of Mexico's best fighting bulls are raised near here, and the town is renowned for basket-weavers and lapidaries (opals and amethysts).

Nearby, on Highway 120, is the picturesque village of **Tequisquiapan ⓭**, another weekend resort with thermal springs, fine climate, watersports and a popular wine and cheese festival in the summer. ❑

BELOW: El Jardín Obregón, the main plaza in Querétaro.

JALISCO AND MICHOACÁN

Maps
Area 236
City 250

*Guadalajara and Morelia are very Spanish cities,
but indian traditions and culture are still strong in many of the
Purépecha and Huichol villages of Michoacán and Jalisco*

Jalisco, northwest of Mexico City and the Central Highlands, is one of the most important states in the country. It has agriculture, a booming industry, and popular coastal resorts. Its capital, **Guadalajara** ⓴, is the second biggest city in Mexico, with a population of over 4 million. Jalisco is also the home of tequila, the hat dance and *mariachi* music.

Perched on a "mile-high" plain (actually 1,524 meters/5,000 ft high), Guadalajara has been called "the biggest small town in Mexico"; it is a busy metropolis that manages to retain a provincial atmosphere. The city is said to have the best climate in North America, with temperatures averaging over 20°C (70°F) all year round.

The pearl of the west

Guadalajara is a city of parks and monuments, cool shady plazas with pretty fountains, gracious buildings, flower-filled patios and quaint white *trolebuses* that glide along on rubber tires. It also has gourmet restaurants and luxury hotels that are as sophisticated as any in North America. There are art galleries, bookstores and some of the best murals in the country.

Founded in 1532 by Nuño de Guzmán, Guadalajara was not recognized by the Spanish Crown until 10 years later. A cruel and ambitious conquistador, Guzmán, who intended Guadalajara to be the capital of the kingdom of New Galicia, was sent back to Spain in disgrace. Guadalajara managed to remain independent of Mexico City, and its archbishopric was as rich and powerful as that of the capital itself.

Guadalajara has long been an important commercial center and it always retained some political and judicial autonomy; it is strategically situated near one of the few passages leading through the mountains to the fertile Pacific coast. Its university was founded very early on, and students were drawn from as far away as southern Texas, then part of New Spain.

Most of the interesting sights in Guadalajara are downtown. Its landmark, the huge **Cathedral** Ⓐ, with its yellow-tiled spire, exhibits a mixture of styles, from neo-gothic to baroque and neoclassical. Surrounded by four plazas, it provides a welcome oasis amidst the bustle of the big city.

A fountain in the **Plaza de los Laureles** Ⓑ, in front of the cathedral, commemorates the founding of the city; along its north side is the porticoed Presidencia Municipal (City Hall). Some of Jalisco's most distinguished men are buried beneath the Greek-style **Rotonda de los Hombres Ilustres** Ⓒ, which stands, surrounded by Doric columns, in the center of another plaza to the north of the cathedral. Statues of famous

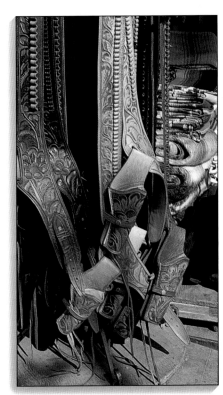

LEFT: a *campesino* shapes a hat from a rolled cactus fiber called *ixtle*.
BELOW: imitation *charro* trappings for sale.

Guadalajara is at its prettiest in March, when the jacarandas are flowering. However, the liveliest time of year is during the Fiestas de Octubre (October), when there are mariachis, charros, processions and fireworks every night.

jalicienses are dotted along the plaza's shady paths. The **Museo Regional** **D** (open Tues–Sun; entrance fee) occupies an attractive 18th-century building, a former seminary, on the east side of the square. The museum has galleries dedicated to archeology, colonial history, painting and ethnography.

To the south of the cathedral is the pretty **Plaza de Armas** **E**, originally Guadalajara's main market square, and ancient execution site. The French bandstand in the center hosts concerts every Thursday and Sunday evening. Facing the plaza, the late-baroque **Palacio de Gobierno** **F**, houses a magnificent mural by **José Clemente Orozco** (*see page 110*). The mural is a striking homage to Padre Miguel Hidalgo, the "father of Mexican Independence."

The **Plaza de la Liberación** **G**, to the east of the cathedral, is the largest of the four squares. Designed by contemporary Guadalajara architect Ignacio Díaz Morales, the plaza blends with the buildings framing the rear of the cathedral and the façade of the 19th-century **Teatro Degollado** **H**. The recently restored theater has a sumptuous red velvet and gilt interior and a ceiling painted with a scene from Dante's *Divine Comedy*.

Hospicio Cabañas

Behind the theater, the **Plaza Tapatía** **I** is a long pedestrian precinct which leads down to the elegant **Hospicio Cabañas** **J** (open Tues–Sun; admission fee), which was founded and financed by one of Guadalajara's great benefactors, Bishop Juan Ruiz de Cabañas. Over 20 patios interconnect the different sections of this neoclasssical building, which was designed by Manuel Tolsá in 1805. At the center is the Capilla Tolsá, whose walls and ceiling were decorated in the late 1930s with what are considered to be Orozco's finest murals. These

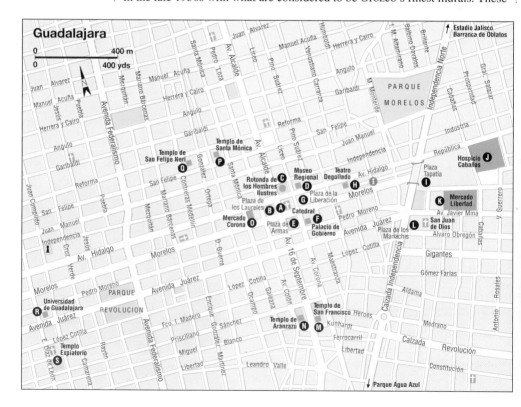

dramatic, symbolic works depict, among other things, the destruction and suffering caused by the Spanish conquest. There is also a museum which displays a collection of drawings and paintings by Orozco – who was a native of Jalisco – as well as temporary exhibitions by other mostly contemporary artists. As the city's most important cultural center, the institute also organizes many other artistic activities such as theater, concerts and films.

Market stalls and mariachis

Just south of the Hospicio Cabañas, at the core of Guadalajara's traditional center, the **Mercado Libertad** Ⓚ is a vast, colorful, undercover market. Better known as San Juan de Dios after the nearby church, the market sells everything from herbal remedies, fresh food and handicrafts, to imported jeans and stereo systems. Beside the church, the **Plaza de los Mariachis** Ⓛ comes alive in the evening when the musicians gather in the square to play traditional songs and *corridos* (ballads) outside the cafés and restaurants.

In the southern part of the downtown area, **San Francisco** Ⓜ and **Aranzazú** Ⓝ are two remarkable colonial churches built by the Franciscans in their ambitious attempts to extend their missions all the way to the Californias. Now located in a busy financial district, these churches, with their attractive *jardines*, were once at the heart of one of the city's best neighborhoods. The Templo de Aranzazú has a highly elaborate interior with three golden churrigueresque altarpieces. The *retablos* in the older San Francisco church were destroyed by arson in the 1930s.

Further south, towards the train station, the large, well-kept **Parque Agua Azul** (open Tues–Sun; entrance fee) offers relief from the city noise with an

Map on page 250

TIP

A huge range of leather goods, including belts, bags and *huaraches* (rough leather sandals) are on sale in the Mercado Libertad. Traditional handmade sweets are another specialty; try the ones made of tamarind fruit and the ultra-sweet coconut, *cocada envinada*.

BELOW: traditional carriages in Guadalajara.

Map
on page
250

aviary, butterfly dome and orchid house. The **Casa de las Artesanías de Jalisco**, on the north side of the park, sells excellent handicrafts from all over the state. Two blocks west of the cathedral is another interesting market, the **Mercado Corona** , which sells every kind of herbal tea and natural remedy imaginable. The streets in this part of town are some of the best for exploring.

Many are lined with orange trees, and some brightly painted houses have pretty wrought-iron grilles leading into patios overflowing with bougainvillea, jasmine and songbirds. Two often overlooked churches in this area are **Santa Mónica** and **San Felipe Neri**; the former, a convent church, has a prodigiously carved, late-baroque façade. Inside, women still pray to St Christopher to help them find a husband (or to get rid of the one they've got). Nearby, 18th-century San Felipe is a very grand church with an exotic belfry and well-proportioned dome.

The university and beyond

Further west, on Avenida Juárez, is the **University of Guadalajara**, whose central building dates from the 1920s. More impressive Orozco murals decorate the dome and back wall of the *Paraninfo* (main hall). The building also houses the **Museo de Arte Contemporáneo** (open Tue–Sat; entrance fee), which exhibits a permanent collection of mainly local modern art, and temporary shows from further afield. Behind the university, the big neo-Gothic church modeled on the cathedral of Orvieto in Italy is known as the **Expiatorio**. The area just beyond the university, along Vallarta and Chapultepec, offers relief from the downtown noise and traffic with its broad, tree-lined streets and inviting sidewalk cafés.

BELOW: mariachis in miniature.

Tequila & Co.

Like Jerez, Curaçao, Champagne and a handful of other places, Tequila has achieved a reputation far out of proportion to its size. Millions of drinkers who never dream of going to this small town wax rhapsodic about its name. Less than an hour's drive northwest of Guadalajara, Tequila lies almost under the shadow of an extinct 2,950-meter (9,700-ft) volcano. It is surrounded by thousands of acres of bluish-green, spear-like, cultivated agave plants.

Although there are hundreds of different species of the maguey plant, under Mexican law at least 51 percent of any tequila must be from the tequila weber agave, which grows only in this region. The best kinds of tequila use pure juice; cheaper brand liquors are supplemented with cane juice.

After growing for eight to ten years, the tequila maguey is trimmed down to its 50-kilo (100-lb) heart or *piña*, which is steamed, then shredded and squeezed. Sugar is added and it is allowed to ferment for four days before undergoing two distillations. Most of this colorless liquid is then bottled; the rest is aged in oak casks for up to seven years, during which it assumes the golden color and mellow flavor of *tequila añejo*.

Mezcal and *pulque* are also derived from the maguey cactus. *Pulque* – the only alcoholic drink known to the pre-Hispanic indian civilizations – is fermented rather than distilled (the distillation process was unknown before the Conquest). Said to be mildly hallucinatory, *pulque* is a cloudy, milky drink with a pungent odour and an acquired taste. *Pulquerías*, with their sawdust-covered floors tend to a predominantly male, blue-collar clientele. However, when it is "cured" with fruits such as guava, pineapple or strawberries, *pulque* becomes much more palatable and is sometimes served at weddings or other fiestas. *Mezcal*, on the other hand, is a fiery high-proof alcoholic drink, which, like tequila, is distilled, but the methods used are different. The small worm in the *mezcal* bottle is considered a delicacy – possibly because it absorbs the alcohol.

But tequila is the only one of the three to have taken its place with top-flight liquors, especially in the US, which, by the late 1980s, was importing 5 million cases a year from its southern neighbor. Tequila became popular as long ago as the 17th century, but its international reputation got its major boost from American servicemen on leave in Tijuana and the other border towns during World War II. Now more than 600 million *margaritas* are reportedly drunk in the US every year – that's about 1.5 million every day.

The ritual of correct tequila drinking begins with placing grains of salt between the thumb and forefinger, licking them then, after sucking some drops of lime, taking a drink from a *caballito* (the small glass used for tequila). The idea is to establish a precise and satisfying balance of strong flavors in which the tequila's pure, sweet fire is complemented by the acidity of lime, and the relief given by those grains of salt. Lesser purists prefer their tequila accompanied by Sangrita, a spicy mixture that contains tomato and orange juice, or in the now world popular *margarita*. ❑

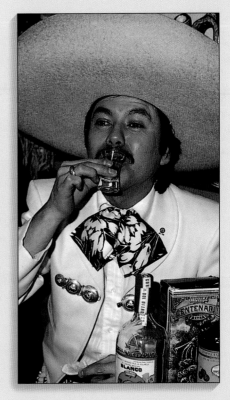

RIGHT: taking a tequila break.

Jalisco is the home of the Mexican cliché: the mustachioed macho wearing a broad-rimmed hat and riding a horse (although today it is just as likely to be a pick-up truck).

Calzada Independencia is the backbone of popular Guadalajara. It is not a beautiful street, but it is busy and full of life. Due north along the *calzada* is a huge soccer stadium, the **Estadio Jalisco**, a shrine to Mexico's most popular – some might say fanatical – sport. A few kilometers further north is the **Barranca de Oblatos**, a superb 600 meter (1,970 ft) canyon whose dramatic stone walls are softened by lush vegetation, and which has an impressive waterfall, the **Cola de Caballo**. At the bottom of the canyon the Santiago river slides into the tropics and towards the distant Pacific. There's a great view of the Barranca from the nearby zoo at **Huentitán Park**, which also features an amusement park and planetarium.

In the northwestern suburbs of Guadalajara, **Zapopán** is visited for its Basílica, a baroque church that houses the miraculous image of the Virgen de Zapopan. Every summer, the Virgin is paraded from church to church through the streets to Guadalajara; then, on October 12, in what must be among the best-attended pilgrimages in the world, the image is brought back to Zapopan. Next door to the church is the small but interesting **Museo Huichol** (open daily; entrance free), with displays that relate to the art, crafts and traditions of the Huichol indians.

Tlaquepaque and Tonalá

San Pedro Tlaquepaque, in the southeastern suburbs, is nationally famous for its ceramics, although much of the quality and style has deteriorated as so many pieces are now mass produced; however, there are still many beautiful, handmade crafts to be found and the **Museo Regional de Cerámica y las Artes Populares** (open Tues–Sun; entrance free) is worth visiting for its display of

BELOW: the felt hats worn by *charros* are very expensive.

local pottery. But the best thing to do in Tlaquepaque is to wander along its cobbled streets and browse around the 19th-century houses that have been turned into shops and restaurants. **El Parián**, the covered market on the central Jardín Hidalgo, is especially favored by *tapatíos* – the name given to people from Guadalajara – who flock here at weekends to drink beer, eat *birria* (a local kid-goat barbecue dish) and listen to the *mariachis*.

Much of the pottery and glassware sold in Tlaquepaque and Guadalajara is produced in the *fábricas* (factories) of nearby **Tonalá**. On Thursdays and Sundays practically the whole town becomes a street market, although many of the stalls sell factory seconds and sometimes it is better to go directly to the shops.

Chapala and beyond

Southeast of Guadalajara is **Lake Chapala**, Mexico's biggest lake, renowned for its glorious sunsets. The comfortable weekend homes of wealthy *tapatíos* and retired *norteamericanos* line its north shore. The town of **Chapala ⓯**, only 40 minutes from Guadalajara, can get crowded at weekends; you can hire a boat to take you to one of the tiny islands for a drink or lunch. Further west along the shore is the attractive, sleepy village of **Ajijic ⓰**, largely poulated by US expatriates, and the thermal spa at **San Juan Cosalá**.

The town of **Tapalpa ⓱**, with its delightful old wooden-balconied houses in the cool pine-forested hills southwest of Lake Chapala, offers a complete change of scenery, and makes a delightful weekend escape from the city.

But for anyone seeking a few leisurely days at the beach, **Puerto Vallarta** – Jalisco's sophisticated Pacific Coast resort – is just minutes away by plane and three hours by car. For those who prefer less activity and more privacy, there are

Map on pages 236–7

BELOW: quiet town of Tapalpa.

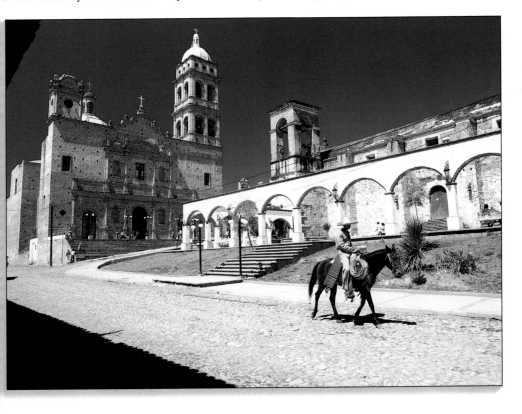

Holy postcards for sale.

long stretches of creamy sand beaches north of Puerto Vallarta and romantic rocky coves to the south (*see pages 265–73*).

Michoacán

Everyone has a favorite state in Mexico and many would choose mountainous **Michoacán**. With its lakes, rivers, indian villages, volcanoes and colonial cities, it is like a miniature model of Mexico. In the northeast part of the state, the capital, **Morelia** , formerly known as Valladolid, was renamed in 1828 for José María Morelos, one of the heroes of the Independence movement. The roads (toll and *libre*) from Mexico City are marvelously scenic. The *libre* winds its way over the **Mil Cumbres** (Thousand Peaks – there are a thousand curves too), through pine forests and past cool waterfalls.

The climate is mild and life moves at a slow tempo in Morelia, a pretty colonial town built of rose-colored stone. The **Cathedral** Ⓐ, which took over a century to build (1640–1744) is a grand combination of Herrerian, baroque and neoclassical styles. Sadly, much of the baroque relief work inside was replaced in the 19th century. However, there is a magnificent German organ, and a corn-paste statue of Christ wearing a 16th-century crown, a gift from King Philip II of Spain. In the **Palacio de Gobierno** Ⓑ, a former seminary on the other side of Avenida Madero, local artist Alfredo Zalce has painted colorful murals which reflect the beauty of Michoacán and its rich history.

The **Casa Natal de Morelos** (open Mon–Sat; entrance free) on the corner of Corregidora and Obeso, is the birthplace of José María Morelos y Pavón, hero of the Independence movement, who studied under Padre Hidalgo and also became a priest. One block east, the **Museo Casa de Morelos** Ⓒ (open daily;

BELOW:
Morelia at dusk.

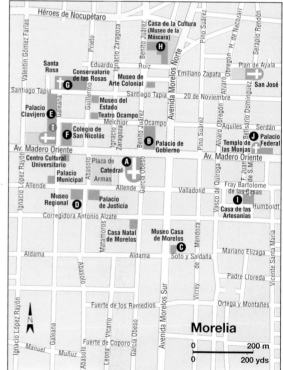

entrance fee), where Morelos lived from 1801, has exhibits on his life and memorabilia, such as the blindfold he wore when he was executed in 1815. Just off the zócalo, the **Museo Regional** D (open Tues–Sun; entrance fee) has exhibits of archaeology, history, ethnology, and, most interestingly, a complete pharmacy dating from 1868.

The elegant **Palacio Clavijero** E, a former Jesuit seminary founded in 1660, now houses the **tourist information office**. It was named in honor of Francisco Xavier Clavijero, a Jesuit who taught here and who wrote what many believe to be the best history of Mexico. The nearby **Colegio de San Nicolás** F, where Morelos studied as a young man, is one of the oldest universities in the Americas. One block north, facing a peaceful plaza with a statue of Miguel de Cervantes, is the pretty baroque church of **Santa Rosa** G and the adjoining 18th-century **Conservatorio de las Rosas**, which still functions as a major music academy.

Marvelous masks

A small but fascinating collection of ceremonial masks associated with dances from different regions of Mexico is on display at the **Museo de la Máscara** H (open daily; entrance free). The museum is part of the Casa de la Cultura, a lively cultural center in the converted **Convento del Carmen** which hosts arts workshops, performances and temporary exhibitions.

Three blocks east of the zócalo, in the converted Convento de San Francisco, the **Casa de las Artesanías** I (open Tues–Sun; entrance fee) has devoted separate rooms to handicrafts from different Michoacán villages, whose dazzling craftsmanship is rivalled only perhaps by that of Oaxaca. Further east, beyond

Maps
Area 236
City 256

Anyone with a sweet tooth should try ordering chongos zamoranos, *a local specialty with a sugar content that is hard to beat; you can even buy them in cans to take home with you.*

BELOW: a Tarascan market.

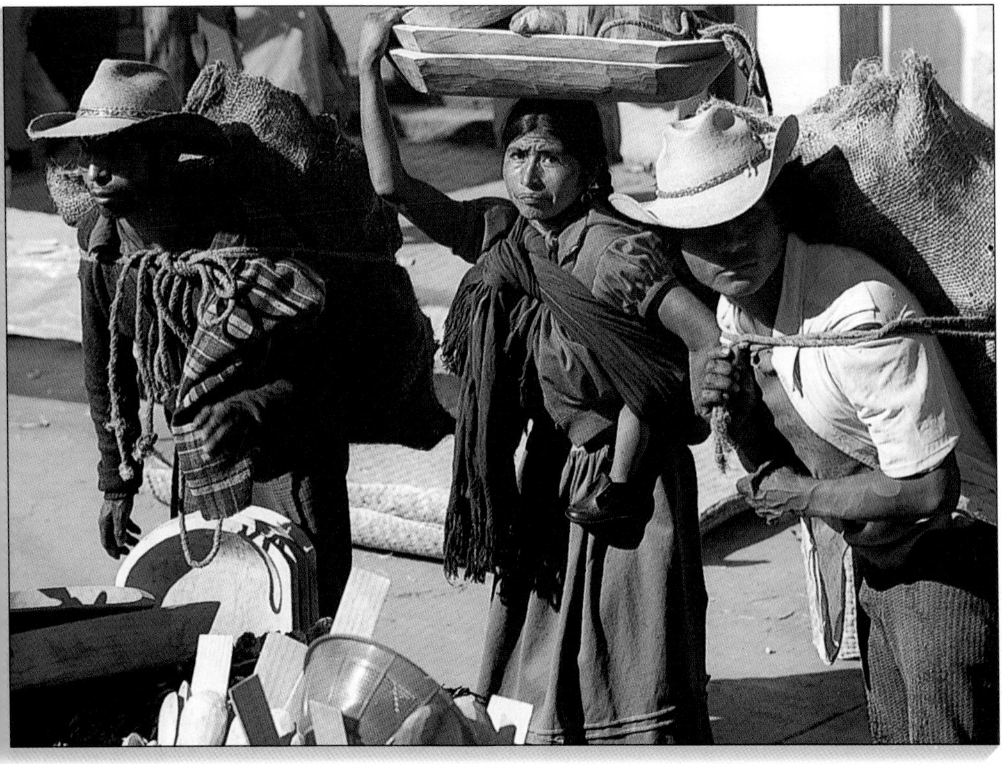

Ice-cream bar in Morelia.

the beautiful **Templo de las Monjas** ❶, on Avenida Madero, is the 18th century **aqueduct**, with 253 arches. South of the aqueduct, in Morelia's largest park – the Bosque de Cuauhtémoc – is the **Museo de Arte Contemporáneo** (open Tues–Sun; entrance free), which has very good contemporary exhibitions of modern art.

Every year, between 30 and 100 million Monarch butterflies fly all the way from Canada and the USA, to their breeding ground in the east of Michoacán. Near the village of Angangueo, and not far from the Mexico City-Morelia highway, the **Santuario de Mariposas El Rosario** ❶ (open daily; entrance fee) can be visited between November and mid-April, when the butterflies blanket the entire landscape in soft velvety orange. It is best to visit the sanctuary in the morning when the butterflies flutter from the trees to the humid ground as the day becomes warmer; it is a truly spectacular sight.

Lake Pátzcuaro and Janitzio

The very Spanish city of Morelia is uncharacteristic of the rest of Michoacán, which has remained strongly indian. Directly west of Morelia, surrounded by indian villages, is **Lake Pátzcuaro** ❷⓿, where the fishermen use distinctive butterfly-shaped fishing nets. There are boat trips to the island of **Janitzio**, in the middle of the lake, with its giant 40 meter (130 ft) sculpture of Independence hero, José María Morelos. You can climb inside the statue, right up to the clenched fist, for a wonderful panoramic view.

Janitzio is especially known for its **Day of the Dead** celebrations (*see pages 262–3*) on November 1–2, when local people cross the lake in a procession of candlelit canoes, bringing flowers, food and other offerings to the cemetery in

BELOW: fishing on Lake Pátzcuaro.

commemoration of their loved ones. In order to preserve the intimacy of the occasion, tourists are discouraged from attending the all-night vigil in Janitzio, but there are other cemeteries in the region where visitors are more welcome to observe the celebrations.

Pátzcuaro

The town of **Pátzcuaro** ㉑, on the south side of the lake, has whitewashed adobe houses with overhanging red-tiled roofs, colonial mansions with balconies and coats-of-arms, cobbled streets, and the smell of wood smoke in the air. This is the heart of Purépecha indian country; the Friday market is especially lively, although indian wares are being overtaken by imported goods.

All the main sights of Pátzcuaro, or Tarascan, are on or near the two central squares: firstly, the shady **Plaza Vasco de Quiroga** and which, is named after the 16th-century bishop who dedicated his life to the welfare of the Purépecha, or Tarascan, indians, and his statue stands in the center. On the east side of the square is the 17th-century **Casa del Gigante** (House of the Giant), former residence of the Counts of Menocal and still a private home. Other mansions have been converted into hotels, restaurants and craft shops.

The **Plaza Gertrudis Bocanegra**, one block north, is named after an Independence heroine. The busy town market is on the west side, while on the north side, the 16th-century Biblioteca occupies the former church of **San Agustín**. Inside, murals by the celebrated Juan O'Gorman illustrate the history of Michoacán. East of the plaza is the **Basílica de Nuestra Señora de la Salud**, a shrine for health-seekers from all over Mexico, who come to revere the statue of Our Lady of Health. Quiroga planned the basilica to be a vast, five-nave

Map on pages 236–7

TIP

On Wednesday and Saturday nights you can attend the *Noche Mexicana* and watch the *Baile de los Viejitos* (Dance of the Old Men) at the Posada de Don Vasco hotel.

BELOW: a typical street corner in Pátzcuaro.

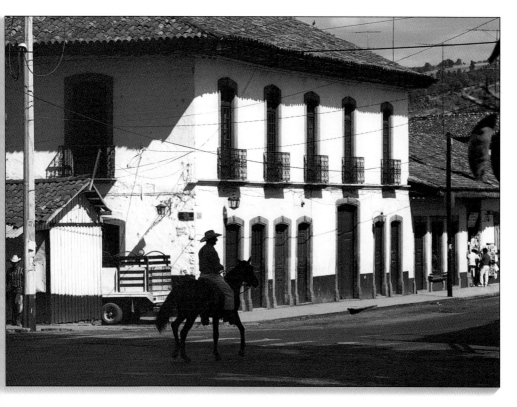

Map on pages 236–7

TIP

Michoacán's hand-painted wooden toys make wonderful ornaments; however, take your own safety precautions as the paint may well be lead-based.

RIGHT: the band-stand, Santa Clara del Cobre.
BELOW: making a song and dance.

cathedral, but unfortunately most of Quiroga's plans were never completed.

The **Museo Regional de Artes Populares** (open Tues–Sun; admission fee), south of the basilica, on Alcantarillas, was founded in 1640 as the Colegio de San Nicolás by Don Vasco de Quiroga. The museum has a fine collection of regional handicrafts, including lacquerwork, pottery, textiles and copperware from Santa Clara. The **Casa de los Once Patios**, southeast of the main square, is a craft center, with workshops and boutiques set around the courtyards of an old Dominican convent built in the 18th century.

The villages of Michoacán

On the eastern shore of Lake Pátzcuaro, the village of **Tzintzuntzán** (Place of Hummingbirds) is the ancient capital of the Purépecha, or *Tarascos* as they were called by the Spanish. The Tarascans, unconquered until the Spanish arrived with their armor plate and cannons, have preserved their traditions, language and way of life to this day, especially in the mountain redoubts.

The ruins, also called **Tzintzuntzán** (open daily; entrance fee), and one of the the chief ancient sites in Michoacán, consist mainly of a group of five *yácatas*, or round-based temples, on a reconstructed terrace which offers wonderful views of the lake and surrounding countryside. In the village, there is a large 16th-century Franciscan monastery in peaceful gardens; the olive trees are deemed the oldest in Mexico, said to have been brought from Spain by Quiroga himself.

The area is dotted with indian villages, each known for its own special handicraft. Many of these are sold in the market town of **Quiroga**, which itself produces brightly painted wooden furniture and masks. South of Pátzcuaro, for instance, **Santa Clara del Cobre** (sometimes called Villa Escalante) is famous for its copperware; and guitars are made in the workshops of **Paracho**.

The town of **Uruapan** ㉒, 62 km (39 miles) west of Pátzcuaro, marks the beginning of another Michoacán – the *tierra caliente*, or tropical lands. It is the center of a rich agricultural area known for its avocados. The town itself is famous for its lacquered trays and boxes; there is a good display of this *artesanía* in the **Museo Regional de Arte Popular** (open Tues–Sun; entrance free), which is housed in one of the oldest buildings in Uruapan, the 16th-century **Huatapera**.

A few blocks west of the zócalo, along Calle Independencia, is the entrance to the delightful **Parque Nacional Eduardo Ruiz**, a luxuriant tropical park which surrounds the source of the Río Cupatitzio. The countryside around Uruapan is remarkable. One popular excursion, just 10 km (6 miles) south, is to see the river Cupatitzio cascading 25 meters (82 ft) through lush tropical forests, over the **Tzararácua** waterfall.

Even more impressive is a trip to the still smouldering **Paricutín**, a volcano which erupted in 1943, leaving whole villages buried in an extraordinary moon-like landscape which is slowly sprouting with green life again. You can walk or hire a pony and guide in the Purépecha village of **Angahuan**, 30 km (18 miles) northwest of Uruapan. ❑

IN HONOR OF THEIR ANCESTORS

Every year on the first two days of November, the people of Mexico recall their dead relations in a serious but festive ceremony

Of the many religious festivals celebrated throughout the year in Mexico, the *Día de los Muertos* (Day of the Dead) is probably the most fascinating to any outsider and the one that is truest to the country's *mestizo* spirit.

The original celebration can be traced to pre-Hispanic rituals dedicated to Mictlantecuhtli, the Mexica lord of the under-world, and Huitzilopochtli, the Aztec war deity to whom so many were sacrificed. After the conquest, in a vain attempt to turn the fiesta into a Christian celebration, Spanish priests moved the date to coincide with that of All Souls' Day.

CHANGING WITH THE TIMES

Nowadays the fiesta blends both pre-Hispanic and Christian rituals, and celebrations vary from state to state. The most commented are the Purépecha traditions in Michoacán, where all-night vigils in the cemeteries and candlelit boat processions across the lake to the tiny island of Janitzio attract visitors from all over the world.

Skeletons and skulls, whether papier maché, chocolate, sugar, or in the form of macabre masked dancers, are most prominent around the capital.

In the big cities, wonderful exhibitions of *ofrendas* are organized as a way of keeping alive Mexico's unique ritual, which is being threatened by monster masks, pumpkins and the American "trick or treat."

▽ **FLOWERS OF DEATH**
The bright orange *cempasúchil* flower, similar to the marigold, is the "flower of death" and figures prominently during Day of the Dead rituals all over the country.

▷ **LIVELY SKELETONS**
José Guadalupe Posada's powerful engravings (*see picture top left*) reflect the humor and tragedy of the occasion and have inspired craftsmen and artists for over a century.

▽ **SWEET SKULLS**
Market stalls fill up with sugar and chocolate skulls – reminiscent of the Aztec *tzompantli* (skull racks). There are also lively and humorous skeletons and coffins made of clay and papier mâché.

◁ **LIFE AND DEATH**
The concept of duality – such as that of life and death shown in this pre-Hispanic skull – was present all over Mesomaerica, and is apparent in this ritual today.

◁ SPIRITS RETURN

Some people prepare an altar at home, others visit the cemeteries to share the festivities with the spirits of their loved ones.

△ TIME FOR THOUGHT

It is a festive occasion for the whole community, but also deeply spiritual; a time of personal contemplation, of shared memories, and for reuniting the living with their dead relations.

LITTLE ANGELS RETURNING HOME

It is believed that the souls of the children who have died (called *angelitos* – "little angels") return to their earthly homes on November 1, while those of the adults arrive the following day. A candle is lit for each returning soul and beautiful *ofrendas*, or shrines are made in homes all over the country.

Photos of the loved ones are placed around the table along with a variety of their favorite foods or *antojitos*, the traditional *pan de muerto* (bread of the dead) and a glass of tequila or mug of *atole* (cornmeal drink). The shrine is decorated with ornately cut tissue paper and orange *cempasúchil* flowers. Little chocolate or sugar skulls, and other decorations are placed around the *ofrenda*, and an incense called *copal* is burned. Sometimes a path of orange petals is strewn from the street to the shrine to help the souls find their way home, in this intimate tribute to lost loved ones.

△ EDIBLE OFFERINGS

Ofrendas, or offerings, vary from state to state and from family to family, but *pan de muerto*, bread decorated with bone shapes, is traditional everywhere.

▽ DIE LAUGHING

Mexicans dread death but also laugh at it. The ritual is neither morbid nor mocking, but an effort to laugh at the tragically inevitable.

ACAPULCO AND THE PACIFIC BEACHES

Map on pages 236–7

The Pacific Coast has glamorous beach resorts with luxury hotels and all the facilities but there are still secluded bays where you can just slip into a hammock and watch the tequila sunrise

Acapulco, with its dramatic mountains sweeping down to the Pacific, was the first of the coastal resorts to achieve international fame as a mecca for the "beautiful people." Later, when the value of tourism as a major industry became apparent, Ixtapa was developed about 257 km (160 miles) northwest. Gradually this whole Pacific coast achieved far-reaching fame.

Romantic Vallarta

Puerto Vallarta ㉓ owes its name to Hollywood. It leaped to fame with the 1964 filming of John Huston's *Night of the Iguana* on Mismaloya beach, just south of town. Richard Burton, who starred in the film, subsequently bought a home nearby; his relationship with bride-to-be Elizabeth Taylor attracted much media attention, and it wasn't long before the tourists started arriving. Their house – at Zaragoza 445, in a residential area known as "Gringo Gulch" – still has its original furnishings and is open to the public daily (entrance fee). Many other, less-memorable movies have also been filmed here since, including *Predator* with Arnold Schwarzenegger in 1987.

Vallarta lines the shore of **Bahía de Banderas**, one of the world's ten largest bays. Sometimes known as Humpback Bay because of the migrating whales that gather here each spring, it is also a breeding ground for dolphins. The town has several different faces: straddling the **Río Cuale**, the relatively unspoiled **old town** has white adobe houses with red-tiled roofs, donkey traffic, and cobblestones.

The **Templo de Guadalupe**, a central landmark, is topped by an imposing crown, a replica of that worn by Maximilian's wife, Charlotte. Attractive bridges cross the river to an island, where there are art galleries, shops, restaurants and a small **archeological museum** (open Tues–Sun; entrance free).

North of the old town, the **Zona Hotelera** is a long stretch of coast lined with luxury hotels which terminates at **Marina Vallarta**, a 178-hectare (440-acre) upscale resort area with even more luxurious hotels, condos and an 18-hole golf course. Parasailing, an easy and spectacular parachute ride behind a speedboat, is a popular pastime on several of Vallarta's beaches. Other watersports include snorkelling, scuba diving, jet-skiing, windsurfing, sailing and deep-sea fishing for marlin, dorado and tuna.

Playa Olas Altas and **Playa de los Muertos**, on the south side of Río Cuale, are the most crowded beaches, but there are several others further south, beyond the city limits at **Mismaloya** or **Boca de**

LEFT: diving off La Quebrada, near Acapulco's old town.
BELOW: keeping a beady eye open.

Tomatlán. Boat or catamaran excursions can be arranged from Los Muertos Pier to **Las Animas**, a tiny community with inexpensive hotels; **Quimixto**, where movie director John Huston built a house, and which is popular with divers; or **Yelapa**, further round the bay, where you can choose between staying in a palm-thatched *palapa* or a small hotel. It is also possible to rent a horse or *burro* and venture into the jungle to the nearby waterfalls.

Manzanillo claims to be "the sailfish capital of the world." The fishing season runs from November to March.

South of Vallarta

The road runs inland for a while and then passes **Playa Blanca**, a loud and busy Club Med facility, and **Pueblo Nuevo**, a budding American-style resort community. Then comes **Bahía Chamela** and the **Costa Alegre** ㉔, a 96-km (60-mile) strip of relatively undeveloped coastline where the delightful bays have changed little since the Spanish galleons sailed these waters 400 years ago. The next resort along the coast is **Barra de Navidad** ㉕, a sleepy beach town which is aimed mainly at vacationers from Guadalajara. These same people also head for **San Patricio Melaque**, just 2 km (1 mile) along the beach. It was from this bay that Miguel López Legazpi sailed in 1564 to conquer the Philippines.

Manzanillo ㉖, just an hour away in the state of Colima, is a busy railhead and port, with narrow, traffic-choked streets. There are a few good hotels in town, although the resort hotels and the best beaches are to the west of the bay around the **Santiago Peninsula**. For the affluent, the top-of-the-line **Las Hadas** (The Fairies) complex, built by a Bolivian tin-magnate, is a mixture of pseudo-Moorish, Mediterranean and Disney.

A short ride inland through lemon groves is the colonial city of **Colima** ㉗,

BELOW: view of Puerto Vallarta's tourist area.

Map on pages 236–7

the state capital and first Spanish city to be built in the west of Mexico. There are two good museums in Colima: the **Museo Regional de Historia** (open Tues–Sun; entrance free) and the even better **Museo de las Culturas de Occidente** (open Tues–Sun; entrance free), which exhibits a large and varied collection of pre-Hispanic pottery from the cultures of western Mexico. Most notable are the pot-bellied Itzcuintli dogs for which Colima is renowned. It is a pleasant city of parks and gardens and the surrounding countryside is dramatically dominated by two volcanoes: the still rumbling **Volcán de Fuego**, and its larger, extinct neighbor, the often snowcapped **Nevado de Colima**, which is popular with climbers.

Twin resorts

As they are served by the same airport and are only a few kilometers apart, Ixtapa and Zihuatanejo tend to be listed and lumped together as a unit, and indeed their boundaries have almost blended; but the characters of these two resort towns are wildly different. **Ixtapa ㉘**, like Cancún in the Yucatán and Huatulco, is the result of government-planned tourism. It came into existence only in the 1970s, but now attracts almost 400,000 visitors each year, three-quarters of whom are Mexican. The luxury high-rise resort hotels are strung out along the dramatic Playa del Palmar and around the Punta Ixtapa.

Across a beautifully manicured roadway that runs past the hotels is a cleverly constructed mall that manages to feel a little more like a village than just a strip shopping center. There are restaurants and juice shops interspersed with stores offering necessities and fripperies of all kinds. Shopping here is a major activity; there are more than 1,000 stores in these two resort towns, including trendy

The Green Roller, a monster of a wave 10 meters (33 ft) high, comes rumbling in at Cuyutlán, south of Manzanillo, in April or May each year.

BELOW: a rococo Beetle.

Selling colorful woven bags, made of ixtle fiber.

boutiques, a good silver shop (Platería Roberto's) with more planned, and three handicraft markets.

In addition to its hotel zone, Ixtapa has luxury condominiums, two golf courses (one designed by Robert Trent Jones), a sheltered marina and all the most popular watersports. Boats leave from Playa Quieta (and less frequently from Zihuatanejo) for **Isla Ixtapa**, an island wildlife sanctuary a couple of kilometers offshore, with good swimming, excellent snorkeling and a handful of beach restaurants.

A real town

Zihuatanejo – or Zee or even Ziwa, as it's known to anyone who has been there for more than a few hours – does more than merely cater to tourists; it is a real town with real people engaged in real activities. Getting around in either place or from one to the other is fairly easy; the hotels know what the prices for cabs should be, and the drivers rarely take advantage of the tourists.

Unlike the sport fishing in the waters off Ixtapa, fishing is still a livelihood in Zihuatanejo as it provides food for both locals and visitors, although tourism is creeping in at a stern and steady pace. Sometimes it is possible to strike a deal with one of the local fishermen and tag along for the ride; most of the boats leave from the beach in the center of town, and a tasty lunch may be included in the overall price.

Facing the sea, on Paseo del Pescador in the center of town, is the small **Museo Arqueológico de la Costa Grande** (open Tues–Sun; entrance fee), which offers an insight into the interesting culture and archeology of the coast of Guerrero. Ziwa is full of little restaurants of all kinds, and those serving

BELOW: getting to the surf on time.

seafood are particularly popular. In a tiny open kitchen on 5 de Mayo, across from the little handicraft market (which does a good line in trendy rubber shoes that are perfect for the beach), the Swiss chef-owner of **Paul's** produces more sophisticated dishes, such as herb-scented chanterelles and sautéed quail, rare treats in a country that does not excel in foreign food.

Many of the hotels in Ziwa qualify as "budget" (Villas Miramar and Bungalows Pacíficos are both good value), with a few notable exceptions such as La Casa Que Canta, a stunning building that cascades down the hill overlooking **La Ropa** beach, and the older, beautifully maintained and exquisitely landscaped Villa del Sol.

For a change of pace, the tiny village and beach of **Playa Troncones** is half an hour's drive northwest of the resorts. The beachfront Burro Borracho and Casa de la Tortuga make relaxing and secluded hideaways, and their co-owner provides transportation to and from both Ixtapa and Zihuatanejo.

Gate to the Orient

In the 16th century, the large natural harbor of **Acapulco ③** was the only port authorized by Spain to receive the treasure-filled galleons arriving from China and the Philippines. The goods were transferred overland via Mexico City to the Gulf coast port of Veracruz, from where they were shipped on to Spain. Over the next couple of centuries, something like 200 million pesos worth of silver was shipped out of Acapulco as payment for the silk, porcelain, spices and ivory of the Orient. Naturally, the flourishing trade and rich shipments attracted pirates, freebooters and the enemies of Spain.

The Mexican War of Independence brought an end to the galleon trade and the

Map
on pages
236–7

TIP

Playa Escolleras, at the west end of Ixtapa's Playa del Palomar, is a favorite beach for surfers; large waves and a strong undertow make swimming dangerous on this beach, though.

BELOW: sand-carrying mules.

In the late 1950s Acapulco became known as "The Riviera of the West".

town was forgotten until it was discovered as a resort in the 1930s. Nowadays, everybody has heard of Acapulco, even if they have never been there.

Bahía de Acapulco

At the west end of the the large, sheltered Bahía de Acapulco is the traditional **old town**. Clustered around **Playa Caleta Ⓐ**, the original resort beach, some of the older hotels (reliable, but not luxurious) are still in operation. The rocky promontory of **La Quebrada Ⓑ** and the traditional Hotel Mirador rises above the old town before the bay sweeps past the *malecón* (seafront promenade) and east towards the strip of modern resort hotels. Acapulco continues to grow every year, and its rapid expansion eastwards, in an area not far from the airport, has been influenced by the arrival of the new toll road from Cuernavaca and Mexico City.

The local population of Acapulco suffered a tragic blow in October 1997 when the dreaded Hurricane Pauline swept through its streets, stacking cars one on top of another, covering the city in deep mud, and killing more than 120 people. The five-star hotels that line the bay were largely unaffected, however, and the city lost no time in reassuring the agents of its lucrative tourist trade that all was well.

The **zócalo**, in the heart of town, is a reminder that this is Mexico and not just resortland. There are parks with benches and shade, a 1930s **cathedral** with a mosque-type dome, open-air cafés, inexpensive restaurants, plenty of stores and the town's largest **craft market**. There are also small eateries that serve up wonderful fresh fish; they mostly cater to locals and Mexican tourists, but also welcome others: be sure to ask for the catch of the day. Across the boulevard is

BELOW: the curving Bay of Acapulco.

the **malecón** **C** and the docks where the deep-sea fishing vessels moor.

One event that sticks in the memory of all visitors to Acapulco, is the emotion of watching the **high divers** at La Quebrada. At 1pm every day, and several times at night, young men execute dazzling swallow dives from a dramatic 40-meter (130-ft) cliff into a narrow channel below; split-second timing is imperative for the divers to hit the water on the swell and not get dashed on the jagged rocks.

Acapulco's most historic landmark, the **Fuerte de San Diego** **D**, was built in 1616 to protect the port from mainly Dutch and English pirates. The fort was leveled by an earthquake in 1776, but was quckly rebuilt and has now been restored to house the small but interesting **Museo Histórico de Acapulco** (open Tues–Sun; entrance fee).

Leaving the warren of streets in old Acapulco, most tourists head along the 11-km (7-mile) **Costera Miguel Alemán** **E**, a broad boulevard that stretches along the bay and is lined with high-rise hotels and restaurants and little thatch-roofed bars advertising *la hora feliz* (happy hour) with drinks priced at "3 x 1".

Shops and shopping malls abound in Acapulco. There are also art galleries galore, as well as restaurants catering for every taste and nationality, and in every price range. Great fun for kids is the **CICI Recreation Center** **F** on the Costera, which offers a wave-pool with slides, a large aquarium and a dolphin show. Another option, the **Parque Papagayo** **G**, has boating, its very own Manila galleon, a cable car and toboggan.

Hotel prices vary greatly with the time of year. The peak season with the best weather and highest prices is between mid-December and Easter and reservations should be made well ahead of time. The jet-set favors February, while the

Maps
Area 236
City 271

Thursday is pozole day in Guerrero. Restaurants serving the regional specialty, a red or green hominy soup (depending on the seasonings used), display signs or advertize in the local press.

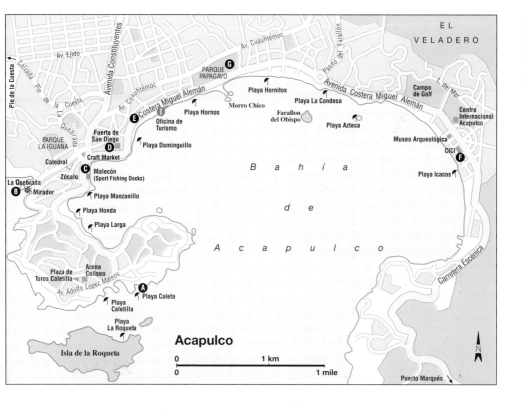

Acapulco

0   1 km

0   1 mile

smartest people come in November and early December, when the weather is ideal but the prices haven't yet peaked. But even in the rainy season, from June to October, there's plenty of sun most mornings, with the showers generally falling only in the afternoon. The best fishing months are November–May. Boats for big- and small-game fishing can be chartered for $200 a day or more (less off-season) through the hotels or directly at the downtown *malecón*. Sailboats, motor boats, pedal boats and canoes can all be hired too; Acapulco caters to its tourists well.

Some sections of the beaches can be polluted in Acapulco, although generally the sea is cleaner towards the east end of the bay; however, many tourists prefer to stick to the hotel swimming pools. All the usual water sports, from water- and jet-skiing to "bananas" and parasailing (easier than it looks), are readily available around the bay, while snorkeling is best in the shallow waters near **Isla Roqueta**. A glass-bottomed boat to the offshore island leaves from Playas Caleta and Caletilla; en route you can see the **Capilla Submarina** (Underwater Chapel), which is a wonderful a submerged statue of the Virgen de Guadalupe (*see page 118*).

Sunset at Pie de la Cuesta

Eight kilometers (5 miles) north of town is **Pie de la Cuesta**, a fishing village with an open beachfront and restaurants. It is the best place to watch the sunset but is definitely not a good place to swim, as the undertow is vicious. A long sand-bar peninsula sheltering the **Laguna de Coyuca** (abounding in catfish, snook and mullet) is gradually filling up with modern villas and hotels catering to tourists. The lagoon is also very popular for waterskiing and fishing trips.

TIP

The Voladores de Papantla *(see page 281)* perform several nights a week at the Convention Center. Ask at your hotel for days and times.

BELOW: tequila served in generous measures.

ACAPULCO NIGHTLIFE

Acapulco's glamour image as the number-one playground for the jet set may have faded somewhat, at least during the daylight hours, with the rivalry of other big-time resorts; however, the glitz and the sparkle are there after dark, when the city takes on an entirely different cast. After 10 o'clock, most people head for the many discos and nightclubs such as **Extravaganzza**, **Baby'O** and **Fantasy** (the latter even has its own laser lights and fireworks display). Other options are the newer **Palladium**, or **Andrómeda**, a favorite among the younger set. **Salon Q** is the spot for *salsa* aficionados, while **The Gallery** offers a twice-nightly transvestite cabaret. The choice can be overpowering and fashions change, but the length of the lines outside is one way of testing which club is flavor of the month. Otherwise, ask around.

If a more sedate evening is in order, there is a **Fiesta Mexicana** twice a week at the **Convention Center** and in some hotels. These feature traditional dances, a buffet of toned-down Mexican food and *margaritas* or tequila sunrises. Perhaps the most romantic option is a nighttime trip around Acapulco Bay in one of many cruise boats which provide open bars, dinner, disco dancing, a running commentary and a show.

Luxury hotels

Getting from one part of Acapulco to another isn't as difficult as it may first appear. Taxis are pretty reasonable, and most hotels list the prices for the usual destinations. Otherwise, if you're on a budget, there are buses that run regularly along the Costera.

On the way southeast to another popular beach at **Puerto Marqués**, in the next bay, you'll pass some of Acapulco's fanciest hotels such as **Elcano, Las Brisas** and the **Camino Real** located at the bottom of a villa-studded hill. These high-class resorts enjoy views of its own small bay, but people pay plenty for the privacy.

About 19 km (12 miles) southeast of downtown Acapulco, on the way to the airport, a stunning metal sculpture by the renowned metalsmith and jeweler Pal Kepenyes marks the "gateway" to the **Acapulco Diamante** development. Landmark hotels in this area are the **Princess** and the **Pierre Marqués**, sister hotels and local monuments in this area, which offer isolated splendor and two golf courses, a score of tennis courts, plus swimming pools, restaurants, nightclubs and bars. The Princess, awash with tropical flowers, is architecturally the more striking of the two, and is built to resemble a pre-Hispanic pyramid; next door, the elegant Pierre Marqués was built by the late John Paul Getty as one of his fun palaces in the sun.

A short way beyond the Princess, the **Vidafel Mayan Palace** is a spectacular new hotel complex where Mayan-style thatches are interspersed with glass-roofed pavilions and reflecting pools, strung out along a series of canals. Spread out over 4.5 hectares (11 acres), the complex includes several buildings of time-share suites, and a dozen sheltered tennis courts with a variety of surfaces. ❑

Map on page 271

TIP

The once remote fishing village of Barra Vieja is locally famous for its delicious *pescado a la talla,* where the fish is slathered in a time-honored, secret mixture of chilies, and then grilled over an open fire.

BELOW: young fiesta-goers.

THE SOUTH

With its beautiful beaches, lush forests and ancient cultures, southern Mexico has something for everyone

The south of Mexico offers more for the visitor in terms of varied landscape and in its range of cultural attractions and outdoor activities than possibly any other region in Mexico. The tropical plantations of Veracruz and the steamy jungles of Tabasco contrast with the cool, misty highlands or the dense Lacandón forest of Chiapas, the craggy, eroded hills of Oaxaca or the flat limestone shelf of the Yucatán Peninsula.

Hugging the Gulf Coast, Veracruz, is one of Mexico's greenest and most beautiful states. Although its beaches are not a scratch on those of the Caribbean or Pacific coasts, this state has much to offer: including the awe-inspiring ruins of El Tajín (city of the God of Thunder); the thrill of white-water rafting, and the historical trail of Hernán Cortés and his conquistadores. For those who want to delve further into the region's past, Xalapa's anthropology museum is state-of-the-art; but if music, dance and festivities are the order of the day, then head for Veracruz city, a popular holiday resort for Mexicans and the most atmospheric and appealing city of the whole coast.

The rugged, rocky and remote landscapes of Oaxaca are very different; the conditions of dire poverty in which many of the indigenous communities live is only emphasized by the fact that it is they with their wonderful handicrafts and the pyramids of their forefathers – that are the principal "tourist attraction." As well as the indian villages, there is the cosmopolitan colonial city of Oaxaca, as well as a wealth of wildlife, some delightfully offbeat Pacific beaches and Huatulco, Mexico's latest mega resort .

Humid, oil-rich Tabasco, Mexico's wettest state, and home to the oldest Mesoamerican cultures, is the gateway to the highlands of Chiapas and the threshold of the ancient Mayan world. Chiapas is an extraordinarily varied state. There are quaint colonial towns; traditional indian villages; the dramatic Sumidero Canyon; the changing colors of the Montebello Lakes or the jungle waterfalls at Agua Azul; and then there is Palenque, the most sensational of all the Mayan ruins (this is the land of the Zapatista activists – *see page 90*).

After Chiapas, the flatness of the Yucatán Peninsula comes as a shock. This is the land of the Maya, and visitors can alternate the azure of the Caribbean – and Mexico's most popular seaside resorts – with the allure of Mayan ruins, comparable to the great cities of the ancient Greek and Roman empires. The Yucatán is also known for its elegant colonial cities and for its reserves, which aim at protecting the region's fantastic diversity of flora and fauna. ❑

PRECEDING PAGES: a group of Tzeltal officials from the state of Chiapas.
LEFT: a reflection of the booming oil industry of Tabasco state.

THE GULF COAST

There's plenty to see in Mexico's greenest state: the highest mountain, the fastest rapids, the oldest civilization, the best museum outside the capital and the liveliest zócalo in the country

Map on pages 280–1

México City

Veracruz is a long, narrow, tropical state that extends down the Gulf of Mexico. Its coast, including the historic port of Veracruz, is hot, humid and still relatively unknown to large-scale international tourism.

As well as being the center of three important pre-Hispanic cultures – Olmec, Totonac and Huastec – Veracruz was the Spanish gateway to the wealth of New Spain and subsequently the route to the riches of China and the Orient. It was very near the modern port of Veracruz that the conquistador Hernán Cortés and his men landed in 1519 before marching on to conquer the Aztecs in Tenochtitlán (*see page 42*).

Nowadays it is "black gold" that sails out of the port of Veracruz; some of Mexico's biggest oil refineries are in the extreme north and south of the state, in Tampico (which is on the border with neighboring Tamaulipas), Minatitlán and Coatzacoalcos (near Tabasco). However, with a population of 6 million, including an indian population of 350,000, Veracruz remains essentially an agricultural state, growing much of the country's sugar cane, vanilla, tropical fruits, coffee, cocoa and other crops.

LEFT: the voladores show bungy jumpers a trick or two.
BELOW: all dressed up for Mardi Gras.

The Huasteca

The northern third of the state, between **Tampico** and Poza Rica, both oil refining towns, has little to attract or detain most tourists. Tampico, with its huge new harbor complex, has a lively seaport atmosphere and the seafood is excellent. South of town is the vast **Laguna de Tamiahua** whose islands and mangrove swamps can be explored in rented boats.

The region known as **La Huasteca ❶** covers a fertile area west of Tampico, and touches on the states of Tamaulipas, Hidalgo, San Luis Potosí and Veracruz.

The ancient Huastec culture, thought to pre-date the Toltecs of Tula (*see page 33*), was at its strongest from about AD 800 to 1200. Little archeological exploration has been carried out in the region and although several sites can be visited (for example at Tamuín or Tampamolón), none is especially revealing or spectacular to the non-specialist. In fact, the best place to see the superb art work of the Huastec culture is probably at the Xalapa Museum of Anthropology (*see page 286*).

The descendants of the ancient Huastecs who live in this area speak a language related to the Mayan tongue. South of Ciudad Valles, through jungles of bamboo and banana trees, the remote Huastec village of **Xilitla** is where English eccentric Edward James (1907–84) built his Dalíesque palace. Further south still, the town of **Tamazunchale** has a colorful Sunday market.

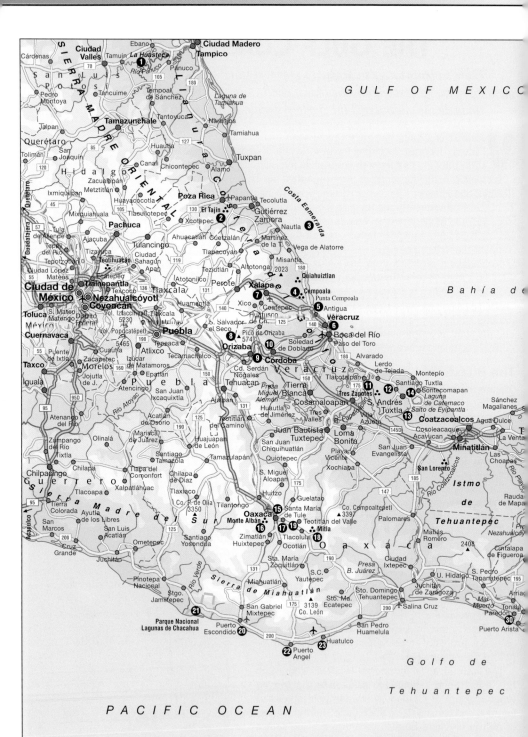

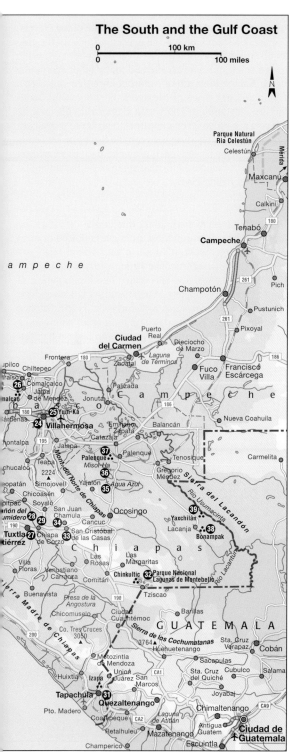

The South and the Gulf Coast

0   100 km
0   100 miles

N

Colorful too is the Day of the Dead (*see pages 262–3*) when the streets are carpeted with confetti and petals. Rare species of birds and butterflies can be found in the tropical vegetation here, attracting nature enthusiasts; and local shops sell mounted butterfly specimens.

Flying men

The little town of **Papantla**, probably the best stopover for visitors traveling to the ruins of El Tajín, has two claims to fame: it is Mexico's main vanilla-growing center, and it is the home of the **Voladores de Papantla**. The famous dance involves five "flying men," dressed in exotic birdlike costumes.

With ropes attached to one leg, four of the men, representing the cardinal points, launch themselves backwards from the top of a 32-meter (105-ft) pole. The *voladores* revolve slowly around the pole and the rope unwinds until they gracefully reach the ground. Meanwhile, on a tiny platform at the top, the fifth man dances and plays a reed flute and a little drum.

Originally the spectacular dance was the culmination of a solemn and symbolic pre-Hispanic ritual closely related to the cult of the fertility gods. These days it provides a means of economic survival and the *voladores* perform daily outside the ruins of El Tajín and at other more touristic venues.

Close to Papantla, **El Tajín ②** (open daily; entrance fee) was the vast religious and political center of a pre-Totonac civilization. The luxuriant tropical surroundings and the fact that it is off the main tourist tracks, almost hidden in the jungle, makes El Tajín all the more wonderful to visit. It must have inspired even greater awe during its period of splendour (AD 800–1150) when all the buildings were brightly painted and decorated with reliefs and sculptures.

In the lower part of the city, buildings were used for religious and ceremonial purposes. The **Pirámide de los Nichos**, with its 365 square insets or niches – one for each day of the solar year – is the finest example of Tajín architecture. The *pelota* ballgame played an important part

Highway maintenance in operation.

in the lives of these people; six relief panels along the walls of the **Juego de Pelota Sur** illustrate the ritual and ultimate sacrifice of one or more of the players.

Above the ceremonial center, **El Tajín Chico** was a residential area for the elite ruling classes and, higher up still, with a superb view over the entire city, is the governor's palace. There is a small museum on site and many other sculptures and reliefs can be seen in the Xalapa Museum of Anthropology (*see page 286*).

Although the state of Veracruz has some of Mexico's most beautiful countryside, few of its beaches are outstanding. The **Costa Esmeralda ❸**, in spite of its enticing name – part of a recent government effort to promote tourism in the area – is a stretch of very straight coastline between the towns of Tecolutla and Nautla. For those who prefer to be by the sea, it is an alternative to Papantla as a base for visiting El Tajín, but be prepared for a string of two- and three-star hotels, a few trailer parks and very little else.

Totonac–Spanish alliance

There are dozens of small archeological sites along this coast – such as the Totonac cemetery at **Quiahuiztlán** – although most are not signposted or even marked on local maps. If you're interested, it's best to ask around once you arrive in an area. Of particular historic significance is the fortified ceremonial center at **Cempoala ❹** (open daily; entrance fee) which had a population of some 30,000 at the time of the Spanish Conquest. When they first landed in New Spain in 1519, Hernán Cortés and his men were well received by the Totonac indians of Cempoala (sometimes spelt Zempoala), and their chief soon struck an alliance with the Spaniards against the powerful Aztecs who had been exacting hefty tributes from the Cempoalans for many years.

BELOW: stop for a fruitful bargain.

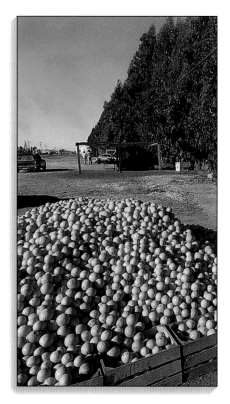

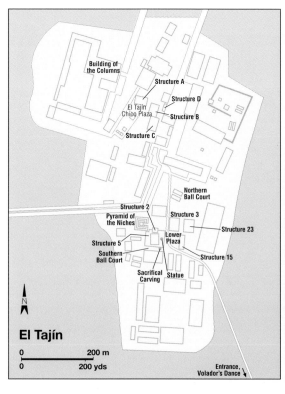

Building of the Columns

Structure A

Structure D

El Tajín Chico Plaza

Structure B

Structure C

Northern Ball Court

Structure 2

Pyramid of the Niches

Structure 3

Structure 23

Lower Plaza

Structure 5

Southern Ball Court

Structure 15

Sacrificial Carving

Statue

N

El Tajín

| 0 | 200 m |
| 0 | 200 yds |

Entrance, Volador's Dance

South of Cempoala, the town of **Antigua** ❺, founded in 1525, was one of the earliest Spanish settlements in New Spain and, hard as it is to believe now, it was for a time the hub of commercial activity between Europe and New Spain. The tiny **Ermita del Rosario** church dates from this period, as do the ruins of the **Casa de Cortés** (in fact, the conquistador never actually lived here).

Map on pages 280–1

Song and dance in Veracruz

When it comes to atmosphere, effervescence, music and gaiety, **Veracruz** ❻ is the place to be. Its zócalo is the liveliest in Mexico. By day, and for much of the night, the **Plaza de Armas**, as it is called, vibrates with trios, marimbas, salsa and danzón. It is a pretty, palm-shaded square lined with elegant white 18th-century buildings and *portales* filled with restaurants and cafés along the north side. The entertainment goes on late into the night; there is organized music and dance several evenings a week and then the itinerant musicians play their hearts out while people eat and drink and often succumb to the irresistible rhythms and just get up and dance. The merrymaking reaches a crescendo in February each year during **Carnaval**, the week before Ash Wednesday. Here duing those festive days, people stream into town from all over Mexico and from other parts of the world to watch and take part in Veracruz's colorful song and dance performances.

A stroll along the waterfront **Paseo del Malecón** is another favorite pastime in Veracruz. Big ships come and go and you can take a boat trip round the harbor; stalls and street vendors sell toys and souvenirs as well as cigars – both local and Cuban – amber jewelry, leather belts and carvings from neighboring Chiapas. No trip to Veracruz is complete without a visit to the **Gran Café la Parroquia** (Gómez Farías 34). This unpretentious café is a national institution

BELOW:
El Tajín's Pyramid
of the Niches.

TIP

Try ordering a *lechero* at the Gran Café la Parroquia: the waiter serves you a glass with strong black coffee, then, by clinking the side of the glass with your spoon, you call the *lechero* (milkman) who arrives with a kettle full of steaming milk.

and has been the traditional location for socializing and coffee drinking in the area for well over a century.

A long (and well-reported) family feud meant that the café had to move in 1994 from its traditional zócalo location to its present site on the Malecón; fortunately, as the waiters, the regular customers and the beautiful Italian coffee machines have moved too, it's business as usual.

Traditional sightseeing in Veracruz is somewhat limited. The spanking new **Museo Histórico Naval** (Arista; open Tues–Sun; entrance free), inaugurated in 1997, houses exhibits related to the port's fascinating naval history. One block south, the **Baluarte de Santiago** (open Tues–Sun; entrance fee) is the only bastion that remains of the fortified wall that surrounded the city until the late 19th century. Inside is a small collection of beautifully intricate pre-Hispanic gold jewelry; the pieces, which had been thought lost in a shipwreck as they left Veracruz for Spain hundreds of years previously, were discovered by a fisherman in 1976.

The small, rather run-down **Museo de la Ciudad** (Zaragoza 397; open Tues–Sun; entrance fee) has an interesting section on slavery and the caste system in colonial Mexico. South along the *malecón* (seafront promenade), towards the city's beaches, the fine new **Acuario de Veracruz** (open daily; entrance fee) is said to be the largest and best aquarium in Latin America.

City under siege

BELOW: for seafood, Veracruz is hard to beat.

Across a causeway, on what was once an island, forbidding **San Juan de Ulúa** (open Tues–Sun; entrance fee) guards the mouth of the harbor; the last 500 years of Mexican history can be told from the forbidding walls of this fortress which has borne the brunt of many attacks – from the likes of Sir Francis Drake, the

Dutch pirates and the powerful navies of France, England and the United States. During the dictatorship of Porfirio Díaz (*see page 58*), San Juan de Ulúa was a notorious, high-security prison, used especially for political prisoners. The damp cells are indeed formidable, and the final irony is that the dictator himself then fled into exile from the same fortress at the beginning of the Mexican Revolution.

Map on pages 280–1

Boca del Río

In front of the large hotels at **Mocambo** and **Playa de Oro**, a few miles south of town, the beaches tend to be cleaner and not quite as crowded as those nearer the town center. However, while the ocean water is warm, and leisurely waves roll in from the Gulf of Mexico, these beaches are really no match for the white expanses of sand on the west coast or the Caribbean. But for seafood, Veracruz is hard to equal. About 10 km (6 miles) south of downtown Veracruz, **Boca del Río** is a fishing village famed for its seafood restaurants (open for lunch only, until about 6pm).

TIP

Try fresh oysters on the half-shell, exotic shrimp soup or *huachinango* (red snapper) *a la vera-cruzana* in one of Boca del Río's lively seafood restaurants.

In the state capital and university town of **Xalapa** ❼ (sometimes spelt Jalapa), 135 km (84 miles) inland from Veracruz, the climate is cool and damp, and the city is often shrouded in mist. But Xalapa enjoys a privileged setting: from the central **Parque Juárez** there are spectacular early-morning views of the nearby Cofre de Perote volcano and, more distant, the Pico de Orizaba, Mexico's highest mountain (*see page 287*).

Down some steps from the square, **El Agora** is the center of Xalapa's lively arts scene (there is a theater, art gallery, cinema and café). Uphill from the center the remaining old barrios have cobbled streets where the colorful houses have sloping tiled roofs and wrought-iron balconies.

BELOW: the cool and elegant Plaza de Armas, Veracruz.

Countless varieties of orchids grow in the Veracruz region

El Museo de Antropología de Xalapa

In the south of the city, away from the fumes and noise of the traffic, is the university campus and the pretty lakeside **Paseo de los Lagos**. But the main reason for visiting Xalapa is in the northwest suburbs: the outstanding **Museo de Antropología de Xalapa** (open daily; entrance fee) is the best anthropology museum outside Mexico City. Located on Avenida Xalapa, the façade of the modern building is stark and fairly uninspiring. Inside, however, the museum is spacious and light, with nine marble exhibition halls and sunny patios displaying many and priceless treasures of the three major pre-Hispanic cultures of the Gulf coast.

The first halls are dedicated to the **Olmecs**, the mother culture, the oldest and one of the most brilliant civilizations of Mesoamerica. The most obviously striking pieces in this section are the famous Colossal Heads, which date from 1200–400BC and are thought to be gigantic portraits of the elite Olmec rulers. The museum has seven of the 17 heads discovered so far, but anthropologists are hopeful that, in time, more will be found.

The next group of galleries is devoted to the cultures from **Central Veracruz** (often referred to as Totonac). These include the haunting Cihuateotl – the terracotta figures of women deified after dying in childbirth – and the enchanting smiling figures, the most characteristic pieces of the Central Veracruz culture. The last room contains examples of finely delineated **Huastec** sculpture and delightful terracotta figurines where were found and brought to the museum from the north of the region.

It is definitely worth staying in Xalapa for a couple of days, if only to explore the surrounding countryside and towns. It is possible to visit Xalapa and the

BELOW: saddled up and ready to go.

museum from neighboring **Coatepec**, best known for its fine coffee and orchid gardens. The Posada de Coatepec, a charming converted hacienda, makes a peaceful alternative to the hotels of Xalapa. The picturesque town of **Xico** is a short but beautiful drive away, through plantations where coffee grows under the shade of banana trees. Nearby, the **Cascada de Texolo**, is a spectacular waterfall where Michael Douglas and Kathleen Turner filmed their action-adventure movie *Romancing the Stone* in 1984.

The highest peak

Mexico's highest mountain, the **Pico de Orizaba** ❽ (5,747 meters/18,855 ft) is the third highest peak in North America (after Mount McKinley in Alaska and Mount Logan in the Yukon Territory). Known to the Aztecs as Citlatépetl, or "Star Mountain," this extinct volcano last erupted in 1546. The first foreign climbers to reach the crater were American soldiers in 1848, part of General Winfield Scott's invading army. Only two of the 16 climbing routes are suitable for inexperienced climbers, and even then pre-climb training and a local guide are highly recommended.

Industrial **Orizaba** ❾, south of Xalapa, on the main Mexico City-Veracruz highway has some fine colonial and neo-classical architecture, and the **ex-Palacio Municipal** is an extraordinary Art Nouveau construction in iron that was shipped over from Belgium in the late 19th century. Also worth seeing is a 1926 mural by José Clemente Orozco (*see page 110*) in the present Palacio Municipal, and the collection of paintings, colonial to contemporary, at the **Museo de Arte del Estado de Veracruz** (open Tues–Sun; entrance fee), next door to the pretty church of **La Concordia**.

Map on pages 280-1

 TIP

The small town of Coatepec has two memorable restaurants: El Tío YeYo (for a meal of mountain trout) and Casa Bonilla, for its great atmosphere and mouth-watering langoustine.

BELOW: the cloud-shrouded slopes of the Pico de Orizaba.

Map on pages 280–1

Two of Mexico's most popular beers, Dos Equis and Superior, are brewed by the Cervecería Moctezuma, in the town of Orizaba.

BELOW: traditional weaving skills are adapting to modern demands, as with these colorful belts.

A few miles further east, busy commercial **Córdoba** ⑩, is one of the centers of Mexico's coffee industry, and is remembered historically for the Tratados de Córdoba, the 1829 treaties which finalized Mexico's Independence from Spain. The most interesting buildings are on or very near the zócalo, but best of all is the **Portal de Zevallos**, located along the north side, where several cafés serve the aromatic local coffee. (Side trips to a local coffee plantation can be organized if you're a true coffee fan.)

Beautiful and unspoilt **Tlacotalpan** ⑪, on the edge of the vast River Papaloapan, was an important internal port during the era of steamships. Arriving at Tlacotalpan is like stepping straight into the past; this delightful town with its brightly painted houses and Arabic-style portals has managed to retain its charm and elegance despite having been discovered, over the years, by quite a few visitors. For most of the year Tlacotalpan is an exceptionally peaceful town; however, its Candlemas festival in January is one of the most colorful and best attended in Mexico, with bull-running through the streets and lots of activities on the river. Book up early if you want to be here.

Los Tuxtlas

The small town of **Santiago Tuxtla** ⑫ nestles in the tropical foothills of the Sierra de los Tuxtla. This is the land inhabited over 3,000 years ago by the Olmecs, the earliest civilization in Mesoamerica. At one end of the zócalo standing 3.5 meters (11 ft 6 inches) high, is the largest of the 17 colossal Olmec heads found to date. The huge monument weighs almost 50 tons. The small but well organized **Museo Tuxtleco** (open daily; entrance fee) has another of these heads and a fine collection of pieces from nearby **Tres Zapotes** and other Olmec sites.

Not far from **San Andrés Tuxtla**, a sprawling commercial town and center for cigar production, is the turn-off for the **Salto de Eyipantla** ⑬. The paved road passes through papaya, sugar cane, banana and tobacco fields before reaching this stunning waterfall - almost as wide as it is high - throwing up a perpetual cloud of mist.

The **Laguna de Catemaco** ⑭ is a picturesque lake, 16 km (10 mile) long, in the crater of an extinct volcano; this is the land of the *brujos* (witch doctors), as you will soon find out from the touts and witch-related souvenirs that are for sale everywhere.

The dividing line between authentic *brujos* and charlatans cashing in on the tourist trade is very fine, but the tradition is real and goes back centuries. Outsiders are not welcome at the annual gathering that is held by the *brujos* on the first Friday of March every year. Sean Connery filmed *Medicine Man* in nearby **Nanciyaga**, a 40-hectare (100-acre) "ecological park" set in tropical rainforest.

Attractions include hanging bridges, "pre-Hispanic" steam baths, mud baths and pools of mineral spring water to swim in. You can reach the park by road or boat from Catemaco. Boat trips also go round the **Isla de los Monos**, which is inhabited by a colony of Macaque monkeys brought here from Thailand for research purposes. ❑

Adventure Tourism

Mexico has long been renown as an ideal holiday destination, mainly for its beautiful beach resorts and year-round sunshine. In recent years, however, with the opening up and expansion of national parks in the country's vast interior, more adventurous travelers have come looking for a challenge – for some, the more rugged and demanding the better. The breadth and depth of Mexico's wilderness is matched only by its rich cultural heritage.

So, put on your hiking boots and take a trek into the mammoth Copper Canyon (dwarfing the Grand Canyon, only a quarter of its size) or the Selva Lacandona tropical forests in Chiapas, part of the great Maya Forest. Kayakers can island-hop through the Sea of Cortés or paddle through the mangroves of the Yucatán.

The rivers, once the lifeblood of ancient empires, now carry adventurers from distant countries. Rafting hit Mexico by storm only recently. A decade ago only the fearless white-water enthusiasts took on the rivers in Veracruz. Now there are four major companies running tours, using the state's capital city, Xalapa, as the base of operations, with branches throughout the state. Tours range from one-day excursions to longer expeditions. Veracruz seems to offer a bit of everything – just two hours away from Xalapa is the Río Filobobos which takes rafters to the ruins of El Cuajilote, one archeological site best visited via river.

While Veracruz is the heartland of Mexico's river trips, rafting is also becoming popular in the state of Morelos, just south of Mexico City. The rivers are less crowded here, but offer the same challenges. The Río Amacuzac is best run during the rainy season, which lasts from from June to October.

On the Caribbean coast, you'll find some of the best scuba diving shops in the hemisphere. Cozumel's Paradise Reef is aptly named. There are more than 32 km (20 miles) of reef, some composed of rare black coral, more than 200 species of tropical fish,

and hundreds of underground caverns.

Mexico also offers great hiking and mountain climbing. Intrepid adventurers can ascend dormant volcanoes, such as the Pico de Orizaba near Puebla or Iztaccíhuatl, also known as "Smoking Mountain." The access point for "Izta" is the town of Amecameca, just one hour southeast of Mexico City. The town is also the gateway to less strenuous hikes on the lower slopes of the volcano.

There are plenty of rock climbing opportunities throughout the country, but some of the best areas are just a stone's throw away from the US border.

El Gran Trono Blanco is a few hours southeast of Tijuana. This area is renowned among climbers, with its colossal rock wall and any number of possible routes. Alternatively, the Cumbres de Monterrey National Park surrounds the city of Monterrey, Mexico's largest industrial center. You can climb the 300-meter (1,000-ft) high walls of the Huasteca Canyon in this park.

(*See Travel Tips pages 344-5 for details of specialist local agencies.*)

RIGHT: white-water rafting is just one of Mexico's white-knuckle activities.

OAXACA

This southern state is rich in history, from the archeological magnificence of its pre-Hispanic cultures to its native-born leaders, Benito Juárez and Porfirio Díaz

Map on pages 280–1

Oaxaca is indian country *par excellence*. Though the Zapotec and Mixtec indians dominate the state, 16 other linguistically and culturally distinct groups live here too. No other Mexican state is as diverse.

There's so much to see in wild and wonderful Oaxaca: major archeological sites, tiny rural villages where people actually produce many of the country's best handicrafts, and the exquisite seashore that lies over the mountains from the high valley of the capital, also called Oaxaca.

Mountain vistas

The city of Oaxaca is 548 km (341 miles) from Mexico City and you can fly, go by train or take the excellent and reasonably inexpensive toll road. The drive through the mountains is beautiful whichever road you take. If you don't want to take the toll road and go through Puebla you can stop at **Atlixco**, known for its bandstand and tiled benches and a dance festival held in September. The "tree of life," often thought to be from Metepec near Toluca (*see page 194*), originated in **Izúcar de Matamoros**, which is a center for ceramics located a little further south.

The state of Oaxaca was also the birthplace of two of Mexico's most prominent leaders: Benito Juárez, the country's first liberal president, was a Zapotec indian born in the hill village of San Pablo Guelatao, about 65 km (40 miles) north of Oaxaca; and Porfirio Díaz, who seized the presidency in 1877 and stayed in power until the Mexican Revolution in 1910.

The Spanish city of Villa de Antequera de Guaxaca, now known simply as **Oaxaca ⓯** (pronounced *wa-ha-ca*), was founded in 1529 near an indian settlement called Huaxyacac, which means "Place of Gourds." At an altitude of about 1,500 meters (4,920 ft) high, its mountain climate is splendid – never too hot and never too cold.

The city has a population approaching 500,000 inhabitants and an unexpectedly cosmopolitan atmosphere. The indian influence is stronger here than in any other state capital, the Spanish colonial architecture is superb and well-preserved and there are some fine museums and a thriving artistic community.

Oaxaca is justly famous for its markets. The **Mercado de Abastos**, the Saturday market, is where the locals come to do their weekly shop. The buying frenzy takes place on a huge plot of ground next to the second-class bus station south of town, on the *Periférico* (ring road). The fruit, vegetables and pottery sections are particularly interesting. Otherwise, there's a hodge-podge of furniture, clothing and kitchen equipment.

LEFT: a glorious array of colors.
BELOW: talking turkey.

The more adventurous can try eating chapulines *(fried grasshoppers) which are sold in the central markets.*

The **Benito Juárez** market and the adjacent **Mercado 20 de Noviembre** , both open daily, are more varied and attractive to visitors. Located on Calle 20 de Noviembre, just a few blocks south of the main square, they offer crafts (many of which are found in stalls on the street outside the market), souvenirs of all sorts, flowers and food, both raw and prepared. Photographers and cooks will find it particularly interesting for its huge mounds of dried peppers in a range of subtle colors and not-so-subtle flavors.

A shady bench in the beautifully planted **zócalo** , the social hub of Oaxaca, is an excellent place to start a tour of the city. Alternatively, you can watch the world go by from the tables outside the many cafés and restaurants under the *portales* that line the square. The history of Oaxaca is illustrated in a mural which adorns the staircase inside the imposing 19th-century **Palacio de Gobierno** , on the south side of the zócalo.

To the north of the zócalo, facing the adjacent **Alameda**, the vast **cathedral**, has a fine baroque façade; building started in 1554 but was only completed in the 18th century. In addition to its regular services, the cathedral is often used for concerts; dates and details are posted at the **tourist office** on the corner of 5 de Mayo and Morelos.

Baroque churches

Two blocks west of the cathedral, on Independencia, the church of **San Felipe Neri** , with its green stone baroque façade, is where Benito Juárez (*see page 57*) got married. Further along the same street, the 17th-century **Basílica de Nuestra Señora de la Soledad** , also of green stone, has a lavish baroque interior and houses a bejeweled statue of Oaxaca's much-revered patron saint,

BELOW:
a quiet back street
in Oaxaca.

believed to possess miraculous healing powers. There is a small religious museum in the convent buildings behind the church (open daily; donation requested), and delicious ice-creams for sale on the plaza in front.

Map
on page
292

Ancient and modern art

Concentrating on aesthetic rather than historical value, it took the 20th-century artist Rufino Tamayo (*see page 111*) over 20 years to assemble his superb collection of pre-Hispanic artefacts. He then donated the pieces to his native city and even supervised their installation in the select **Museo Rufino Tamayo ❻** (open Wed–Mon; entrance fee).

A more recent donation was made by Francisco Toledo, a contemporary artist also from Oaxaca. Housed in his elegant former home, the **Instituto de Artes Gráficas de Oaxaca ❼** (open Wed–Mon; donation requested) displays a small but important collection of prints by internationally famous artists as well as the prominent Mexican muralists Rivera and Orozco (*see pages 109-110*). The institute also has temporary exhibitions of graphic art.

The recently restored **Museo Regional de Oaxaca ❽** (open Tues–Sun; entrance fee), housed around the handsome cloisters of a Dominican monastery, is most noted for its spectacular collection of intricate Mixtec jewelry and other objects in gold, turquoise, obsidian and glass. The pieces, dating from approximately AD 500, were found in Tomb 7 at nearby Monte Albán when it was uncovered in 1932. (They are often faithfully copied by local jewelers in gold or gold-washed silver, and sold in several of the city's better shops.)

The museum also has good displays of textiles, clothing, household implements and archeological relics. The adjacent 16th-century former monastery

TIP

Oaxaca is an easy city to get around on foot; or take taxis, which are cheap and plentiful.

BELOW: Oaxaca's baroque church of Santo Domingo.

There are so many archeological sites in Oaxaca that someone once suggested putting a roof over the whole state and calling it a museum.

of **Santo Domingo** 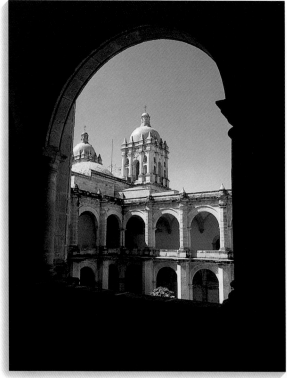, the most outstanding of Oaxaca's churches, has two handsome belltowers and a magnificent gilt and colored stucco interior. The main altarpiece is especially beautiful (although a replica of the original, replaced in 1959), and on the ceiling just inside the main entrance door there is an elaborate family tree of Santo Domingo de Guzmán, the 13th-century founder of the Dominican order. The exquisite giltwork reaches a crescendo in the dazzling 18th-century **Capilla del Rosario.**

Shopping opportunities

Oaxaca is a wonderful and exciting town for shopping. It is possible to buy handicrafts directly from the indian craftsmen and women, who come to town to sell their wares, chiefly hand-woven rugs or serapes. A certain amount of bargaining is expected although prices are often so low that it would seem insulting to beat them down any further.

From Santo Domingo, it is a short five-block walk back to the zócalo along **Macedonio Alcalá**, a street lined with beautifully maintained colonial buildings and excellent shops selling crafts and jewelry, such as **La Mano Mágico** or **Yalalag de Oaxaca**. On nearby García Vigil, **Artesanías Chimalli** has authentic folk art and is reliable for shipping purchases.

It costs very little to join the **Biblioteca Circulante de Oaxaca**, a private library with a fine selection of books in English and Spanish, many of them on Oaxaca and Mexico; the resident librarian, Ruth González, is an invaluable source of information and is helpful to people who just drop in to read a magazine or two.

Probably the most colorful of Oaxaca's legendery religious festivals is the

BELOW LEFT:
Atzompa pottery.
BELOW RIGHT:
shady view of Santo Domingo church.

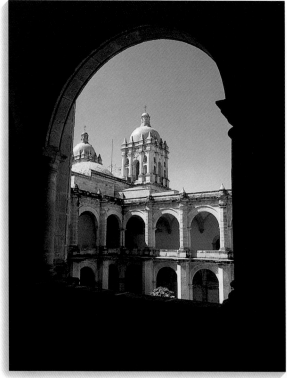

Guelaguetza, which takes place in the Cerro del Fortín amphitheater on the first two Mondays after July 16th. On December 23rd, the **Noche de los Rábanos** (Night of the Radishes), the zócalo is filled with an extraordinary display of sculptures which are made out of these exquisitely carved vegetables (*see photo, page 115*).

Monte Albán

What draws many people to Oaxaca is the proximity of its archeological wonders. Early morning is the best time to see the ruins of **Monte Albán** 🟤 (open daily; entrance fee). The grand Zapotec ceremonial center stands, about 10 km (6 miles) west of the city, on an artificially leveled mountain-top commanding compelling 360-degree views.

Monte Albán was established around 500 BC although the city did not peak until 1,000 years later, when the population reached 25,000. The entrance to the **Gran Plaza** is at the northeastern corner located between the **ball court** and the **Plataforma Norte**. In the center of the plaza, **Edificio J** is known as the Observatory, while at the south end is the towering **Plataforma Sur**, Monte Alban's tallest building.

The **Palacio de los Danzantes** is on the west side of the square. Archeologists have not yet agreed upon the meaning of the strange low-relief "dancers" carved on the walls of this building; the figures, which bear definite Olmec influence, have been interpreted as ball players, medical specimens, deformed persons, sacrificial victims or slain enemies.

It is possible to descend into some of the tombs to see the ancient frescoes. In **Tomb 104**, in the northwest, there is a fine figure of Cocijo, the rain god, whose

Maps
Area 280
City 292

Even today... this high place of the Zapotecs remains extraordinarily impressive.
– ALDOUS HUXLEY

BELOW: the solid masonry of Monte Albán.

forked tongue represents lightning; the treasures of **Tomb 7**, which belonged to a 14th-century Mixtec dignitary, can be seen in the **Museo Regional de Oaxaca** (*see page 293*).

Mitla and the Tule tree

TIP

The price of car rentals is so high these days that it's actually more economical to rent a taxi for several hours; establish a fair price before you leave.

About 10 km (6 miles) from Oaxaca, on the road to Mitla, is the village of **Santa María de Tule** ⑰, which has a small craft market and a pretty church but, most of all, it has an enormous, 2,000-year-old *ahuehuete* tree which, with a girth of 50 meters (164 ft), is thought to be the widest in the Americas.

Following the decline of Monte Albán, **Mitla** ⑱ (open daily; entrance fee) became one of the most important centers of the Zapotecs. The site's main structures, however, are Mixtec in style. The buildings, with their complex technique of inlaid stone, are highly reminiscent of the geometric friezes of the ancient Greeks.

The most intricate of the "mosaics" are in the **Patio de las Grecas**. In the **Patio de las Tumbas** there are two underground, cross-shaped tombs, one of which contains the **Columna de la Vida**; it is said that if you embrace this Column of Life, the gap left between your hands represents the years you have left to live. Unlike most ceremonial centers, Mitla was not abandoned after the Spanish Conquest, but remained inhabited well into the 16th century.

The church next to the site is built of stones taken from the ceremonial center. Outside the site entrance there is an extensive craft market with some white, lacy hand-woven shawls. Just off the plaza, the **Museo Frissell** (open daily; entrance free), a research center for the University of the Americas, has a collection of Zapotec artefacts on display and handicrafts for sale. The trip to

BELOW: Oaxaca's indians bring goods to sell in the city's markets.

CRAFT VILLAGES IN OAXACA

Although there are many excellent craft shops in the city of Oaxaca, it is often more interesting to visit the villages in the surrounding countryside where the crafts are still made:

☛ **San Bartolo Coyotepec** is known for its surprisingly light and highly-polished black pottery.

☛ **San Martín Tilcajete** is the center for fancy, carved and brightly painted wooden *animalitos.*

☛ **Ocotlán de Morelos** is the home of many renowned pottery artists. Friday is market day and occasionally it is possible to find outstanding baskets.

☛ **Santo Tomás Jalieza** is the center of backstrap weavings in the form of belts, bags, placemats and napkins, usually decorated with plant and animal designs.

☛ **Santa María Atzompa** is famous for intricate pottery renditions of the Virgen de la Soledad and other raw clay figures. Much of the pottery is glazed with a green finish, which, owing to its lead content, is unsafe for cooking.

☛ **Teotitlán del Valle** is famous for its blankets, rugs, serapes and other woven goods. Motifs range from traditional geometric shapes to portraits of Che Guevara, copies of pre-Hispanic sculpture or even of paintings by Picasso or Miró.

Mitla can be combined with other, less extensive, but nonetheless impressive ruins at **Dainzu**, **Lambityeco** and **Yagul.**

Several tour companies run minibuses with English-speaking guides to the various archeological sites. The one to Monte Albán operates from the Mesón del Angel, and to Mitla from the Camino Real, Victoria and Marqués del Valle hotels. People who prefer to explore on their own can drive, negotiate an hourly rate with a taxi driver, or take a local bus that goes near but not directly to the sites. Many hotels and city bookshops sell specific guidebooks providing background and directions to the more established locations.

Map on pages 280–1

Exploring the area

For an insight into life in this mountainous region, there are second-class buses to villages, several jolting hours away, where many indian groups live in relative isolation. Oaxaca is one of the poorest states of Mexico; erosion is devastating and the *campesinos* do not have enough land to go around. To supplement what they earn from farming, many Oaxacans have become craftsmen, and villages in the area surrounding Oaxaca offer opportunities to see the artisans at work. (Prices are much the same as they are at city market stalls, but much less than in Mexico City or other tourist towns.)

In **Teotitlán del Valle** ⓳, a couple of kilometers off the main road to Mitla, it is sometimes possible to watch weavers creating designs from wool spun and dyed by the women of the household. Some people also come to the village specifically to eat at **Tlamanalli**, a restaurant featuring updated versions of traditional Zapotec food.

The fine Dominican church at nearby **Tlacolula** was built in the 16th century;

TIP

Ben Traven's short stories make excellent reading for anyone traveling in Oaxaca or southern Mexico. (*See Further Reading, page 380.*)

BELOW: Huatulco in Oaxaca state.

particularly note the indian influence in the riotously decorated interior and the antique, tubular pipe organ. The town also has the best Sunday market in the region and is the place to get top-quality **mezcal** sometimes flavored with herbs; bottles often include the coveted worm that lives in the maguey plant.

South of Oaxaca, in the Mixtec town of **Cuilapan**, are the ruins of an early Dominican church and monastery. Independence hero Vicente Guerrero was executed here in 1831. Cuilapan was once a center for the production of cochineal, the scarlet dye made from female insects that feed on cactus. Used as a base for magenta hues in Europe, and even in the red coats of the British army, this dye was once so highly prized that its export was strictly controlled under Spanish rule.

Oaxaca's coast

Oaxaca has 480 km (298 miles) of Pacific coastline with excellent beaches, quiet lagoons and good surfing. The highway from Acapulco (in neighboring Guerrero) to Salina Cruz (in Oaxaca) has been resurfaced, although it is still rough in many places. Puerto Escondido, Puerto Angel and now Huatulco are the three best-known destinations.

International surfing tournaments in Puerto Escondido attract expert surfers from all over the world.

Of these three resorts, **Puerto Escondido** has been in the business of tourism the longest, although it is by no means a sophisticated destination. Fishing is still an important source of revenue and the daily catch turns up fresh in the marketplace and on the table in local seafood restaurants.

The atmosphere in Puerto Escondido is low-key and relaxed with little to do but enjoy the sun, sea and surf. The **old town** is on a hill above the bay. The main tourist area stretches from **Playa Principal**, where the fishing boats are berthed, to **Playa Marinero**, the swimming beach.

BELOW: going with the flow.

Around the curve is the long, sandy beach at **Zicatela**, a magnet for surfers who come to ride the famous "Mexican Pipeline." Unfortunately, Playa Zicatela has a lethal undertow which makes swimming a pretty dangerous activity.

Most tourist facilities are on or near the beach. The pedestrian walkway that parallels the bay through the tourist part of town is lined with shops selling silver, jewelry and other trinkets.

There are simple but excellent seafood restaurants, such as **La Perla Flamante** and **Nautilus**, as well as bars that have live jazz and dance music starting at about 10pm and continuing far into the night. The most outstanding hotel in Puerto Escondido, the **Santa Fe**, stands at the point where the surf beach and the swimming beach converge. On the hill at the other end of town, **El Aldea del Bazar** is a new and handsomely designed hotel, although a taxi is needed to get to or from anywhere else.

Spectacular wildlife

Anyone with an interest in birds and other wildlife should consider a 60 km (37 mile) detour west of Puerto Escondido to the **Parque Nacional Lagunas de Chacahua** ㉑. *Lanchas* (small motor boats) can be hired in the village of Zapotalito to tour the lagoons and their mangrove-edged islands.

It is best to come in the early morning or late afternoon to see the ibis, spoon-bills, parrots, alligators, turtles and many other animals that inhabit the lagoons. There are also fine sandy beaches and sheltered coves; but bring insect repellent as the mosquitoes can be fierce.

Map on pages 280–1

Puerto Angel and Huatulco

Even more than Puerto Escondido, **Puerto Angel** ㉒ is a sleepy resort with a tropical setting and superb sheltered beaches for people who want to relax, swim and lie in the sun. The fishing village is on the east side of the bay, while swimming is better at **Playa del Panteón**, on the west side. Fresh seafood abounds and there are several comfortable, though no luxurious, hotels in the town. And if you want to get right back to basics, the long, sandy, palm-fringed beach of Zipolite is only 5 km (3 miles) along the coast.

In contrast, the beautiful bays of **Huatulco** ㉓, are rapidly being developed as a mega-resort, complete with marina, golf courses, scuba diving and horse-riding. Beaches sprawl along 35 km (22 miles) of glorious coastline. Several hotels have been completed, including the Sheraton, Holiday Inn and Crowne Plaza together with Club Med and the Royal Maeva complexes; more are on the drawing-board, and eventually there will be 30,000 rooms available. For the moment, at least, not all of the seven bays have been developed and Huatulco is a pleasant, reasonably uncrowded resort.

There are boat trips from the harbor in the main Bahía de Santa Cruz to some wonderful beaches with excellent snorkeling The new, purpose-built town of **La Crucecita**, 2 km (1 mile) inland, is complete with a central plaza, a range of restaurants, a couple of inexpensive hotels and a delightful marketplace. ❑

TIP

Take good care of your belongings at all times, but especially in Puerto Escondido and Puerto Angel where theft is fairly common; it is also a good idea to stick to well-lit streets at night.

BELOW:
fishermen of Puerto Escondido.

TABASCO AND CHIAPAS

This chapter reflects the broad dissimilarity between these two neighboring states: flat, humid, tropical Tabasco, and the mountainous isolation of Chiapas

The two very different states of Tabasco and Chiapas span the country from the Gulf of Mexico to the Pacific Ocean, just east of the Istmo de Tehuantepec, Mexico's narrow waist.

Green, tropical **Tabasco** is often dismissed as an oil state you pass through on the way to Chiapas and the Yucatán Peninsula. This steamy, low-lying coastal area is criss-crossed with wide, meandering rivers which were used as trading highways by the Ancient Olmecs who inhabited this land 3,000 years ago.

Boom town

The conquistador Hernán Cortés landed on the Gulf coast of Tabasco on March 23, 1519 (*see page 42*) and founded the original Spanish settlement at the mouth of the Río Grijalva; but pirate raids soon forced its removal inland. Now called **Villahermosa ㉔**, it is the capital of Tabasco and has a population of more than a quarter of a million people.

The oil boom of the 1970s changed the face of Villahermosa and, even more recently, huge sums have been invested in developing tourism in and around the city; there are new parks and gardens, several museums and a glitzy shopping mall, **Tabasco 2000**, complete with planetarium, convention center and up-market boutiques.

The city's greatest attraction is still the vast **Parque Museo La Venta** (open Tues–Sun; entrance fee), to the northwest of town. The museum re-creates the jungle setting of the ancient Olmec center at **La Venta**, 130 km (80 miles) west of Villahermosa, which flourished from 1000–400 BC.

After initial excavations by archeologist Franz Blom in 1925 and then by Matthew Sterling in the 1940s, La Venta (the original site) became threatened by oil drilling. A mammoth operation, headed by Tabascan poet and anthropologist Carlos Pellicer, organized the transportation of 32 monumental Olmec pieces to the open-air museum in Villahermosa. Most impressive of all are the three colossal heads, over 2 meters (6 ft) tall, believed to represent the powerful leaders of Mexico's *cultura madre*.

The **Museo Regional de Antropología Carlos Pellicer** (open Tues–Sun; entrance fee), in the south of town, provides an excellent introduction to the Olmec and Mayan cultures of this region. There is a section on the ruins at Comalcalco, and a good reproduction of the murals at Bonampak.

"Eco-tourism" is a fast-spreading trend in Mexico these days. There are hiking tours in the remote southwest of Tabasco or boat trips down the Usumacinta and Grijalva rivers. The not-so-remote **Yum-Ká ㉕** (open daily; entrance fee) – named after the dwarf

LEFT: masked performers at the fiesta of San Sebastián.
BELOW: a dog knows its place.

Many people don't realize Tabasco is the name of a state in the south of Mexico – not just a chili sauce.

who protects the jungle – is a fairly new safari park and center for environmental studies rolled into one. The guided tour of the enormous park, just 18 km (11 miles) east of Villahermosa, includes a walk through the jungle, a train ride over the "savannahs of Africa" and a boat trip round a lagoon. On the way you'll see everything from monkeys and parrots, to elephants, wildebeest and hippopotamuses.

Relatively few people visit the beautiful Mayan ruins at **Comalcalco ㉖** (open daily, entrance fee), 62 km (39 miles) northwest of Villahermosa. There are three groups of buildings here – the Plaza Norte, the Gran Acrópolis and the Acrópolis Este – most of which date from AD 700–900. The Palenque influence is palpable; but, for practical reasons (namely, lack of stone in the area), these Mayans used baked bricks for building. The cacao bean with which they traded is still an important part of the region's economy today; in the town of Cárdenas, an enormous plant processes most of the cacao grown in the region, for distribution to chocolate manufacturers throughout the world.

Chiapas

In contrast to the flatness of Tabasco, neighboring **Chiapas** is a mostly mountainous state; much of the scenery is spectacularly beautiful, with crystalline rivers, and waterfalls gushing down the mountains, but some of the steep, switchback roads are not for the faint-hearted. Chiapas is a land of many climates. In some areas there is almost continuous rain throughout the year, although mostly the rainy season lasts from May until October (July and August are the wettest).

Like Oaxaca, Chiapas is a strongly indian state; in fact, the different indige-

BELOW: the inscrutable features of the massive Olmec stone heads.

Map on pages 280-1

nous groups comprise about a third of the population, the majority living in conditions of dire poverty. Spurned as second-class citizens, they have gradually (and violently) been pushed out of their land and into the least productive areas of the state. In spite of the Zapatista uprising of 1994 (*see page 90*), which was centered in the highlands of Chiapas, tourists are still visiting the area; however, as the situation is still unresolved, it is a good idea to get up-to-date information before traveling here.

Tuxtla Gutiérrez

The state capital **Tuxtla Gutiérrez** ㉗ ("Place of the Rabbits"), is 290 km (180 miles) south of Villahermosa. It is a city with few major attractions, although the **Museo Regional de Chiapas** (open Tues–Sun; free entry, but donations welcome), in Parque Madero, has fine pre-Hispanic and colonial exhibits, and some interesting explanatory maps. The **Zoológico Miguel Alvarez del Toro** (open Tues–Sun; donation welcome), is also fascinating as it houses only animals native to Chiapas, such as tapirs, jaguars, and ocelots, in natural settings along a wooded trail. Another popular attraction is the cathedral's German-style glockenspiel that features musical movements by the 12 apostles every hour.

The most memorable way of exploring the **Cañón del Sumidero** ㉘ is to take a boat trip along the Grijalva River through the dramatic gorge where the sheer cliff walls rise to a height of over 1,000 meters (3,280 ft). The water is calm, thanks to the dam at Chicoasén which has tamed the once fierce rapids. The round trip lasts for over two hours and the motorboats set off from the town of **Chiapa de Corzo** ㉙, 15 minutes east of Tuxtla. This was the site of the

BELOW: the still waters of the Sumidero Canyon.

TIP

Take a hat and suntan lotion for the canyon trip, and bring a wide-angle lens if you're a photographer.

first Spanish settlement in Chiapas and, in fact, it had been occupied for about 3,000 years before the Conquest. The 16th-century octagonal fountain in the town center, **La Pila**, is said to have been inspired by the shape of the Spanish crown. Nearby the huge **Templo de Santo Domingo** is also 16th-century and has one of the oldest church bells in Latin America. Chiapa de Corzo is famous for its lacquerware, and the **Museo de la Laca** (open Tues–Sun; free entry) exhibits the different techniques used. Other crafts (mainly embroidered clothing) are for sale in shops around the plaza.

Another way to see the canyon is from one of the lookout points; Volkswagen minibuses called *combis* leave from Madero Park and drive up the highway to clifftop *miradores*. Just west of Tuxtla there is a turnoff north to the huge **Chicoasén Dam**, some 40 km (25 miles) away on a well-paved road. Just after a tunnel the road emerges above the dam where there is a turning marked *Mirador*. A couple of kilometers along there is a spectacular viewpoint. On one side is the imposing **Grijalva Canyon** (the Sumidero is further back at the top of the cliffs); on the other side is the top of the dam, with an artificial lake in between. There are buses from Tuxtla to Chicoasén.

The coast of Chiapas

Southwest of Tuxtla are Arriaga and Tonalá, supposedly the hottest place in Chiapas. From here you can drive to **Paredón** ❸ on the Mar Muerto (Dead Sea), which is really a lagoon with excellent fishing and calm water for year-round swimming. There are no hotels but plenty of seafood restaurants. Alternatively, **Puerto Arista** is a quick 19-km (12-mile) drive away. This is where the well-to-do of Chiapas have their weekend homes. Again, the seafood is excellent

BELOW: Tzeltal officials sharing a ritual drink, or two.

and inexpensive, and it is possible to rent a hammock under a palm-thatched *palapa*, but bring a light blanket in winter.

The Pearl of the Soconusco

Near the Guatemalan border, **Tapachula** ㉛ is the center of the region's banana, cotton, cacao and coffee plantations, operated by people of German origin who moved en masse into Chiapas from Guatemala during the Díaz administration (*see page 58*). When these German descendants were interned during World War II, coffee production dropped drastically. Of course many are now fully-fledged Mexican citizens and the names of the plantations have been localized. Still there is the town of Nueva Alemania (New Germany) in the coffee-growing district near Tapachula.

From **Huixtla**, 42 km (26 miles) north of Tapachula, the road begins an incredible climb, then drops along Highway 190 which follows the Guatemalan border to the crossing point at **Ciudad Cuauhtémoc**. The drive is worthwhile for the scenery alone, but it is not advisable to attempt it at night. There are checkpoints along the way where customs officials regularly stop travelers. They are on the lookout for contraband drugs, arms and illegal Guatemalan immigrants.

Lakes of many colors

As the Pan-American highway climbs into the central highlands of Chiapas, there are superb views across a broad valley towards Guatemala's imposing mountains, looming hazily in the distance. Before reaching the town of **Comitán**, there is a turnoff east to the **Parque Nacional Lagunas de Monte-**

Map
on pages
280-1

TIP

If you intend to cross the border into Guatemala at Ciudad Cuauhtémoc, have your visa ready. Cross before 1pm or between 4pm and 6pm. Most problems, however, can be resolved by the payment of an extra "fee".

BELOW: celebrants at the fiesta of San Sebastián in Chiapa de Corzo.

Ciudad Cuauhtémoc is at the end of the Mexican part of the Pan-American Highway, which begins in the north at Ciudad Juarez, just across the border from Texas.

bello **32**. Located in a peaceful setting very near the Guatemalan border and on the edge of the **Lacandón** rainforest, there are some 60 lakes in all. The group known as the **Lagunas de Colores**, straight ahead as you enter the park, range spectacularly in color from turquoise and amethyst to dark emerald green and steely gray. These shades are the result of vast mineral deposits in the water. There is a campsite near here, and the *Albergue Turístico* (hostel) is in the village of **Tziscao**.

Between the Pan-American highway and the national park, a dirt track branches left and leads to the pre-Hispanic Mayan ruins of **Chinkultic** where a large temple, El Mirador, stands high over the valley. Only part of the extensive site has been cleared and restored, but the setting and views are wonderful.

Tzeltal potters

The town of **Comitán** is known for its fiery liquor, steep streets, numerous varieties of orchid and ears of corn that measure almost half a meter (20 inches) long. It has a pleasant plaza, good hotels and is a 45-minute drive from the Lagunas de Montebello to the southeast.

The Tzeltal indian women in **Amatenango del Valle** specialize in making beautiful unglazed pottery which they fire in the same way as their pre His-panic ancestors; they do not use a baking oven, but simply light a fire around the sun-dried clay vessels. The natural colors will not fade, although the pottery does need to be transported carefully as it is quite brittle and not as hard as pottery which has been fired in high-temperature kilns.

Continuing north from Amatenango, 80 km (50 miles) east of Tuxtla Gutiérrez (*see page 303*), is the popular destination of **San Cristóbal de las Casas** **33**.

BELOW: the church of Santo Domingo in San Cristóbal de las Casas.

At an elevation of 2,300 meters (7,550 ft) it is believed by many visitors to be the most agreeable town in Mexico; it has a leisurely atmosphere and a cool, healthy climate. There are numerous clean, inexpensive hotels and good food at reasonable prices; almost every other storefront along Calle Madero, off the zócalo, houses a different restaurant.

San Cristóbal was the capital of Chiapas, under the administration of Guatemala, until the 19th century. Founded in 1528, it was named after the Dominican bishop Fray Bartolomé de las Casas who defended the indians against the excesses of the colonists. It is a place of immense colonial charm; the houses are mostly whitewashed one-story buildings with red-tiled roofs, and an agreeable smell of wood smoke lingers in the air.

Several important churches dominate the town, most notable is the baroque **Templo de Santo Domingo**, begun in 1547, and whose intricate pink façade dates from the 17th century. Inside the church are religious paintings, elaborate gilt altarpieces and an ornate pulpit.

Objects from amber

Outside Santo Domingo, indian women sell an amazing variety of brightly colored clothing and other woven items. Pottery and leather goods are also widespread, as are woolen and cotton clothing and objects made out of amber. Nearby, in the cooperative at **Sna Jolobil** (Tzotzil for "Weavers House"), there is a display of backstrap weaving and other crafts.

The indians come to San Cristóbal de las Casas from the villages in the surrounding hills; each highland village has its own traditional dress. In Chamula, the men wear long white woolen tunics, whereas their civic or religious leaders

Map on pages 280-1

TIP

The indians in San Cristóbal and the surrounding villages rightly resent being treated as a tourist attraction. Always ask their permission before taking a photograph.

BELOW: a finely carved perch.

MAYAN CALCULATIONS

The Maya excelled in the fields of mathematics and astronomy and invented a complex system of hieroglyphics, which they used, together with a bar and dot system, to record history and rituals. They also devised an astrological calendar of amazing accuracy, to plan the agricultural and ceremonial year. Their 260-day cycle (called Tzolkin) formed a basic part of all Mesoamerican calculations while, at the same time, they used another cycle, similar to our 365-day solar year (Haab). The two cycles ran concurrently, like intermeshed cog-wheels, and it took 52 years to return to any given date.

The 52-year cycle, called the Calendar Round or the Sacred Round, had been used by earlier Mesoamerican peoples. who also developed a more elaborate calendar, the Long Count. But it was the Maya, even more demanding in their calculations, who refined the Long Count to its highest levels of accuracy, measuring time from the beginning of their calendar (3113 BC). At the completion of 104 years, several time-cycles coincided spectacularly: the 584-day Venus cycle (also of considerable significance to the Maya), the 365-day solar year, the 52-year cycle and the Tzolkin, and the event was celebrated with great rejoicing and special ceremonies.

TIP

Most of the villages
around San Cristóbal
hold their weekly mar-
ket on Sunday morn-
ing and this is the best
time to visit.

wear black. Tzotzil men from Zinacantán wear red and white striped tunics and flat hats with colorful ribbons; longer flowing ribbons are for unmarried men. The elaborate decorations on the women's *huipiles* (short smocks) often represent stylized animals and birds and are highly symbolic.

Na-Bolom, the "house of the jaguar"

A visit to San Cristóbal has to include the **Na Bolom** (open Tues–Sun; entrance fee), the center was founded by the late Gertrude Duby-Blom, a Swiss writer, photographer and linguist, and her husband Franz Blom, a Danish archeologist and excavator of La Venta who died in 1963. "Trudi" devoted half a century to the study of the customs, languages and history of the people of this region, for whose rights she also campaigned rigorously. She died in her nineties in 1993. In a large house with flower-filled patios, beautifully furnished rooms and log fires, the center – containing a library, a museum, and a guesthouse – is dedicated to the preservation of the Lacandón region.

Indian villages

Probably the most accessible of the indian villages in the hills to the north of San Cristóbal is **San Juan Chamula ㉞**, 9.5 km (6 miles) away on a paved road. You can either drive, take a bus or rent a horse and ride across country. A permit must be obtained (for a small fee) from the local visitors' office before entering the church, and it is strictly forbidden to take photographs inside the building. The Chamulan religion is a combination of Catholic and pre-Hispanic Mayan beliefs.

Inside, the floor is carpeted with branches of pine and the church is lit with

BELOW:
brotherly love.

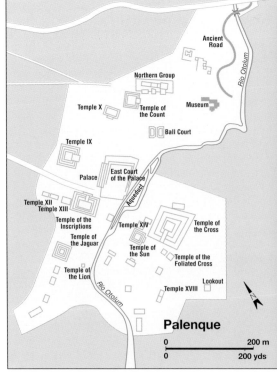

Palenque

0   200 m
0   200 yds

hundreds of candles which are dazzlingly reflected in the many mirrors that surround the statues of saints.

Other villages to visit are **Zinacantán**, which is reached by taking the same paved road that goes to San Juan Chamula, then branching off to the left, and **Tenejapa**, some 29 km (18 miles) away. The drive to Tenejapa passes through spectacular scenery and the weaving, embroidery and brocaded crafts are excellent, especially at the Sunday market.

Agua Azul and Misol-Ha

It is worth making two stops en route from San Cristóbal to Palenque. The dozens of breathtakingly beautiful jungle waterfalls at **Agua Azul ㉟**, on Río Tulijá, are only 4 km (2½ miles) off the main road. During the spring is the best time to visit, as the pools of water beneath the falls really are clear aquamarine. Safer for swimming in than the thundering cascades at Agua Azul is the pool beneath the 35 meter (115 ft) waterfall at **Misol-Ha ㊱**, which is 22 km (14 miles) from Palenque.

Looming out of the dense, jungly undergrowth of Chiapas, the Mayan ruins at **Palenque ㊲** are, for many visitors to the area, the highlight of their trip to Mexico. The complex site inspires both awe and wonder, and yet what one sees today represents barely ten percent of the incredible complex of chambers, terraces, staircases, temples, palaces and other structures that graced Palenque in its heyday in the 7th century AD. During that time the stucco and limestone relief panels would have been polychromed, and the effect of the colors and the white plaster – set off against the backdrop of dark green foliage – must have been truly dazzling.

Map on pages 280-1

TIP

The archeological site at Palenque opens at 8am; arrive early to miss the heat and the crowds.

BELOW: the Pyramid of the Inscriptions at Palenque.

Map
on pages
280-1

This is the site of the famous tomb within the **Templo de las Inscripciones**, a superb example of Classic Mayan architecture. It is in fact a pyramid with a temple on top, dominating the whole site. The hieroglyphic inscriptions on the walls, with the date AD 692, give the temple its name. In 1952, archeologist Alberto Ruz Lhuillier discovered a sealed stone passageway that led to the burial chamber 25 meters (82 ft) down, at the center of the pyramid. It contained the skeleton of the deified king, Pakal, wearing a mosaic jade death mask.

Almost directly opposite the pyramid, and in the center of the site is the **Palacio**, a complex of buildings with courtyards, passages and tunnels, crowned by a unique four-story reconstructed tower which may have been used as an observatory. Its walls are embellished with detailed stucco panels, and its courtyards have low walls decorated with stone sculptures and hieroglyphics, many of which have yet to be deciphered.

There is a **ball court** and another group of temples, the **Grupo del Norte** to the north of the Palacio, while to the east, across the stream, and on the edge of the encroaching jungle are the **Templo de la Cruz**, the **Templo del Sol** and the **Templo de la Cruz Foliada**.

There is a visitors' center with a museum at the entrance to the site (open Tues–Sun 10am–5pm) which can be reached by frequent VW bus service from the nearby town of Palonque. The best of the town's numerous hotels, which are mostly located around the zócalo, is the Chan Kah; all the hotels near the site are exorbitantly expensive.

BELOW: a Lacandón smokes a home-made cigar.
RIGHT: Tzoltales gathering for a religious festival outside their church in Tenejapa, Chiapas.

Ruins in the rainforest

The other two important Mayan sites, **Bonampak** 🟟 and **Yaxchilán** 🟟, are

located deep in the heart of the rainforest near the Usumacinta River, which marks the international border with Guatemala.

During the dry season Bonampak can be reached by truck from Palenque, 140 km (87 miles) northwest. Archeologists, who only "discovered" the site in 1946, were excited by the vividly colored murals (*see photo, page 32*), depicting wars, ceremonial rites and festivals, which have taught us so much about the ancient Mayan way of life.

The floor-to-ceiling frescoes present a running historical narrative of ceremonial activities, battles, festivals, celebrations and dances, depicted in tiny, fascinating detail. For those who cannot reach the remote ruins of Bonampak, there are reproductions of the murals in the Museo de Antropología Carlos Pellicer, in Villahermosa, and in the Museo Nacional de Antropología in Mexico City.

An even stronger spirit of adventure is needed to reach the much larger (and, to many, more wonderful) Mayan site of Yaxchilán on the banks of the Usumacinta River, most admired for its intricate stucco carvings and roof decorations.

Yaxchilán is accessible only by boat or plane. Boats can be hired from Frontera Echeverría (also called Corozal) or else organized tours by plane can be booked through travel agencies in Palenque or San Cristóbal de las Casas. ❏

THE UNDERWATER OASIS OF THE YUCATAN

Mexico's Caribbean harbors some magnificent natural treasures: hundreds of species of colorful marine and shore life – a diver's paradise

While most visitors to the Yucatán Peninsula are busy clambering over its mysterious Mayan ruins or sunning themselves on its gorgeous beaches, divers and snorkelers flock here to view the region's diverse marine life. Puerto Morelos, a fishing village just 32 km (20 miles) south of the international resort city of Cancún, is one of the bases from which underwater adventures can be made to the Great Maya Reef. The reef here is part of the second longest coral reef system in the world, stretching for some 350 km (218 miles) along the east coast of Mexico's Yucatán Peninsula and south to Belize and Honduras. Although much narrower than the Australian Great Barrier Reef system, the Great Maya Reef reaches depths of over 40 meters (130 ft) around Cozumel Island. The remarkable transparency of the water provides visibility up to 27 meters (90 ft) in places, making it one of the most popular diving locations in the world.

TEEMING WITH LIFE

The Caribbean is one of the richest regions on earth in coral formations. Reefs, in turn, harbor an incredible variety and density of marine life. Over 50 species of corals, 400 of fish and 30 gorgonians have been identified to date on the Yucatán reef system, along with hundreds of mollusks, crustaceans, sponges and algae. The size of its importance is comparable to the discovery of a virgin forest. The long term effect of hurricanes on the reef favors a greater diversity of species as they suppress dominant types, while creating spaces for new species.

△ **UNIQUE BIRDLIFE**
The Yucatán is known for its unique avian diversity, with 530 species,such as this Great Egret, and others found only here.

▽ **BIOSPHERE RESERVE**
Near to Tulum, the Sian Ka'an Reserve covers tropical forest, savanna and coastline, protecting a host of land and aquatic animals.

▽ **NESTING GROUND**
The loggerhead is one of five species of sea turtle that come to the Yucatán to nest on the beaches between the months of May and September

◁**AMERICAN VISITOR**
Several thousand of Mexico's only American Flamingo colony can be easily viewed at Celestún on the northwest coast.

THE DELIGHTS OF DIVING

Renowned for its spectacular underwater scenery and well preserved reef system, Cozumel Island, off the east coast of the Yucatán attracts scuba divers from all over the world. The best diving areas are found within the National Underwater Reserve on the southwest shore of the island and on the Maracaibo reef at the sounthern point of the island. Sheer walls drop down into the depths, covered with exotic flora and fauna.

The importance of coral reefs has made them a focal point for conservationist efforts. Amigos de Sian Ka'an, a Cancún based charity, is mapping the entire Quintana Roo reef in order to provide the necessary information for sustainably managing it for the benefit of all.

◁ **SACRED WATERS**
Dozens of natural sinkholes, called *cenotes*, dot the Yucatán, such as this one in Valladolid. Some *cenotes* were sacred to the Maya, for receiving offerings.

△ **UNDERWATER OASIS**
The Great Maya Reef serves as an oasis in an otherwise nutrient poor sea. It is home to several thousand plant and animal species, from exotic fish to rare turtles.

△ **FOOD FROM THE SEA**
Whether it's pink conch, shrimp, spiny lobster, stone crab, squid, grouper or *boquinete*, the warm local waters serve up a tasty seafood platter.

▷ **VERSATILE CONCH**
Valued for its edible as well as its decorative use, local fishermen and scientists are now trying to protect the pink conch.

THE YUCATÁN

Mexico, bordering the Gulf, is shaped like a fish-hook and the Yucatán Peninsula is the bait which has lured many a traveler to the sparkling Caribbean beaches and Ancient Mayan cities

Map
on pages
318–9

México City

After the Spanish conquest, the Yucatán Peninsula was not governed by the viceroys in distant Mexico City but directly from the mother country, Spain. Over a period of nearly 300 years of colonial rule, the region developed its own particular syncretism of Mayan and Spanish cultures. Its isolation from the center of Mexican power also meant that it took little part in the 19th-century Independence movement.

War of the Castes

If one word could be used to sum up the colonial history of the Yucatán, it would be "strife." Mayan resistance to the Spanish invasion was fierce and battles were frequent, as were attacks by pirates; and friction persisted between the Franciscan monks, the civil authorities and the clergy. Drought often struck and hunger ravaged the land. The Mayas, like other indian groups, were treated shamefully by the Spanish; their lands were taken away, they were abused and despised. As a result of mistreatment and epidemics from European diseases, their population plummeted.

After Independence in 1821, the Yucatán reacted by declaring its own independence from Mexico. The ensuing contretemps with central government led to local *hacendados* arming thousands of indians who overran the very Spanish city of Valladolid and expelled federal troops from Campeche. This was the start of the **War of the Castes** (1847).

But the pent-up anger of the Mayas was not only against central government and federal troops, but against all white settlers. After months of violence and killings the planting season arrived and the Mayas – who were farmers, not soldiers – returned to their villages to plant the year's corn.

When the Mayas left, the whites recovered their strength and retaliated. From Cuba, came rifles and artillery. The federal government sent troops and supplies, and some 1,000 mercenaries came from the US. Over the next five or six years the indian population in the Yucatán Peninsula was slashed by half.

The Yucatán did not submit to the control of central government until Porfirio Díaz took power in 1876. At the beginning of the century the economy was boosted by the production of *henequén* (a fibrous plant used to make rope) which increased ten-fold between 1879 and 1916. Today, as synthetic fibers have reduced the importance of henequén, oil, sulfur and tourism are the major industries in the Yucatán peninsula.

From Villahermosa (*see page 310*), in the state of Tabasco, there are two possible routes into the Yucatán Peninsula: one goes directly east towards Chetumal and the Caribbean coast; the other heads north to

PRECEDING PAGES: the Mayan site of Tulum. **LEFT:** Mexico's multi-feathered creatures. **BELOW:** fine colonial façade, Campeche.

The Yucatán

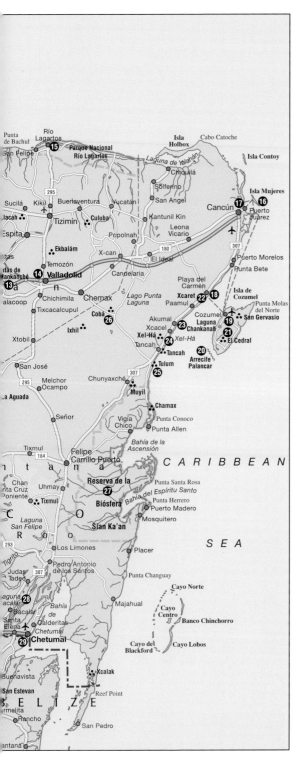

Ciudad del Carmen and the colonial cities of Campeche and Mérida.

From **Isla del Carmen**, an island that was once a pirate stronghold, the barely signposted and unreliable coastal road proceeds north to **Champotón ❶**. It was there, in 1517, that Spanish blood was shed for the first time in Mexico, when an expedition under the command of Francisco Hernández de Córdoba fought the Mayas. Córdoba was wounded and died a short while afterwards in Havana.

A fortified city

It is an easy 62-km (40-mile) drive along the coast to **Campeche ❷**, a city which has retained much of its colonial character. As it developed, Campeche, capital of the state which bears the same name, proved to be an attractive target for pirates. After one particularly devastating attack in 1663, when the buccaneers of several nations joined forces in a fierce and ferocious onslaught, the Spanish authorities ringed the city with around 2.5 km (1.5 miles) of 2.5-meter (8-ft) thick walls, turning it into a hexagonal stronghold guarded by eight towers. In 1717 an attack against the pirates on Isla del Carmen finally wiped them out.

In the decades after Mexico's independence in 1821, when the lucrative shipping industry to Spain was reduced to nothing more than a trickle, Campeche became little more than a backwater, and fishing became of necessity its main source of income. The city's walls saved it yet again in the mid-1800s during the War of the Castes, when the Maya insurgents took over every town in the peninsula except Campeche and Mérida.

By the end of the 19th century, Campeche was expanding beyond its city walls, which no longer served as defence, and demolition began. However, most of the *baluartes* (bulwarks) are still standing. The **Puerta del Mar** (Sea Gate), which was demolished in 1893 was rebuilt in the 1950s when its historical value was realized.

The Baluarte Santiago is now the site of a glorious tropical garden, the **Jardín Botánico Xmuch Haltún** (open Tues–

Good quality handwoven Panama hats, made near Campeche, can be rolled up and will immediately resume their shape.

Sun; free entry). The **Museo de las Estelas Mayas** (open Tues–Sun; free entry), in the Baluarte de la Soledad, exhibits stelae from the Mayan site at Edzná (*see page 321*) whose hieroglyphs have been of key importance in deciphering the ancient language. The modern **Congreso del Estado** (State Congress) – whose curious shape has earned it the nicknames UFO, the flying saucer, and the sandwich – is next door to the **Baluarte San Carlos** (open daily; free entry), which contains a small **armaments museum**. The **Baluarte de San Juan** is still connected to a stretch of the old city walls and to the **Puerta de Tierra**, the former city gates for travelers arriving by land.

Nearby is the **Museo Regional de Arqueología** (open Tues–Sun; entrance fee), which has an extensive collection of Mayan artefacts including clay figures and even a wooden contraption used to re-shape the heads of the Maya children to give them the sharply sloping forehead that, at the time, was considered a mark of great beauty.

Elegant mansions

In Campeche, as in most Mexican towns, the old colonial plaza, or **Parque Principal**, is the center of social life, where people congregate to enjoy the shade of the trees, listen to concerts and attend mass in the **Catedral de la Concepción.** The plain façade and tall twin towers of the cathedral are typical of the earliest churches on the peninsula, and the dome has curious flying buttresses. Note also the old **Portales** building, an elegant structure with its graceful façade and arcade.

Campeche's array of beautiful stately houses attest to the wealth that once flowed into the city. One of the most luxurious is the **Mansión Carvajal** (at

BELOW: Puerta de Tierra, Campeche.

BUCCANEER ATTACKS

Soon after the arrival of the Spanish, Campeche became the main port of the Yucatán Peninsula. Pirates – mainly Dutch, French and English – cottoned on to the riches that were being exported to Europe and challenged the Spanish supremacy of the Caribbean seas. The first attack on Campeche came just six years after the city had been founded in 1540. For over 100 years, the people of Campeche lived in fear, for the pirates did not limit their attacks to the ships leaving the harbor, but plundered property and killed many Campechanos. In one historic onslaught in 1633, the rival pirates combined forces and attacked the city in one huge flotilla. In response, massive coastal fortifications were built, such as the imposing fortress of San Juan de Ulúa at the port of Veracruz, and the whole of Campeche was eventually surrounded by thick ramparts. The wealth of men like John Hawkins and Sir Francis Drake was largely accumulated from the Spanish ships plundered in the Caribbean. Although Drake was knighted by Queen Elizabeth I and held the respected post of Mayor of Plymouth, his reputation in Mexico as a notorious pirate and swashbuckler has persisted.

Calles 10 and 53) with its Moorish arches, black-and-white marble floors and sweeping staircase.

Map on pages 318–9

The oil boom of the 1970s brought new life to Campeche and the Mexican oil industry is still a major source of income. Famous both for its hospitality and its seafood, it is a good place to shop for Panama hats (locally known as *jipis*), cattle horn jewelry, which looks rather like tortoiseshell, Maya-style clothing and handicrafts, and objects with nautical themes, such as ships in bottles.

Edzná, "the house of grimaces"

Most of the ruined temples of **Edzná** ❸ (open daily; entrance fee) some 65 km (40 miles) southeast of Chetumal, date from around AD 500–800 when the city was at its height. The most impressive structure is the huge **Templo de los Cinco Pisos** (Temple of Five Levels) which has chambers at each level and a roof comb on the top. The buildings at Edzná resemble the so-called Puuc style of architecture from the sites further north around Uxmal and Kabah.

Uxmal's architecture

Although the name means "thrice built" in the Mayan language, archeologists have in fact found as many as five different construction periods represented at **Uxmal** ❹ (open daily; entrance fee). Building began in the Classic period, in the 6th and 7th centuries, and the city reached its zenith between AD 600–900; some of the original sapodilla-tree lintels are still in place thanks to the hardness of the wood and the relatively dry climate.

The magnificent, oval-based **Pirámide del Adivino** (Pyramid of the Magician) is the first building encountered at the entrance to the site. According to

BELOW: Catedral de la Concepción, Campeche.

Yucatán license plate.

legend, it was built in a single night by a sorceress's son, a dwarf who had hatched from an egg. In fact, the structure consists of five superimposed pyramids built over a period of centuries. For the fit, energetic and fearless of heights, some very steep and narrow steps lead to the top, 35 meters (115 ft) up; a chain at the side serves as a handrail.

The **Cuadrángulo de las Monjas** (Nunnery Quadrangle), a plaza formed by four buildings immediately to the west of the pyramid, was so named by its Spanish discoverer in the 17th century because it reminded him of the cloister of a convent. Archeologists believe that the 74 chambers may have been used as a residence or school of some sort.

The Nunnery Quadrangle

It was this quadrangle that inspired Mexico's best known architect, Pedro Ramírez Vázquez, when he designed the Museo Nacional de Antropología (*see page 164*) in Mexico City. The entire complex is built on an elevated, man-made platform and is typical of of Puuc-style architecture, which is based on the Mayan hut, or *na*, with its smooth walls and high-peaked thatched roof. Particularly admirable is the complexity of the stonework, which was created piece by piece following a master plan, and then interlocked like a three-dimensional jigsaw puzzle. Scores of masks of **Chaac**, the rain god, adorn the façades, his curved nose silhouetted against the sky seems to pierce the clouds to bring life-giving rain.

It is no accident that Chaac has been given such a prominent place, since this part of the peninsula has no rivers or even *cenotes* (sinkholes), which are found at sites further north. In Uxmal, rain water was collected and stored in *chaltunes*, bottle-shaped cisterns carved out of stone and lined with thick, heavy coats of plaster.

BELOW: the Nunnery Quadrangle, Uxmal.

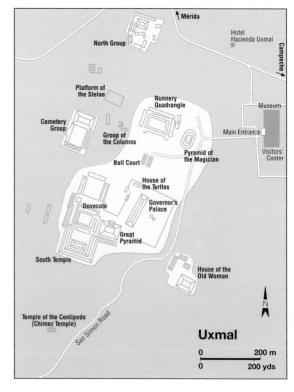

Between the Quadrangle and the **Palacio del Gobernador** (Governor's Palace), to the south, are the remains of an unrestored **ball court**, with a stone ring still embedded in one wall. The Palacio, on a high platform which provides a panoramic view, is considered one of the masterpieces of all Mayan architecture, with its corbelled arches, delicate proportions and the light and shadow created by its gently sculptured decoration. The façade has some 20,000 hand-carved stones fitted together in geometric friezes.

The Maya expert Sylvanus Morley called this palace "the most magnificent, the most spectacular single building in all pre-Columbian America." The adjacent **Casa de las Tortugas** (House of Turtles) is adorned with carved turtles, an animal the Mayas associated with the rain god Chaac. Behind the Palace stand the partially restored **Gran Pirámide** and **El Palomar** (the Dovecote) with a series of perforated triangular roof combs, which may have been designed for astronomical sightings.

The Puuc Route

At **Kabah** ❺ (open daily; entrance fee), the façade of the **Palacio de las Máscaras** (Palace of the Masks) is literally covered with inlaid stonework representing masks of the rain god Chaac. The **Arco de Kabah**, which has been compared to a Roman triumphal arch, once marked the start of a processional route leading to the ceremonial center of Uxmal.

Nearby, other Puuc Maya sites are located at **Sayil** and **Labná**, on the road to the **Grutas de Loltún** ❻ (open daily; entrance fee), the highly important and most impressive caves in the Yucatán. Apart from the huge Jaguar Warrior at the caves' entrance, there are stalactites, stalagmites and wonderful rock forma-

Map on pages 318–9

TIP

A bus tour of the Ruta Puuc leaves from Mérida every morning and stops at Uxmal, as well as the other Mayan sites of Kabah, Sayil, Labná and Loltún.

BELOW: Pyramid of the Magician overlooking the Nunnery Quadrangle, Uxmal.

tions, as well as ancient carvings and fine paintings on the walls. Carbon-dating indicates the vast network of caves were inhabited at least 2,500 years ago.

Not far away, the village of **Ticul** is a good place to buy hats, footwear, ceramics and jewelry. A little further east is the small town of Mani. It was here, in 1562, in front of the huge Franciscan monastery, that Bishop Diego de Landa burned hundreds of priceless Mayan writings, denouncing them as "lies of the devil."

Paris of the New World

Monumento a la Patria, Maya-inspired modern art, Mérida.

Residents of **Mérida** ❼ once liked to think of it as the "Paris of the New World." At the turn of the century, thanks to profits from *henequén*, the city had more millionaires per capita than anywhere else in Mexico. They built fabulous homes in Mérida but spent much of their time in Paris or New York.

Throughout the colonial period, Mérida was by far the most important city in the province. As the seat of civil and religious authority, it had a fine cathedral, a monastery and civic buildings. The Spaniards lived in the center of town, while the indians and *mestizos* lived in the segregated areas outside. It was the most aristocratic of towns, proud of its pure Spanish blood.

Mérida's downtown area is compact; its narrow streets and close-together buildings fill the limited space available within the ancient fortifications. Of the 13 Moorish-style gates erected in the 17th century, only two remain: **La Ermita** and the **Arco de San Juan**.

BELOW: fast-food stall, Mérida.

Mérida, often referred to as La Ciudad Blanca (White City), is an excellent town for a self-guided walking tour; many sights are near each other and the streets are laid out on a grid plan: even-numbered streets run north–south; and the odd-numbered run east–west.

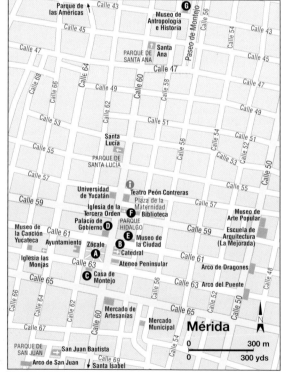

The laurel-shaded **zócalo** , or Plaza de la Independencia, is an inviting place for a stroll and to begin a tour of the city. On the east side, the massive, rather stark but elegant **Catedral de San Ildefonso** Ⓑ was built with the stones of a dismantled temple that had previously occupied the site.

The **Casa de Montejo** Ⓒ, on the south side of the zócalo, was built in the mid-1500s by Francisco de Montejo el Mozo, the conqueror of Mérida, and was lived in by successive generations of his family until the 1980s. After this, the house was taken over by Banamex. The elaborate plateresque façade depicts two conquistadores symbolically standing on the heads of the defeated indians. Each window of the house bears the coat of arms of a branch of the Montejo family.

Vivid murals

In the 19th-century **Palacio de Gobierno** Ⓓ, at the north end of the plaza, are some impressive and vivid murals by Fernando Castro Pacheco depicting the history of Yucatán. Historic photographs, on the other hand, can be viewed in the **Museo de la Ciudad** Ⓔ (open Tues–Sun; entrance fee), housed in the former church of San Juan de Dios, which is one block away and at the corner of Calle 58.

Inside the Franciscan **Iglesia de la Tercera Orden**. Ⓕ (also called Iglesia de Jesús) a panoramic painting depicts a formal visit made by Tutul Xiu, the Mayan ruler of Mani, to the conquistador Montejo. The tall twin towers are topped by a shingle design that coils under the crosses. One local guide maintains this embellishment was introduced by the indian stonemasons as a symbol of the Mayan god Kukulcán, the plumed serpent. If that is so, the god occupies the place of honor he might have held in a temple at the summit of a pyramid.

Maps
Area 318
City 324

TIP

If you're shopping in Mérida, look out for guayabera shirts, embroidered blouses, Panama hats, shoes and hammocks.

BELOW: a mansion on Paseo de Montejo, Mérida.

The road to the ruins.

An alternative to walking are the horse-drawn carriages called *calesas*, which can be hired downtown; be sure to agree on a route and price with the driver before setting off. A popular ride is along the chic, shaded **Paseo de Montejo** to see some of the palatial mansions built at the turn of the century by the wealthy *henequén* tycoons. One of the grandest, the Palacio Cantón, now houses the **Museo de Antropología e Historia** Ⓒ (open Tues–Sun; entrance fee). The museum covers the history of the Yucatán from prehistoric times, with displays on ancient Mayan rituals and culture, and provides a good background to the archeological sites of the region.

Day-trips from Mérida

The bird sanctuary at **Celestún** ❽, 90 km (56 miles) west, is famous for its flamingos, and *lanchas* (boats) can be hired to see them and other birds that migrate here in the winter.

North of Mérida, the ancient site of **Dzibilchaltún** ❾ (open daily; entrance fee), was once an important Mayan city, and is one of the oldest continuously occupied settlements in the Americas; people have lived here since 1500 BC. The main structure is the **Templo de las Siete Muñecas** (Temple of the Seven Dolls), named for the deformed clay figurines found there. Thousands of other offerings have been retrieved from the deep *cenote* **Xlacah** (ceremonial well); some of these finds can be seen at the site museum. A few kilometers on, the beach at **Progreso** ❿ makes an easy outing from Mérida; the seafood is good.

A short detour about halfway between Mérida and Chichén Itzá leads to the peaceful town of **Izamal** ⓫, once an important Mayan center of worship.

BELOW: the long, straight highway across the flat Yucatán.

Remains of unrestored pyramids can still be seen, but the most important temple was destroyed by the Spanish, who used its stones to build the massive **Convento de San Antonio de Padua**, which has the largest atrium in Mexico.

Maps
Area 318
City 324

The Mayan-Toltec fusion

Chichén Itzá ⓬ (open daily; entrance fee), the most visited of all the Mayan sites, is built on a grand scale. Many of the important buildings bear little evidence of classical Mayan refinements, for the architects were mostly Toltecs who arrived in the Yucatán in the late 10th century, and introduced the worship of Quetzalcóatl. The result is a unique fusion of Mayan and Toltec art, and there are images throughout the city of Chac, the Mayan rain god, and Quetzacóatl, the plumed serpent of the central highlands (called Kukulcán in Maya).

Dominating the site is the Temple to Kukulcán which the Spaniards called **El Castillo**. The pyramid incorporates key measurements of time in its structure: its four staircases have 91 steps each which, including the platform at the top, total 365, the number of days in a year; each side has 52 panels, representing the 52-year cosmic cycle; this was the point at which the religious and secular calendars coincided and when, it was believed, time ended and began anew (see box page 307).

Every year, at the spring equinox (March 21), thousands of people come to Chichén Itzá to witness the astonishing play of sunlight on the balustrade of the northern staircase. The effect created is that of a serpent creeping down to the foot of the pyramid, where it slithers into the ground. The Mayan priests claimed this phenomenon was Kukulcán's signal that it was time for the citizens to sow the crops. In contrast, at the fall equinox (September 21st) the "snake"

TIP

Staying overnight at Chichén Itzá has advantages: you can visit the ruins early in the morning or late in the afternoon, avoiding the midday heat and tourist rush.

BELOW: the jaws of Quetzalcóatl, the plumed serpent, at the ball court, Chichén Itzá.

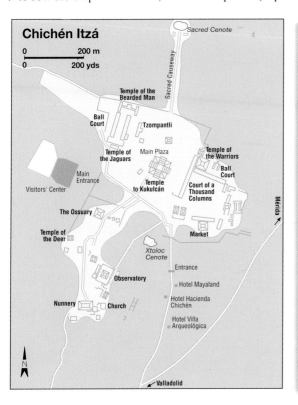

Chichén Itzá

0 — 200 m
0 — 200 yds

Sacred Cenote

Sacred Causeway

Temple of the Bearded Man

Ball Court

Tzompantli

Temple of the Jaguars

Main Plaza

Temple of the Warriors

Main Entrance

Ball Court

Visitors' Center

Temple to Kukulcán

Court of a Thousand Columns

The Ossuary

Mérida

Temple of the Deer

Market

Xtoloc Cenote

Entrance

Observatory

Hotel Mayaland

Nunnery

Church

Hotel Hacienda Chichén

Hotel Villa Arqueológica

N

Valladolid

appears to ascend the pyramid, indicating the time for the crops to be harvested.

Next to the pyramid is the **Templo de los Guerreros** (Temple of the Warriors) and the adjoining **Patio de las Mil Columnas** (Court of a Thousand Columns), where the forest of "Atlantean" columns (reminiscent of Tula – *see page 178*) were used to hold up the roof. On top of the temple, between two massive stone snakes, reclines what may be the most photographed statue in the Americas. He is the **chacmool** whose lap once held a receptacle for receiving the hearts of sacrificial victims.

One of the most intriguing structures in Chichén Itzá is the restored **Juego de Pelota** (Ball Court), the largest and best preserved anywhere in Mesoamerica. The ritual game played here is still somewhat of a mystery. What is known for sure is that the players propelled a heavy rubber ball without using their hands or feet, bouncing it off their hips or shoulders and through one of the rings on either side of the court. A relief panel along the wall of the court shows a headless kneeling figure with writhing snakes symbolizing blood coming out of his neck; this has led experts to suppose that the losers were decapitated.

Sacred Well

The **Cenote Sagrado** (Sacred Well) is a short walk away. These natural sinkholes which dot the landscape of the northern Yucatán lowlands were the only source of water, and some, such as this one, were used for ritual purposes. Offerings thrown to the rain god Chaac have been retrieved from the well, such as statues and precious objects of jade and gold, brought here from afar, as well as the bones of human sacrificial victims, including children under the age of 12.

The most important structure in **Chichén Viejo** (Old Chichén), south of the

BELOW: *El Castillo, the Temple to Kukulcán, Chichén Itzá.*

road, is the **Observatory**, known as **El Caracol** (The Snail). Particularly fascinating because of its resemblance to modern observatories, the circular building has windows aligned with points of specific astronomical observation.

Several hotels are within walking distance of the site: the **Hotel Mayaland** is the oldest and most gracious; the **Hotel Hacienda Chichén** belonged to Edward H Thompson, the American consul who excavated the Cenote Sagrado; and the **Hotel Villa Arqueológica**, which offers the usual "fun and sun" Club Med amenities.

Towards the coast

A network of caves can be visited 6 km (4 miles) east of Chichén Itzá in the **Grutas de Balankanché** ⓭ (open daily; entrance fee). Offerings to the Toltec rain god Tlaloc have been found in the caves. Visits include *luz y sonido* (light and sound), views of stalactites, stalagmites and an underground pool. There is also a small museum and a botanical garden at the entrance.

Valladolid ⓮ is a charming colonial town whose wealthy inhabitants were nearly wiped out during the War of the Castes (*see page 57*) in the mid-19th century. Most tourists pass it by, but Valladolid's proximity to Chichén Itzá and the generally lower hotel prices make it an alternative base for visiting the ruins 40 km (25 miles) away. The most interesting of the town's many churches are the **Catedral**, on the main square, and the church of **San Bernardino de Siena** next to the fortified **Convento de Sisal**, constructed in 1552.

Of the two local *cenotes* (limestone sinkholes), the most beautiful is not the Cenote Zací near the town center, but the Cenote Dzitnup, 7 km (4 miles) away.

On the coast north of Valladolid is **Río Lagartos** ⓯, famous for the thousands

Map
on pages
318–9

Isla Mujeres (Island of Women) is thought to have been named after the many female figurines found by the Spanish conquistadores in the Mayan temple dedicated to Ixchel, goddess of fertility.

BELOW: flamingos flying in formation over the Yucatán.

Cancún has seafood restaurants galore.

of pink flamingos that gather there. There is an inexpensive hotel in town and good tarpon fishing close by.

From Valladolid, most travelers head straight for the beaches of Quintana Roo. **Puero Juárez**, just north of Cancún, is the ferry port for **Isla Mujeres** ⓰. No longer the cheap, low-key paradise it once was, the little island is still fairly laid-back and a far less glitzy alternative to buzzing Cancún, just 13 km (8 miles) away. Mopeds and boats can be hired to explore the island which is only 8 km (5 mile) long. The best beach is **Playa los Cocos**, while snorkeling is popular at **El Garrafón**, an underwater coral garden on the southern tip (sadly most of the coral is now dead). There are giant turtles at the **Parque de las Tortugas**, and a pirate ship graveyard known as **El Dormitorio** under 10 meters (30 ft) of clear water. Boat trips to the bird sanctuary at **Isla Contoy** are also available.

Pot of gold

Virtually every architectural concept of modern high-rise luxury can be found among the 50 or so hotels that span the 23-km (14-mile) long hotel zone of **Cancún** ⓱: from the verdant tropical lobby of the Meliá Cancún to the cosmopolitan ambience of the Ritz Carlton, and everything in between; domed, Mexican neo-colonial complexes rub shoulders with a number of buildings clearly inspired by the sloping walls of Mayan pyramids. Luxury is at your beck and call: gourmet meals, bright nightlife, drinks on the beach while lazing under the shade of a thatched *palapa* shelter.

BELOW: turquoise waters off Cancún beach.

Protected from crashing waves by coral reefs, Cancún's turquoise sea and powdery white beaches (that never get unbearably hot) are legendary. The sea is Cancún's raison d'être and all forms of watersports are on offer including snor-

keling, scuba, jet-skiing, water-skiing, windsurfing and fishing. Boat trips, plane tours and rides in ultralights are also available.

Construction began in Cancún during the administration of President Luis Echeverría (1968–76) after a computer study determined that the best site in the nation for creating a new, world-class resort was this narrow sandstrip enclosing a brackish lagoon on the Yucatán Peninsula. Unlike the port city of Acapulco, Cancún was created from scratch, with a complete infrastructure, including modern housing for all personnel providing services in the hotel zone. The first hotels opened in 1972 and the building boom has continued ever since.

Malls galore

For getting around Cancún, you can drive, take a tour, rent a car, take a taxi (be sure to agree on the price before setting out) or go by local bus (look for those with signs saying *Hoteles* or *Turismo*). There are shops and restaurants in the business section of downtown Cancún, although most of the malls are in the hotel zone along **Boulevard Kukulcán**.

Plaza Caracol has 200 shops, restaurants and cafés; while upscale Plaza Kukulcán, adorned with a frieze inspired by Mayan hieroglyphs, is the newest mall offering 350 locales. For Mexican arts and crafts, try Plaza La Fiesta and Plaza Mayfair, whereas Plaza Flamingo provides shopping in a setting with a Mayan flavor. It is worth visiting the impressive Convention Center which has a museum with Mayan artefacts.

The coastal highway known as the Cancún-Tulum Corridor runs south past newly developed beach resorts almost all the way to Chetumal. About 32 km (20 miles) beyond **Puerto Morelos** – the car-ferry port for Cozumel – is the turn-

Map on pages 318–9

Cancún is the Mayan word for "pot of gold."

BELOW: strapped up and raring to go.

The Palancar Reef, off the coast of Cozumel, is considered one of the world's top diving destinations.

off for idyllic **Punta Bete**, at the end of an unpaved road running through a banana grove.

Although no longer the fishing village it once was, **Playa del Carmen** , with its sidewalk cafés and relaxed atmosphere, is still relatively unspoilt by tourism, and its reef diving is as good or better than any along this coast. Playa del Carmen is also the port for the passenger ferry to Cozumel, 19 km (12 miles) offshore.

Island of the Swallows

Cozumel ⑲, the "Island of the Swallows," was a sacred place to the Mayas, who came to pay tribute to the moon goddess, Ixchel. Women would travel here seeking her divine intervention in matters of love and fertility. Later, it was an important trading port and a haunt for pirates.

The island has some of the clearest water in the world, with visibility often reaching some 70 meters (200 ft) deep. The **Arrecife Palancar** ⑳ (Palancar Reef), where French explorer Jacques Cousteau filmed in the 1960s, is still a mecca for divers. The island's tiny capital, **San Miguel**, has an attractive museum, the **Museo de la Isla de Cozumel** (open Sun–Fri; entrance fee) and a score of modest places to stay, although many visitors just come here for the day.

About 8 km (5 miles) south of town is the **Laguna Chankanab** ㉑, recently designated a national park, where reproductions of Mayan buildings are set in a botanical garden. The bay with its clear water and colorful marine life is the most popular on the island and gets very crowded when the cruise passengers arrive around midday. There are other beaches further south, such as Playa San

BELOW: Punta Celarain, Cozumel.

Francisco, and some quieter stretches, which are only accessible through hotels.

Back on the mainland, the coastal highway heads past **Xcaret ㉒**, a privately owned "eco-archeological" theme park where you can don a mask and fins to explore an underground river system. Further south, **Akumal ㉓**, the "Place of the Turtles," is famous for its snorkeling and diving, as is the beautiful but thoroughly overcrowded **Xel-Há ㉔** lagoon, a large natural aquarium full of iridescent tropical fish.

Tulum

The archeological site at **Tulum ㉕** (open daily; entrance fee) is one of the few enclosed settlements built by the Mayas, and virtually the only one with such an extensive boundary still standing. Dating from the post-Classic period after 900 AD, when the main Mayan ceremonial centers had been abandoned, the site was undoubtedly a port, and it may also have served as a fortress protecting sea trade routes. Even at its height, prior to the Spanish Conquest, it is estimated to have had a population of no more than 600; the priestly and noble classes would probably have resided within the walls, and the rest of the population would have live outside the walls.

It has been suggested that **El Castillo** (the Castle), Tulum's watchtower perched on the edge of the cliff (*see photo page 312–3*), might once have been a lighthouse. Archeologist Michael Creamer came to the conclusion that it was a navigational station: "We placed a lantern on shelves behind each of two windows located high on the face of the Castillo. At sea, where the two beams can be seen at the same time, there is a natural opening in the reef." In support of this theory, some Spanish conquistadores wrote in their diaries that they

Map on pages 318–9

Peaceful lookout, Laguna Bacalar.

BELOW: beachside bar, Cozumel.

Map
on pages
318–9

TIP

Take insect repellant, sturdy shoes and a site map for visiting the ruins at Cobá: it is a fair distance along jungle paths between groups of buildings.

BELOW: the Great Pyramid, Cobá.
RIGHT: keeping in the shade, Isla Mujeres,
FOLLOWING PAGE: two-faced devil mask

could clearly see the light of a flame coming from the building as they sailed by.

The **Templo de los Frescos** (Temple of the Frescoes) is a two-story structure with columns on the bottom level and a much smaller room on top. The frescoes inside bear Toltec influence and the masks extending around the corners of the façade are believed to represent the rain god Chaac. The **Templo del Dios Descendente** (Temple of the Descending God) is decorated with a relief which may have represented Ab Muxen Cab, the Mayan bee god.

Cobá

It is a 40-km (25-mile) drive inland to **Cobá** ㉖ (open daily; admission fee), hub of the famous Mayan system of roads called *sacbeob* (*sacbé* in singular). The longest of these roads ran nearly 100 km (60 miles) straight through the jungle and swamp to Yaxuná, near Chichén Itzá (*see page 327*). It is believed that Cobá, with a population of 50,000, may once have been the largest of all the Mayan cities.

Near the entrance, between two lakes, is the **Grupo Cobá**. There are fine views over the lakes and other pyramids from the top of the nine-terraced pyramid, which is 24 meters (80 ft) high and topped by a Toltec-style temple. However, you may want to save your energy for the 120 steps of the **Great Pyramid** (42 meters/138 ft high) in the **Nohoch Mul** group, 2 km (1 ¼ mile) to the east.

Footpaths lead through the jungle connecting the 6,000 structures that have been identified in Cobá. The site extends over 77 sq km (30 sq miles), although few buildings have been restored.

South of Tulum, the vast **Reserva de la Biósfera Sian Ka'an** ㉗, one of the UNESCO World Network of Biosphere Reserves, seeks to save the region from

overdevelopment while providing a living for the local people. The reserve contains a wide range of wetlands and coastal habitats, such as seasonally flooded forest, savanna, mangrove and coral reef. It is home to a huge variety of flora and fauna such as spider and howler monkeys, tapir, crocodiles, several species of wild cat, manatee, peccaries, deer and over 300 species of birds.

Visitors are welcome in the reserve, and there is also a research center here (tel: 98-84 9583, fax: 98-87 30 80). At the fishing village of **Punta Allen**, on the tip of a slender peninsula, you can rent a hammock and sleep on the beach.

Beside the lovely **Laguna Bacalar** ㉘ is the Fuerte San Felipe Bacalar, which was built for protection against pirates in the 18th century, and was used as an indian stronghold during the Caste Wars. Just beyond the lagoon is the turnoff east to the ancient port of **Chetumal** ㉙, the jumping-off point for visitors moving on to Belize.

Highway 186 heads west across the peninsula through thick jungle to complete the circle of the Yucatán Peninsula at **Escárcega**, which is directly south of Champotón. There are several archeological sites along the way, the best being **Kohunlich**, on a side road out of Francisco Villa, containing the Pyramid of the Masks - unique of its kind - dating from 250–600 AD. ❏

INSIGHT GUIDES 👁

Travel Tips

Simply travelling safely

American Express Travellers Cheques

- are recognised as one of the safest and most convenient ways to protect your money when travelling abroad

- are more widely accepted than any other travellers cheque brand

- are available in eleven currencies

- are supported by a 24 hour worldwide refund service and

- a 24 hour Express Helpline service provides assistance and information when travelling abroad

- are accepted in millions of shops, hotels and restaurants throughout the world

Travellers Cheques

CONTENTS

Getting Acquainted

Area: 1,958,202 sq. km (756,066 sq. miles).
Capital: Mexico City, also known as the Distrito Federal (DF).
Population: 93 million, with 35 percent under the age of 15.
Languages: Spanish (92 percent), various Indian languages.
Religions: Roman Catholic (89.7 percent), Jewish and various Protestant Evangelical Churches (10 percent).
Time Zones: Mexico is divided into three time zones – Central, Mountain and Pacific – each separated by 1 hour. Most of the country follows Central Standard Time (GMT minus 6 hours) year-round. The northern Pacific coast states follow Mountain Standard Time (GMT minus 7 hours) year-round; and Baja California Norte follows Pacific Standard Time (GMT minus 8 hours, but GMT minus 7 hours from 1 April to end October.)
Currency: Mexican peso. This comes in denominations of 10, 20, 50, 100, 200 and 500 peso bills. Coins come in denominations of 1, 2, 5, 10 and 20 pesos and 5, 10, 20 and 50 centavos. The peso coins have a contrasting-colored metal border, while the centavos are small, thin and silver-colored.
Weights and measures: Metric.
Electricity: 110 volts; flat two-pronged plugs.
International Dialing Code: 52
Local Dialing Codes: Mexico City (5); Guadalajara (3); Monterrey (8); Acapulco (74); Ixtapa-Zihuatanejo (755); Puerto Vallarta (322); Cancún (98); Los Cabos (114); Mazatlán (69).
Highest Mountain: Pico de Orizaba 5,747 meters (18,855 ft).

Climate

Central Mexico

Mexico City, Guadalajara and many other Mexican cities lie in the central plateau where the climate is temperate year-round. Summer is the wet season – in July and August, Mexico City has rain nearly every day, usually for a couple of hours in the afternoon.

High altitude keeps these cities from becoming really hot, even at midsummer. In an average year, Mexico City's highest temperature will be around 31°C (88°F); Guadalajara's around 35°C (95°F). In Mexico City, the hottest months are April and May, when temperatures are on average in the upper 20s°C (low 80s°F). In midsummer and autumn, temperatures are in the low 20s°C (70s°F), and in winter around 20°C (68°F). Night-time temperatures may fall to 0°C (32°F) in winter.

Baja California

Baja has very low annual rainfall, mostly falling in late autumn and winter. Temperatures are more comfortable where the land is cooled by sea breezes, on the southern tip of the peninsula and along the Pacific coast. In an average year Ensenada's temperature will not rise above 35°C (95°F); but San Felipe, on the Gulf of California, may soar to 48°C (118°F). Desert areas are cold at night.

Northern Mexico

Northern Mexico is largely desert. The days are very hot in summer – well over 38°C (100°F). Mountainous areas are cooler. In winter, temperatures may drop below freezing at night. As you go east toward Monterrey, the climate is wetter and more moderate, but still very hot in summer.

The Pacific Coast

Along the Pacific coast, the temperature is cooler at night than in the south, but otherwise similar. In an average year, the maximum temperature experienced by Mazatlán or Puerto Vallarta will be in the mid-30s°C (mid-90s°F).

North of Mazatlán, the coast becomes a desert, and summer weather is hotter. In Guaymas, the maximum temperature in an average year is 44°C (112°F). Typical summer temperatures are in the upper 20s°C (80s°F) to 30s°C (90s°F). In winter it is usually in the 20s°C (70s°F) in the daytime.

Southern Mexico and the Yucatán Peninsula

This area has some of the most variable weather in Mexico: some regions are dry, others have nearly 5 meters (16 ft) of rainfall a year.

In Oaxaca, over 1,500 meters (5,000 ft) above sea level, the night-time temperature in winter can fall below freezing but in summer, at midday, it can rise to nearly 38°C (100°F). Acapulco has daily highs of 27–32°C (80–90°F) year-round, seldom falling much below 21°C (70°F) at night. Pacific breezes keep temperatures bearable. As in most of Mexico, the rainy season is summer and early autumn; there is little rain in winter.

On the peninsula, expect daily temperatures in the upper 20s°C (low 80s°F) year-round; night-time temperatures seldom go below 16°C (60 °F). Mérida's temperature can rise as high as 42°C (108°F); Cozumel, just off the coast, has a maximum just above 32°C (90°F).

Business Hours

Opening hours vary throughout the country. Banks are open Monday–Friday 9am–1.30pm. In larger towns and cities, the main offices of some banks are open in the afternoons and on Saturday mornings until noon. Office hours are widely variable; they are generally open 9am–2pm, then close for lunch, reopening from 4–6pm. Stores open at 9 or 10am and stay open until 7 or 8pm; in provincial towns shops may close between 2pm and 4pm.

SURF BEFORE YOU FLY

Surf the Lufthansa Internet web site and you'll soon be at the gateway to Lufthansa's global network of flights, including detailed information on the airline's worldwide services. As well as checking timetables and booking tickets, you can also access the latest Lufthansa travel information, including updates on Star Alliance, the Young Europe Special and Miles & More, our frequent flier programme. So the next time you fly, don't forget to surf.

http://www.lufthansa.co.uk

STAR ALLIANCE
The airline network for Earth

Lufthansa

Probably the <u>most</u> <u>important</u> TRAVEL TIP you will ever receive

Before you travel abroad, make sure that you and your family are protected from diseases that can cause serious health problems.

For instance, you can pick up *hepatitis A* which infects 10 million people worldwide every year (it's not just a disease of poorer countries) simply through consuming contaminated food or water!

What's more, in many countries if you have an accident needing medical treatment, or even dental treatment, you could also be at risk of infection from *hepatitis B* which is 100 times more infectious than AIDS, and can lead to liver cancer.

The good news is, you can be protected by vaccination against these and other serious diseases, such as *typhoid, meningitis* and *yellow fever.*

Travel safely! Check with your doctor at least 8 weeks before you go, to discover whether or not you need protection.

Consult your doctor before you go... not when you return!

SB
SmithKline Beecham
V A C C I N E S

Produced as a service to public health

Public Holidays

- **1 January** New Year's Day
- **5 February** Constitution Day
- **21 March** Birthday of Benito Juárez
- **March/April** Good Friday, Easter Monday
- **1 May** Labor Day
- **5 May** Battle of Puebla
- **May (Last Monday)** Spring Bank Holiday
- **1 September** President's Annual Message
- **16 September** Independence Day
- **12 October** Día de la Raza/ Columbus Day
- **20 November** Revolution Day
- **25 December** Christmas Day

Unofficial Holidays

Many businesses close or operate on a half-day schedule on the Epiphany (6 January), Mother's Day (10 May), All Souls' Day – Day of the Dead (2 November), and the Feast Day of the Virgin of Guadalupe (12 December). Except in beach resorts, business almost slows to a standstill during Easter Week and between Christmas and New Year.

Planning the Trip

Visas & Passports

Citizens of the following countries, wishing to enter Mexico as tourists, do not need a visa. Instead, they will be given a tourist card, known as the FMT form, valid for a maximum of 180 days, which can be obtained on the aeroplane, at the port of entry into Mexico, from travel agents or airline companies, or at the nearest Mexican consulate:

Andorra, Argentina, Australia, Austria, Belgium, Bermuda, Canada, Chile, Costa Rica, Denmark, Finland, France, Germany, Greece, Hungary, Iceland, Ireland, Israel, Italy, Japan, Korea (South), Liechtenstein, Luxembourg, Monaco, Netherlands, Norway, New Zealand, Portugal, San Marino, Singapore, Spain, Sweden, Switzerland, United Kingdom, United States (naturalized US citizens should also bring their naturalization papers or a US passport), Uruguay and Venezuela.

US citizens can visit Mexican border towns (and Baja California, as far south as Ensenada) for up to 72 hours without even a tourist card. Visitors from other countries may need a valid passport with visa (obtainable from any Mexican embassy or consulate). Visitors from any country, including Britain, Canada and the USA, traveling on business need a business visa.

Unless you are flying into Mexico, try not to enter the country at night. Waiting for a border official to wake up is a waste of your time and, having been inconveniently disturbed, he or she is less likely to accommodate your request for a 180-day tourist card.

Requirements for a Tourist Card

All visitors will need the following: a passport that is valid for at least six months from the date of travel; a return airline ticket, or other online ticket; proof of financial means (if staying for six months).

Deciding How Long to Stay

When you first enter Mexico, the immigration official who stamps your tourist card will decide how long you can stay: 30, 60, 90 or 180 days. Since getting an extension is a chore, ask for more time than you think you will need. It is impossible to predict whether the border official will give you what you want – the decision may be based in part on how you look.

Once you're in the country, you can extend the time available on your card at the Mexican Immigration Service (Dirección General de Servicios Migratorios) – there is one in most major towns. This is a time-consuming procedure, especially outside Mexico City, so begin at least a week before the expiry date. In Mexico City the office is at Homero 832, in Polanco (tel: 5-626 7200). You must fill out a form, then take it to another office where they will want to see how much money you have (in traveler's checks or an international credit card in your name, not cash). This takes about an hour. Another option, if you are near a border, is to cross into the US or Guatemala, then renew your tourist card on re-entry into Mexico.

Keep your tourist card with you at all times. You will have to return the card to Immigration on departure. If you lose the card, report the loss immediately to the nearest Mexican Tourism Office.

Children

Children over 15 years of age must have their own proof of citizenship and tourist card. Children under 18 traveling with one parent must have written, notarized consent from the other parent to travel or, if applicable, carry a decree of sole custody for the accompanying parent or a death certificate for the other parent. A child traveling alone or in someone else's custody must have notarized consent from both parents to travel or, if applicable, notarized consent from a single parent plus documentation that the parent is the only custodial parent. Note that these requirements do not apply to British minors, who can now travel on their own passport and are thus given the same rights as adults.

Useful Information

Tips for Travelers to Mexico is a helpful pamphlet issued by the US Department of State Bureau of Consular Affairs. It can be ordered from the Superintendent of Documents, US Government Printing Office, Washington, DC 20402. Tel: 202-783 3238.

Customs

All articles brought into Mexico may be subject to duty and require an import permit. Visitors are given an allowance of exempted goods (*see box*). Business visitors require special permits for portable computers. Penalties for smuggling in items is a high percentage of their cost.

Pets may enter Mexico with you only if you have a certificate of good health, signed by a veterinarian, and a certificate of rabies vaccination, dated within the previous 6 months. Both must be stamped by a Mexican Consul.

When leaving Mexico, it is forbidden to take narcotics or pre-Columbian artifacts. Visitors from

the US are permitted to bring home some 2,700 different items duty-free from Mexico, under the General System of Preferences. These items include pottery, folk art, handmade clothing and so on. For items not on the GSP list, each traveler may bring back up to US$400 worth of purchases duty-free, as long as they are not expressly limited or prohibited from entering the US. Keep hold of your receipts, to substantiate the value of your purchases. Family members may pool their exemptions. The brochure *GSP and the Traveler* is available at the border or by mail (with an SAE) from the US Customs Service, Dept of the Treasury, Washington, DC 20229.

Health & Insurance

As with travel to any country, you should never leave home without travel insurance, for yourself and your belongings. Rates vary, so shop around, but ensure you are covered for accidental death, emergency medical treatment, trip cancellation, cash and baggage loss. Many credit card companies also provide limited coverage for medical and/or legal emergencies for trips paid for with their card.

Health Precautions

Malaria is present in remote areas, and visitors to such regions should take a course of anti-malaria pills. It is also advisable to be inoculated against polio, tetanus and hepatitis, and, if necessary, a typhoid booster shot. Aids is widespread, and rabies is prevalent. Cholera is also present, so look for cleanliness

Cactus Protection

If you'll be traveling through cactus country, bring a candle and some tweezers. When you encounter the type of cactus spines that are too fine to tweeze out, pour melted but slightly cooled wax over the affected area. When the wax has solidified, pull it off and the tiny spines will come away embedded in the wax.

when choosing eating places.

Take it easy for the first few days if flying into the capital city. Many visitors arrive in Mexico City jet-lagged, then begin walking for miles, eating and drinking heavily and immersing themselves in unfamiliar customs – all of this in the low-oxygen environment of a smoggy, high-altitude city. Any ability to resist infection takes a plunge, and one result is the infamous Moctezuma's revenge (diarrhea).

It's a good idea to bring a basic medical kit, including medication for diarrhea and stomach cramps, insect repellent, aspririn or an equivalent, antiseptic cream, plasters, sunscreen and any prescription drugs you may need.

See pages 347–8 for advice on medical treatment in Mexico.

Drinking Water

Tap water in Mexico is not safe to drink. All hotels and restaurants catering for foreigners provide purified water although make sure you are not paying for a bottle of commercial water (unless, of course, that's what you want). In restaurants, ask for *agua purificada*. If you are in any doubt about its purity, ask for *agua mineral* (mineral water), or drink beer, soft drinks, or fruit juice. It is a good idea to ask for drinks without ice *(sin hielo)*. Be aware of the difference between fruit juice *(jugo)* and fruit drink *(agua fresca)* which is made with water – probably not purified.

Brush your teeth with the same water you drink. Wash fruits and

Customs Allowance

Articles brought into Mexico are subject to duty and require import permit. Visitors, however, are given an allowance of exempted goods. These include:
● **Cigars and cigarettes:** Up to 20 packets of cigarettes, or 25 cigars or 200 grams (7 oz) of tobacco.
● **Alcohol:** Visitors over 18 can

bring in up to 3 litres (100 fl. oz) of wine or liquor.
● **Electrical equipment:** One photo camera, a movie or video camera (except professional equipment); one pair of binoculars, one portable TV, one portable radio/cassette recorder, one video recorder, one portable computer.

vegetables with purified water, or peel them. If you are camping out or traveling in remote areas, be prepared to purify water yourself: either boil it for 20 minutes or more (depending on altitude), or use purification tablets. Be especially careful when eating lettuce, strawberries and dishes prepared with pork or raw fish such as *ceviche*.

Money Matters

The safest and easiest way to bring money to Mexico is as dollar traveler's checks from a well-known issuer, in fairly large denominations. They can be cashed in banks. If you are bringing cash, the best place to change your money is a bank or a *casa de cambio* (money exchange). You can also change money at hotels. American Express will cash personal cheques for card-holders. Avoid carrying large amounts of cash; Mexican pickpockets are efficient.

Major credit cards are widely accepted in tourist areas but for public markets and many smaller, less expensive hotels, restaurants and shops you will have to pay cash.

In border towns patronized by large numbers of US day-trippers, many visitors use American currency instead of changing money. Stores here often have price tags in both pesos and dollars; but you will still be better off changing your money in advance, since the stores are unlikely to give you the best rate of exchange. Those going further into Mexico, or staying more than a day, will want to change their money into pesos; and those coming from other countries must do so.

Taxes

If not already included in your airline ticket, an airport departure tax of US$17 or the peso equivalent must be paid in cash at airports for domestic and international flights.

Mexico has a value added tax (IVA) of 15% (10% in the states of Quintana Roo, Baja California Norte and Baja California Sur) and most states charge a 1% tax on accommodation, the funds from which are used to promote tourism.

What to Wear

Mexico's climate is diverse, and you should be at least minimally prepared for the weather of every area you pass through (see Climate, page 340). You should pack a sweater if you are visiting mountain or desert areas. May to October is the rainy season in much of Mexico, so you may want to take an umbrella or waterproof coat if you are visiting at this time. Long-sleeved shirts or tops are good to protect against sunburn and insect bites; a hat will also help keep off the sun. No matter where you plan to travel, bring a pair of comfortable walking shoes that are already broken in. A decade ago, any woman traveling in Mexico needed a hat or scarf (or at least a handkerchief) to cover her head when visiting churches; now this is considered unnecessary. However, your best approach will always be to observe what the people around you are wearing.

In cities, except for resorts, dress tends to be quite formal. For most occasions a shirt and pants should be adequate for men, and women can wear anything reasonably respectable. For elegant restaurants a man will need a jacket and tie, and a woman a smart dress or trousers. Women traveling alone should bear in mind that they may be more likely to be hassled by Mexican men if they wear skimpy clothes.

Advance Tourist Information

Mexican Tourist Offices abroad are now moving into the nearest Mexican Embassy or Consulate. Until addresses are finalized, contact the Embassy or Consulate in your country for tourist details:
UK: Mexican Consulate, 8 Halkin St, London SW1X 2DW; tel: 0171-235 6393. Embassy; 0171-499 8586
Australia: Mexican Embassy, 14 Perth Ave, Yarralumla, 2600 ACT; tel: 616-273 3905, fax: 616-273 1190
Canada: Mexican Embassy, 44 O'Connor Street, Suite 1500, K1P 1A4 Ottawa, Ontario; tel: 613-233 8988, fax: 613-235 9123
US: Mexican Embassy, 1911 Pennsylvania Avenue, Washington DC 20006; tel: 202-728 1600, fax: 202-728 1698

In the country and in provincial towns, shorts and casual clothes are fairly widely seen; but going to public places shirtless or in bathing suits is frowned upon and should be avoided. Most visitors are not likely to require formal dress, but it is useful to take something besides jeans. Baggy cotton pants are cooler than denim, and more comfortable for hiking in, especially in humid tropical forest.

Standards are different in resort areas such as Acapulco, Ixtapa/Zihuatanejo, Puerto Vallarta, Mazatlán, Cozumel, Cancún, and the beach towns of Baja frequented by Californian surfers. Shorts and bathing suits are acceptable on the street in these areas, even in restaurants (except the more formal ones). For men a suit and tie is not likely to be necessary – a shirt and pants should be enough to look more dressed up. For women long, loose, cotton dresses are both cool and comfortable.

Maps

Patria maps are available for each state, and they are excellent driving maps; Guía Roji maps are also good for driving. The Guía Roji and Detenal maps are the clearest and most detailed for Mexico City.

In Mexico you can buy maps from some of the bigger supermarkets (like Superama) and bookshops in large Mexican cities. If you are driving to Mexico from the US, petrol stations and bookshops near the border should also have Mexican maps.

Photography

Cameras, film and camera batteries are expensive in Mexico, so bring what you think you will need for your trip. Similarly, having film developed is expensive; if you do decide to have film processed, stick to places in the larger cities. Keep your films cool and ask to have your camera and film inspected by hand rather than through an airport X-ray machine – one passage through the machine may not ruin your film; but several inspections might.

There are a few restrictions on photography in Mexico. Tripods and flashes are not permitted in museums, archeological zones, or colonial monuments without a special permit. A fee is required for video cameras. Special permits must be obtained from the Instituto Nacional de Antropología e Historia for anyone wishing to conduct professional photo or film shoots.

Getting There

By Air

Mexico City can be reached by direct flights from many US cities, as well as major cities in Europe, Canada, and Central and South America. The American airlines, some of which serve several Mexican cities in addition to Mexico City, include American, Continental, Delta, Alaska Airlines, America West, and North West, TWA, United. European carriers include Air France, Aeroflot, Alitalia, British Airways, Iberia, KLM, Lufthansa and Swissair. Mexico City is also served by Air Canada and Canadian Airlines International, El Al, Japan Airlines and Singapore Airlines. Some of these carriers fly to other Mexican cities, such as Acapulco, Cancún, Puerto Vallarta, and Guadalajara.

If you cannot fly direct to your destination, connections can be made with AeroMéxico, Mexicana or TAESA, which have numerous domestic flights. All three national airlines also fly to the US.

There is a proliferation of discount air fares at different times of the year. Shop around for the

Airline Numbers

American Airlines: 800-433 7300 (US and Canada); 0345-789789 (UK).
British Airways: 0345-222111 (UK).
Continental: 800-231 0856 (US and Canada); 0800-776464 (UK).
Delta: 800-241 4141 (US and Canada); 0800-414767 (UK).
Northwest: 800-241 6522 (US and Canada); 0181-990 9900 (UK).
US Airways: 800-428 4322 (US and Canada).

best prices for both international and domestic flights. In addition to scheduled airline services, there are also some reduced-rate charter air-fares from the US and Canada.

When you arrive at Mexico City airport, porters will direct you to the taxi-stand. Fares from the airport are fixed according to zones, and prices are posted. The coupon is valid for four people and luggage that fits in the trunk. Don't forget to keep a sharp eye on your luggage.

By Sea

Round-the-world cruise ships frequently include Acapulco and other Pacific ports of call on their voyages, as well as Mexico's Caribbean resorts. From the US, a selection of 1- to 3-week cruises is available. Caribbean cruises departing from New Orleans, Tampa, Miami and Fort Lauderdale may stop at Cancún and Cozumel. Numerous cruises along the west coast of Mexico start from Los Angeles; some of these can be boarded in San Francisco, Portland, Seattle and Vancouver, British Columbia: these may stop at Acapulco, Ixtapa, Manzanillo, Puerto Vallarta, Mazatlán, and in Baja, at Cabo San Lucas and Ensenada. Cruises are a leisurely, comfortable way of getting to Mexico, but often leave little time for travel within the country.

Traveling to Mexico in your own boat requires clearance papers,

obtained at a Mexican Consulate or a marine customs broker before you leave home. You must present them at ports of entry and departure; sanitary inspection is also made at the port of entry. In addition, each passenger and crew member needs a multiple entry tourist card (*see Visas and Passports, page 341*). The boat, all passengers and crew must leave Mexico at the same time.

By Rail

If you travel by rail from the US, you must transfer at the border to the Mexican rail system, which is relatively slow and rarely on time.

By Bus

Bus travel within Mexico has many advantages, and those visitors coming from the US have the option of making their entire journey by bus. However, unless you live near the border or have more time than money, flying to the area you want to visit and then using buses is a better bet. For more information regarding bus travel within Mexico, see Getting Around.

Bus tours to Mexico from the US are available through:
Sunset Coaches, Inc, 1317 W Main, El Paso, Texas 79902.
Red Star America Tours, 4121 N 10 St, McAllen, Texas 78504.

By Car

Many visitors, particularly Americans living in the border states, drive to Mexico. To enter, you need a temporary automobile permit. Ask the Mexican Embassy or consulate for details of how to apply for one of these before you go. Ensure you have good insurance.

Specialist Holidays

A few companies offer tours of remoter areas of Mexico or ones that focus on outdoor adventure activities. These tours are often a good way to explore less visited areas for those with limited time. The following is a selection:
American Wilderness Experience are based in Boulder, Colorado (tel: 800-444 0099). They specialize in

camping and hiking trips through the Copper Canyon.

Trek America, Rockaway, NJ (Tel: 800-221 0596) offer two to six-week camping excursions in both northern and eastern Mexico.

The Association of Ecological and Adventure Tourism, Insurgentes Sur 1981–251, Col. Guadalupe Inn, Mexico, DF (Tel: 5-663 5381) offers a number of excellent adventure and wilderness tours throughout Mexico.

Baja Expeditions (Tel: 800-843 6967) specialize in the 1,600-km (1,000-mile) Baja Peninsula.

Club de Exploraciones de México (Tel: 5-740 8032) offers guides for hiking through the urban jungle that is Mexico City.

Language Institutes

You can stay in Mexico and study Spanish at the following places:

Cetlalic, Apdo Postal 1–20, Cuernavaca, Morelos 62000; tel: 73-13 3579.

Spanish Language Institute, Apdo Postal 2–3, Cuernavaca, Morelos; tel: 73-17 5294.

Centro Internacional de Estudios para Extranjeros, Tomás V. Gómez 125, Guadalajara, Jal. 44000; tel: 3-616 4399.

Centro de Idiomas S.A., Belisario Domínguez 1908, Mazatlán, Sin; tel: 69-82 2053.

Instituto Falcón, Moral 158, Guanajuato, Gto 36000; tel: 473-2 3694.

Instituto Allende, Ancha de San Antonio No. 20, San Miguel de Allende, Gto; tel: 465-2 0190.

Instituto Allende (Puerto Vallarta), Apdo Postal 201-B, Puerto Vallarta, Jal. 48350; tel: 322-3 0801.

Instituto Cultural Oaxaca, Apdo Postal 340, Oaxaca, Oaxaca 68000; tel: 951-5 1323.

Instituto Jovel, A.C., Apdo Postal 62, Ma. Adelina Flores 21, San Cristóbal de las Casas, Chiapas 29200; tel: 967-8 4069.

Practical Tips

Media

Newspapers and Magazines

Mexico fares well for daily newspapers, both national and regional. Mexican nationals include *Reforma, Excelsior, El Universal* (which has an English-language section), *UNO más UNO, La Jornada* and *El Financiero* (business-oriented). *Tiempo Libre*, on Thursdays, lists the week's cultural activities in Mexico City. In English, *The News* is a daily aimed at English-speaking foreigners. The *Mexico City Times* carries full US stock exchange reports. The free *Mexico Daily Bulletin* (which always carries a downtown map) is an institution and can be found in many hotels.

Time and *Newsweek* are readily available, as well as other US magazines and newspapers. European publications, such as *Der Spiegel* and *L'Express* are also often found. Many newsstands carry some foreign-language publications; but you can always count on a Sanborns, or the hotel shops, to have a good selection.

Radio and Television

Mexico has numerous radio stations, both FM and AM, ranging from *mariachi* music to heavy metal; all broadcasts are in Spanish.

Television broadcasts are also in Spanish, with the exception of late-night movies in English and cable TV channels. Bigger hotels feature cablevision or satellite dishes with programs from America, including ABC, CBS, NBC and CNN. If you want to watch sports events originating in the US, your best bet is to go to one of the large hotels or, on

Mexican channels, you can listen for the English narration beneath the louder narration of the Mexican commentators. US and British serials are shown, either with Spanish dubbed in or with subtitles, and Spanish-language soap operas produced in Mexico and South America are extremely popular.

Postal Services

Post offices are usually open Monday–Friday 9am–7pm and Saturday 9am–1pm. In smaller towns the hours vary: most will be closed on Saturday afternoons.

Mark all your correspondence to go air mail *(correo aéreo)*; surface mail is very slow. You can mail out packages of up to 20 kg (44 lbs) – go to the central post office of a large town, and have the package registered. Registered mail *(correo certificado)* must be sent before 5pm on weekdays, before noon on Saturdays.

MEXPOST, Federal Express, United Parcel Service and other courier services will pick up your packages for shipping on request; your hotel can usually make arrangements. You may find it easier to ask the store to send your purchases home. Most large stores are experienced at this and are reliable, though over Christmas delays and some losses have been known.

The surest way to receive mail in Mexico is to have it sent to a hotel at which you have a reservation, marked "Please hold for arrival". You can also receive mail at post offices if it is addressed to *Lista de Correos*, with your last name in capital letters and underlined. When you go to the post office where you are expecting mail, ask for the *Lista*; take some identification with you. Mail addressed to *Lista de Correos* will be held for 10 days before being returned to the sender. If you leave town before receiving mail that you know is on its way, fill out a change-of-address form at the post office. Packages sent to Mexico are subject to Customs duty, which can be substantial.

Telecommunications

Telephone

Mexico's telephone company, Telmex has installed Ladatel phones in all but the remotest spots in the country. To use one you'll need a phone card, available at news stands and convenience stores for 20, 30 and 50 pesos. You can make both local and long distance calls with these cards, if you have enough credit left (shown automatically when you insert the card in the phone). Occasionally you'll even find a coin-operated machine that takes a peso or 50 centavos, but these are exclusively for local and collect calls.

Directory Enquiries

Operators in Mexico speak Spanish; the international operators are English-speaking:
● For directory enquiries within Mexico City, dial 040.
● For long-distance directory information within Mexico, dial 020.
● For international enquiries, dial 090.

One of the least expensive ways to make long-distance calls is at the *Caseta de Larga Distancia* office – there's one in almost every town. Write out the area code and number, the city and country. If the call is to be person-to-person, write the name clearly. Specify *persona a persona*; station-to-station is called *con quien contesta* (literally, "to whomever answers"). When the operator puts your call through, your name will be called and you will be assigned to one of the phone booths. When making a collect call (*por cobrar*), be aware that if the answering party refuses to accept the call you will be charged for a one-minute call. The operator in your hotel will place long-distance calls for you, but will usually add a hefty surcharge to your bill.

Long-distance calls can be dialed direct from Mexico to most other countries. If you are making the call from a private phone and want to know the cost of the call, you will need to make the call via an operator and will not, therefore, be entitled to the cheaper direct-dial rates.

The prefix for long distance calls within Mexico is 01 (followed by the area code and number); for the US and Canada, dial 00+1; for the rest of the world, dial 00 followed by the country code.

Telegrams

To send a telegram, you can telephone it in from a private phone or send it from a telegraph office (*Oficina de Telégrafos*); you can't telephone it in from your hotel. Telegraph offices are usually open from 9am until the early evening on weekdays, sometimes closing for *siesta*, and will be open at least in the morning, if not all day, on Saturdays. If you require rapid delivery, ask for urgent service (*urgente*); regular service (*ordinario*) is cheaper. Write out your message and the address of the recipient clearly to minimize errors. To send an international telegram, phone 5-709 8625.

To receive a telegram in Mexico, if you're not staying at a hotel or home where it can be sent, ask for it to be addressed to you at *Lista de Correos* (to receive it at the post office) or at *Lista de Telégrafos* (to receive it at the telegraph office).

Western Union Financial Services have introduced a money-transfer service, *Dinero en Minutos* (Money in Minutes), whereby money can be sent from any Western Union office in the US and picked up in pesos at any of the 300 furniture-and-electronic stores in the Elektra, SA de CV chain throughout Mexico.

Faxes

Fax bureaux are not particularly common, although they can be found in most cities and resorts, in some stationery stores and telegraph offices. Some luxury hotels also have fax machines, and you may be able to use their facilities. Do note, however, that fax services can be very expensive.

Local Tourist Offices

In Mexico, each state capital has an office of the Secretariat of Tourism (*Secretaría de Turismo*). There is also a tourist information office (*Oficina de Información Turística Nacional*) at Mexico City Airport, section "A", where domestic flights are located. They can be contacted on tel: 5-762 6773, and can deal with queries in English as well as Spanish. Below is a list of the tourist offices in Mexico:

Mexico City (main office): Av. Presidente Masaryk 172, 11587, México, DF; tel: 5-250 0123 (24-hour standard information such as directions, details of special events)/ 5-250 0151 or 5-250 8555.

Mexico City (Distrito Federal): Amberes 54, 06000 México, DF; tel: 5-533 4700

Aguascalientes: Av. Universidad 1001, 8º Piso, 20127 Aguascalientes, Ags; tel: 49-12 3511.

Baja California Norte: Blvd Díaz Ordaz, Edif. Plaza Patria, 3er Piso, 22440 Tijuana, BC; tel: 66-81 9492.

Baja California Sur: Carretera al Norte Km. 5.5, Fraccionamiento Fidepaz, 23090 La Paz, BCS; tel: 682-4 0100.

Campeche: Calle 12 No. 153, entre 53 y 55, 24000 Campeche, Camp. Tel: 981-6 6767.

Chiapas: Blvd Belisario Domínguez 950, 4º Piso, 29060 Tuxtla Gutiérrez, Chis; tel: 961-2 4535.

Chihuahua: Libertad 1300, 1er Piso, 31000 Chihuahua, Chih; tel: 14-29 3421.

Coahuila: Periférico Luis Echeverría 1560, Piso 11, 25286 Saltillo, Coah; tel: 84-15 2182.

Colima: Portal Hidalgo 75, Colonia Centro, 28000 Colima, Col; tel: 331-2 4360.

Durango: Hidalgo 408 Sur, Col. Centro, 34000 Durango, Dgo; tel: 18-11 3166.

Estado de México: Urawa 100, Puerta 110, 50150 Toluca, Edo de México; tel: 72-19 6158.

Guanajuato: Plaza de la Paz 14, Col. Centro, 36000 Guanajuato, Gto; tel: 473-2 7622.

More colour
for the world.

HDCplus. New perspectives in colour photography.

http://www.agfaphoto.com

AGFA *Agfa*

When you're
bitten by the travel bug,
make sure you're protected.

Check into a British Airways Travel Clinic.

British Airways Travel Clinics provide travellers with:
- A complete vaccination service and essential travel health-care items
- Up-dated travel health information and advice

Call **01276 685040** for details of your nearest Travel Clinic.

BRITISH AIRWAYS
TRAVEL CLINICS

Guerrero: Costera Miguel Alemán 4455, 39850 Acapulco, Gro; tel: 74-84 2423.
Hidalgo: Carr. México-Pachuca Km. 93.5, 42080 Pachuca, Hgo; tel: 771-1 3806.
Jalisco: Morelos 102, Plaza Tapatía, 44100 Guadalajara, Jal; tel: 3-614 0123.
Michoacán: Nigromante 79, Palacio Clavijero, 58000 Morelia, Mich; tel: 43-12 0415.
Morelos: Av. Morelos Sur 157, 62050 Cuernavaca, Mor; tel: 73-14 3794.
Nayarit: Av. de la Cultura 74, 63157 Tepic, Nay; tel 321-4 8071.
Nuevo León: Zaragoza Sur 1300, Edif. Kalos, Desp. 137, Nivel A-1, Colonia Centro, 64000 Monterrey. NL; tel: 8-344 4343.
Oaxaca: Independencia 607, 68000 Oaxaca, Oax; tel: 951-4 0570.
Puebla: 5 Oriente No. 3, 72000 Puebla, Pue; tel: 22-46 2044.
Querétaro: Av. Luis Pasteur 4 Nte, 76000 Querétaro, Qro; tel: 42-12 1412.
Quintana Roo: Carr. a Calderitas 622, 77010 Chetumal, QR; tel: 983-2 8661.
San Luis Potosí: Alvaro Obregón 520, 78000 San Luis Potosí, SLP; tel: 48-12 9939.
Sinaloa: Av. Camarón Sábalo esq. Tiburón, 82100 Mazatlán, Sin; tel: 69-16 5166.
Sonora: Comonfort & Paseo del Río, 83280 Hermosillo, Son; tel: 62-17 0076.
Tabasco: Av. Paseo Tabasco 1504, Tabasco 2000, 86000 Villahermosa, Tab; tel: 93-16 3633.
Tamaulipas: Calle 16 y Rosales 272, 87000 Ciudad Victoria, Tamps; tel: 131-2 1057.
Tlaxcala: Av. Juárez 18 esq. Lardizábal, 90000 Tlaxcala, Tlax; tel: 246-2 0027.
Veracruz: Blvd Cristóbal Colón 5, 91190 Xalapa, Ver; tel: 28-12 8500, ext 124.
Yucatán: Calle 59 No. 514, entre 62 y 64, Colonia Centro, 97000 Mérida, Yuc; tel: 99-24 8013.
Zacatecas: Prol. González Ortega y Esteban Castorena, Edif. Marzes, 98000 Zacatecas, Zac; tel: 492-40552.

Embassies and Consulates

Some embassies and consulates in Mexico City:
Austraila: Rubén Darío 55, Polanco; tel: 5-531 5225.
Canada: Schiller 529, Polanco; tel: 5-280 9682.
Ireland (Honorary consulate): Av. San Jerónimo 782-A; tel: 5-595 333.
New Zealand: J.L. Lagrange 103, Piso 10, Los Morales, Polanco; tel: 5-281 5486.
UK: Río Lerma 71, Cuauhtémoc; tel: 5-207 2089.
USA: Reforma 305, Cuauhtémoc; tel: 5-209 9100.

Women Travelers

Women traveling alone or with another woman in Mexico are likely to attract a lot of attention from Mexican men, although in large cities attitudes are changing. Groups of three or more women are less likely to be bothered, and women with men are unlikely to receive more than whistles.

To minimize unwanted attention, avoid making eye contact or responding to comments from strangers, and walk purposefully. If you want to take a long walk alone, try to recruit fellow visitors to come along.

Women traveling in Mexico, with or without men, should also be aware that some drinking places admit only men. Bars in hotels and restaurants, cocktail lounges and many other bars admit women, but true *cantinas* do not. *Pulquerías* not only don't admit women, they usually don't take too well to strange men.

Tipping

In restaurants, the usual tip is 15 percent before IVA (Value Added Tax). Porters and bellboys are tipped at least 12 pesos per person. The same is appropriate for a taxi-driver who helps with your luggage; otherwise, there is no need to tip taxi-drivers. The usual tip for chambermaids is about 8–10 pesos per night. Tour guides are tipped according to the amount on the bill and the quality of their performance, but the usual is a minimum of 10 pesos for the day, per person. In barber shops and beauty salons the usual tip is about 15 percent of the bill before tax.

Petrol station attendants are usually given a small tip – many Mexicans, for example, ask for 95 pesos worth of petrol, then give the attendant 5. Boys who guard your car when you park on the street may be given 2–5 pesos; be sure to remember what the boy looks like or you may feel compelled to tip the whole group surrounding the car on your return. Parking attendants are tipped 2–5 pesos.

Keep in mind that many people in Mexico depend almost exclusively on tips for their livelihood.

Medical Treatment

If you need medical assistance, ask your hotel for a list of local English-speaking doctors (or dentists). In Mexico City, you can also call the embassy of your home country (see box). In other cities, ask at the government tourism office. If you are in a remote area you will have to depend upon a hotel manager or other appropriate individual to give you a referral. Larger cities have 24-hour pharmacies. In smaller cities and towns, the pharmacies use a rotation system. Your hotel should be able to direct you to one that is open all night.

Hospitals

Both Mexico City and Guadalajara have hospitals that cater for the English-speaking foreigner:
Mexico City: Hospital Inglés-ABC (American British Cowdray Hospital), Calle Sur 136, No. 201, Colonia Américas, 01120 México, DF; tel: 5-230 8000.
Guadalajara: Hospital México-Americano, Colomos 2110, 44610 Guadalajara, Jalisco; tel: 3-641 3141.

Security and Crime

The best recommendation for a safe holiday in Mexico is to use your common sense and follow a few simple rules:
● don't drive or walk on dark streets at night.
● wear a money belt and don't carry all your credit cards or large amounts of cash with you.
● always lock your car.
● keep valuable jewelry, watches and video or camera equipment locked away safely and out of sight.
● keep a sharp eye on your baggage, especially at airports.

In Mexico City and Guadalajara, particularly, do not flag down a cab on the street, especially at night. Call a *sitio* cab or take an authorized *turismo* taxi at the hotel taxi stands – it will be more expensive, but much safer. Do not pick up hitch-hikers, not even fellow countrymen, to avoid not only possible robbery but also the unwitting transport of narcotics. If you are travelling long distances by bus (occasionally subject to bandits), choose a bus that heads to its destination without making any stops.

One sure way to get arrested is to buy marijuana from strangers (or smoke it in public). Until recently, many Mexicans associated marijuana almost exclusively with criminals. Near the Guatemalan border, and in remote areas elsewhere, you can expect to have police descend on your car for a search. Don't forget: Mexico has some pretty stringent rules regarding drugs, and they're not limited to marijuana alone.

Etiquette

Most visitors like to leave a good impression on the country they are visiting. One way is to be polite. Asking for directions in the street, for example, might be prefaced by a simple *buenas tardes* (good day) or *por favor* (please). You can improve the impression you make by trying to speak Spanish and shaking hands. Mexicans shake hands not only when first introduced, but whenever they meet again, and when they take leave of one another. Women almost always greet each other with a kiss on the cheek.

Mexicans believe it is less rude to accept an unwanted invitation, and fail to appear, than to refuse it. Don't be too offended by being stood up in this way. Most visitors needn't be warned that Mexicans are not always punctual. In fact, the few times Mexicans take time seriously they refer to it as *"hora inglesa"* ("English time"). As in any country, some remarks should not be taken literally. When you ask a Mexican where he is from, he will often give the name of the town or the address, followed by *"donde tiene su casa"* ("where your home is"), implying that "my home is your home." Respond *"muchas gracias"* but don't take him up on this; he is only being polite – unless, of course, he specifically invites you over.

Mexicans are often very seriously offended by nudity. Avoid any public exposure that might offend people – for example, short shorts are considered inappropriate by many Mexicans, especially in cities and small inland villages, and the same goes for shirtless men.

Getting Around

Domestic Transport

Almost 250,000 km (150,000 miles) of free and toll roads make Mexican cities, towns and most villages accessible by car, and bus travel has been upgraded in recent years making road travel a comfortable and economical way to see the country. Most of Mexico's cities are served by three major domestic airlines. Except for the Chihuahua-Pacífico railroad, which is not luxurious but is well main-tained, passenger trains tend to be slow and inefficient. Mexico's long coastline and some good ferry services make going by boat an easy way to travel in some areas.

By Air

For domestic flights there are three major airlines, AeroMéxico, Mexicana and TAESA. They have reservations offices in cities throughout the country; ask at your hotel, or phone the airline direct (see box) to find the nearest office. Domestic airline tickets and information are also available at the ticket desks in airports, at travel desks in many

Domestic Airlines

For information on domestic flights, contact the following:
Aeroméxico: Reforma 445, Col. Cuauhtémoc, 06500 México, DF; tel: 5-133 4455.
Mexicana: Paseo de la Reforma 312, 03100 México, DF (timetable information); tel: 5-5110424 (reservations).
TAESA: Paseo de la Reforma 30 Mexico, DF; tel: 5-705 0880.

hotels, and through travel agents.

Air fares are generally the same whether you fly Mexicana or AeroMéxico on routes served by both. TAESA fares tend to be lower. These airlines offer package flights to more major destinations that usually include air fare and hotel at considerable savings.

On domestic flights, each passenger is permitted to check in two bags, with neither weighing more than 32 kg (70 lbs) and with the total weight not exceeding 50 kg (110 lbs). You are also permitted to take one carry-on bag (small enough to fit under a seat) and a garment bag.

By Boat

Ferries run between Baja California and the mainland, and between the Caribbean islands of Cozumel and Isla Mujeres, and the Yucatán Peninsula. The latter are mainly passenger ferries, traveling short distances. The Baja ferries make long journeys across the deep Gulf of California, which gives the traveler the chance to appreciate both the peninsula and the mainland without making the extremely long and hot drive around the Gulf.

Baja California ferries

For these ferries, make sure you have the latest timetable as boats don't leave every day. They are run by SEMATUR (see box). Write to the main office or contact local offices for reservations not more than two months and not less than two days in advance of travel. Alternatively, ask at your hotel for ferry information, preferably a few days before you want to leave. If you are coming from the US, ask a travel agent or insurance agent at the border for an up-to-date timetable.

The northernmost route connects Santa Rosalía with Guaymas, leaving Santa Rosalía on Tuesdays and Wednesdays, and returning from Guaymas on Thursdays and Fridays. A similar schedule applies between Mazatlán and La Paz. There are cabins on the ferries running from Topolobampo to La Paz and from Guaymas to Santa Rosalía, as well as a public (not very comfortable) salon area. Food and drink are available on the ferries. Double-check schedule information as boats are sometimes delayed.

Yucatán ferries

Reservations and schedules are not a problem for the frequent, short-distance ferry-trips from the Yucatán Peninsula to the offshore islands of Cozumel and Isla Mujeres. The passenger-only ferry to Cozumel departs from Playa del Carmen 12 times a day; if you are driving, there is a car park near the ferry landing. If you want to take your car on to the island – not a bad idea, for Cozumel is fairly large – the departure point is Puerto Morelos, further north. This ferry goes in each direction once a day.

For the shorter trip to Isla Mujeres, you can take a car ferry from Punta Sam or a passenger-only ferry from Puerto Juárez. Passenger-only ferries also operate from 9am to 5pm between Cancún and Isla Mujeres.

There are no ferries to Isla Contoy, a bird refuge popular with fishermen and snorkelers as well as bird-watchers; but you can book an excursion.

Ferry Information

For timetable information and reservations on the Baja California ferries, contact:
SEMATUR, Texas 36, Col. Nápoles, Mexico City. Tel: 5-382 7043. Numbers of local offices are:
Guaymas: 622-2 3390.
La Paz: 682-5 3833.
Pichilingue: 682-2 9485.
Mazatlán: 69-81 7020.
Santa Rosalía: 685-2 0013.
Topolobampo: 686-2 0141.

By Bus

One can go virtually anywhere in Mexico by bus. Hundreds of bus companies criss-cross the country, their vehicles ranging from the very clean, modern and fast to the

Bus Companies

There are numerous bus companies in Mexico, all providing a different selection of destinations. Ring around the companies to find out which routes they are offering and the terminal from which they start. The following are the major first-class bus companies:

ADO, tel: 5-133 2424.
Enlaces Terrestres Nacionales (**ETN**), tel: 5-273 0251.
Estrella Blanca, tel: 5-729 0707
Estrella de Oro, tel: 5-549 8520.
Estrella Roja, tel: 5-522 0269.
Flecha Amarilla/Primera Plus, tel: 5-587 5200.
Omnibus Cristóbal Colón, tel: 5-756 9926.

opposite extreme. The deluxe, first-class buses, which are air-conditioned, have comfortable reclining seats, a video screen showing movies and a toilet in the back. Seats are assigned, and you can usually purchase the right to use the seat next to yours for your bags or to stretch your legs, and pay the charge for excess luggage. These buses stop only at major centres. Second- and third-class buses may stop whenever someone flags them down. If you are going to a remote area you will need to take a second or third-class bus, but it is a good idea to use a first-class bus to reach the nearest major destination more quickly. On long hauls, drivers usually stop for a break at meal-times (especially around 2pm).

There have been hold-ups of buses, so it's safer, if you're going a long way, to travel on buses that head straight to their ultimate destination without stopping. ADO, for example, travels overnight non-stop between Mexico City and Villahermosa, showing a movie, providing blankets, pillows, free soft drinks and coffee, and offers wide, reclining seats. The cost is higher than first-class but you may consider it worth it.

Buying tickets

Reservations can be tricky. You cannot reserve a seat by telephone, or buy a round-trip ticket, nor can you buy a ticket to your ultimate destination if you are breaking your journey. At busy times of the year, make reservations well ahead. Around Christmas and Easter, buses are very crowded and you should reserve your seat at least two weeks in advance. If you make several stops, buy your seat for the next stage of your trip as soon as you arrive – otherwise, you may have to stay a day or two longer than you intended.

If you are traveling from the US, Greyhound will arrange your reservations from the border as far as Mexico City. In Mexico City, Greyhound has a ticket office at Reforma 35, tel: 5-592-3766. Otherwise, make reservations and buy tickets at the local bus station.

Bus stations

In most cities, the bus station is conveniently located. In Mexico City, you must go to one of four stations: **Terminal de Autobuses del Norte:** Av. de los Cien Metros 4907 (Metro: Terminal de Autobuses del Norte). Buses for the northern part of the country – beyond Manzanillo on the Pacific side, or beyond Poza Rica on the Gulf side. **Terminal de Autobuses del Sur:** Av. Tasqueña 1320 (Metro: Tasqueña). Buses bound for points south and southwest of Mexico City, such as Cuernavaca, Taxco, Acapulco and Zihuatanejo. **Terminal de Autobuses del Occidente:** Avenida Sur 122, Colonia Tacubaya (Metro: Observatorio). All other points to the west of the city. **Terminal de Autobuses de Pasajeros de Oriente (TAPO):** Zaragoza 200 (Metro: San Lázaro). Buses to the east and southeast, including the Yucatán Peninsula.

All of these bus stations are well away from downtown to avoid traffic problems. If you go there by taxi, the taxi-driver can probably tell you which of the many bus companies (see box) at that terminal will take you to your destination.

Baggage

This is limited to 25 kg (55 lbs) on first-class buses, but the limit is not usually enforced. On second-class buses there is virtually no limit, although you may have to load it yourself. Live baggage is also permitted on second-class buses: this includes pigs and chickens on their final journeys, as well as pets.

By Train

Rail used to be a good way of traveling within Mexico, but the railways are now in the process of being privatized and passenger service has almost come to a halt. It is limited to four routes: Mexico City to Veracruz; Mexico City to Nuevo Laredo; Mexico City to Oaxaca; and the Chihuahua al Pacífico. Only the latter, a spectacular ride which travels from Chihuahua city to Los Mochis on the Pacific coast, passing through Mexico's famed Copper Canyon, is recommended.

Mexico City Transport

Buses

City buses are often convenient, and in Mexico City – where driving is a nightmare for the visitor – they are highly recommended. The fare is quite low, about 20 US cents. Buses and mini-buses run up and down main boulevards such as Insurgentes and the Paseo de la Reforma. There are other buses which run only on the system of *Ejes Viales* or main thoroughfares. This makes them more efficient; they are also more comfortable and more clearly labeled.

Metro

Mexico City has an excellent subway (Metro) system, operated by STC (Sistema de Transporte Colectivo, tel: 5-709-1133). A free, if small, map of the network is available at most stations. Stay away from the Metro at rush hour and don't plan on using it for a trip to the airport or bus station with all your luggage; no large bags are permitted, especially at peak traveling times. Metro tickets are very cheap – buy a strip of five at a time.

Taxis

Mexico City has a bewildering variety of taxis. Fares are fairly low, but if you are going some distance you should tell the driver your destination and ask the fare: *Cuánto cuesta?* For an idea of what is reasonable, ask at your hotel.

The easiest Mexico City taxis for the non-Spanish speaking traveler to use are those waiting outside hotels. Drivers often speak English but their fares are very expensive by Mexican standards. Somewhat less expensive than hotel cabs are the *sitio* taxis, which work out of cab-stands, usually found on street corners. You can telephone them to pick you up, but you will need to speak some Spanish to do so. Some *sitio* stands accept advance reservations; and some even offer a 24-hour service, like Servitaxis (tel: 5-516 6020).

Many cruising taxis are Volkswagen Beetles which charge about half as much as hotel cabs. The green ones (usually cleaner and in better condition) use unleaded petrol. There are drawbacks with cruising cabs, however: it is virtually impossible to hail one if it is raining, and due to the numerous robberies in cruising cabs, it is advisable to use either hotel or *sitio* cabs, especially after dark. Always look for the driver's photo ID which should be displayed on the dashboard of the cab. Also check that the driver has turned on the meter or you will find yourself paying what he estimates is the right amount.

The cheapest cabs are collective taxis, *colectivos*. Those called *peseros* travel only on set routes, using the main thoroughfares. They are VW vans, usually white with colored stripes painted down the side. The driver will take two passengers in front, six in the back – sometimes more. You will be charged according to the length of your ride. Special *colectivos* carry passengers leaving the Mexico City bus stations. Tickets are sold in the bus stations for rides in these taxis. The first passenger in determines the direction the cab will take; the driver will then wait for a full load before leaving. During holiday periods, there is a mad rush for each taxi as it pulls into the loading zone; you may find it more convenient to pay for a private cab.

If your Spanish is good and you want to do some touring in Mexico City, settle on an hourly rate with a taxi driver. You could try to hire a street cab for less, but be sure to ask, negotiate and agree a price before starting out.

Sightseeing Tours

There are a number of organized tours around Mexico City. Contact the Mexican Tourist Office 24-hour hotline (Tel: 5-250 0123 or toll free from outside Mexico City: 5-91 800 90 392) for up-to-date details. Alternatively try a tour company (*see box below*).

Tour Companies

American Express: Paseo de la Reforma 234; tel: 207 6745. Tours throughout Mexico.
Grey Line: Londres 166; tel: 208 1163. Numerous one-day excursions from Mexico City.
Komex Tours: Benjamin Hill 243, Col. Condesa; tel: 272 9913, fax: 272 0648. Tours all over Mexico, from whale watching in the Baja Peninsula to beach resort packages.
Mundo Joven: Insurgentes Sur 1510; tel: 661 3233, fax: 663 1556. Specializes in discount travel for students and teachers.
Turiste: Reforma 19; tel: 592 7661. For Spanish-speakers; relatively inexpensive tours throughout Mexico.
Viajes Americanos: Reforma 87; tel: 566 9179. Tours throughout Mexico.

Driving

Roads & Regulations

Exploring Mexico by car is a popular option as the major roads are of a very high standard, although tolls can be expensive. For the necessary documents, see Getting There, page 344. Many visitors coming from the US bring their car over the border. It is also relatively straightforward to hire a car once you get to Mexico.

Car Hire

There are car hire agencies in most cities and resorts. You'll need a major credit card as well as a valid driving license. During peak holiday times, ensure you book your car in advance. Costs vary according to the location and type of car but are not cheap and it is costly to drop off the car in any place other than where it was rented. All the major companies are represented in Mexico, including Hertz, Avis and Budget. Check in the phone book (under *Automóviles – Renta de*) or ask in your hotel.

Insurance

If you are hiring a car, the insurance will probably be automatically arranged – check that it is fully comprehensive. If you are bringing your own car, buy Mexican auto insurance before you arrive. You may be able to arrange this via your own insurance company, or you can buy insurance at the border. Buy a policy for the longest period you might stay; if you leave the country sooner, you can arrange for a pro-rata partial refund.

Good insurance is vital because Mexican law is based on the Napoleonic Code – guilty until proven innocent – and if you have an accident, you could be jailed until fault is established. With the insurance, damages will be paid regardless of fault. However, keep in mind that motor vehicle insurance is invalid in Mexico if the driver is found to be under the influence of alcohol or drugs.

When you buy the policy, or if you hire a car, be sure to get the names and addresses of the company's adjusters, or of the local rental offices in the areas you plan to visit. Contact them immediately if you are involved in an accident of any kind.

Gas

When driving long distances, fill up on gas every chance you get. Pemex is the government oil monopoly. Until recently they owned and operated all petrol stations in the country, but now many of them have been franchised, resulting in better service. Leaded and non-leaded (*premium* or *magna sin*) gas and diesel fuel are sold. Gas prices do not vary from one station to the next, but check that the attendant sets the pump at zero before filling your car to avoid being overcharged. Most gas stations don't accept credit cards.

Safety Tips

Avoid driving at night in Mexico. There are animals and people on every road at all hours, and you will be less likely to see potholes.

When visiting some mountainous regions – such as Chiapas – you should be aware that there is a growing tendency for remote villages to set up impromptu "toll booths" by stretching a rope across the road.

Breakdown Services

The Green Angels are Mexican tourism employees in green-and-white radio-equipped vehicles which patrol some major highways. They are ready to offer first-aid, minor repairs to your vehicle, or an emergency supply of petrol and oil. You pay only for the parts used and for petrol and oil. The Green Angels operate daily 8am–8pm. Most speak some English. In time of need, just raise your hood, wait and hope.

Always carry water for the radiator, a jack and spare tire (or two, in rugged and remote areas of the country), fuses and any other spare parts that might need replacing – even if you're not prepared to do the repair yourself. You can count on the Green Angels for mechanical know-how but not for parts specific to your make and model (and remember, away from the main roads you may well be on your own).

Mexican mechanics are to be found in nearly any village, and at the ubiquitous Pemex gas stations. They are familiar with American-made and some other foreign made cars, especially Renaults and Volkswagens.

Road Signs

Many road signs are international, others assume a knowledge of Spanish. If you don't understand a road sign, slow down and be prepared to stop. Here are some key words that can be found on road signs:

Alto – Stop
Despacio – Slow
Peligro – Danger
Precaución – Warning
Ceda el paso – Yield right of way
Puente angosto – Narrow bridge
Curva peligrosa – Dangerous bend
Tránsito Circulación – One way (usually on an arrow)
Estacionamiento – Parking (also abbreviated E; E with a diagonal line through it means no parking)
Vado – Dip; in wet weather, a ford.
Conserve su derecha – Keep right
Altura máxima – Vertical clearance (in meters)
Ancho libre – Horizontal clearance (in meters)
Maneje despacio, neblina – Drive slow, fog (seen on toll booths – lights up when the warning applies).

Una hora, Dos horas – One hour, two hours (parking time limits, printed beneath a large circled E).

Day Without a Car

In an effort to combat pollution, Mexico City has instituted a "Day Without a Car" *(Hoy No Circula)* program based on the last number of your license plate and applicable to foreign-plated and most rental cars as well as local vehicles. The program restricts circulation to cars with plates ending in 5 and 6 on Mondays; 7 and 8 on Tuesdays; 3 and 4 on Wednesdays; 1 and 2 on Thursdays; and 9 and 0 on Fridays. This regulation is rigidly enforced between 5am and 10pm. On certain public holidays, restrictions are lifted and all cars are allowed to circulate.

Parking

If you park illegally you may return to find your license plates missing. Usually the policeman will be nearby and you can retrieve them by offering him some money. The same technique is effective if you commit a minor traffic violation. Try to think of it as an on-the-spot fine, rather than as a *mordida* ("bite", meaning bribe). The same goes for the tow-truck, if you're lucky enough to see it before it drives off to the pound (*corralón*) with your car.

In Mexico City your wheels get clamped if you overstay your time at a parking meter (you pay the fine to a traffic warden who is never far away). If you drive to Mexico City, your best chance of avoiding parking violations is to leave your car in the garage of your hotel – both parking and driving are best avoided in the city.

Where to Stay

Hotels

Hotels in Mexico number in the thousands, and range from luxurious suites in opulent surroundings to small rooms costing as little as 70 pesos per night. The cheaper rooms are ideal for those with a tight budget and plenty of time, but they are difficult or impossible to reserve in advance.

Most hotels have local publications that provide information about activities, sights and restaurants nearby.

Hotel Listings

MEXICO CITY
Downtown

Casa de los Amigos
Ignacio Mariscal 132.
Tel: 5-705 0646.
Friendly hostel near Monumento a la Revolución. Low-budget hideaway, ideal for students, writers, academics. Two-night minimum, 15-night maximum stay. **$**

De Cortés Best Western
Av Hidalgo 85, behind the Alameda.
Tel: 5-518 2182.
Former 18th-century hospice has colonial charm with modern comfort. Patio restaurant. **$$**

Gillow
Isabel la Católica 17.
Tel: 5-518 1440.
19th-century building refurbished in 1997. Good central location; large, clean rooms. Restaurant, bar, TV. **$**

Howard Johnson Gran Hotel
16 Septiembre 82.
Tel: 5-510 4040.
Just off the Zócalo, in a splendid shell of an ornate former department store, complete with gilded elevators and awesome ceiling. **$$–$$$**

Sevilla Palace
Reforma 105, near Colombus statue.
Tel: 5-705 2800.
Pool, sauna, restaurants. **$$$**

Roma/Insurgentes Sur
La Casona
Durango 280.
Tel: 5-286 3001.
Renovated early 20th century
mansion now run as a B&B.
Individual-style rooms. **$$–$$$**
Roosevelt
Insurgentes Sur 287.
Tel: 5-208 6813.
Low-key, budget-priced place about
2 km (1 mile) from the Zona Rosa. **$**

Zona Rosa & Chapultepec
Camino Real
Mariano Escobedo 700.
Tel: 5-203 2121.
Huge, modern complex with many
restaurants, pool and dramatic
whirlpool, just across from
Chapultepec Park. **$$$–$$$$**
Century
Liverpool 152.
Tel: 5-726 9911.
Highrise anchoring the southern
side of the Zona Rosa. **$$$**
Four Seasons
Reforma 500.
Tel: 5-230 1818.
US tel: 1-800-332 3442.
Luxurious, built around a patio
garden. Restaurant, bar, pool,
gym. Outstanding food. **$$$$**
María Christina
Río Lerma 31, Col. Cuauhtémoc.
Tel: 5-703 1787.
Classy mansion-style hotel with
garden. Restaurant, bar. **$$**
Marquís Reforma
Reforma 465.
Tel: 5-211-3600.
High-class lodgings in distinctive
building. Health club, sauna. **$$$$**

AGUASCALIENTES
Aguascalientes
Fiesta Americana
Paseo de los Laureles.
Tel: 49-18 6010.
Near San Marcos park and
convention centre, this has 192
air-conditioned rooms, a pool, rest-
aurant, gym, and obliging staff. **$$$**

La Vid
Blvd José Chávez 1305.
Tel: 49-13 9150.
This budget hotel has 68 rooms, a
restaurant and a pool. **$**
Quinta Real
Av Aguascalientes Sur 601.
Tel: 78-5818.
This is as luxurious as
Aguascalientes gets. 85 suites,
restaurant, pool. **$$–$$$**

Price Guide

Price categories are based on
the cost of a double room for one
night in high season:
$$$$ Over 1,700 pesos
$$$ 850–1,700 pesos
$$ 500–850 pesos
$ Less than 500 pesos

BAJA CALIFORNIA
Cabo San Lucas
Hotel Cabo San Lucas
PO Box 48088,
Los Angeles CA 90048.
Tel: 114-3 3458.
Fountains and statues dot the
gardens of this out-of-town hotel
with a private beach, sports facil-
ities and its own airstrip. **$$$–$$$$**
Mar de Cortés
Calles Guerrero & Cárdenas.
Tel: 114-3 0232;
Downtown, near marina. Pool,
restaurant, bar. **$**

Ensenada
La Pinta
On the Ensenada highway.
Tel: 61-76 2601.
Small hotel with restaurant, bar;
organizes excursions to see the
gray whales and salt mines. **$$**

La Paz
La Concha Beach Resort
Carr a Pichilingue Km 5.
Tel: 112-1 6344.
Good beach resort with lots of
activities. **$$$**
La Posada de Engelbert
Av Reforma & Playa Sur (10
minutes along road to airport).
Tel: 682-2 4011.

Owner Engelbert Humperdink rarely
being there, Mlle Jacqueline
presides over beachside suites and
a fine restaurant. **$$**
Perla
Paseo Obregón 1570.
Tel: 682-2 0777.
Irresistible friendly place on the
seafront (*malecón*). Popular
restaurant, pool. **$$**

Loreto
Diamond
Blvd Misión de Loreto.
Tel: 113-3 0700.
This is a hacienda-style all-inclusive
resort. **$$$**
Misión de Loreto
Blvd López Mateos 113.
Tel: 113-5 0048.
On the seafront. Attractive neo-
Colonial style with bar, restaurant,
pool. **$$**
Plaza
Hidalgo 2.
Tel: 113-5 0280.
One block from the mission. Attractive
rooms around a small patio, with
bar/restaurant and pool. **$**

Mexicali
Crowne Plaza
Blvd López Mateos and Av. de los
Héroes 201.
Tel: 65-57 3600.
Nicely appointed modern low rise
with restaurant, bar, pool, gym. **$$**

Mulegé
Hacienda
Calle Madero 3.
Tel: 115-3 0021.
Small, comfortable and great value.
Restaurant (breakfast only) and
pool. No credit cards. **$**
Serenidad
Apdo Postal 9, Mulegé.
Tel: 115-3 0530.
Situated where the river meets the
sea. Comfortable and attractive
with bar, restaurant and pool. Offers
tours to cave paintings. **$–$$**

Rosarito
La Fonda
Km 59 Carr. Tijuana–Ensenada
Highway, where Libre and Cuota
highways meet. Reservations: PO
Box 430268, San Ysidro, CA 92143.

Charming ocean-front hacienda with bar and restaurant on a tropical patio. Four-person studios with kitchens. **$$**

Rosarito Beach Hotel
Blvd Benito Juárez 31.
Tel: 661-2 1106.
Legendary resort, with pools, restaurant, spa, tennis, shops. **$$**

San Felipe
Las Misiones
Av Misión de Loreto 148.
Tel: 657-7 1280.
On the beach with restaurant, bar, pool and tennis. **$$**

Las Palmas
Mar Báltico.
Tel: 657-7 1333.
The hotel has 45 rooms with pool, restaurant and tennis. **$**

San Ignacio
La Pinta
Tel: 115 4 0300.
Downtown, colonial-style hotel, with pool and restaurant. **$$**

San José del Cabo
Howard Johnson Plaza Suites
Paseo Finisterra 1.
Tel: 114-2 0999.
Distinctive architecture, with a pool in tropical gardens. Restaurant, gym. **$$**

Presidente Inter-Continental
Blvd Mijares.
Tel: 114-2 0211.
All-inclusive resort on a secluded beach next to the lagoon. **$$$$**

Tropicana Inn
Blvd Mijares 30.
Tel: 114-2 1580.
This hotel has a pool, fountain, resident parrot and a charming patio restaurant. **$$**

Westin Regina Resort
Transpeninsular highway Km 22.5.
Tel: 114-2 9000.
A spectacular luxury resort with restaurant, bar, pool and tennis. **$$$$**

San Quintín
La Pinta
Playa Santa María.
Tel: 61-76 2601, in Ensenada.
Charming hotel on the beach. Restaurant. **$$**

Santa Rosalia
Hotel del Real
Av. Manuel F. Montoya on seafront.
Tel: 115-2 0068.
Attractive wooden building with terrace, restaurant and long-distance phone. **$**

Hotel Francés
Calle 11 de Julio.
Tel: 115-2 0829. Dominates the hill near the mining office at the north end of town. **$$**

Tecate
Hacienda Santa Verforni
Highway 2, 4 km (2 miles) east of Tecate.
Tel: 619-298 4105; toll free: 1-800-522 1516.
Lots of activities, including a motorbike track, but the hotel area is peaceful. **$$**

Rancho La Puerta
Highway 2, 5 km (3 miles) west of Tecate.
Tel: 619-744 4222; toll free: 1-800-443 7565.
Luxurious health spa and resort with restaurant, pool, massages and tennis. Seven day minimum stay. **$$$$**

Tijuana
Camino Real
Paseo de los Héroes 10305.
Tel: 66-33 4000.
Deluxe, with 250 rooms, restaurants, bars and a gym. **$$$**

Grand Hotel Tijuana
Blvd Agua Caliente 4558.
Tel: 66-81 7000.
Modern skyscraper with 422 rooms and suites. Restaurant, nightclub, pool, tennis, gym, spa, and movie theaters. **$$–$$$**

Lucerna
Av. Rodríguez & Paseo de los Héroes.
Tel: 66-34 2000.
Situated near the river, away from the crowds. Restaurant, attractive coffee shop, pool, tennis. **$$**

CAMPECHE
Campeche
Hotel América
Calle 10 No 252.
Tel: 981-6 4588.

A converted colonial home in a downtown location, with rooms around a patio. This makes a good budget choice. **$**

Ramada
Av. Ruíz Cortines 51.
Tel: 987-6 2233.
The city's luxury hotel on the waterfront has been refurbished. Pool, restaurant. Rate includes breakfast. **$$**

CHIAPAS
Ocosingo
Central
On the plaza.
Tel: 967-3 0024.
A dozen simple rooms with bath, plus a sidewalk restaurant. **$**

Price Guide

Price categories are based on the cost of a double room for one night in high season:
$$$$ Over 1,700 pesos
$$$ 850–1,700 pesos
$$ 500–850 pesos
$ Less than 500 pesos

Palenque
Chan-Kah Centro
Juárez 2, on the main square.
Tel: 934-5 0318.
Small, cosy hotel with balconied rooms and restaurant. **$**

Plaza Palenque Best Western
Blvd Pakal.
Tel: 934-5 0555.
Modern, comfortable hotel at the entrance to town. Restaurant, pool. Free transport to archeological zone. **$$**

San Cristóbal de las Casas
Casa Mexicana
28 de Agosto No 1.
Tel: 657-8 0698.
Small colonial-style hotel, in center. Restaurant, spa, tennis. **$–$$**

Ciudad Real Teatro
Diagonal Centenario 32.
Tel: 657-8 0187.
Charming, colonial building with patio restaurant, comfortable rooms. **$**

Flamboyant Español
Calle 1º de Marzo 15.

Tel: 657-8 0726.
Colonial building, with restaurant, and interior patios filled with pottery and greenery. $$

Tuxtla Gutiérrez
Camino Real
Blvd Belisario Domínguez 1195.
Tel: 961-7 7777.
A modern hilltop hotel with gorgeous grounds. Restaurant, bar, pool, tennis. $$
Flamboyant
Blvd Belisario Domínguez Km 1081.
Tel: 961-5 0888.
Situated 4 km (2 miles) west of town, with rich and exotic decor, restaurants, bar, disco, tennis and car rental. $$

CHIHUAHUA
Chihuahua
Camino Real
Barranca del Cobre 3211.
Tel: 14-29 4000.
A beautiful hotel about 15 minutes from downtown. $$$
Holiday Inn Hotel & Suites
Escudero 702.
Tel: 14 3350.
Fully equipped kitchens in suites, pool, jacuzzi, steam bath, tennis. $$

Ciudad Juárez
Plaza Juárez
Av Lincoln and Coyoacán.
Tel: 16-13 1310.
Colonial-style hotel with a restaurant, bar and pool. $$

Ciudad Valles
Hotel Valles
Blvd México-Laredo 36 Norte.
Tel: 138-2 0050.
Set in attractive grounds, with a pool and children's play area. $

Copper Canyon (Barranca del Cobre)
Mansión Tarahumara
Posada Barrancas station.
Tel: 14-15 4721, in Chihuahua.
Fifteen cabins in the heart of the Copper Canyon with a restaurant and bar. Manager María Barriga is very friendly and knowledgeable. Recreational vehicles (RVs) can park here. $$$

Margaritas
Creel.
Tel: 145-6 0245.
Twenty-six cabañas; the price includes breakfast and dinner. $
Posada Barrancas Rancho
Posada Barrancas railroad station.
Reservations in Los Mochis, Sinaloa.
Tel: 68-18 7046.
Country inn with 36 rooms with fireplaces, restaurant, bar. $$
Riverside Lodge
Batopilas.
US tel: 1-800-776 3942.
Restored 19th-century hacienda in the heart of the Copper Canyon. Fourteen rooms and a fine dining room. $$$$

COAHUILA
Saltillo
Camino Real
Blvd Los Fundadores 2000.
Tel: 84-30 0000.
Very good, 140-room motor inn on top of knoll on Highway 57 southeast of town. Pool, restaurant, bar, tennis and putting green. $$
Rancho El Morillo
Prolongación Obregón & Echeverría.
Tel: 84-17 4078.
Popular guest ranch 3 km (2 miles) southwest of town. Beautifully landscaped grounds around old hacienda. Pool, tennis, horses. $$

COLIMA
Manzanillo
La Posada
Lázaro Cárdenas 201, Las Brisas Peninsula.
Tel: 333-3 1899.
A friendy place with a high reputation. Pool, coffee shop. $$
Las Hadas Resort
Av de los Riscos & Vista Hermosa.
Tel: 333-4 0000.
Gorgeous location overlooking sea. Restaurants, pools, tennis, golf. $$$$
María Cristina
Calle 28 de Agosto No 36.
Tel: 333-3 0966.
Spotlessly clean motel a short walk from the beach. All the 21 rooms have TV and two are air-conditioned. Pool. $

ESTADO DE MEXICO
Ixtapan de la Sal
Bungalows Lolita
Blvd Arturo San Román 33.
Tel: 714-3 0016.
One block from public baths and water park, with restaurant, bar, pool and gardens. Good value. $
Hotel Ixtapan
Plaza San Gaspar.
Tel: 714-3 0125.
Immense spa in landscaped grounds with mineral baths, health club, pools, tennis, restaurant. $$$

Toluca
Quinta del Rey
Paseo Tollocán Km 5.
Tel: 5-11 8777.
Colonial style with 66 rooms, restaurant, bar, pool, gym. $$–$$$

GUANAJUATO
Celaya
Hotel Celaya Plaza
Blvd López Mateos Pte.
Tel: 461-4 6677.
Restaurant, pool, tennis. $$

Guanajuato
La Casa de Espíritus Alegres
Ex-Hacienda de la Trinidad 1, Marfil.
Tel: 473-3 1013.
An artist couple have converted an 18th-century mansion into a charming B&B. $$
Las Embajadoras
Parque Embajadoras.
Tel: 473-2 0081.
Somewhat hidden, 27 units around a patio. Good restaurant. $

León
Comanjilla Termas Spa
Carr. Panamericana 385.
Tel: 12 0091.
Comfortable spa resort with thermal water springs. $$

San Miguel de Allende
Aristos
Calle del Cardo 2.
Tel: 465-2 0149.
Next door to the Instituto Allende, San Miguel's famous art school. There are 60 units and bungalows set in a lovely garden, with a pool, tennis court and a restaurant. $

Casa de Sierra Nevada
Hospicio 35.
Tel: 485-2-0415.
50 exquisitely furnished units divided among several colonial mansions, refined, friendly service, a fine restaurant, pool and spa. $$$

La Puertecita
Santo Domingo 75.
Tel: 465-2 2250.
Charming, small hilltop hotel, exquisitely furnished with wonderful views. 25 minutes from downtown. 25 suites (two with jacuzzi). Pool, gardens, good restaurant, music room. $$$

Rancho El Atascadero
Prolongación Santo Domingo.
Tel: 465-2 0206.
Former hacienda converted into 51 units, in extensive grounds about 2km (1 mile) east of town. Popular with families. $–$$

GUERRERO

Acapulco

Acapulco Princess
Playa Revolcadero, Acapulco Diamante.
Tel: 74-69 1000.
The largest hotel in Acapulco, with two 18-hole golf courses, seven tennis courts and five pools. $$$$

Boca Chica
Playa Caletilla.
Tel: 74-66 1010.
A small hotel on a private swimming cove, with pool, restaurant and beach club. $–$$

Elcano
Costera Miguel Alemán 75.
Tel: 74-84 1950.
Across from the municipal golf course, this old favourite has been completely renovated and has a beautiful pool and beach. $$$

Los Flamingos
Calle López Mateos.
Tel: 74-82 0690.
Almost a historical landmark – the favored hangout of the "Hollywood gang" in the 1950s. Stunning views, restaurant and pool. $–$$

Misión
Calle Felipe Valle 12.
Tel: 74-82 3643.
A charming budget hotel, downtown. No air-conditioning, but ceiling fans

and plenty of hot water. No credit cards. $

Vidafel Mayan Palace
Playa Revolcadero 39000.
Tel: 74-69 0201.
Stunning Mayan-style architecture including thatched roofs and glass pavillions. Large complex with 18-hole golf course, 12 tennis courts, canals connecting facilities. $$$

Westin Las Brisas
Carr. Escénica 5255.
Tel: 74-84 1580.
Secluded *casitas* set on a hillside with individual or shared pools. Superb service. Restaurants, tennis, beach club. $$$$

Ixtapa/Zihuatanejo

Casa Elvira
Paseo del Pescador 8.
Tel: 755-4 2061.
A long-time Zihua favorite. $

Ixtapa Sheraton
Paseo de Ixtapa, Zona Hotelera.
Tel: 755-3 1858.
Soaring lobby atrium with glass elevators. Close to Ixtapa golf course. $$$$

Villa del Lago
Adjoins golf course.
Tel: 755-3 1482.
B&B in a luxurious colonial-style villa with pool. $$$

Villa del Sol
Playa La Ropa, Villas Miramar, Playa Madera, Zihuatanejo.
Tel: 755-4 2106.
Small colonial-style hotel, popular with seasoned visitors; book well in advance. $$

Taxco

Agua Escondido
Guillermo Spratling 4.
Tel: 762-2 1166.
Very centrally located with rooftop terrace above the noise of the city. $

Monte Taxco
Lomas de Taxco.
Tel: 762-2 1300.
Situated high above the city which can be reached by cable car. Restaurants, bar, disco, pool. $$

Posada de la Misión
Cerro de la Misión 32.
Tel: 762-2 0063.
This hotel houses the famous O'Gorman mural and also has a

pool and excellent restaurant. Rate includes breakfast. $$

Posada San Javier
Ex-rastro 4.
Tel: 762-2 3177.
Very secluded with a lovely garden and pool. $

JALISCO

Chapala

La Nueva Posada
Donato Guerra 9.
Tel: 376-6 1344.
16 spacious suites in a colonial-style inn overlooking the lake. Pool, excellent restaurant. $$–$$$

Quinta Quetzalcóatl
Zaragosa 307.
Tel: 376-5 3653.
Luxurious 8-suite bed and breakfast where D.H. Lawrence wrote *The Plumed Serpent*. $$

Costa Alegre

Aldea El Tamarindo
Carr. Melaque-Puerto Vallarta Km 7.5, Cihuatlán.
Tel: 335-1 5032.
An exquisite luxury resort in a rustic beachfront setting with 14 villas and an 18-hole golf course. $$$$

Guadalajara

Aranzazú
Av. Revolución and Degollado.
Tel: 3-613 3232.
Commercial hotel with friendly staff. 500 units, popular nightclub and restaurant. $$

Hotel Francés
Maestranza 35.
Tel: 3-613 1190, fax: 3-658 2831.
Attractive colonial building in the center of the city. Restaurant, bar and good atmostphere. $$

Presidente Inter-Continental
López Mateos Sur and Moctezuma.
Tel: 678-1234.
14-storey glass pyramid with atrium lobby and outstanding facilities. $$$

Puerto Vallarta

Camino Real
Playa Las Estacas.
Tel: 322-1 5000.
Secluded resort on one of Vallarta's prettiest beaches. Restaurant, bar, pool, tennis. $$$

Costa Azul Adventure Resort
30 miles north of Puerto Vallarta in San Francisco (affectionately known as San Panchito), Nayarit.
Tel: 322-2-0450.
Ecologically-friendy resort. with Watersports, biking, hiking, horse riding. **$$–$$$**

Los Cuatro Vientos
Matamoros 520.
Tel: 322-2-0161.
Charming hostel located downtown atop a steep hill. Restaurant, bar. Rate includes continental breakfast. **$**

Marriott Casa Magna
Paseo de la Marina 5, in Marina Vallarta.
Tel: 322-1 0004.
Bayfront property with 433 rooms and suites, excellent restaurants, and fine service. Pool, tennis, gym, children's activities. **$$$$**

Quinta María Cortéz
Calle Sagitaro 132.
Tel: 322-5 2322.
Eccentric accommodation cluttered with antiques, interesting junk and paintings. Great baths, no TVs, pool. Rate includes breakfast. **$$**

MICHOACAN

Morelia

Posada Vista Bella
Santa María.
Tel: 43-14 0284.
Motel with apartments and rooms, pool, restaurant and a great view. **$**

Villa Montaña
Patzimba.
Tel: 43-14 0231.
On the outskirts of town. 40 units, all uniquely decorated. Private patios, pool, outstanding view. No children under 8. **$$$**

Virrey de Mendoza
Portal de Matamoros 16.
Tel: 43-12 0633.
The first floor dates from the 16th century. Perfect location on the main square, restaurant. **$$**

Pátzcuaro

Hostería San Felipe
Lázaro Cárdenas 321.
Tel: 434-2 1298.
Colonial-style inn with a restaurant. Each room has a fireplace. **$–$$**

Los Escudos
Portal Hidalgo 73.
Tel: 434-2 0138.
The 16th-century home of the Count de la Loma is now a charming hotel with a restaurant. **$$**

Mesón del Gallo
Dr José María Coss 20.
Tel: 434-2 1474.
25 small, well-maintained rooms, restaurant and pool. **$**

Zitácuaro

Rancho Motel San Cayetano
Carr Zitácuaro - Huetamo Km 3.5.
Tel: 715-3 1929.
Nine-room hotel with pool; convenient for Monarch butterfly sanctuary. **$$**

Price Guide

Price categories are based on the cost of a double room for one night in high season:
$$$$ Over 1,700 pesos
$$$ 850–1,700 pesos
$$ 500–850 pesos
$ Less than 500 pesos

MORELOS

Cuernavaca

Camino Real Sumiya.
Tel: 73-20 9199.
Woolworth's heiress Barbara Hutton's former estate is the setting for this lavish new hotel, which contains her prized collection of oriental art and furniture. 163 rooms in a cluster of four-storey modules connected by roofed corridors. Fully equipped business centre in large gardens. **$$$–$$$$**

Las Mañanitas
Ricardo Linares 107.
Tel: 73-14 1446.
Luxurious converted mansion with pool, fountain and peacocks. Restaurant and bar. **$$$–$$$$**

Papagayo
Motolinía 3.
Tel: 73-14 1711.
Three long blocks below the cathedral but bargain-priced and with twin pools. **$**

Posada Maria Cristina
Juárez 300.
Tel: 73-18 5767.

Set in a beautiful estate with luxurious gardens, a fine dining room and pool. Rate includes breakfast. **$$**

Tepoztlán

Posada del Tepozteco
Paraíso 3.
Tel: 739-5 0010.
Charming, rustic hotel on a hill overlooking town. Lovely grounds, restaurant and bar. **$–$$**

NAYARIT

Bucerías

Royal Decameron
Lázaro Cárdenas 150.
Tel: 329-8 0226.
All-inclusive colonial-style beach-front hotel. **$$–$$$**

Nuevo Vallarta

Diamond Resort
Flamingos Nayarta Golf Development.
Tel: 329-7 0400.
Deluxe all-inclusive hotel on Banderas Bay. Non-stop activities plus restaurant, bar, tennis, kids' club, land and water sports. **$$$$**

Sierra Nuevo Vallarta
Paseo de los Cocoteros 19.
Tel: 329-7 1300.
All-inclusive hotel located on the beach, just minutes away from Puerto Vallarta. **$$$–$$$$**

Rincón de Guayabitos

Los Cocos
Retorno Las Palmas.
Tel: 327-4 0190.
All-inclusive resort on seafront. **$$**

San Blas

Bucanero
Juárez 75.
Tel: 328-5 0101.
About 10 blocks from the beach, a clean budget downtown hotel with pool, disco and pool table. **$**

Garza Canela
Paredes Sur.
Tel: 328-5 0112.
Formerly known as Las Brisas and still the nicest place in town. 42 air-conditioned rooms and a pool. Breakfast is included. English, French and German spoken. **$$**

NUEVO LEON
Monterrey
Colonial
Hidalgo 475.
Tel: 8-343 6791.
Six-storey, 100-room downtown hotel across from Ancira. Reasonably priced but sometimes a bit noisy. $$
El Paso Autel
Zaragoza 130 Nte.
Tel: 8-340 060.
Good air-conditioned three-storey, 64-room drive-in hotel, conveniently situated 10 blocks north of the business district. $$
Gran Hotel Ancira
Ocampo 440 Ote.
Tel: 8-345 1060.
Monterrey's most famous landmark hotel: Pancho Villa stabled his horse in the lobby in 1913. Distinguished, five-story building with 240 rooms, restaurants, bar and pool. $$$
Quinta Real
Diego Rivera 500.
Tel: 8-368 1000.
A stunning property in the Garza García district. Restaurant, bar, spa. $$$$
Santa Rosa Suites
Escobedo 930 Sur.
Tel: 8-342 4200.
Beautiful, elegant suites each with refrigerator, sofa etc. $$$

OAXACA
Huatulco
Casa del Mar
Balcones de Tangolunda 13.
Tel: 958-1 0203.
Beautifully appointed suites set on a cliff. Steps lead to the beach. $$$
Villablanca
Blvd Benito Juárez and Zapoteco.
Tel: 958-7 0606.
Colonial-style hotel with a restaurant, bar and pool. $$
Zaachilá Resort
Playa Rincón Sabroso, Tangolunda Bay.
Tel: 958-1 0460.
A spectacular resort with all amenities. $$$$

Oaxaca
Camino Real Oaxaca
5 de Mayo 300, north of Zócalo.
Tel: 951-6 0611.
A former 16th-century convent with cloisters and courtyard, now a national monument. $$$$
Fiesta Inn
Av Universidad 140.
Tel: 951-6 1122.
Comfortable, well-run hotel on the outskirts of town with a good restaurant and beautiful pool. Free transport to downtown. $$–$$$
Hacienda de la Noria
La Costa 100.
Tel: 951-4 7555.
Well run, about a 15-minute walk from the main square, has a restaurant and pool. Their more centrally-located **Hostal de la Noria** (tel: 951-4 7844), a block from the main square in a colonial building, has a good restaurant. $–$$
Parador Plaza
Murguía 104.
Tel: 951-4 2027.
Very attractive colonial-style hotel built around a patio, 3 blocks from the main square. $

Puerto Escondido
Aldea del Bazar
Av Benito Juárez.
Tel: 958-2 0508.
Set on a bluff over Bacocho Beach. Comfortable rooms in a pre-Hispanic-style, with eucalyptus sauna and massages, restaurant, bar and pool. Ramp access to the beach. $$$
Santa Fe
Calle del Morro.
Tel: 958-2 0170.
A delightful hotel on Zicatela beach. Each room is unique. Excellent restaurant with seafood and vegetarian specialities. $$
Arco Iris
Calle del Morro.
Tel: 958-2 0432.
Simple clean rooms, some with kitchenettes. Large pool, restaurant. $

PUEBLA
Puebla
Camino Real
7 Pte No. 105.
Tel: 22-29 0909.
Two blocks from the main plaza in a converted 16th-century convent, rooms are decorated with original colonial art and antiques. Fine restaurant and bar featuring 13th-century Hindu balcony. $$$
Mesón Sacristía de la Compañía
6 Sur No 304, downtown.
Tel: 22-32 4513.
Stunning colonial hostelry with restaurant. $$–$$$
Posada San Pedro
3 Ote. No. 202, downtown.
Tel: 22-46 5077.
Colonial-style hotel with a restaurant, bar and small pool. $

QUERETARO
Querétaro
Hacienda Yextho
Carr. Las Adelitas-La Rosa, Tecozautla Km 20.5, in nearby state of Hidalgo.
Tel: 5-550-8656, in Mexico City.
25 suites in former hacienda. Restaurant, thermal water pool, horseback riding, Jacuzzi. $$
La Casa de la Marquesa
Madero 41.
Tel: 42-12 0092.
A unique luxury hotel housed in an 18th-century mansion. $$$
La Mansión Galindo
Carr. a Amealco Km 5.
Tel: 427-5-0250 (San Juan del Río).
Sprawling yet charming resort. 166 rooms and suites, restaurants, pools, tennis, horses. $$–$$$
Sol y Fiesta
H. Colegio Militar 4, Tequisquiapan.
Tel: 427-3-1504.
Small hotel with 19 units, jacuzzi, pool, hot springs and restaurant. $

QUINTANA ROO
Akumal
Club Oasis Akumal
Carr. Chetumal Puerto Juárez Km. 251.
Tel: 987-3 0843.
Once a private fishing camp started by the late Pablo Bush Romero, friend and associate of Jacques Cousteau, now a luxury all-inclusive hotel. Restaurant, bar, pool, tennis, dive shop, beach. $$$

Cancún
Antillano
Av. Tulum and Claveles.
Tel: 98-84 1532.

One of the older and also one of the better economy hotels, situated downtown. **$$**

Camino Real Cancún
Blvd Kukulcán, Punta Cancún.
Tel: 98-83 0100.
Surrounded by the sea on three sides, the hotel is architecturally dramatic, with truly private balconies. **$$$**

Casa Turquesa
Blvd Kukulcán Km 13.5.
Tel: 98-85 2924.
Small, elegant and very private residence; a favorite hotel of celebrities. **$$$$**

Fiesta Americana Coral Beach
Blvd Kukulcán.
Tel: 98-83 2900.
A dazzling all-suite resort with every amenity. **$$$$**

Ritz-Carlton Cancún
Retorno del Rey 36, Zona Hotelera.
Tel: 98-85 0808.
Traditional Ritz-Carlton continental elegance and refinement, with an introspective air. **$$$$**

Tankah
Av. Tankah 69, Cancún City.
Tel: 98-84 4446.
Simple lodgings downtown for a modest price. **$**

Tropical Inn
Av. Yaxchilán 31.
Tel: 98-84 3078.
A well-maintained hotel with rooms set around pretty courtyard. **$$**

Villa Deportiva Juvenil
(Youth Hostel), Blvd Kukulcán Km 3.2 Zona Hotelera.
Tel: 98-83 1337.
Economical lodgings in the exclusive Hotel Zone, in communal dorms divided by gender. **$**

Chetumal
Holiday Inn
Av. Héroes 171-A.
Tel: 983-2 1607.
A modern downtown hotel with a restuarant, bar and pool. **$$**

Cobá
Villa Arqueológica
Zona Arqueológica.
Tel: 987-4 2087.
Set at the edge of the archeological site, this villa has 40 rooms with Club Med amenities. **$$**

Cozumel
Casa del Mar
Carr. a Chankanaab Km 4.
Tel: 987-2 1900.
Great swim-up bar, on-site dive shop for top diving facilities and pier. **$$–$$$**

Galápago Inn
Carr. a Chankanaab Km 1.5.
Tel: 987-2 1133.
Expert staff make this a favorite with divers. **$$$**

Meliá Mayan Paradisus
Carr. Santa Pilar Km 3.5.
Tel: 987-2 0411.
Secluded setting on a very long beach, luxurious lobby and rooms, all with an ocean view. **$$$$**

Safari Inn
Av. Rafael Melgar, between Calles 5 and 7 Sur, San Miguel.
Tel: 987-2 0101.
A prime budget choice for a pleasant room, adjoining dive-shop premises and offering diving packages. **$**

Tamarindo Bed & Breakfast
Calle 4 Norte 421.
Tel: 987-2 3614.
Downtown, simple, colorful, friendly, and very comfortable. **$$**

Price Guide

Price categories are based on the cost of a double room for one night in high season:
$$$$ Over 1,700 pesos
$$$ 850–1,700 pesos
$$ 500–850 pesos
$ Less than 500 pesos

Isla Mujeres
Na-Balam
Zazil-Ha 118.
Tel: 987-7 0279.
Quiet location for 12 junior suites with ocean views. Restaurant, bar, pool. **$$$**

Hotel Martínez
Madero 14.
Tel: 987-7 0154
Fan-cooled, simple rooms, in a small, older hotel. **$**

Perla del Caribe
Av. Madero 2.
Tel: 987-7 0444.
This downtown hotel has

comfortable air-conditioned rooms each with a balcony. Restaurant, bar, pool. **$$**

Playa del Carmen
La Posada del Capitán Lafitte
Carr. Puerto Juárez-Tulum Km 62.
Tel: 987-3 214.
Cluster of *cabañas* with air-conditioning or ceiling fans. Beautiful beach. Breakfast, dinner and tips included. **$$$–$$$$**

Maroma
30 minutes south of Cancún airport.
Tel: 987-4 4729.
A luxurious secluded resort in a former coconut plantation. Rate includes breakfast. **$$$$**

Puerto Aventuras
Continental Plaza
Caleta Xel-ha and Privada Xel-ha.
Tel: 98-73 5133.
Small hotel in the marina section of a marina and golf resort. 5 minutes from the beach. **$$$**

Oasis
Carr. Chet - Pto Juárez Km 269.
Tel: 98-3 5050.
An all-inclusive resort on the beach with restaurant, bar, disco and pool. **$$$$**

Tulum
Cabañas Ana y José
On dirt road off Highway 307 between entrance to ruins and town.
Tel: 98-80 6021.
Retreat at the edge of the Sian Ka'an Biosphere Reserve. Good restaurant. Electricity from 5pm to 10pm. No credit cards. **$**

SAN LUIS POTOSI

San Luis Potosí
Fiesta Inn
Carr. 57, Hotel Zone.
Tel: 48-22-1995.
Comfortable rooms situated around a large central pool. **$$**

Westin San Luis Potosí
Lomas 1000.
Tel: 48-25-0125.
Colonial-style property beautifully decorated with antiques and authentic art. Pool, jacuzzi, restaurant, bar. **$$$**

SINALOA
Los Mochis
Plaza Inn
Leyva & Cárdenas.
Tel: 69-18 1043.
A modern air-conditioned downtown hotel with restaurant, bar, pool and disco. **$$**

Mazatlán
El Cid
Av. Camarón Sábalo.
Tel: 69-13 333.
1310-room hotel on the beach with restaurants, bars, tennis, 18-hole golf course, eight pools. **$$–$$$**
Hacienda Las Moras
Reservations: Av. Camarón Sábalo 204–6.
Tel: 69-16 5045, in Mazatlán.
A former 19th-century tequila ranch at the foot of the Sierra Madre mountains, 30 miles (48 km) inland from Mazatlán. Renovated with authentic furnishing and art. Over 3,000 acres (1,200 ha). No TVs, clocks or phones. Rate includes all meals. Pool, tennis. **$$$$**
Las Palmas
Av. Camarón Sábalo 305.
Tel: 69-13 4255.
Two-story, eight-room hotel with restaurant, bar and pool. **$**
Playa Mazatlán
Rodolfo T. Loaiza 202.
Tel: 69-13 4444.
This beachfront hotel is a Mazatlán institution. Restaurant, pool, bar. **$$**
Pueblo Bonito
Camarón Sábalo 2121.
Tel: 69-14 3700.
Beautiful beachfront property with full amenities. **$$$**

SONORA
Alamos
Casa de los Tesoros
Alvaro Obregón 10.
Tel: 642-8 0010.
Romantic, converted 18th-century convent with restaurant, bar and pool. **$$$**

Guaymas/San Carlos
Flamingos
North Highway 15.
Tel: 622-1 0961.
Surprisingly nice air-conditioned 55-unit motel. Restaurant, bar, pool. **$**

Playa de Cortés
Bacochibampo Bay.
Tel: 622-1 0142.
Famous hotel, built by Southern-Pacific Railroad, with restaurant, bar, pool, tennis, boat ramp. **$$–$$$**

Hermosillo
Kino
Pino Suárez Sur 151.
Tel: 62-13 3131.
Comfortable hotel with restaurant and pool. Rooms have refrigerator and TV. **$**

Bahía Kino
Kino Bay
Tel: 624-2 0216.
Six two-story units (with kitchenettes) at north end. Restaurant across the street. **$**
Posada Santa Gemma
Mar de Cortés and Rió de la Plata.
Tel: 624-2 0001.
14-unit air-conditioned motel: two-bedroom split-level units with bath, kitchen and fireplace. **$$$**
Saro
Tel: 624-20007
Simple but very neat 16-roomer on the beach, with laundry. Saro speaks English, Italian and Spanish. **$$**

Puerto Peñasco
Costa Brava
Malecón Kino & 1ero de Junio.
Tel: 638-3 4100.
Downtown hotel - small and clean. **$**
Plaza Las Glorias
Playa Las Glorias.
Tel: 638-36010.
US-style beachfront hotel with restaurant and pool. **$$–$$$**

San Carlos
Club Mediteranée
Playa Los Algodones.
Tel: 622-6 0176.
17-hectare (43-acre) village-like complex with Club Med amenities. **$$$**
Fiesta San Carlos
Carr. San Carlos Km 8.
Tel: 622-6 0229.
Three-storey, 33-unit, air-conditioned motel in Mayan temple-style, on the beach, with pool. **$$**
Las Playitas
Carr. Varadero Nacional Km 6 by the naval base.

Tel: 622-1-5196.
30 air-conditioned cottages on Las Playitas Peninsula in conjunction with RV facility of same name. Boat ramp. **$**
San Carlos Plaza
Mar Barmejo 4.
Tel: 622-6 0794.
As luxurious as San Carlos gets, complete with marble floor atrium. **$$$**

TABASCO
Villahermosa
Casa Real
Paseo Tabasco 1407.
Tel: 931-16 4400.
Modern hotel adjacent to golf course in Tabasco 2000 complex, with pool, restaurants and bars. **$$$**
Cencali
Av. Juárez and Paseo Tabasco.
Tel: 93-15 1999.
Hacienda-style hotel on a park. Excellent views. **$$**
Don Carlos
Francisco I. Madero 418.
Tel: 93-12 2499.
Near the main plaza, this unpretentious, clean hotel offers good service, a restaurant and bar. **$**

TAMAULIPAS
Nuevo Laredo
El Río
Reforma 4402.
Tel: 87-14 3666.
An attractive motel 7 km (4 miles) south of the international bridge. Pool, restaurant, bar. **$–$$**

Tampico
Inglaterra
Díaz Mirón 116 Ote.
Tel: 12-12 5678.
Very nice two-story 126-room air-conditioned downtown hotel across from the plaza. **$$**
Posada del Rey
Madero 218 Ote.
Tel: 12-14 1024.
Downtown hotel, the oldest in town but has been renovated. It has 60 rooms with ceiling fans and air-conditioning. No elevator. Inner rooms are quiet. **$**

TLAXCALA
Tlaxcala
Posada San Francisco
Plaza de la Constitución 17.
Tel: 246-2 6022.
19th-century building on the town's main square, run by Club Med as an archeological villa. Restaurant and pool. **$–$$**

VERACRUZ
Catemaco
Gran Hotel Playa Azul
Carr. Sontecomapan Km 2.
Tel: 294-3 0001.
Completely renovated resort on gorgeous Lake Catemaco. **$**

Coatepec
Posada Coatepec
Hidalgo 9.
Tel: 28-16 0544.
Charming conversion of a 19th-century hacienda. **$$-$$$**

Papantla
Premier
Enríquez 103.
Tel: 784-2 2700.
Situated on the Zócalo, this is the best place in town. **$**
Tajín
Nuñez and Domínguez.
Tel: 784-2 0644.
One block from Zócalo, this hotel has spacious rooms. **$**

Poza Rica
Plaza
Juárez 39.
Tel: 782-4 0738.
57-room air-conditioned hotel whose Vintage photographs of Tuxpan give it a historic atmosphere. **$$**
Poza Rica Best Western
2 Norte and 10 Orient.
Tel: 782-2 0112.
Modern downtown hotel with restaurant and bar. **$–$$**

Tuxpan
Club Maeva
Carr. a Cabos Km 2.5.
Tel: 783-4 2519.
All-inclusive resort, with 163 air-conditioned rooms, wonderful views and beautiful grounds. **$$$**

Florida
Juárez 23.
Tel: 783-4 0222.
Old but serviceable. Mostly air-conditioned. Resembles a ship, with wrap-around balconies overlooking the river. **$$**

Price Guide

Price categories are based on the cost of a double room for one night in high season:
$$$$ Over 1,700 pesos
$$$ 850–1,700 pesos
$$ 500–850 pesos
$ Less than 500 pesos

Veracruz
Emporio
Insurgentes Veracruzanos 210.
Tel: 29-32 0200.
Downtown on the harbor. Most rooms have balconies with splendid views. **$$**
Mocambo
Blvd A. Ruiz Cortines 4000.
Tel: 29-22 0205.
Grand old tourist hotel on Mocambo Beach. Ten-minute taxi-ride to the Zócalo. **$$–$$$**
Torremar Resort
Blvd A. Ruiz Cortines 4300.
Tel: 292-1 3466.
A modern hotel, particularly popular amongst Mexican tourists. **$$$**

Xalapa (Jalapa)
Fiesta Inn
Carr. Xalapa-Veracruz Km 2.5.
Tel: 28-12 7920.
A new and comfortable hotel, on the outskirts of town. **$$**

YUCATAN
Celestún
Eco Paraíso Xixim
Km. 9 Camino Viejo a Sisal.
Tel: 991-6 2100.
15 *cabañas* on seafront. **$$$$**

Chichén-Itzá
Hotel Dolores Alba
Km 122 Carr. Valladolid-Chichén-Itzá.
No phone. For reservations, contact its sister hotel the Hotel Dolores

Alba in Mérida; tel: 99-28 5650, clearly specifying a room at the Chichén-Itzá establishment. Modest, clean rooms and restaurant with moderately priced meals, 2 km (1 mile) from ruins. Pool. **$**
Hotel Mayaland
Zona Arqueológica.
Tel and fax: 985-1 0077.
Dignified old hotel, with three pools, three restaurants, and accommodation in 92 units including 12 Mayan-style villas. **$$$**
Hotel Villa Arqueológica
Zona Arqueológica.
Tel: 985-6 2830.
Attractive rooms, near to the ruins, with a library, Club Med amenities and excellent French and Yucatecan food. **$$**

Mérida
Caribe
Calle 59 No. 500 & Calle 60.
Tel: 99-24 9022.
Lovely historic building on attractive plaza downtown. **$$**
Casa San Juan Bed & Breakfast
Calle 62 No. 545A.
Tel: 99-23 6823.
Beautifully restored 18th-century house, declared a historic site in 1982. Three blocks from the main square. Some rooms have air-conditioning and/or private bath. Rate includes breakfast. **$**
Fiesta Americana Mérida
Av. Colón 451.
Tel: 99-42 11.
Built to resemble one of the city's colonial-era mansions. Excellent restaurant, bar, pool and tennis. **$$$**
Hacienda Katanchel
Carr. a Cancún Km. 25.5.
Tel: 99-23 4020.
A restored 17th-century hacienda, 15 minutes from Merida. **$$$$**

Progreso
Club Maeva Mayan Beach
Carr. Progreso Telchac Km 32.
Tel: 99-49 3383, in Mérida.
All-inclusive beach resort with non-stop activities. **$$–$$$**
Sian K'an Hotel & Beach Club
Yucalpeten.
Tel: 993-5 4017.
Attractive beachfront hotel with 10

suites, restaurant, bar, pool and water sports. **$$$**

Uxmal
Hacienda Temozón
35 km (22 miles) from Mérida, in the town of Temozón.
Tel: 99-49 5001.
Spacious, elegantly decorated rooms in former hacienda. Air-conditioning and ceiling fans. Pool, spa, gym, restaurant and bar. Also offers tours. **$$$$**
Hacienda Uxmal
Km 78 Carr. Mérida-Campeche.
Tel: 99-24 7142.
Uxmal's oldest and most traditional hostelry. **$$$**
Villa Arqeológica
Ruinas Uxmal.
Tel: 99-28 0644.
The full range of Club Med amenities, located right by the ruins. **$$**

Price Guide

Price categories are based on the cost of a double room for one night in high season:
$$$$ Over 1,700 pesos
$$$ 850–1,700 pesos
$$ 500–850 pesos
$ Less than 500 pesos.

Valladolid
San Clemente
Calle 42 No. 206.
Tel: 985-6 2208.
On the main plaza. Restaurant, pool and parking. **$**

ZACATECAS
Zacatecas
Continental Plaza
Hidalgo 703.
Tel: 492-2 6183.
Well situated on the main plaza. Restaurant, bar. **$$**
Mesón de Jobito
Jardín Juárez 143.
Tel: 492-4 1722.
A beautifully renovated 19th-century building. Restaurant, bar, pool. **$$$**
Posada de la Moneda
Av. Hidalgo 413.
Tel: 492-2 0881.

Clean budget hotel, centrally located. No credit cards. **$**

Camping

Mexico's trailer-park industry has experienced a boom. Almost every city has a trailer-park or motel with amenities including modern hook-ups, laundries, cafeterias, showers, small grocery stores, and even gas stations. Many National Parks (*Parques Nacionales*) have at least parking areas for recreational vehicles (RVs) or areas for tents, plus 24-hour vigilance. They charge very modest fees for overnighting. Bear in mind that campgrounds, like hotels, can be extremely crowded during the peak tourist season.

There are several good sources of information for campers, whether you have a trailer or a tent. The Mexican Tourist Office can supply information and lists of campsites. You can also order campground directories from KOA (PO Box 30558, Billings, MT 59114, USA); and from Climatic Data Press (PO Box 413, Lemont, PA 16851, USA). Write well in advance for a price list, specifying that your interest is in Mexico.

It is definitely not a good idea to camp in wild, off-the-beaten-track areas. For the sake of safety, stick to campsites or beaches where others are already camping.

Where to Eat

Cafés & Market Stalls

Low-price restaurants are called *cafés*, *fondas*, *merenderos*, *comedores* or *loncherías*. The *lonchería* may specialize in sandwiches, or *tortas*. In any of these places, however, the food will be inexpensive; in some, it will be very good indeed; in others, it will be contaminated. The safest course is to look carefully before ordering. Some travelers avoid eating in the marketplace, supposing that a regular restaurant is safer. However, the *fondas* in the market have the advantage that you can see the kitchen and the food before committing yourself (plus, you can get breakfast here when most other places are still closed). At these stalls, there is unlikely to be a menu.

Restaurant Listings
MEXICO CITY
Downtown
Café Tacuba
Tacuba 28.
Tel: 5-518 4950.
Go for the atmosphere, enhanced by the vaulted ceilings, tiled walls, large paintings and mural. **$–$$**
Cícero Centenario
República de Cuba 79.
Tel: 5-521 7866.
A beautifully decorated, turn-of-the-century mansion offering excellent Mexican cuisine. **$$$**
Los Girasoles
Tacuba 8, on Plaza Tolsá.
Tel: 5-510-0630.
Creative Mexican dishes in a stunning setting. **$$**
Sanborns Casa de los Azulejos
Madero 4.
Comfortably familiar dishes served in a dramatic patio. **$–$$**

Insurgentes Sur
Arroyo
Insurgentes Sur 4003, Tlalpan.
Tel: 5-573 4344.
Huge and very popular, especially
for lunch and at weekends. Serves
good Mexican dishes, including
tacos, mole and *cabrito* (baby
goat). **$–$$**
La Taberna del Lees
Altamirano 46, in Plaza Loreto.
Tel: 5-616 3951.
Fine international cuisine served in
a refurbished turn-of-the-century
home. **$$–$$$**
Le Petit Cluny
Av. de la Paz 58, San Angel.
Tel: 5-616 2288.
European-style bistro and bakery.
Crêpes and Italian specialties. **$$**

Polanco/Lomas de Chapultepec
Crêperie de la Paix
Anatole France 79, Polanco.
Tel: 5-280 5859.
Delicious crêpes with a Mexican
flair. **$–$$**
Hunan
Reforma 2210, Lomas.
Tel: 5-596 5011.
Bamboo, a pond and some of the
best, most authentic Chinese
Hunan-style cuisine to be found in
Mexico. **$$–$$$**
La Valentina
Presidente Masaryk 393, Polanco.
Tel: 5-282 2297.
Hacienda-style interior decor and
traditional cuisine from all over
Mexico. **$$**
Sir Winston Churchill's
Avila Camacho 67, Polanco.
Tel: 5-280 6070.
Exceptional beef and seafood
dishes served in an English
Tudor-style mansion. Never
disappoints. **$$–$$$**

Zona Rosa/Condesa area
Bellinghausen
Londres 95.
Tel: 5-207 4049.
Steaks and seafood specialties with
an old-fashioned ambience and
service. **$$–$$$**
Specie
Amsterdam 241.
Tel: 5-564 9576.
Polish cuisine, including the

specialty of crisp duck served
with baked apple and blueberry
sauce. **$$**
Tezka
Amberes and Liverpool.
Tel: 5-228 9918.
Excellent Basque cuisine with an
emphasis on seafood. **$$$**
Yug
Varsovia 3.
Tel: 5-533-3296.
Vegetarian restaurant, a favorite
with people from nearby offices. **$**

BAJA CALIFORNIA
Cabo San Lucas
Cavendish
Playa El Medano.
Tel: 114-3 0901.
On the beach with superb
seafood and a great view of
El Arco. **$$**
Da Giorgio
Misiones del Cabo.
Tel: 114-3 3988.
On a hill about 5 km (3 miles) east
of town. Excellent Italian dishes
include pizzas baked in a brick
oven. **$–$$**
The Giggling Marlin
Matamoros at Marina.
Tel: 114-3 0606.
Lively bar with lots of dancing, fun
and games. **$$**

Breakfast in Mexico

The Mexican breakfast menu can
range from specialties to more
familiar items. Expect the unex-
pected. Mexican dishes may
include *menudo* (tripe),
chilaquiles (fried tortilla strips
with cream and chilli sauce),
puntas de filete (spicy beef
stew), and hot chocolate and
sweet rolls.
   If you want the usual
breakfast staples, look on the
menu for *huevos al gusto* (eggs
prepared as you like), *tortilla de
huevos* (omelette), *huevos
revueltos/ estrellados*
(scrambled/fried), *tocino* (bacon),
jamón (ham), *avena* (porridge),
pan tostado (toast), *mermelada*
(jelly) and *mantequilla* (butter).

The Shrimp Factory
Marina Blvd across from Plaza Las
Glorias Hotel.
Tel: 114-3 5066.
Shrimp only, served by the kilo **$$**
Señor Sushi's
Opposite Plaza Las Glorias.
Tel: 114-3 1323.
Serves everything from BBQ ribs to
chicken teriyaki. **$$**
Tacos Chidos
Zapata and Guerrero.
Tel: 114-3 0551
A old favourite for *tacos, tortas* and
tamales. No credit cards. **$**

Ensenada
China Land
Av. Riveroll 1149.
Tel: 61-8 8644.
More than 100 Asian dishes are of-
fered in this delightful restaurant. **$$**
El Charro
Av. López Mateos 475.
Tel: 61-78 3881.
Chickens roasted over a wood fire. **$**
El Rey Sol
Av. López Mateos 1000.
Tel: 61-8 1733.
French and Mexican dishes in a
charming setting. A favorite for
years. **$$–$$$**
La Embotelladora Vieja
Av. Miramar 666.
Tel: 61-74 0807.
Baja-French cuisine served in a
converted wine-aging room at the
Santo Tomás winery. **$$–$$$**

La Paz
Bismark
Santos Degollado & Av. Altamirano.
Tel: 112-2 4854.
Excellent Mexican dishes and
seafood. Family-style ambience. **$$**
La Terraza
Obregón 1570.
Tel: 112-2 0777.
Hotel Perla's sidewalk hangout
opposite the *malecón* (seafront
boulevard). The best place to watch
the sunset. **$$**

Loreto
Cafe Olé
Madero.
Tel: 113-5 0496.
Just off the plaza. Perfect for
breakfast and people-watching. **$**

El Embarcadero
Blvd Mateos, opposite the fishing harbour.
Tel: 113-5 0132.
The owner operates the adjoining fishing-tackle store, so fresh fish is a specialty. **$$**
El Nido
Salvatierra 154, opposite the bus station.
Tel: 113-5 0284.
Cozy atmosphere, with fish-nets, oak beams and an open fireplace/grill. Good food, mostly steak and seafood. **$$**

Mexicali
Misión del Dragón
Blvd Lázaro Cárdenas 555.
Tel: 65-66 4320.
A beautifully decorated Chinese restaurant. **$$**
Mezzosole
Blvd Benito Juárez 2151.
Tel: 65-66 1000.
A varied menu of Italian Tuscan dishes. **$$**

Mulegé
Los Equipales
Moctezuma, near Zaragoza.
Tel: 115-3 0330.
A spotless and attractive restaurant with soft music and a cool airy terrace upstairs. **$$**
Las Casitas
Hotel Las Casitas, Callejón de los Estudiantes.
Tel: 115-3 0019.
Seafood specialists. A Mexican *mariachi* band plays on Friday night. **$**

Tijuana
Carnitas Uruapan
Paseo de los Héroes & Av. Rodríguez.
Famous for their *carnitas*, fried pork served with *tortillas*, *salsa*, onion, cilantro, and *guacamole*. **$**
Señor Frog's
Vía Oriente 60, Pueblo Amigo.
Tel: 66-82 4662.
Good food and drinks in a fun, casual setting. **$$**
Tía Juana Tilly's
Av. Revolución & Calle 7.
Tel 66-85 6024.
Lively ambience and generous portions of Mexican specialties. **$$**

CAMPECHE
Campeche
La Pigua
Miguel Alemán 197-A.
Tel: 981-1 3365.
Excellent regional food – the specialty is a delicious local fish called *pejelagarto*. **$$**
Marganzo
Calle 8, No. 267.
Tel: 981-1 3898.
An upmarket favorite where Mexican food is served by waitresses in regional costumes. **$$**

CHIAPAS
San Cristóbal de las Casas
Casa del Pan Cantante
Belisario Domínguez y Dr Navarro.
Tel: 657-8 0468.
Imaginative vegetarian dishes, fresh baked breads, and tempting desserts. **$**
La Selva Café
Crescencio Rosas 9.
Tel: 657-8 7268.
Excellent varieties of regionally grown coffee and good food. No credit cards. **$–$$**

CHIHUAHUA
Chihuahua
La Casa de los Milagros
Victoria 812.
Tel: 14-37 0693.
A colonial-style restaurant with a bohemian ambience. **$$**
Los Parados de Tony Vega
Av. Juárez 3316.
Tel: 14-15 3333.
A fabulous restaurant in an old mansion. Steaks and seafood are the specialties. **$$$**

COAHUILA
Saltillo
El Tapanco
Allende Sur 225.
Tel: 84-14 4339.
This superb downtown restaurant in a converted 17th-century home serves excellent international cuisine and Mexican specialties. **$$–$$$**
Regio
Carr. Monterrey-Saltillo Km 3.5.
Tel: 84-15 2662.

Known for their charbroiled steaks and *cabrito*. **$$**

COLIMA
Manzanillo
El Bigotes
Blvd Miguel de la Madrid 3157.
Tel: 333-4 0831.
The specialty is the spicy *pescado sarandeado* (whole fish marinated and grilled over hot coals). **$$**
Legazpi
Las Hadas Hotel.
Tel: 333-4 0000.
White-gloved service and continental cuisine with a Mexican touch. Dinner only. **$$$**
Rosalba's
Blvd Miguel de la Madrid, Km 13.
Tel: 333-3 0488.
American and Mexican-style breakfasts and tasty seafood, steaks and tacos served under a *palapa*. **$**
Willy's
Crucero Las Brisas.
Tel: 333-3 1794.
French-inspired cuisine accompanied by a relaxing sea view. **$$**

ESTADO DE MEXICO
Toluca
La Cabaña Suiza
Paseo Tollocán, Km 63.
Tel: 5-16 1877.
Good hearty food and lots to keep children occupied. **$$**
Hacienda de San Martín
Carr. México - Toluca, Km 44.
Tel: 5-7 6337.
Excellent international and Mexican dishes. Gorgeous setting and a breathtaking view. **$$$**

GUANAJUATO
Guanajuato
Casa del Conde de la Valenciana
Km. 5, Carr. Gto-Dolores Hidalgo.
Tel: 473-2 2550.
Beautiful 18th-century building houses a fine restaurant and wonderful crafts shop. **$$–$$$**
La Hacienda del Marfil
Arcos de Guadalupe 3, in the suburb of Marfil.
Tel: 473-3 1148.

Traditional French dishes and nouvelle Mexican cuisine served in an elegant yet rustic restaurant and bar in a former hacienda. **$$**

San Miguel de Allende
Casa de Sierra Nevada
Hospicio 35.
Tel: 465-2 0415.
Fine dining at one of Mexico's most beautiful hotels. **$$$**
El Mesón de San José
Mesones 38.
Tel: 465-2 3848.
A delightful patio setting for Mexican, international and vegetarian dishes. **$$**
Mama Mía
Umarán 8.
Tel: 465-2 2063.
Very popular for international and Italian dishes. Live music. **$**

GUERRERO
Acapulco
Betos Tradicional
Costera Miguel Alemán, at Playa Condesa.
Tel: 74-84 0473.
Try the red snapper and lobster while enjoying a good view of Condesa beach. **$–$$**
Carlos and Charlie's
Costera Miguel Alemán 112.
Tel: 74-84 0039.
A pleasant terrace and always a lively, noisy crowd as at all restaurants in this chain. **$$**
Casa Nova
Carr. Escénica 5256.
Tel: 74-84 6819.
Southern Italian cuisine including homemade pasta. Reserve a table at weekends. **$$–$$$**
El Amigo Miguel
Benito Juárez 31.
Tel: 74-83 6981.
A favourite with the locals, serving excellent seafood and fish. **$–$$**
El Cabrito
Costera Miguel Alemán, near the Hard Rock Café.
Tel: 74-84 7711.
Real Mexican food and ambience. *Cabrito* (baby goat) is a specialty. **$–$$**
Kookaburra
Highway to Las Brisas;

Tel: 74-84 1448.
The name is Australian but the food is international, with an emphasis on shellfish. Views are magnificent. **$$**
Madeiras
Highway to Las Brisas.
Tel: 74-84 6921.
Excellent fixed-price menu, good value and offers a great view. Reservations are a must. **$$**
100% Natural
Costera Miguel Alemán 200.
Tel: 74-85 3982.
Open 24 hours for vegetarian dishes, fondues and juices. **$**
Zorrito's
Costera Miguel Alemán and Antón de Alaminos.
Tel: 74-85 3735.
Specialty of *pozole*, a pork and hominy stew served with fresh vegetables and spices. **$$**

Price Guide

Price categories are based on the cost of a meal for one person without drinks:
$$$ Over 250 pesos.
$$ 130–250 pesos.
$ Less than 130 pesos.

Ixtapa/Zihuatanejo
Beccofino
Marina de Ixtapa.
Tel: 755-3 1770.
Stunning Italian preparation of local ingredients, specializing in fish and seafood. **$$–$$$**
Casa Elvira
Paseo del Pescador 8, Zihuatanejo.
Tel: 755-4 2061.
An old favorite serving seafood and Mexican dishes. **$–$$**
Coconuts
Paseo Agustín Ramírez 1.
Tel: 755-4 2518.
The oldest building in town with an excellent menu of fish, seafood and choice meats. Fun bar. **$$**
La Casa Que Canta
In the hotel of the same name in Zihuatanejo.
Tel: 755-4 2722.
Perfectly prepared French-inspired cuisine served in romantic surroundings. **$$$**

La Sirena Gorda
Paseo del Pescador 20-A, Zihuatanejo.
Tel: 755-4 2687.
Good breakfasts and unusual seafood tacos. **$**
La Valentina
Blvd Ixtapa.
Tel: 755-3 1250.
Traditional Mexican dishes served in a hacienda-style setting. **$$**
Villa de la Selva
Paseo de la Roca, Ixtapa.
Tel: 755-3 0362.
Good international menu and a spectacular view. Great spot for watching the sunset. **$$$**

Taxco
Hostería el Adobe
Plazuela de San Juan 13.
Tel: 762-2 1416.
Original decor and excellent food. Wait for a window seat to view the busy plaza below. **$–$$**
Pizza Pazza
Calle del Arco 1.
Tel: 762-2 5500.
A cheery place decorated with plaid tablecloths and hanging plants serving tasty pizza and outstanding *pozole*. **$**
Santa Fé
Hidalgo 2.
Tel: 762-2 1170.
Mexican home cooking featuring Puebla-style *mole* sauce, and *enchiladas*. **$**

JALISCO
Puerto Vallarta
Chef Roger
Agustín Rodríguez 267, downtown.
Tel: 322-3 5900.
The Swiss owner and chef combines European techniques with Mexican ingredients and the results are superb. **$$–$$$**
Don Pedro's
Sayulita town beach, north of Puerto Vallarta.
Tel: 322-5 2029.
A huge *palapa* serving an array of fish, seafood and poultry grilled over *mesquite*. Worth the trip. **$$**
Pancake House
Basilio Badillo 289.
Tel: 322-2 6272.

Only breakfast, but the hefty portions can get you through the day. Pancakes, waffles, eggs, and great coffee. No credit cards. **$**

Rito Baci's
Ortiz de Domínguez 181.
Tel: 322-2 6448.
Twenty-four varieties of pizza and other Italian favorites. **$–$$**

MICHOACAN

Morelia

El Rey Tacamba
Portal Galeana 157.
Tel: 43-12 2044.
Popular spot on the Plaza de Armas, serving local specialties such as *pollo de plaza* (chicken in a red chilli sauce served with *enchiladas*). **$–$$**

Fonda Las Mercedes
León Guzmán 47.
Tel: 43-12 6113.
Restored colonial mansion with a varied menu including soups, crêpes and pastas. **$$**

MORELOS

Cuernavaca

Las Mavaca
Ricardo Linares 107.
Tel: 73-14 1466.
Exceptional restaurant in a beautiful garden setting. One of Mexico's best. **$$$**

La India Bonita
Morrow 106-B.
Tel: 73-12 5021.
Former residence of US Ambassador Dwight Morrow is very popular for authentic Mexican fare. **$$**

La Strada
Salazar 38, around the corner from Cortés' Palace.
Tel: 73-18 6085.
Fine Italian cooking served on a delightful patio. **$$**

Tepoztlán

Casa Piñón
Revolución 42.
Tel: 739-5 2052.
Open-air restaurant serving French cuisine with a Mexican touch. **$$**

Luna Mextli
Revolución 6.
Tel: 739-5 1114.
Bohemian ambience, good food. **$–$$**

NAYARIT

San Blas

McDonald's
Calle Juárez 36.
Good restaurant (no relation of the fast-food chain) a block west of the main plaza. Mexican-style beef fillets and fish, lobster, shrimp, *tacos,* and *enchiladas*. A gathering place for local expat gringos. **$**

Tony's Inn La Isla
Paredes Sur.
Tel: 328-5 0407.
Decorated with nets and shells, serves excellent seafood. **$–$$**

NUEVO LEON

Monterrey

El Tío
Hidalgo 1746 Pte & México, Col. Obispado.
Tel: 8-346 0291.
Very popular for charbroiled steak, *cabrito,* and other Mexican dishes. **$$**

Luisiana
Av. Hidalgo 530 Ote.
Tel: 8-343 1561.
Old-time favorite on Hidalgo Plaza mall near Ancira. Elegant modern decor. International cuisine, including fillets, game and seafood, with top-notch service. **$$–$$$**

Regio
Regio Gonzalitos, Av. Gonzalitos and Insurgentes.
Tel: 8-346 8650.
One of a chain of good restaurants, open late and well known for their tasty charcoaled steaks and *cabrito* (*baby goat*). **$$**

Señor Natural
Mitras.
Tel: 8-378 4815.
Good assortment of healthy dishes including fruit salads, yogurt, granola, natuaral juices, and tasty soy dishes. **$**

OAXACA

Huatulco

Avalos
Bahía Santa Cruz.
Tel: 958-7 0128.
Also known as Doña Celia, this beachfront restaurant serves fresh seafood. **$$**

Casa del Mar
Balcones de Tangolunda 13.
Tel: 958-1 0203.
Good Continental and Mexican fare and a lovely setting. Beautiful view. **$$–$$$**

María Sabinas
La Crucecita, on the plaza.
Tel: 958-7 1039.
This place, named after the magic mushroom lady of the 1960's, serves good fish and steaks. **$$**

Oaxaca

El Asador Vasco
Portal de Flores 11.
Tel: 951-4 4755.
Located on the second floor facing the Zócalo, specializing in Basque and Paxacan dishes. Reserve a front-row table on the balcony – the view makes up for the notoriously bad service. **$$**

El Refectorio
Camino Roal Hotel, Cinco de Mayo 300.
Tel: 951-6 0611.
Good international and regional specialties. Wonderful Saturday-night buffet. **$$–$$$**

Flamanalli
Av. Juárez 39, Teotitlán del Valle.
Tel: 956-2 0255.
Charming village restaurant serving Zapotec food (somewhat overpriced) and also selling attractive hand-woven rugs. **$$**

La Asunción
Hostal de la Noria Hotel;
tel: 951-4 7844.
Nouvelle Oaxacan cuisine beautifully presented. **$$**

La Casita
Av. Hidalgo 612.
Tel: 951-6 2917.
Some people consider this the best Oaxacan food in town. **$**

Los Jorge
Pino Suárez 806.
Tel: 951-3 4308.
Outstanding fish and seafood. A real treat. **$$**

Puerto Escondido

Perla Flameante
Av. Pérez Gasca.
Tel: 958-2 0167.
Tropical island ambience, specializing in fish and seafood. **$$**

Santa Fe
Calle del Morro.
Tel: 958-2 0170.
Restaurant of the Sante Fé Hotel with a great view. Serves excellent Mexican, seafood, chicken and vegetarian dishes. **$$**

PUEBLA

Puebla

Fonda de Santa Clara
3 Poniente 307.
Tel: 22-42 2659.
Serves traditional dishes such as *chiles en nogada* (green chillis stuffed with meat, fruit and spices, white walnut, cheese and cream sauce and ruby red pomegranate seeds, representing the Mexican flag). **$$**

Las Bodegas del Molino
Molino de San José del Puente.
Tel: 22-49 0399.
Excellent restaurant set in a beautifully restored 16th-century hacienda. **$$$**

QUERETARO

Querétaro

Josecho's
Dalia 1, next to Plaza de Toros Santa María.
Tel: 42-16 0229.
Hefty portions of steak and seafood in a real macho atmosphere. **$$$**

La Mariposa
A Peralta 7.
In business for more than 50 years, La Mariposa is spotlessly clean, serving tasty Mexican food. **$**

QUINTANA ROO

Cancún

Casa Rolandi
Blvd Kukulcán Km 8, Plaza Caracol Shopping Center, Hotel Zone.
Tel: 98-83 1817.
Italian and Swiss dishes in a lively atmosphere. **$$**

La Habichuela
Margaritas 25.
Tel: 98-84 3158.
Longtime favorite situated downtown serving international and regional fare in a romantic setting. **$$–$$$**

La Joya
Fiesta American Coral Beach, Hotel Zone.
Tel: 98-83 2900.
Among Cancún's finest. Excellent local and international dishes. **$$$**

Lorenzillos
On the lagoon across from the Continental Plaza Hotel.
Tel: 98-83-1254.
Seafood served in a huge *palapa* setting. **$$–$$$**

Los Almendros
Av. Bonampak Sur 60 (corner Sayil, front of bullring).
Tel: 98-83 3093.
This downtown restaurant serves Yucatecan dishes such as lime soup and *cochinita pibil.* **$$**

100% Natural
Plaza Terramar, Hotel Zone.
Tel: 98-83 1180.
Delicious health food 24 hours a day in a pleasant atmosphere. **$**

Yamamoto
Uxmal 31.
Tel: 98-87 3366.
Traditional Japanese cuisine. **$$$**

Zuppa
Plaza Flamingo, Hotel Zone.
Tel: 98-83 2966.
Superb Italian cooking. Desserts are a real treat. **$$–$$$**

Price Guide

Price categories are based on the cost of a meal for one person without drinks:
$$$ Over 250 pesos.
$$ 130–250 pesos.
$ Less than 130 pesos.

Cobá

El Bocadito
Main street in village.
Casual place, popular with tour groups. **$**

Villa Arqueológica
Near entrance to ruins.
Tel: 9874 2087.
Refined Gallic atmosphere and cuisine, plus Yucatecan dishes. **$$**

Cozumel

El Arrecife
Presidente Inter-Continental Hotel.
Tel: 987-2 0322.
Excellent Italian and Mediterranean specialties with an ocean view. **$$–$$$**

La Choza
Calle R. Salas 198 y Av. 10 Norte.
Tel: 987-2 0958.
Some of the best home-cooked Mexican food in town. **$$**

Las Palmeras
Av. Juárez and Av. Rafael Melgar.
Tel: 987-2 0532.
Very popular spot for good eating and people-watching. **$$**

Prima
Calle Rosado Salas 109.
Tel: 987-2 4242.
Trattoria serving pizzas including the Chicago black-pan variety and excellent north Italian dishes. **$–$$**

Isla Mujeres

María's Kan Kin
Km 4 Carr. al Garrafón.
Tel: 987-7 0015.
French cuisine under a *palapa* overlooking the sea. Live lobsters for your selection. **$$**

Mirtita
In town on Av. Rueda Medina, across from ferry dock. Favorite local hangout for seafood and Yucatecan specialties. **$**

Pizza Rolandi
Hidalgo between Abasolo and Madero.
Tel: 987-7 0430.
Lively atmosphere for delicious Italian dishes besides pizza. **$–$$**

Zazil-Ha
Na-Balam Hotel.
Tel: 987-7 0279.
The fine cuisine includes regional specialities, seafood and vegetarian dishes in a beachside setting. Gracious service. **$$**

Tulum

Casa Cenote
On dirt road off Highway 307, between Xel-Há and Tulum.
An exceptionally fine restaurant beside a *cenote*. Delicious *fajitas* and seafood kebabs. **$$**

Cabañas Ana y José
On dirt track off Highway 307, between entrance to the ruins and town. One of the best local restaurants. **$$**

SINALOA

Mazatlán

Angelo's
Pueblo Bonito Hotel.
Tel: 69-14 3700.
Outstanding food and decor. The best in Mazatlán. **$$–$$$**

Doña Dona
Av. Camarón Sábalo, opposite the Holiday Inn.
Tel: 69-14 2200.
US-style donut and coffee shop; especially good for breakfast. **$**

Doney
Av. Mariano Escobedo 610.
Tel: 69-81 2651.
Downtown landmark restaurant since 1959. Mexican food including *cabrito*, seafood and steaks. Good desserts. **$–$$**

El Parador Español
Camarón Sábalo 714, next to El Cid.
Tel: 69-13 0767.
Spanish restaurant whose specialty is *paella*. **$$**

El Paraíso Tres Islas
Av. Rodolfo T. Loaiza 404, across from Sea Shell City.
Tel: 69-14 2812.
Good seafood restaurant on beach. Very popular. **$–$$**

El Shrimp Bucket
Olas Altas 11 in La Siesta.
Tel: 69-81 6350.
The original restaurant of the Anderson chain. Live music. **$$**

Miyiko
Av. del Mar 70.
Tel: 69-81 6590.
Japanese food and drinks, including *sushi, teppan yaki, sake* and beer. **$$$**

Pastelería Panamá
Av. Camarón Sábalo & Av. de las Garzas.
Tel: 69-13 6977.
Good food and pastries. **$**

Sr Peppers
Av. Camarón Sábalo opposite the Camino Real Hotel.
Tel: 69-14 0101.
Steaks, lobsters and shrimp, all delicious. **$$$**

SONORA

Guaymas

Baja Mar
Av. Serdán & Calle 17.
Tel: 622-4 0225.

Downtown restaurant with great seafood, wonderful clam and fish soups. Prime cuts from Sonora. Cocktails. **$–$$**

Kino Bay

El Pargo Rojo
Av. del Mar 1426, across from beach.
Tel: 622-2 0205.
Pleasant seafood and steak restaurant. **$$**

Kino Bay
On the beach.
Tel: 622-2 0049.
One of the few spots for breakfast. Mexican food in a pleasant atmosphere. **$**

San Carlos

Jax Snax
Carr. San Carlos.
Tel: 622-6 0270.
Good Mexican-American fast and not-so fast food.

Rosa's Cantina
Carr. San Carlos.
A casual place, popular with young people, serving *cabrito*, steak and *enchiladas*. Bulletin-board for buying, selling, renting or local events. Good value. **$$**

Terraza
Carr. San Carlos Km 5.
Tel: 622-6 0039.
Overlooking San Carlos Bay. Specializes in seafood. Also serves Sonoran beef and chicken. **$$$**

TABASCO

Villahermosa

Los Tulipanes
Carlos Pellicer Cámara Cultural Center.
Tel: 931-12 9209.
Features Villahermosa's outstanding – and little known – cuisine. **$$**

TAMAULIPAS

Tampico

Diligencias
H. del Cañonero & López de Lara, one block off Plaza de la Libertad.
Tel: 12-13 7642.
Absolutely the best seafood in town. Reasonable prices. **$$**

VERACRUZ

Catemaco

La Finca
Costera del Golfo Km. 147.
Tel: 294-3 0322.
One of the best places in town. **$**

Los Sauces
Paseo del Malecón.
Tel: 294-3 0548.
Fish restaurant near the lake front. Its specialty is *mojarra* (perch from Lake Catemaco). **$**

Coatepec

Casa Bonilla
Juárez and Cuauhtémoc.
Tel: 28-160374.
A local institution famous for its langoustine and shrimp. Well worth a detour. **$$**

El Tío Yeyo
Santos Degollado 4.
Tel: 28-16 3645.
Lively bar and restaurant serving local specialties. Excellent mountain trout – 21 varieties. Also crayfish and shrimp. **$$**

Santiago Tuxtla

El Trapiche de Ximagambazca
Km 114 Carr. Costera del Golfo, Popotepec.
Great roadside restaurant between Alvarado and Santiago Tuxtla. Smoked meats a specialty. **$$**

Tuxpan

Posada Don Antonio's
Av. Juárez & Garizurieta, next to the Hotel Reforma.
Tel: 783-4 1602.
Excellent fish dishes, especially the shellfish stew. **$$**

Veracruz

El Gaucho
Costilla 187.
Tel: 29-35 0411.
Popular for quality beef and pasta. **$$**

Gran Café de la Parroquia
Gómez Faríasm 34, on the *malecón* (seafront boulevard).
Tel: 29-32 2584.
According to a local saying, if you haven't been to La Parroquia, you haven't been to Veracruz. This café is a national institution. **$**

Gran Café del Portal
Independencia & Zamora.

Tel: 29-31 2759.
Popular coffee house and restaurant that preserves period decor. Originally the location of the famous Café de la Parroquia. **$**

La Fuente de Mariscos
Hernán Cortés 1524.
Tel: 29-38 2412.
Mecca for seafood lovers. **$$**

La Mansión
Blvd Avila Camacho & Ruiz Cortines, Boca del Río.
Tel: 29-37 1363.
Argentine-type steak-house. Good wine-list. **$$$**

Xalapa (Jalapa)
La Casa de Mamá
Avila Camacho 113.
Tel: 28-17 6232.
Extremely popular for fish, shrimp, steaks and good desserts. **$$**

Churrería del Recuerdo
Guadalupe Victoria 158.
Tel: 28-18 1678.
This lively and very popular restaurant (evenings only) serves the best authentically Mexican food you'll find anywhere (no alcohol).

YUCATAN
Chichén-Itzá
Hotel Hacienda Chichén-Itzá
Near southern entrance to site.
Tel: 985-1 0045.
Enjoy a meal where this century's first archeological teams stayed, in a beautiful setting. **$$**

Hotel Mayaland
Just outside southern entrance to site, next to Hotel Hacienda Chichén.
Tel: 985-1-0077.
A choice of three restaurants in a hotel with dignified ambience. **$$**

Mérida
Alberto's Continental Patio
Calle 64 and Calle 57.
Tel: 99-28 6336.
International and Lebanese cuisine, for an eleganat evening. **$$**

Los Almendros
Calle 50 No. 493 between Calles 57 and 59.
Tel: 99-23 8135.
Traditional Yucatán specialties. **$$**

Santa Lucía
Calle 60 No. 481, next to Santa

Lucía park.
Tel: 99-28 8135.
Full course meals featuring Yucatecan favorites. **$**

Uxmal
Hotel Hacienda Uxmal
Carr. 261 Km 80, across from ruins.
Tel: 99-24 7142.
A choice of restaurants in a beautiful 4-star hotel, the former headquarters of archeologists. **$$**

Price Guide

Price categories are based on the cost of a meal for one person without drinks:
$$$ Over 250 pesos.
$$ 130–250 pesos.
$ Less than 130 pesos.

Valladolid
El Mesón del Marqués
Calle 39 No. 203.
Tel: 985-6 2073.
Newly renovated, on the main plaza, next to the Hotel del Marqués, for Mexican and Yucatecan dishes. **$$**

Hotel María de la Luz
Calle 42 No. 195.
Tel: 985-6-2070.
Good Mexican/Yucatecan eating in a hotel setting, where you can look out on the street happenings. Very popular with the locals. **$**

ZACATECAS
Zacatecas
La Cuija
Mercado González Ortega.
Tel: 492-2 8275.
Zacatecas specialties, very well prepared. **$$**

Quinta Real
González Ortega, at the aqueduct.
Tel: 492-2 9104.
This beautiful restaurant offers fine Continental cuisine. **$$$**

Drinks

Mexicans tend to drink copiously at fiestas and in times of great calamity or great good fortune. Otherwise, the vast majority are relatively sober folk.

Beer
A cool beer is very popular as an accompaniment to the heavy *comida* in mid-afternoon, and you would be well advised to adopt this custom as beer complements Mexican flavors and helps take the bite out of chillis. Mexican beers are excellent, as good as any in the world. Try drinking canned beer (eg. Tecate) in the local fashion: squeeze lime and sprinkle salt on the lid of the can. The best dark beers are Bohemia, Negra, Modelo, Dos Equis, Noche Buena and Negra León. For light lagers, try Carta Blanca, Corona, Sol, Victoria and Dos Equis lager.

Wine and Spirits
Wine is rarely drunk, although there are vineyards in some areas of Mexico. Some Mexican wines are quite good, especially those produced in the vineyards of Baja California. Imported wines, especially French wines, are quite dear in Mexican restaurants.

Mexico's own deservedly famous liquor is tequila. There are other liquors, besides tequila, made from varieties of the *maguey* plant; the generic term is mezcal. The most traditional of Mexican drinks is *pulque*. For better or for worse, you will probably not have a chance to try it. Made from a type of *maguey*, *pulque* is not distilled as are tequila and other mezcals. It must be drunk when freshly fermented, because it cannot be canned or bottled without being ruined. Undiluted, it is highly nutritious and only mildly alcoholic, about the same in strength as beer. In pre-Columbian Mexico, *pulque*

Coffee

Coffee served in the big cities is often good, and cafés are proliferating. In villages instant coffee is usually what's served. Coffee with sugar and cinnamon is known as *café de olla*. *Café con leche* is mostly milk with a little coffee in it. To order coffee with milk served separately, ask for *café americano*.

was reserved for use in rituals and healing and is still highly valued by Mexicans (*see page 253*).

Bars

In addition to the usual hotel bars and international-style drinking places found in cities, there are some with a distinctively Mexican flavour. *Pulquerías* are special bars (like informal men's clubs) where *pulque* is drunk. Strangers are not generally welcome, but if you have a male Mexican friend, ask him to invite you to a *pulquería*. Women are virtually never allowed in, except to the special ladies' bar, and if they are they might well attract unwanted attention. Likewise, some *cantinas* still don't welcome women, but trends are changing and nowadays most *cantinas* welcome men and women.

Soft Drinks

A wide variety of non-alcoholic beverages is available in Mexico; soft drinks are called *refrescos*. Some of the Mexican ones are worth a try, including apple-flavored *Sidral* and *Sangría*, a mixed-fruit drink. Fruit juices, whether ordered in restaurants, in markets or from street vendors, are often freshly squeezed for you. *Jugo* is the word for juice. while *agua fresca* is a fruit juice mixed with a lot of water. It is much cheaper but more risky.

Licuados are shakes, made with chocolate or fruit and water or milk, often with raw eggs added (but only if you ask for them). A popular one is a *licuado de coco* (coconut shake). If you're after authenticity, try *atole* – cornmeal mixed with water or milk, sugar, and some flavouring (chocolate, vanilla, strawberry) to taste – or *horchata*, made from ground rice, cinnamon and water. Another pre-Columbian drink is chocolate.

Culture

Diary of Events

The following list gives some of Mexico's hundreds of fiestas and fairs month by month. Check dates before you go as many vary slightly from year to year.

January
6: *Día de los Santos Reyes*, Feast of Epiphany; the traditional day for children to receive Christmas gifts (instead of Christmas Day).
17: *Día de San Antonio Abad*, blessings of animals at parish churches.
18: *Fiesta de Santa Prisca*, at Taxco, Guerrero.
20: *Fiesta de San Sebastián*, at Chiapa de Corzo, Chiapas; León and Guanajuato.

February
February or March: *Carnaval* during the week before Lent, notably in Acapulco, Guerrero; Mazatlán, Sinaloa; Mérida, Yucatán; Huejotzingo, Puebla: Tepoztlán, Morelos; and Veracruz. Street parades, floats and dancing.
2: *Candelaria* feast (Candlemas) especially in Tlacotalpan, Veracruz.
5: Fair at Zitácuaro, Michoacán.
21: Folk dances celebrating the spring festival at Chichén-Itzá.

March
March or April: *Xochimilco* (festival queen elections, usually the week before Easter); *Semana Santa* (Holy Week).
19: *Dia de San José*, patron saint of San José del Cabo, Baja California, where they hold street parties with dancing, firework

displays, cock-fights, horse races and foodstalls.

April
April–May: San Marcos national fair in Aguascalientes.
5: Fair at Ticul, Yucatán.
23: Aztec Day of Tezcatlipoca.
25: San Marcos Fair at Tuxtla Gutiérrez, Chiapas.
29: Fair at Puebla.

May
1: Fair at Morelia, Michoacán.
2: Fair at Cuernavaca, Morelos.
3: Fair at Valle de Bravo;
Corpus Christi Day. Papantla, Veracruz, including a dance of the flying men (*Voladores de Papantla*).
5: Cinco de Mayo; national holiday, commemorating the mexican defeat of the French army at Puebla de los Angelesin 1862.
20: Festival of the Hammocks, Iecoh, Yucatán.
31: Crafts fair at Tehuántepec, Oaxaca.

June
1: Navy Day (*Día de la Marina*); national holiday
13: Fair at Uruapan, Michoacán.
29: Street fiesta at Tlaquepaque, Guadalajara.

July
7: Fair at Comitán, Chiapas.
Last two Mondays in July: Lunes del Cerro, the **Guelaguetza**, an indian festival in Oaxaca.
25: Santiago Tuxtla, Veracruz.

August
During August: **International Surfing Competition** at Puerto Escondido, Oaxaca; **Guadalupe Valley Wine Festival**; annual regatta at Todos Santos (south of Ensenada).
1: Fair at Saltillo, Coahuila.
8: Fair at Mérida, Yucatán.
15: Assumption of the Virgin Mary – many towns have fiestas, most notably, one in Huamantla, Tlaxcala.

September
During September: Rosarito–Ensenada 50-mile fun bicycle ride.

Annual State of the Union, address by the president.
1: Fair at Tepoztlán, Morelos.
4: Fiesta at Santa Rosalía and Mulegé.
6: Fair at Zacatecas.
8: *La Virgen de Loreto*: procession through the streets of many towns.
10: Fair at Chihuahua.
12: Seafood fair at Ensenada.
14: Charro Day.
15–16: Independence Day, celebrated nationally.
21: Autumnal equinox celebrated at Chichén-Itzá.
Late September: San Miguel de Allende: fiesta on the Saturday following **Día de San Miguel** (29 Sept).

October
During October: Annual Lobster and Wine Festival in Rosarito; Cervantino Festival in Guanajuato; Mole Fair in Milpa Alpa district of Mexico City.
4: Día de San Francisco de Assisi: many towns have fiestas; coffee-growers' fair in Cuetzalán, Puebla;
Fair at Pachuca, Hidalgo.
5: Día de La Virgen de Zapopan, Guadalajara.
12: month-long fair at Guadalajara; *Día de la Raza* (Columbus Day).

November
1–2: All Saints and **Day of the Dead** celebrated nationally. Graveside vigils at Janitzio, Michoacán and processions in San Andrés Mixquic, in Mexico City.
20: National holiday celebrating 1910 Revolution.

December
1: Fair at Compostela, Nayarit.
8: Día de Nuestra Señora de Guadalupe, many pilgrimages to La Villa, the shrine of Our Lady of Guadalupe in Mexico City.
18: Día de Nuestra Señora de la Soledad; fair at Oaxaca.
23: *Noche de Rábanos* (Radish fair), Oaxaca.

Music and Dance in Mexico City

The prime venue for music and dance in the Mexican capital is the **Palacio de Bellas Artes** at Eje Central Lázaro Cárdenas, at the eastern end of the Alameda. A wide range of Mexican dances are performed here by the **Ballet Folklórico de México**, including on Wednesday and Sunday evenings, and Sunday mornings. The theatre also stages performances by Mexico's classical and modern ballet companies, as well as opera and classical concerts. Tickets are available at the box office (to reserve seats in advance you have to go in person.)
A newer Mexican dance company worth seeing is the **Ballet Folklórico Nacional Aztlán**, which performs at the refurbished **Teatro Histórico de la Ciudad** at Donceles 36 (tel: 510-2197).

Nightlife

Mexico City

The Zona Rosa in Mexico City, with its plethora of bars and sidewalk cafés, is the area which probably has the most to offer after dark. The following is a selection of nightclubs in the capital:
• **Bar León**, República de Brasil 5. Tel: 5 510 3093. Tropical music.
• **La Boom**, Rodolfo Gaona 3. Tel: 5-580 0708. Large, lively disco.
• **La Llorona**, Mesones & 5 de Febrero downtown. Tel: 5-709 8420. Trendy nightclub.
• **Mesón Triana**, Oaxaca 90. Tel: 5-525 3880. Flamenco shows and dancing with a Latin flavour.
• **Pervert Lounge**, Uruguay 70, downtown. Tel: 5-518 0976. Music and decor inspired by the 60s.
• **Salón México**, Segundo Callejón de San Juan de Dios 25. Tel: 5-518 0931. Two blocks from Alameda Park. Sounds of danzón, salsa, swing and mambo.

Yucatán Peninsula

Outside of Mexico City, some of the country's liveliest nightlife can be found in the Yucatán Peninsula.
The two main centers for entertainment on the peninsula are Cancún (glitzy) and Mérida (rather more cultural), although Cozumel is also good for discos. This is a selection of some popular places.

CAMPECHE
This is a true provincial city, and entertainment options for late nights are few but dancing is one possibility.

Discos
Try **Disco Atlantis**, Hotel Ramada, Av. Ruíz Cortínes, 51; **El Olones**, Hotel

Baluartes, Av. Ruíz Cortínes and Calle 61 is open Fridays and Saturdays.

Check at your hotel or the tourist office for dates and times of folk music and dance performances at different plazas in the city.

CANCUN

Cancún's nightlife is generally expensive (in particular, be prepared for stiff cover charges) but the sheer variety of options will keep you busy every night, if you manage to keep up the pace.

Bars/Restaurants

In downtown Cancún, the following restaurants all have dance floors: **Carlos 'n' Charlie's**, lagoon side of Blvd Kukulcán, near Calinda Beach hotel; the ever-popular **Señor Frog's**, lagoon side of Blvd Kukulcán, near Casa Maya hotel; **Carlos O'Brian's**, Av. Tulum.

If you would like to combine eating out with a romantic cruise, there are several companies offering floating dinner cruises. Pleasant options include **Columbus**, on a galleon-style boat (tel: 83-14-88); **Lobster Sunset Cruise** (tel: 83-04-00); **Pirate's Night Adventure** (tel: 83-14-88).

Performance Art

Ballet Folklórico Nacional de México, Hotel Continental Villas Plaza, Blvd Kukulcán (tel: 83-10-22). This is an unforgettable performance of Mexican folk dances executed by some of the region's best professionals. The evening's entertainment also includes supper, and you will need to make reservations as far in advance as possible. There's a dinner show featuring a fine performance by the **Indios Voladores** of Papantla at Xcaret (tel: 83-07-65).

Discos

Coco Bongo, Blvd Kukulcán, Km 9.5; **Fat Tuesday**, Blvd Kukulcán 6.5 (tel: 83-26-76); **Christine**, Hotel Krystal, Blvd Kukulcán, Km 7.5 (tel: 83-11-33); **Daddy'O**, Blvd Kukulcán, Km 9.5 (tel: 83-31-34); and **Daddy Rock**, next door (tel: 83-16-26);

Hard Rock Café, Blvd Kukulcán, Km 8.5 (tel: 83-20-24); **La Boom**, Blvd Kukulcán, Km 3.5 (tel: 83-14-58).

Music

Jazz: **Casis Bar**, Hotel Hyatt Cancún Caribe, Blvd Kukulcán, Km 10.5; **Pat O'Brien's**, Flamingo Plaza, Blvd. Kukulcán, Km 11 (tel: 83-08-32). The Cancún branch of the famous New Orleans bar. One bar is devoted to jazz; the other two offer rock and country.

Reggae: Try **Cat's**, Av. Yaxchilán, 12, Cancún City (tel: 83-19-10).

Romantic music for dancing: Find this at **The Touch of Class**, Centro de Convenciones, Blvd Kukulcán, Km 9 (tel: 83-28-80).

Salsa and other Latin rhythms: Best at **Azúcar**, next to the Hotel Camino Real at Punta Cancún in the hotel zone (tel: 83-04-41); and **Mango Tango**, on the lagoon side of Blvd Kukulcán, near Cancún Palace Hotel (tel: 85-03-03).

The lobby bars of hotels are also good places to find all kinds of live music. **Hotel Camino Real Cancún**, Blvd Kukulcán, Punta Cancún, for Mexican music in the evening or try **Hotel Fiesta Americana Coral Beach**, Blvd Kukulcán, Km 9.5, for easy listening music; the **Hotel Meliá Cancún**, Blvd Kukulcán, Km 14, for Latin rhythms; **Hotel Marriott Casamagna**, Blvd Kukulcán, Km 20, for lively, great mariachi music, or **Hotel Sierra Cancún**, Blvd Kukulcán, Km 10, for Mexican trio music.

Party Center

Party Center, Blvd Kukulcán, Km 9. A whole mall dedicated to parties, with stores open until 10pm, and restaurants, bars and nightclubs serving until 4–5am.

COZUMEL

Visitors to Cozumel are generally more oriented to water sports, especially diving, and nightlife is more low-key than in Cancún. Divers like to retire early and be relatively fresh for the next day's explorations.

Bars/Restaurants

Carlos 'n' Charlie's, Av. Melgar, 11

(tel: 2-01-91); **The Sports Page**, Av. 5 Norte and Calle 2 (tel: 2-11-99). The latter is a well-known video bar for American sports events and reasonable food.

Dance

Forum, Av. Circunvalación. Nightly Mexican fiesta with dance performances and mariachi bands. Check at your hotel for dates, times and reservations.

Discos

Neptuno, Av. Rafael Melgar (tel: 2-15-37); **Hard Rock**, Rafael Melgar 2-A (tel: 2-52-71) has a good atmosphere and very lively dance floor.

ISLA MUJERES

This island resort attracts people looking for a slower pace and so its evening entertainment options are limited. Beach parties are popular with some tourists.

You might try the bar at the **Na-Balam Hotel** or El Pingüino, at the Posada del Mar. Otherwise, the pickings are very slim.

MERIDA

Free performances in the city are scheduled for every evening of the week. The following list is provided by Yucatán Today.

Monday: Regional *vaquería* (cowboy) show, with typical dancing and dress, 9pm at the Palacio Municipal on the main plaza (Zócalo).

Tuesday: 1940s big band music at the Musical Memories Concert, featuring hits by Glenn Miller and Benny Goodman, 9pm in Santiago Park, situated in front of the Rex movie theater.

Wednesday: String instruments and piano concerts at the Casa de Artesanías, 9pm on Calle 63, between Calles 64 and 66.

Thursday: La Serenata (serenade) in Santa Lucía park for a fine display of typical Yucatecan dress, dance, music and folklore, 9pm on Calle 60, corner of Calle 55.

Friday: University students' serenade at the Universidad de Yucatán, 9pm between Calle 60 and Calle 57.

Saturday: Catholic Mass is held in English at the Santa Lucía church in Santa Lucía park. 6pm at Calle 60 and Calle 55.
Sunday: From 9am–9pm the streets surrounding the Zócalo are closed to motor traffic. Concerts are held at nearby municipal buildings, and you will find street theater and sidewalk vendors selling food, balloons, handicrafts and good souvenirs. On that note, don't miss the bazaar in Santa Lucía park.

Discos and Nightclubs

La Hach, Fiesta Americana Hotel, Paseo de Montejo and Av. Colón (tel: 20-21-94); and **Pancho's**, Calle 59 located between Calles 60 and 62 (tel: 23-09-42).

Cinema

Mexico has one of the most prolific film industries in the word and has provided sites for the shooting of innumerable Westerns (especially in Durango). Vintage Mexican films are often shown here, as well as modern ones and the ubiquitous Hollywood mainstream movies.

Two of the most successful films to have come out of Mexico in recent years are **Danzón**, directed by Mariá Novaro, and **Como agua para chocolate**, an adaptation of the novel by Laura Esquivel.

In the cities more and more multiplex cinemas are being built – they are mostly found wherever there are shopping malls.

In Mexico City, the state-sponsored *Cineteca Nacional* (Metro Coyoacán station) is often worth a visit. Mexico City's English-language *Daily News* does not list current movie showings; you'll have to refer to one of the Spanish dailies although the concierge at most larger hotels usually has a list. *Tiempo Libre* offers the most complete listing (look under *cine.*) There are cinemas showing English-language movies (usually with Spanish subtitles, except in the case of animated and children's films) along Reforma between the Cuauhtémoc and Angel statues and also along Hamburgo in the Zona Rosa.

Sport

Spectator Sports

Bullfighting

Bullfighting is popular throughout Mexico and can be experienced at the Plaza de Toros in various cities. Check with your hotel to see if *corridas* are in season at the time of your trip and obtain information on acquiring some tickets.

An afternoon's event usually includes three *toreros* – each fighting and killing two bulls in a highly stylized manner. Two types of seats are available: *sol* (sun), which are cheapest but the least comfortable, and *sombra* (shade).

Football

The site of the 1986 World Cup championships, Mexico is a soccer-playing country, with the huge Aztec Stadium (in Mexico City) its largest venue. Enquire at your hotel about the *fútbol* game on Sunday morning.

Jai Alai

One of the fastest sports alive is the Basque game of jai alai. It is played in Tijuana at the Palacio Frontón on Av. Revolución (Mon–Sat 8pm), and in Acapulco at the Jai Alai Acapulco Race & Sports Book, Costera Miguel Alemán 498, from Thursday to Sunday at 9pm, between December and August. Betting is heavy and fun.

Participant Sports

Fishing

Fishing is permitted in Mexico's lakes and rivers, and along its 8,000-odd km (5,000-odd miles) of coastline. Annual fishing tournaments, usually in May and June, are based in La Paz, Guaymas, Mazatlán, Puerto Vallarta, Barra de Navidad, Manzanillo and Acapulco on the Pacific Coast; in Tampico and Veracruz on the Gulf of Mexico; and in Cancún, Cd. del Carmen and Cozumel on the Caribbean. Fishing seasons and regulations vary according to area and season. For information, write to:
• Departamento de Pesca, Oficina de Permisos de Pesca Deportiva, Anillo Periférico Sur 4209, 14210 México, DF.

Send a large, stamped, self-addressed envelope and they will send you (in English) information and regulations. If you are already in Mexico, tel: 5-628 0600. There are also some 150 branch offices of the Departamento de Pesca.

One license will cover you for freshwater or sea fishing anywhere in Mexico. Licenses are issued for periods of three days, one month, three months or one year. You can purchase a license at any Departamento de Pesca office, from any local fish or game warden, or from the captain of any port or fishing facility.

Water Sports

There are aquatic activities galore along the Mexican coastlines. You will find everything from boat tours, windsurfing and fishing to snorkelling and scuba diving.

The generally calm waters of some hotel beaches are great for beginners and children to learn basic snorkel techniques and most have lifeguards. Equipment can be rented from local marinas and some hotels provide it free of charge.

Diving off Mexico

The Great Maya Reef, the second longest in the world, begins (or ends) its 250-km (155-mile) length near the Club Med resort at Punta Nizuc, Yucatán. All beaches are open to the public in this area, so it is an easy place to enjoy the sights of the reef in shallow water. The most scenic and popular diving spots are the island of Cozumel and Isla Mujeres.

Shopping

What to Buy

Few visitors can resist shopping in Mexico. For some, bargain hunting may be the primary purpose of their visit. The price-range is nearly as wide as the range of craft items available, so take your time and choose wisely. Serious shoppers should plan to travel extensively in the countryside – everything is cheaper at the place where it's made. You may also be lucky enough to watch and photograph the *artesano* at work.

For those limited to one or two cities, the range of possible purchases is still wide. Items from all over Mexico can be bought at the large markets in the capital and other large cities. Prices are well above those paid at the source, but you can bargain the prices down – even where there are signs saying *precios fijos* (fixed prices). Simply ask for a "discount." You'll have to exercise your Spanish, especially numbers. Begin by asking "¿Cuánto cuesta?" (How much?). Then make an offer – half the asking price is usual in a tourist area; perhaps two-thirds elsewhere. Take your time and work down to a mutually agreeable figure.

Handicrafts from all over Mexico are also sold at government-run stores in many cities. These are not particularly cheap, and prices are generally not negotiable, but quality is high. The same is true of many shops and boutiques in the stylish areas of cities.

Some large stores will pack your purchases carefully and mail them to your home, for a reasonable charge. If you are buying gifts for someone in the US, many stores will mail parcels direct to the recipient.

Markets

The markets of Mexico City are fascinating. The best (and cheapest) for handicrafts and souvenirs is **Artesanías de la Ciudadela** (Ayuntamiento at Balderas) displaying a range of Mexican souvenirs and crafts (masks, blankets, blouses, napkins, silver, papier-mâché fruits, toys, leather) and harboring a neat little café in its sunny, central plaza.

The **San Juan market** (on Ayuntamiento at Dolores; walk three blocks south on San Juan de Letrán and turn right) boasts 176 stores selling handicrafts but all of it is familiar stuff. The biggest market is probably the immense **Merced** (La Merced Metro station), where there is as much going on outside as under cover – chicken frying; radios blaring; girls rolling, heating and filling *tortillas* from an array of brightly colored plastic bowls. Itinerant peddlers, arms heavy with garments on hangers, selling razors or cosmetics from carrier-bags. A few blocks away, the **Sonora** market on Fray Servando Teresa de Mier at Rosario, is famous for its magical and herbal remedies.

Almost as large as the Merced is the **Lagunilla** market, also known as the Thieves Market, It is three blocks along Rayón, about three blocks north of the Plaza Garibaldi. Divided by the main street, it offers chicken, fruit, meat and other types of food on one side and clothes – from ballgowns to ranch wear – on the other. It's at its best on Sunday, when the market spills out onto the

Antiques

Don't pay high prices for pre-Columbian artifacts. They are almost certain to be fakes, though possibly well-made. Very fine ceramic figures are made using original types of clay and authentic firing processes. Should the artifact be genuine, you will face serious penalties if you try to take it out of the country.

surrounding streets. You'll need a careful eye to tell the good stuff apart from the junk. Dress discreetly and keep your hand on your wallet or purse.

Ceramics

Beautiful ceramics are available all over Mexico. Except for stoneware, most of the items may not be lead-free, so use them for decoration or for storing dry goods. If the empty article rings like a bell when flicked with the fingernail, it is safe; if it sounds as if you've tapped on wood, it probably contains lead. Glaze and paint often contain lead, too.

In Tlaquepaque, Jalisco there is a variety of ceramics, including replicas of pre-Columbian pieces. In nearby Tonalá, innovative styles are sold alongside the more traditional. The city of Puebla specializes in household crockery, tiles, and Talavera ceramics, while Acatlán and Izúcar de Matamoros, also in Puebla, and Metepec in the State of Mexico, sell "tree of life" ceramics.

In Tzintzuntzan, Morelia and San Miguel de Allende in Guanajuato, as well as San Bartolo Coyotepec in Oaxaca, you will find burnished ceramics. Green-glazed pottery is from Patambán in Michoacán and Santa María Atzompa. Fantastical figures known as *alebrijes* are produced in Arrazola, Oaxaca. In Amatenango, Chiapas, traditional pottery is fired without kilns. Local areas specialize in different woodworking styles and techniques. The Seri indians in Bahía Kino, Sonora make ironwood animals. In Uruapan, Michoacán, masks and lacquerware are the local product, while in Quiroga in Michoacán, painted wooden bowls and household items are widely available. Ixtapan de la Sal in the State of Mexico also specializes in household items as well as carved animals. Colonial-style furniture and wooden bowls can be found in Cuernavaca, Morelos. In Olinalá, Guerrero, you will find jaguar masks, gourd bowls, wooden trays and fine lacquerware.

Ixmiquilpan, Hidalgo is known for

Government Craft Shops

Fonart, a government-sponsored fund for promoting handicrafts is a good source of arts and crafts. Its shops control the quality of all they buy and sell.

In Mexico City **Fonart** has outlets at the following locations:
• Juárez, 89 Av. Juárez, Mexico. Tel: 5-52 0171.
• **Fonart**, Patriotismo 691, Col, Mixcoac. Tel: 5-563 4060.
• **Fonart,** Presidente Carranza 115, Col. Coyoacán. Tel: 5-554 6270.

In other cities, **Fonart** shops include the following:
• **Fonart**, Anillo Envolvente Lincoln y Mejía, Ciudad Juárez, Chihuahua. Tel: 16-13 6143.
• **Fonart**, Manuel M. Bravo 116, Oaxaca. Tel: 951-6 5764.
• **Fonart,** Ángela Peralta 20, Querétaro. Tel: 42-12 2648.
• **Fonart**, Ignacio Allende Sur 225, Saltillo, Coahuila. Tel: 84-12 6936.
• **Fonart,** Jardín Guerrero 6, San Luis Potosí. Tel: 48-12 7521.
• **Fonart**, Hotel Monte Taxco, Taxco, Guerrero. Tel: 762-2 1300.
• Casa del Conde de la Valenciana, SA de CV, Km 5 Valenciana, Carr. Guanajuato-Dolores, Hidalgo. Tel: 2 2550.

its bird cages; Tequisquiapan, Querétaro for its wooden furniture. Painted wooden animals are made in Cuilapan and san Martín Tilcajete, Oaxaca, and masks and other lacquerware in Chiapa de Corzo, Chiapas. Fine mahogany and cedar furniture comes from Mérida in Yucatán, Valladolid in Tabasco; and Campeche.
Wooden musical instruments can

also be a good buy. guitars are made in Paracho, Michoacán, and San Juan Chamula, Chiapas, where they also make harps.
Basketry in a wide range of shapes and sizes is found in Tequisquiapan in Querétaro, Lerma in the State of Mexico and Ihuatzio in Michoacán. In the Copper Canyon the Tarahumara indians also make fine basketry. Cane and reed containers are specialty of San Miguel de Allende and Guanajuato (both in Guanajuato) Puebla, and Otomí indian villages in the Mezquital valley, Hidalgo.
Indian bark paintings can be purchased at Xalitla in Tolima and San Agustín de las Flores in Guerrero. In the Veracruz coastal area palm-leaf mats can be bought, while in the Mixtec area of Oaxaca there are net carrying bags. In Puebla, Veracruz and San Luis Potosí, Huastec indians produce cactus fibre bags. **Panama hats** are made in Becal, Campeche, and **hammocks** in Mérida, Yucatán. When buying a hammock, look for one of pure cotton, of thin thread, tightly woven. Bees-wax on the thread will make it mildew-resistant.
Rugs made with traditional Mexican designs and using Oriental techniques are produced in Temoaya, in the State of Mexico.

Wool and Clothing

You can buy beautiful and colorful clothes in Mexico. Be aware that hand-made items may shrink, so buy a larger size if in any doubt. Cotton (algodón) means pure cotton but wool (lana) is often a blend of fibres.
Good areas for woolen items include Tlaxcala; Cuernavaca and Huejapan in Morelos; Tequisquiapan in Querétaro; San Miguel de Allende in Guanajuato; Teotitlán del Valle, near Oaxaca City; Saltillo in Coahuila, and Zacatecas. Sarapes (blankets), hand-woven belts and clothing are a local specialty for the Otomí indians of Mezquital Valley, Hidalgo; the Tarahumara indians of the Barranca del Cobre, Chihuahua; the Cora and Huichol indians of

Nayarit; and the Tzotzil indians of San Juan Chamula, Chiapas.
Embroidered clothing is widely available and may be produced by hand or machine. Check that you are paying an appropriate price by looking at the reverse to see how it has been made. The Amuzgo indians near Ometepec, Guerrero, and in Oaxaca make cotton huipiles (women's blouses); in Yalalag, Oaxaca indian blouses and wrap-skirts are made with natural dyes.

Jewelry

It is best to buy jewelry from a reputable store, not from a street vendor. In Mexico City plenty of shops sell modern jewelry. Silver is the main material for jewelry in Taxco, Guerrero; Toluca, Mexico state; Yalalag, Oaxaca; Querétaro; Veracruz; and the Yucatán. Oaxacan jewelers produce replicas of some of the gold jewelry found at Monte Albán. In Veracruz, coral jewelry is also made. Make sure you are not buying black coral, as this is one of many listed species – also including turtleshell – protected by CITES, the Convention on International Trade in Endangered Species of Wild Flora and Fauna.

Language

Pronunciation Tips

Although many Mexicans speak some English, it is good to have basic Spanish phrases at your disposal; in remote areas, it is essential. In general, Mexicans are delighted with foreigners who try to speak the language, and they'll be patient – if sometimes amused. Pronunciation is not difficult. The following is a simplified mini-lesson:

Vowels:
a as in *father*
e as in *bed*
i as in *police*
o as in *hole*
u as in *rude*

Consonants are approximately like those in English, the main exceptions being:
c is hard before **a**, **o**, or **u** (as in English), and is soft before **e** or **i**, when it sounds like **s**. Thus, *censo* (census) sounds like *senso*.
g is hard before **a**, **o**, or **u** (as in English), but before **e** or **i** Spanish **g** sounds like a guttural **h**. **G** before **ua** is often soft or silent, so that *agua* sounds more like *awa*, and Guadalajara like *Wadalajara*.
h is silent.
j sounds like the English h.
ll sounds like y.
ñ sounds like ny, as in señor.
q is followed by **u** as in English, but the combination sounds like **k** instead of like **kw**. ¿Qué quiere Usted? is pronounced: Keh kee-er-eh oosted?
r is often rolled.
x between vowels sounds like a guttural **h**, e.g. in Mexico or Oaxaca.
y alone, as the word meaning "and", is pronounced **ee**.

Note that **ch** and **ll** are separate letters of the Spanish alphabet; if looking in a phone book or dictionary for a word beginning with **ch**, you will find it after the final **c** entry. A name or word beginning with **ll** will be listed after the **l** entry (**ñ** and **rr** are also counted as separate letters.)

Useful Words/Phrases

please – *por favor*
thank you – *gracias*
you're welcome – *de nada* (literally, for nothing)
I'm sorry – *lo siento*
excuse me – *con permiso*
yes – *sí*
no – *no*
can you speak English? – *¿habla (usted) inglés?*
do you understand me? – *¿me comprende? / ¿me entiende?*
this is good – *(esto) está bueno*
this is bad – *(esto) está malo*
good morning – *buenos días*
good night/evening – *buenas noches*
goodbye – *adiós*
where is...? – *¿dónde está?*
exit – *la salida*
entrance – *la entrada*
money – *dinero*
credit card – *la tarjeta de crédito*
tax – *impuesto*

At the Bar/Restaurant

In Spanish, *el menú* is not the main menu, but a fixed menu offered each day (usually for lunch) at a lower price. The main menu is *la carta*.
restaurant – *un restaurante, una fonda, un merendero*
café, coffee shop – *un café*
please bring me some coffee – *un café, por favor*
please bring me... – *Tráigame por favor...*
beer – *una cerveza*
cold water – *agua fría*
hot water – *agua caliente*
soft drink – *un refresco*
daily special – *la comida corrida; el especial del día*
breakfast – *desayuno*
lunch – *almuerzo/comida*
dinner – *cena*

first course – *primer plato*
second course – *plato principal*
may I have more beer? – *¿Más cerveza, por favor?*
may I have the bill? – *¿me da la cuenta, por favor?*
To get the attention of a waiter (waitress)– *¡Señor! (¡Señorita! ¡Señora!)*

At the hotel

where is there an inexpensive hotel? – *¿dónde hay un hotel económico?*
do you have an air-conditioned room? – *¿tiene un cuarto con aire acondicionado?*
do you have a room with bath? – *¿tiene un cuarto con baño?*
where is – *¿dónde está?*
the dining room? – *¿el comedor?*
key – *la llave*
manager – *el gerente*
owner (male) – *el dueño*
owner (female) – *la dueña*
can you cash a traveler's cheque? – *¿puede cambiar un cheque de viajero?*

Communications

post office – *el correo; la oficina de correos*
telegraph office – *la oficina de telégrafos*
public telephone – *el teléfono público*
letter – *la carta*
postcard – *la tarjeta postal*
envelope – *el sobre*
stamp – *un timbre*

Places

police station – *la delegación de policía*
embassy – *la embajada*
consulate – *el consulado*
bank – *el banco*
hotel – *un hotel*
inn – *una posada*
apartment – *un departamento*
restroom – *el sanitario/el baño de hombres/mujeres*
(private) bathroom – *el baño privado*
public bathhouses – *los baños públicos*

ticket office – *la oficina de boletos, taquilla*
dry cleaners – *la tintorería*

Shopping

department – *el departamento*
market, market place – *el mercado*
souvenir shop – *la tienda de curiosidades*
what is the price? – *¿cuánto cuesta?*
it's too expensive – *es muy caro*
can you give me a discount? – *¿me puede dar un descuento?*
do you have...? – *¿tiene usted...?*
I will buy this – *voy a comprar esto*
please show me another – *muéstreme otro (otra) por favor*
just a moment, please – *un momento, por favor*

Transport

airplane – *avión*
airport – *el aeropuerto*
ferry boat – *el transbordador*
subway – *el metro*
train station – *la estación del ferrocarril*
train – *el tren*
first class – *primera clase*
second class – *segunda clase*
deluxe – *de lujo/ejecutivo*

Useful Phrases when Traveling

how much is a ticket to...? – *¿cuánto cuesta un boleto a...?*
I want a ticket to... – *quiero un boleto a...*
please stop here – *pare aquí, por favor*
please go straight – *derecho, por favor*
how many kilometers is it from here to...? – *¿cuántos kilómetros hay de aquí a...?*
how long does it take to go there...? – *¿cuánto se tarda en llegar?*
left – *a la izquierda*
right – *a la derecha*
what is this place called? – *¿cómo se llama este lugar?*
I'm going to... – *Voy a...*

On the buses

bus – *autobús/camión de pasajeros*

express bus – *el camión directo*
bus station – *la central camionera*
bus stop – *parada*
reserved seat – *asiento reservado*
where does this bus go? – *¿adónde va este camión?*
I am getting off here! (to call out to a bus driver when you want to get off) – *¡Bajan!*

On the Road

car – *el coche, el automóvil*
where is a petrol station? – *¿dónde hay una gasolinera?*
a repair garage – *un taller mecánico*
auto parts store– *una refaccionaria para coches*
fill it up, please – *lleno, por favor*
please check the oil – *cheque el aceite, por favor*
radiator – *el radiador*
battery – *el acumulador*
I need... – *necesito...*
spare wheel – *la rueda de repuesto*
jack – *un gato*
towtruck – *una grúa*
mechanic – *un mecánico*
tune-up – *una afinación*
tire – *una llanta*
a fuse like this one – *un fusible como éste*
it's broken – *está roto/a*
they're broken – *están rotos/as*

Taxis

taxi – *el taxi*
taxi stand – *el sitio de taxis*
please call me a taxi – *pídame un taxi, por favor*
what will you charge to take me to...? – *¿cuánto me cobra para llevarme a...?*

Months of the Year

January	– enero
February	– febrero
March	– marzo
April	– abril
May	– mayo
June	– junio
July	– julio
August	– agosto
September	– septiembre
October	– octubre
November	– noviembre
December	– diciembre

Days of the Week

Monday – *lunes*
Tuesday – *martes*
Wednesday – *miércoles*
Thursday – *jueves*
Friday – *viernes*
Saturday – *sábado*
Sunday – *domingo*

Numbers

1 – *uno*
2 – *dos*
3 – *tres*
4 – *cuatro*
5 – *cinco*
6 – *seis*
7 – *siete*
8 – *ocho*
9 – *nueve*
10 – *diez*
11 – *once*
12 – *doce*
13 – *trece*
14 – *catorce*
15 – *quince*
16 – *dieciséis*
17 – *diecisiete*
18 – *dieciocho*
19 – *diecinueve*
20 – *veinte*
21 – *veintiuno*
25 – *veinticinco*
30 – *treinta*
40 – *cuarenta*
50 – *cincuenta*
60 – *sesenta*
70 – *setenta*
80 – *ochenta*
90 – *noventa*
100 – *cien*
101 – *ciento uno*
200 – *doscientos*
300 – *trescientos*
400 – *cuatrocientos*
500 – *quinientos*
600 – *seiscientos*
700 – *setecientos*
800 – *ochocientos*
900 – *novecientos*
1,000 – *mil*
2,000 – *dos mil*
10,000 – *diez mil*
100,000 – *cien mil*
1,000,000 – *un millón*
1,000,000,000 – *mil millones*

Further Reading

Ancient Mexico by Frederick Peterson, Capricorn. A good introduction to all the major pre-Columbian cultures.

The Broken Spears: The Aztec Account of the Conquest of Mexico by Miguel León Portilla, Beacon Press, 1962. Read this for its contrast with the Spanish viewpoint of Díaz del Castillo.

Burning Water: Thought and Religion in Ancient Mexico by Laurette Sejourne, Shambhala, 1976. Controversial but stimulating. Argues that local religions were manipulated and distorted by the invading Aztecs to serve their political ends.

A Concise History of Mexico, from Hidalgo to Cárdenas by Jan Bazant. Cambridge University Press, 1977. Emphasis on the struggle for land.

The Conquest of Mexico by William H. Prescott, Modern Library, 1931. This vivid recounting, based on Díaz del Castillo's story, is a gem.

The Conquest of New Spain by Bernal Díaz del Castillo, Penguin, 1963. This simple soldier's tale, delightful to read, has been corroborated by archeological findings, and is now the standard reference on the events of the conquest.

Daily Life of the Aztecs on the Eve of the Spanish Conquest, Stanford University Press, 1961. Just what the title says, and quite fascinating.

Five Letters by Hernán Cortés. Gordon Press, 1977. Long letters in which Cortés recounts his exploits and justifies his actions to his king.

Distant Neighbors: A Portrait of the Mexicans by Alan Riding, Vintage, 1989. An insightful study of Mexico's politics, society, culture and economics. Riding was the New York Times bureau chief in Mexico for six years.

General History of the Things of

New Spain by Bernardino De Sahagún, 12 volumes, University of Utah Press. A gold-mine of information about the Aztecs and neighbouring peoples, written by one of the early Spanish missionaries.

A History of Mexico by Henry Bamford Parkes, Houghton Mifflin, 1969. A hefty tome for those with a serious interest.

Insurgent Mexico by John Reed, International Publishing, 1969. Exciting account of the 1910 revolution by the reporter famous for his coverage of the Russian Revolution.

The Maya by Michael Coe, Thames & Hudson, 1980. A good one-volume summary, with useful details on the major sites and Mayan hieroglyphics.

Maya History and Religion by J. Eric Thompson, University of Oklahoma Press, 1976. Also by the same author, *The Rise and Fall of Maya Civilization*, University of Oklahoma Press, 1977. His explanations are based on decades of excavating Mayan temple complexes.

Los Olmecas (The Olmecs) by Jacques Soustelle. For those who can read Spanish or French, a scholarly yet highly readable account of Mexico's "mother culture."

The People of the Sun by Alfonso Caso, University of Oklahoma Press, 1978. Authoritative source on the Aztecs.

Voyage to the New World: Fact and Fantasy by Nigel Davies, Morrow, 1979. If you are tempted to subscribe to any of the fashionable theories about the Chinese, Middle Eastern or extra-terrestrial origins of Mexican civilization, read this first.

The Wind that Swept Mexico by Anita Brenner and George R. Leighton, University of Texas Press, 1971. Brief account of the revolution, with excellent historical photographs.

Yucatán Before and After the Conquest by Bishop Diego De Landa, Kraus reprint of 1941 Harvard University Peabody Museum Publication. Written by the same man who burned nearly all

the Mayan pictographic accounts. This book is the starting-point for all serious research on the Maya.

Zapata and the Mexican Revolution by John Womack, Knopf, 1968. Readable and well-researched.

American Extremes by Daniel Cosío Villegas, University of Texas Press, 1964. Cosío Villegas, also the author of a 10-volume history of Mexico, provides in these essays an intelligent perspective on Mexico's problems and its relations with its northern neighbour.

La Democracia en México by Pablo González Casanova. Democracy in Mexico. A very good book, unfortunately not available in English. Analyses Mexico's social, political and economic institutions and its overall power structure, and assesses the potential for a more active democratic process.

The Labyrinth of Solitude by Octavio Paz, Grove, 1962. Paz is perhaps the best-known (outside Mexico) of all Mexico's intellectuals. This book is not easy to read, but is a must for anyone who wants to go beyond a superficial understanding of the psychology and culture of contemporary Mexicans.

Mexican Traditions by Sebastián Verti, Editorial Diana, 1993. One of Mexico's strongest cultural advocates writes on religious celebrations, regional festivities, dances and traditions, history and legend, the origins of mariachi and the charrería and the Mexican culinary legacy. Well-illustrated with color photographs, it includes traditional recipes.

Mexico, Profile of a Nation. Mexico, DF: INEGI, Fomento Cultural Banamex, 1989.

Mexico A Biography of Power: A History of Modern Mexico 1810–1996 by Enrique Krauze, Harper Collins Publishers, 1997. Enrique Krauze is one of Mexico's most respected contemporary historians and political analysts.

Last Call by Mauricio González de la Garza. (No English edition). A scathing critique of Mexico's political institutions. The book has been quite controversial and enormously successful in Mexico (over 200,000 copies in print).

Profile of Man and Culture in Mexico by Samuel Ramos, University of Texas Press, 1962. A companion piece to Paz's *Labyrinth of Solitude*. Provides particular insight into the psychology of Mexican indians and their relations with the dominant mestizo culture.

Foreign Writers on Mexico

American and British Writers in Mexico, 1556–1973, by Drewey Wayne Gunn. University of Texas Press, 1974.

Barbarous Mexico by John Kenneth Turner, University of Texas Press, 1969; first published 1908. Turner's reporting of the abject misery and death among the slaves working Mexico's tobacco and henequén plantations led many Americans to question Porfirio Díaz's reputation as a benevolent dictator.

Beyond the Mexique Bay by Aldous Huxley, Vintage, 1960. Erudite observations on the Mayan cultural remains. Mostly concerned with Guatemala, but worthwhile reading for serious archeology buffs.

Five Families by Oscar Lewis, Basic Books, 1959. Lewis spent many years studying Mexico's "culture of poverty" and interviewing its victims. Other books by him are: *The Children of Sánchez* (Random House, 1961); *Pedro Martínez* (Random House, 1964); and *A Death in the Sánchez Family* (Random House, 1969).

The Forgotten Peninsula by Joseph Wood Krutch, William Sloan, 1961. Perhaps the best book about Baja.

Hovering Over Baja by Erle Stanley Gardner, Morrow, 1961 and **Whispering Sands**, Morrow, 1981. Gardner was a passionate outdoorsman who knew Baja California thoroughly from visiting

the area when he was not writing detective stories.

Incidents of Travel in Central America, Chiapas and Yucatán by John L. Stephens, Dover, 1969; first published 1841. Stephens and illustrator Frederick Catherwood had many adventures and made remarkable discoveries. Their book was instrumental in arousing scientific interest in the lost Mayan civilization.

La Capital, The Biography of Mexico City, by Jonathan Kandell, Random House.1988.

The Lawless Roads by Graham Greene, Heinemann, 1950; published in the US as *Another Mexico*, Viking, 1939. Greene tells entertainingly of his travels, though his views of Catholicism in Mexico are debatable.

Life in Mexico: The Letters of Fanny Calderón de la Barca, wtih New Material from the Author's Private Journals by Fanny Calderón de la Barca edited by H.T. and M.H. Fisher, Doubleday, 1966, first published 1913. The author was a Scotswoman living in Spain, whose husband became Spain's first ambassador to independent Mexico. Madame Calderón de la Barca, intelligent and curious, loved to travel and spoke Spanish fluently.

The Log from the Sea of Cortés by John Steinbeck, Viking, 1951. Steinbeck tells of an expedition to gather biological specimens from the Sea of Cortés off Baja California. Recommended for those who boat or fish in these waters.

Many Mexicos by Lesley Byrd Simpson, University of California Press, 1966. A good historical analysis.

Mexico's Agricultural Dilemma by P. Lamartine Yates, University of Arizona Press, 1981. A good source for those interested in Mexico's land problems.

Mexico in its Novel by John S. Brushwood, University of Texas Press, 1966. A useful guide to Mexican fiction.

Mornings in Mexico by D.H. Lawrence, Knopf, 1927. Includes several descriptive essays which

beautifully express Lawrence's feeling for the country.

Peyote Hunt: The Sacred Journey of the Huichol Indians by Barbara Myerhoff, Cornell University Press, 1974. An analysis of Huichol religious symbolism and religious use of hallucinogens.

Political Essay on the Kingdom of New Spain by Alexander von Humboldt, AMS Press, reprint of 1811 edition. Unusual in that it's not the work of a British or American writer. Von Humboldt traveled through Mexico in 1803–04, studying the country's economic resources and pre-Columbian antiquities. His book, the first systematic study of the country, alerted European powers to the mineral wealth of Mexico.

In the Shadow of Tláloc: Life in a Mexican Village by Gregory C. Reck, Penguin, 1978. Full of interesting information, like most anthropological studies, but also unusually expressive of the feelings of village life.

The Tall Candle: The Personal Chronicle of a Yaqui Indian by J. Kelley and William Holden, R. Moises. Lincoln: University of Nebraska Press, 1971.

The Teachings of Don Juan: A Yaqui Way of Knowledge by Carlos Castañeda, Universtiy of California Press, 1968. This and other books by Castañeda provide an imaginative insight into spiritual experience – but don't believe every word. Also *A Separate Reality* (Simon & Schuster, 1971); *Journey to Ixtlán* (Simon & Schuster, 1973); *Tales of Power* (Simon & Schuster, 1975); *The Second Ring of Power* (1980); *The Eagle's Gift* (Simon & Schuster, 1981).

Tortillas for the Gods: A Symbolic Analysis of Zinacanteco Ritual by Evon Z. Vogt, Harvard University Press, 1976. Good source for those interested in the contemporary Mayan indians of Chiapas.

Travelers' Tales Mexico edited by James O'Reilly and Larry Habegger, Travelers' Tales Inc., 1994. An outstanding collection of Mexican experiences.

Travels in the New World by

Thomas Gage, University of Oklahoma Press, 1969; first published 1648. One of the few accounts of colonial Mexico still worth reading. Gage, a Dominican friar from England, traveled widely in Mexico.

Unknown Mexico: Indians of Mexico by Carl Lumholtz, Rio Grande Press. Lumoltz was one of the last of the great explorer-anthropologists. Contains an immense amount of information on the indians of northern Mexico.

Viva México by Charles Macomb Flandrau, University of Illinois Press, 1964; first published 1908. In the same vein as the writings of Madame Calderón de la Barca, but more limited in scope. The style is charming and unhurried, and some of Flandrau's insights into Mexican character are absolute gems.

Fiction by Mexican Authors

The Burning Plain/El Llano en Llamas by Juan Rulfo. University of Texas Press, 1967. The best of Mexican literature. A collection of short stories in which Rulfo's spare, suggestive prose gives the reader a deep understanding of the *mestizo* culture that was formed during the colonial era and then left behind by the nation's progress. Also by the same author, the novel *Pedro Páramo* (Grove Press, 1959).

Almost Paradise/Casi el Paraíso by Luis Spota. A Mexican best-seller, available only in Spanish, in Mexico.

Confabulario by Juan José Arreola, University of Texas Press, 1964. Highly polished short stories.

The Edge of the Storm by Agustín Yáñez, University of Texas Press, 1963. A great novel, set in a small town in Jalisco just before the revolution. The atmosphere is heavy, the characters complex. Also *Lean Lands* (University of Texas Press, 1968).

Like Water for Chocolate/Como Agua para Chocolate by Laura Esquivel; first published 1989; English version, Doubleday, 1992. The 1990 number-one bestseller novel about family life in turn-of-the-

century Mexico. Wit, humour, irony and more blend into an easy-to-read, difficult-to-put-down book. The film based on the novel won 11 awards.

Memoirs of Pancho Villa by Martín Luis Guzmán, University of Texas Press, 1965 and **The Eagle and the Serpent** by Peter Smith. Both books are based on the authors' personal experiences with Pancho Villa and other revolutionary leaders.

The Underdogs by Mariano Azuela, New American Library. An excellent novel (based on the author's own life) with insights into the experiences, ideals and frustrations of ordinary men fighting the Mexican revolution.

Where the Air Is Clear by Carlos Fuentes, Farrar, Straus & Giroux, 1971. Considered by some to be the best novel of modern Mexico. The narrator is a rather mysterious man who spends his life listening to and watching fellow inhabitants of Mexico City, of every social stratum, as they attempt to cope with the various conditions of their lives. Also by the same author, *The Death of Artemio Cruz* (Farrar, Straus & Giroux, 1964), in which the protagonist recalls the revolution and the following years, when he gradually became a cynical opportunist, manipulating old revolutionary contacts to build his fortune.

Fiction by Foreign Authors

The Collected Stories by Katherine Anne Porter, Harcourt, Brace, 1965; and **The Collected Essays** (Delacorte, 1970). Porter understood the oppressive role the Church had played in Mexican history. She also understood the new Constitution and Mexico's intricate political machinery. Further, Porter was one of the first to appreciate and document the difference between pre-Columbian and contemporary indian arts.

Time's Awakening/El Despertar del Tiempo by Carlos Villa Ruiz and Ivonne Carro, Plaza y Valdés Editores. A sort of *Quantum Leap*

involving a Mexica warrior frozen for 500 years on the slopes of one of the volcanoes and two Mexican boys of the 90s. Compulsive reading, it describes the indian-mestizo "encounter", underscoring the gap between Mexicans separated by a 500-year transition in culture.

The Treasure of the Sierra Madre by B. Traven, Hill & Wang, 1967. No other author has written so much and so well about Mexico as the mysterious B. Traven (his identity is still a matter of controversy). Most of his books are set in southern Mexico, and his knowledge of that area is astounding. Other books to look out for are: *The General from the Jungle* (Robert Hale, 1945); *The Rebellion of the Hanged* (Knopf, 1952); *March to Caobaland* (Robert Hale, 1961); *The Bridge in the Jungle* (Hill & Wang, 1967); *The Carreta* (Hill & Wang, 1970).

The Night of the Iguana by Tennessee Williams. New Directions, 1962. Powerful drama made famous by film starring Richard Burton.

The Plumed Serpent by D.H. Lawrence, Knopf, 1951. Lawrence takes on profound problems – the meaning of life and death, the relations of man to man and woman to man – and argues for a profound change in Mexico. One of the best novels ever written about Mexico.

The Power and the Glory by Graham Greene, Viking, 1962. Considered by many critics to be Graham Greene's finest novel, it takes place in Tabasco during the persecution of the Catholic clergy. Its hero is a priest who is faced with choosing marriage, exile or the firing squad.

Under the Volcano by Malcolm Lowry. Lippincott, 1965. Without making any explicit attempt to clarify them, Lowry reveals the hidden forces which move Mexico. In this, his only major work, he tells the deceptively simple story of a British Consul who drinks himself to death during the crisis year when President Cárdenas nationalized the oil industry.

Arts and Crafts of Mexico

Art and Time in Mexico, photographs by Judith Hancock Sandoval, and text by Elizabeth Wilder Weismann, Harper & Row, 1985. Well-illustrated overview of colonial art and architecture.

Casa Mexicana: the Architecture, Design and Style of Mexico, by Tim Street-Porter, New York, 1989.

Crafts of Mexico by Chloe Sayer, Doubleday, 1977. Step-by-step instructions for making traditional Mexican craft items. Excellent photographs.

Ethnic and Tourist Arts by Nelson H.H. Graburn, editor, University of California Press, 1976. Includes articles by anthropologists on three Mexican art forms popular with foreign visitors: the ironwood carvings of the Seri indians, the bark paintings of Xalitla, and Teotihuacán-area pottery. These articles explain the cultural and economic contexts of these so-called "tourist arts."

Indian Art of Mexico and Central America by Miguel Covarrubias, Knopf, 1957; and **Mezcala: Ancient Mexican Sculpture** (Andre Emmerich Gallery, 1956). Covarrubias is a respected authority on Mexican art.

Mexican Churches, by Eliot Porter and Ellen Auerbach, Albuquerque, N.M., 1987.

Mexican Colonial Art by Manuel Toussaint, University of Texas. The best textbook on the subject, covering everything worth knowing about colonial art in Mexico. Toussaint's newspaper columns in the 1930s and 1940s brought new attention to Mexican colonial art.

The National Museum of Anthropology, Mexico: Art, Architecture, Archeology, Anthropology by Pedro Ramírez Vázquez and others, Abrams, 1968. The story of the creation of the National Museum, written by the men responsible and illustrated with excellent photographs of museum exhibits enriching short essays about Mexico's pre-Columbian cultures.

Painted Walls of Mexico by Emily Edward and Bravo Alvarez, University of Texas Press, 1966. Treats Mexican murals from pre-Columbian examples onward, with special emphasis on the post-revolutionary masters.

Popular Art of Mexico by Tonatiuh Gutiérrez and Electra, reprint of a 1960 special issue of the magazine *Artes de México*. Illustrates the crafts of every area of the country. Available in three languages, English, French or Spanish in FONART

stores, Sanborn's bookstores, and museum shops in Mexico.

Popular Arts of Mexico by Porfirio Martínez Peñaloza, Editorial Panorama, 1981. A compact and inexpensive book by one of the outstanding authorities on Mexican art.

The Sculpture of Ancient Mexico by Paul Westheim. Doubleday, 1963. Westheim's writings on the aesthetics of pre-Columbian art are hard to surpass for insight and clarity.

The Traditional Architecture of Mexico, Photographs by Mariana Yampolsky; text by Chloe Sayer, London and New York, 1993.

A Treasury of Mexican Folkways by Frances Toor, Crown, 1947. Covers folk art, fiestas, music and dance. A classic in its field.

Other Insight Guides

Insight Guide: Mexico City provides in-depth coverage of the capital and its surrounding area, with revealing features and stunning photography.

Pocket Guides: Mexico City, the Baja Peninsula and the Yucatán Peninsula are designed for the visitor with limited time to spare and include a selection of carefully timed itineraries and personal recommendations.

ART & PHOTO CREDITS

All photography by Kal Müller except for:
Guillermo Aldana E 84
John Brunton 70, 92, 105, 128/129, 184T, 252, 259, 261, 270T, 285, 290, 291
The Casasola Archive 60/61
Jean and Zomah Charlot Collection 94
Désiré Charney 41, 88
Bruce Coleman Ltd 297
Christa Cowrie 14, 16/17, 36, 69, 71, 78, 157, 164, 169, 170, 171
Mary Evans 42
The Antonio García Collection 52, 58, 64, 65, 67
Jacques Gourguechon 310
Andreas Gross 154, 165
José Guadalupe Posada/from the Jean and Zomah Charlot Collection 299
Blaine Harrington 31
Huw Hennessy 333
Dave G. Houser 289
Piere Hussenot 120/121, 122/123, 124
Archivo Iconográfico 111, 266
Graciela Iturbide 83
Kerrick James 206
Lyle Lawson 126
Bud Lee 155
Buddy Mays Travel Stock 33, 242, 286T
Pablo Ortíz Monasterio 132
Museo Nacional de Antropología, Mexico City 30, 32
Rod Morris 89
Museo Nacional de Historia 59
The National Palace, Mexico City 37
Jorge Nunez/Sipa/Rex 91
Jutta Schütz/Archiv Jutta 63, 163
Schülz 46/47
Spectrum 24/25
Marcus Wilson-Smith 6/7, 12/13, 22, 26/27, 40, 87, 93, 104, 106/107, 125, 127, 131,

136/137, 150, 151, 153, 153T, 159, 161, 161T, 164T, 167, 169T, 170T, 172, 191T, 203, 204, 205, 206T , 207, 208, 208T, 209, 210, 211, 222, 223, 223T, 224T, 244, 227, 238, 256T, 258T, 268, 268T, 272, 273, 279, 282T, 284, 286, 288, 298, 301, 308, 317, 320, 320T, 321, 322T, 324T, 325, 326, 330, 331, 332, 333, 334, 335
David Stahl 39, 249, 302 **Mireille Vautier** 56, 57, 112/113, 115, 235
Jorge Vertíz, Artes de México 43, 48, 49, 53
Tom Servais 212
Topham 66, 73, 257
Washington D.C. 62
Bill Wassman 54, 55, 188, 247
The Jorge Wilmot Collection 102
Woodfin Camp & Associates 68, 198, 276, 304, 306
Norbert Wu 142
Crispin Zeeman 160, 234, 251, 295

Picture Spreads

Beach Resorts, pages 134-5: *Top Row Left to Right:* Buddy Mays Travel Stock: *Top Left, Top Center Left*; Mireille Vautier: *Top Center Right*; Andreas Gross: *Top Right* **Center Row Left to Right:** John Brunton: *Center Left*, Buddy Mays Travel Stock: *Center Right*, **Bottom Row Left to Right:** Buddy Mays Travel Stock: *Bottom Left*, Stephen Trimble: *Bottom Center Left*, Andreas Gross: *Bottom Center Right and Bottom Right*

Copper Canyon, pages 220-1: All pictures by Buddy Mays Travel Stock except: Andreas Gross: *Top Left and Center Right*; John Brunton: *Top Center Left and Bottom Center Right*;

Day of the Dead, pages 262-3: *Top Row Left to Right:* Andreas Gross: *Top Left*, Blaine Harrington: *Top Center Left*, Duggal: *Top Center Right*, Mireille Vautier: *Top Right* **Center Row Left to Right:** Mireille Vautier: *Center Left*, Crispin Zeeman *Center and Center Right* **Bottom Row Left to Right:** Andreas Gross: *Bottom Left*, Blaine Harrington: *Bottom Centre Left*, Crispin Zeeman: *Bottom Center Right*, Mireille Vautier *Bottom Right*

Marine Wildlife, pages 314-5
Top Row Left to Right: Marcus Wilson Smith: *Top Left*, Buddy Mays Travel Stook: *Top Center Left*, Terra Aqua: *Top Center Right and Top Right* **Center Row Left to Right:** Marcus Wilson Smith: *Center* **Bottom Row Left to Right:** Buddy Mays Travel Stock: *Bottom Left, Bottom Center Left*; Andreas Gross: *Bottom Center*; Buddy Mays Travel Stock: *Bottom Center Right and Below Right.*

Map production Berndtson & Berndtson Productions

© 1999 Apa Publications GmbH & Co. Verlag KG (Singapore branch)

Cartographic Editor **Zoë Goodwin**
Production **Stuart A. Everitt**
Design Consultants
Carlotta Junger, Graham Mitchener
Picture Research **Hilary Genin**

Index

Numbers in italics refer to photographs

A
B
C
D
E
F
G
H
I
b
c
d
e
f
g
h
i
j
k
l

The Insight Approach

The book you are holding is part of the world's largest range of guidebooks. Its purpose is to help you have the most valuable travel experience possible, and we try to achieve this by providing not only information about countries, regions and cities but also genuine insight into their history, culture, institutions and people.

Since the first Insight Guide – to Bali – was published in 1970, the series has been dedicated to the proposition that, with insight into a country's people and culture, visitors can both enhance their own experience and be accepted more easily by their hosts. Now, in a world where ethnic hostilities and nationalist conflicts are all too common, such attempts to increase understanding between peoples are more important than ever.

Insight Guides:
Essentials for understanding

Because a nation's past holds the key to its present, each Insight Guide kicks off with lively history chapters. These are followed by magazine-style essays on culture and daily life. This essential background information gives readers the necessary context for using the main Places section, with its comprehensive run-down on things worth seeing and doing.

Finally, a listings section contains all the information you'll need on travel, hotels, restaurants and opening times.

As far as possible, we rely on local writers and specialists to ensure that information is authoritative. The pictures, for which Insight Guides have become so celebrated, are just as important. Our photojournalistic approach aims not only to illustrate a destination but also to communicate visually and directly to readers life as it is lived by the locals. The series has grown to almost 200 titles.

Compact Guides:
The "great little guides"

As invaluable as such background information is, it isn't always fun to carry an Insight Guide through a crowded souk or up a church tower. Could we, readers asked, distil the key reference material into a slim volume for on-the-spot use?

Our response was to design Compact Guides as an entirely new series, with original text carefully cross-referenced to detailed maps and more than 200 photographs. In essence, they're miniature encyclopedias, concise and comprehensive, displaying reliable and up-to-date information in an accessible way. There are almost 100 titles.

Pocket Guides:
A local host in book form

However wide-ranging the information in a book, human beings still value the personal touch. Our editors are often asked the same questions. Where do *you* go to eat? What do *you* think is the best beach? What would *you* recommend if I have only three days? We invited our local correspondents to act as "substitute hosts" by revealing their preferred walks and trips, listing the restaurants they go to and structuring a visit into a series of timed itineraries.

The result: our Pocket Guides, complete with full-size fold-out maps. These 100-plus titles help readers plan a trip precisely, particularly if their time is short.

Exploring with Insight:
A valuable travel experience

In conjunction with co-publishers all over the world, we print in up to 10 languages, from German to Chinese, from Danish to Russian. But our aim remains simple: to enhance your travel experience by combining our expertise in guidebook publishing with the on-the-spot knowledge of our correspondents.

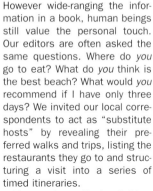

66 I was first drawn to the Insight Guides by the excellent "Nepal" volume. I can think of no book which so effectively captures the essence of a country. Out of these pages leaped the Nepal I know – the captivating charm of a people and their culture. I've since discovered and enjoyed the entire Insight Guide series. Each volume deals with a country in the same sensitive depth, which is nowhere more evident than in the superb photography. 99

Sir Edmund Hillary

The World of Insight Guides

400 books in three complementary series cover every major destination in every continent.